OUT OF THE MOUTHS OF BABES

OUT *of the* MOUTHS *of* BABES

Infant Voices in Medieval French Literature

JULIE SINGER

The University of Chicago Press

CHICAGO AND LONDON

The University of Chicago Press, Chicago 60637
The University of Chicago Press, Ltd., London
© 2025 by The University of Chicago

Published 2025
Printed in the United States of America

34 33 32 31 30 29 28 27 26 25   1 2 3 4 5

ISBN-13: 978-0-226-83801-4 (cloth)
ISBN-13: 978-0-226-83802-1 (paper)
ISBN-13: 978-0-226-83803-8 (e-book)
DOI: https://doi.org/10.7208/chicago/9780226838038.001.0001

The University of Chicago Press gratefully acknowledges the generous support
of Washington University in St. Louis toward the publication of this book.

Library of Congress Cataloging-in-Publication Data

Names: Singer, Julie, 1978– author.
Title: Out of the mouths of babes : infant voices in medieval French literature /
   Julie Singer.
Description: Chicago : The University of Chicago Press, 2025. | Includes
   bibliographical references and index.
Identifiers: LCCN 2024024462 | ISBN 9780226838014 (cloth) |
   ISBN 9780226838021 (paperback) | ISBN 9780226838038 (ebook)
Subjects: LCSH: French literature—To 1500—History and criticism. | Infants in
   literature.
Classification: LCC PQ155.I54 S56 2025 | DDC 840.9/352320902—dc23/
   eng/20240627
LC record available at https://lccn.loc.gov/2024024462

CONTENTS

ILLUSTRATIONS

THE UNIVERSAL ALTERITY
OF THE INFANT

Popular wisdom has long dictated that children should be seen and not heard. When small children are both seen and heard, however, they can make an outsized impression on the adults around them. This much is clear in the Dominican Jean l'Agneau's remarks about children in his Christmas 1272 sermon, delivered at the parish Church of Sainte-Marie-Madeleine on Paris's Île de la Cité:

> Solet dici quod qui fecit puerum fecit ioculatorem, quia delectabilius quod in terra possit videri est unus puer, quando est bene graciosus. Quidquid ipse faciat, etiam si potos et vitreas frangat, non fit nisi ridere, unde etiam isti ioculatores non libenter vadunt ubi sciunt talem puerum.[1]

> It is often said that whoever makes a child makes a jester, for there is nothing on earth more delightful to see than a charming child. Whatever the child may do, even if he breaks cups or glassware, people do nothing but laugh, and therefore jesters are in no hurry to go where they know there are children.

The preacher recognized the amusement to be derived from small children's speech and behavior, belying Philippe Ariès's influential but now debunked view of the Middle Ages as a period devoid of what he called a *sentiment de l'enfant* (typically translated as "concept of childhood").[2] The sermon also confirms that popular wisdom had already anticipated W. C. Fields's famous admonition to his fellow performers ("Never work with children or animals") by at least 650 years.

The comparison between children and jesters or minstrels is

telling. Both the entertaining tots and the adults who risk being upstaged by them are identified as *ioculatores*, a term that, like its vernacular counterpart *jongleurs*, encompasses a variety of performance practices, many of which center on the sung or spoken word.[3] *Ioculatores* are frequently seen by their contemporaries as undignified, morally dubious, or socially marginal—yet they bring joy, providing a service that can cut across class boundaries. Their verbal entertainments are disordered or excessive (at least from the moralists' point of view), sometimes conveying deep meaning and sometimes no meaning at all.[4] Funny, undignified, socially marginal but universally relatable, capable of uttering profound truths amid sheer silliness—such is also the essence of childhood, "l'âge comique par excellence."[5]

Jean l'Agneau's comparison of children to *ioculatores* likewise hints at children's uneasy command of the spoken word. Although *ioculatores* are often verbal artists, the preacher's specific examples of children's antics are seen (*videri*) and not heard. Does the child-*jongleur* speak at all? The question is not as silly as it might seem if we bear in mind that for etymologically minded medieval writers, the notion of "child speech" or "infant speech" is a contradiction in terms. Throughout the Western European Middle Ages, early childhood is constructed as a period of speechlessness. The English *infant* and the French *enfant* ("child") both derive from the Latin *infāns*, literally meaning "unable to speak." As Isidore of Seville explains,

> Infans dicitur homo primae aetatis; dictus autem infans quia adhuc fari nescit, id est loqui non potest. Nondum enim bene ordinatis dentibus minus est sermonis expressio.[6]

> A human being of the first age is called an infant (*infans*); it is called an infant, because it does not yet know how to speak (*in-*, "not"; *fari*, present participle *fans*, "speaking"), that is, it cannot talk. Not yet having its full complement of teeth, it has less ability to articulate words.[7]

Infancy, which in Isidore's view lasts from birth to age seven, is thus a developmental stage defined by a biologically grounded incapacity: the inability to speak is regarded as resulting less from immature cognitive competency than from immature dentition. This biolog-ically unique stage of life is also a period of restricted sociability, as the infant, regardless of its sex, remains largely confined to a feminine domestic sphere: the child's emergent speech develops almost exclu-sively through interaction with women. Any potential for infants to communicate verbally would thus seem to be doubly impeded, by bodily immaturity and by lack of access to a circle of interlocutors. And yet, despite their supposed speechlessness, in medieval French literature babies have quite a lot to say. What are we to make of those moments in medieval literary texts where toddlers, infants, and even fetuses speak? When those who are etymologically and axiomatically mute are endowed with speech, what can these voices tell us?

Children's speech, as represented in medieval texts, is used to con-vey fundamental truths, voicing them at the fine line between sense and nonsense. In a certain respect all child speech is nonsensical, irra-tional, in that it is produced by a creature who (according to medieval developmental theories) has not attained the age of reason. Some-times small children's vocalizations confirm their lack of reason, as in Jean Maillart's *Roman du comte d'Anjou* (1316). When a newborn who is about to be killed laughs, his mother laments:

> Tu ris, et tu plorer deüssez,
> Se point de senz en toi eüssez,
> [...]
> Mes tant as jone aage et tendre
> Que rienz ne pués encore entendre,
> N'avoir senz ne discrecion.[8]

> You laugh, when you ought to be crying,
> If you had any sense in you,
> [...]
> But you are of such a young and tender age
> That you can't understand anything yet,
> Nor do you have sense or discretion.

The child is endowed with a voice, though he cannot yet speak, and all he can vocalize is his own lack of sense. But infants are not speechless in the same way that animals are: they are already laying the foundations for their eventual attainment of reason, as Philippe de Novare notes in his *Des IIII tenz d'aage d'ome* (On the four ages of man, c. 1260–70). God, according to Philippe, "ne vuet mie que li anfant soient paroils as faons des bestes ne as pijons des oisiaus, qui sont sanz loquance et sanz raison et vivent naturelment sanz plus" (does not by any means want children to be like young beasts or chicks, which are without speech and without reason and live according to nature without anything more); once they are about ten years old, they have developed "loquance et raison, [. . .] san et entendement" (speech and reason, sense and intellect).[9]

Even prior to the age of reason, children's speech, like children's play, is both irrational and meaningful.[10] Words that do not signify can still make sense and can be made sense of. And whether or not one accepts Johan Huizinga's contention that speech itself is a form of imaginative play,[11] there certainly is a great deal of imagination at play when a presumably sensible adult writer gives voice to an infant character. This book is an effort to plumb the insights that medieval writers sought to gain by imagining and attending to small children's speech—not just laughing at their antics, but lending them voices. Imagining infant perspectives, these medieval writers make profound questions seem like child's play.

In this book I explore how medieval writers use fictions of infant speech as a means of giving articulate voice to penetrating inquiries into human knowledge and experience. While I am not arguing for a monolithic "medieval view" of childhood,[12] nor even a singular "medieval French view," the French textual evidence shows that across time and genre, infant voices repeatedly serve as vehicles for reflections on weighty questions of personhood, ability, morality, justice, and the origins and symbolic logic of human language. In other words, the imagined speech of children too young to talk proves to be a potent ethical, epistemic, and even epistemological tool. I am not claiming that the mostly French, mostly vernacular writers whom I study in this book are closet epistemologists: few if any of them are setting out *explicitly* to tell their audiences what human knowledge is or how it is constituted.[13] But neither am I convinced that "vernacular knowledge of childhood" is to be held separate from learned debates;[14] vernacular literature, too, is a site of reflection on the origin and nature of human knowledge, often adopting the age schemas and even the vocabulary of learned treatises. Within the imaginative and speculative realms of fiction, infants offer what other human subjects cannot: a way of bypassing experientially acquired particulars (since infants *have* no lived experience to speak of) and acceding directly to more general, even universal knowledge.

The ability of "speechless" infants to communicate about profound topics is a direct consequence of the peculiar alterity of medieval children as imagined by medieval adults. Infants speak as humans in a state-of-becoming, as impaired agents, and as the subjects of thought experiments that cut to the heart of what it might mean to be human. And while my primary object is not to rehash the question of the *sentiment de l'enfant*, it will emerge from these readings that medieval literature is a site where sentimental views of childhood come into contact with theoretical and abstract ones, and it is this convergence that enables imagined children's voices to become instruments for serious intellectual work. If discourses about children and child-rearing are revelatory of societal values and systems of social regulation,[15] they also reveal what a society finds most troubling; and they locate these points of tension not at the social margins, but at the heart of the family. By imagining or adopting infant voices, authors use infants' universal alterity as a tool with which to define difficult-to-grasp dimensions of human experience. Attending to these voices yields important insights into both learned and popular medieval constructs of personhood, nature, innocence, language, ability—in short, *humanity*.

For medieval writers, small children represent a particular blend of universality and alterity, as a result of which their voices become a particularly efficacious instrument for explorations of the human condition. Infants embody the promise of life, but by virtue of their position at one extremity of the human life span, they remain in close proximity to the threshold of life and death;[16] they occupy the heart of the family, but the fringes of social life; all adults were once children, but none are children now. This ambivalent status that I term "universal alterity" cannot be equated to social marginality. Eminent social historians of medieval childhood such as Christiane Klapisch-Zuber and Didier Lett have described children as "marginal" and unable to be integrated into social institutions, and have compared their status to that of women, non-Christians, and the mentally ill[17] — but such comparisons miss a crucial distinction. Through combined pressures of nature and nurture, children are raised to leave behind their marginalized status in a way that the members of other disadvantaged categories cannot; and, likewise, the very people who compose, consolidate, and derive power from the social institutions that fail to integrate children *were once children themselves*. Childhood is an alienated condition, but one through which all of us must pass.

INFANCY AS A LIFE STAGE

In medieval texts, the human life span was conventionally conceived as a series of "ages."[18] The number of ages could vary from three to seven or more, but by the end of the Middle Ages it is the seven-age model that becomes dominant.[19] Of these seven ages, three correspond to modern categories of childhood: *infantia* (lasting until the age of seven), *pueritia* (usually ending at age fourteen), and *adolescentia* (often ending at age twenty-one). The boundaries between the ages are not sharply delineated, though, and the conventional definition of infancy as a period marked both by a lack of speech and a lack of permanent teeth gives rise to some uncertainty. For Thomas of Cantimpré, *infantia* lasts only until a child begins speaking;[20] for William of Conches, infancy ends when a child speaks distinctly, around age five;[21] and the physician Bernard of Gordon specifies that infancy ends with the advent of articulate speech, but he does not assign a precise age to that development.[22]

Many if not most children do come to speak more or less articulately before the age of seven, and so the category of *infantia* in fact includes what modern people tend to recognize as several distinct developmental stages: infancy proper, toddlerhood, and — after weaning and the advent of more complex and comprehensible speech—the phase from about age three to seven that Didier Lett has called the "hidden childhood" or the "second *infantia*."[23] The rapid and dramatic changes that characterize this first phase of human life do not go unnoticed in medieval literary texts, and even brief allusions to the early childhood years signal that learning to talk is the most meaningful infant milestone. For instance, when personified Faith in Alain Chartier's *Livre de l'Espérance* (c. 1430) expounds on the behaviors inculcated in young nobles "des ce qu'ilz sont naiz, c'est a dire dez qu'ilz apprennent a parler" (as soon as they are born, that is, as soon as they learn to speak),[24] her phrasing suggests that the onset of speech marks a second birth—or perhaps the true birth—of the subject. Evidently the inclusion of nonverbal babies and verbal children in the single category of *infantia*, a phase defined by a lack of speech, affords a playful testing of the meanings of "infancy." The indeterminate language with which adults can speak *about* babies and young children also creates a poetic space in which writers can imagine babies speaking for themselves.

On the whole, medieval French is marked by a notably impoverished vocabulary for childhood.[25] Jean Corbechon, the late fourteenth-century translator of Bartholomew the Englishman's thirteenth-century encyclopedia *De proprietatibus rerum*, laments this lexical imprecision in his discussion of the ages of man:[26]

> L'aage d'enfance se fine a .vii. ans. Et là commance le secont aage que nous appellons enfance en françois mais en latin on l'appelle puericia. Et en ce il appert qu'il y a plus grant deffaulte de langage en françois que en latin, car en latin il y a .vii. aages nommez par divers noms des quelz il n'en y a que trois en françois c'est assavoir enfance ieunesce et viellesce. Et par ce on puet penser quelle paine c'est de proprement translater latin en françois. (BnF MS fr. 16993, fol. 76r)

> The age of childhood ends at age seven. And there begins the second age that we call childhood in French but in Latin it is called *puericia*. And in this it is apparent that there is much greater linguistic poverty in French than in Latin, for in Latin there are seven ages designated by [seven] different names, of which only three have equivalents in

French, namely childhood, youth, and old age. And by this one can understand what a grueling task it is to translate Latin properly into French.

Attempts to adopt a new Latinate term to denote the second part of childhood amounted to little. A brief fifteenth-century enumeration called "Les .VII. Eages de l'omme" offers a telling illustration:

> Le premier age de l'omme est enfance et dure jusques a .vii. ans.
> Le .iie. est ditte ~~puricie~~ puericie et a a nom au peuple aussy enffance et dure jusques a .xv. ans.[27]

> The first age of man is infancy and it lasts until seven years of age.
> The second is called ~~chilhood~~ childhood, and it is also called infancy by the people, and it lasts until fifteen years of age.

Not only must the neologism *puericie* be glossed as equivalent to the popular term *enffance*, but the strike-through on the first attempt at the word *puericie* is perhaps a further indication of the term's unfamiliarity.[28] French speakers are thus left with only a single word, *enfant*, that can denote people at a wide range of ages: fetuses, infants, prepubescent children, and youths and young warriors (as in the popular *enfances* subgenre of epic prequels).[29] Sometimes the word *enfant* even excludes infants and toddlers, so that the youngest children not only cannot speak, but cannot be named.[30] However—in contrast to James A. Schultz's interpretation of Middle High German evidence—I do not construe these lexical limitations as reflective of a narrow *imaginary* of childhood. Rather, I propose that the broad set of meanings available for the word *enfance* signals a conceptual capaciousness which makes childhood a productive site for play on the ambiguities inherent in binary constructs of knowledge/ignorance, innocence/culpability, and nature/culture.

In this book I am primarily interested in discourses of and around *infantia*, the fully or partially "speechless" stage of development lasting until age seven. It is notably difficult to recover the experiences of young medieval children: lacking a public voice and the ability to write, "the under-sevens are silent in historical documents" and "have left virtually nothing on the written record."[31] Children under seven are most often captured in historical records if they die young.[32] Few medieval pediatric texts survive, and while infant care is discussed with some frequency in health regimens for women, medical manuals generally "go into greater detail about the infant from birth to 2 years of age than about ages 2–7."[33] The latter period, Lett's "hidden childhood," is in particular thinly documented—but it is richly imagined by medieval writers.

In many respects the study of medieval childhood still lies (as the opening paragraph of this book illustrates) under the long shadow of Philippe Ariès. His *L'enfant et la vie familiale sous l'Ancien Régime* prompted a strong reaction from medievalists and thus inspired a rich body of more nuanced research into medieval attitudes about and representations of childhood.[34] The psychohistorian Lloyd deMause prompted similarly forceful reactions among medievalists.[35] In the wake of these pioneering works published in the 1960s and 1970s, more thorough overviews of childhood in medieval Europe are now available.[36] Doris Desclais Berkvam and Jens N. Faaborg have gathered French literary examples, and Pierre Riché has published an accessible anthology.[37] In her important body of work, Danièle Alexandre-Bidon has shown among other insights that (contra Ariès) young children were depicted quite frequently in late medieval miniatures.[38] Didier Lett and William F. MacLehose have drawn on hagiography, theology, and canon law to produce rich social histories of medieval childhood.[39]

Despite the surge in histories of medieval childhood published in recent decades, there is much we still do not know about the lives of (and adult attitudes toward) children under the age of seven. Ariès was right about children's lives having been made up largely of experiences "trop communes, trop quotidiennes, trop loin de l'accident mémorable, pour que le contemporain les mentionne" (too ordinary, too commonplace, too far removed from the memorable incident for contemporary writers to mention them).[40] And this is where taking a new approach to literary representations of children becomes so vital: while the activities of axiomatically speechless infants may not have entered the historical record, fundamental debates about human nature did enter literary texts, wherein they are expressed "out of the mouths of babes." Literary fictions imagining the speech of child characters have little to tell us about what real, living children may have said or thought; they are not, in this regard, a supplement to the historical record. Instead, they can offer us an entirely different view of the epistemic weight of children's voices.[41] Rather than another cultural history of medieval childhood, then, what I propose here is a conceptual map of the kinds of knowledge work that medieval (mostly French) writers imagine that children's discourse is particularly well suited to perform. There is much to learn—and not just about childhood, but about gender, ability, and personhood as well—by looking at the ways adult writers found children "good to think with."[42]

INFANCY AS A CRITICAL FRAMEWORK

Infancy implies a particular relation to the word—to the unwritten and unspoken word. It has occasionally figured as such in modern literary-historical theory: as a tool with which to think through the limits of language, for Giorgio Agamben,[43] and as a paradigm for the cultural historian's approach to the past, for Jacques Rancière.[44] Infancy also becomes the site for an interrogation of gendered modes of dependency on, care for, and communication with the other, as in the works of such feminist theorists as Adriana Cavarero.[45] All of these questions—inexpressible truths, archival silences, bridging the distance between self and other—are central both to the questions medieval texts pose and to the methods through which modern readers can attend to them. Therefore, infancy is not only the topic of this book, but its central methodological problem.

I have opted to tackle the problem of infant speech from multiple critical angles—including sound studies, sociolinguistics, theories of justice, and disability studies—while simultaneously placing each of these contemporary discourses in conversation with medieval legal, theological, medical, or grammatical concepts. One of the more prominent threads I draw out in this book is the relationality of the infant's voice to that of its female caregiver (usually a mother or a nurse), and the ways that literary imaginings of infant personhood, speech, and identity often rely on a concomitant diminution or erasure of maternal personhood, speech, or identity; thus, questions of gender recur throughout the book. Other critical approaches emerge with reference to the more specific philosophical questions that different kinds of literary infants prompt. In approaching the question of fetal subjectivity and personhood, I have sought to attend to the sonic worlds created by medieval writers, and thus to the effects of infant voices as auditory phenomena. Undertaken in conjunction with medieval embryology, this approach has enabled me to rethink what it is to "ventriloquize"—to cause one's voice to emanate from another's body—and how this medieval ventriloquistic construct enmeshes the personhood of mother and fetus. And in conjunction with medieval grammatical theories, insights from sound studies help situate newborns' cries as the ultimate test case of what language is and how it defines the human experience. From second-wave French feminism, the writings of Hélène Cixous in particular, I derive notions of *écriture féminine* and *languelait* as essentially female communicative modes that elude expression via traditionally masculine modes of writing; in conjunction with medieval discussions of mothers and nurses in their dual duties of nourishment and language teaching, these concepts help me tease out the inherent foreignness—especially from the perspective of male writers—of the domestic sphere. More contemporary feminist thought has informed my inquiries into the relationality of the woman-infant dyad, and the resulting modes by which one may speak *for* the other. When placed in dialogue with recent theorizations of epistemic injustice, literary texts in which very young children testify on adult women's behalf yield new insights into the ability of marginally situated voices to critique unjust systems, as well as the impossibility of proving innocence. Finally, from the field of disability studies I adopt notions of impairment and temporality that, when put in dialogue with medieval French narratives, enable a meditation on the mute orphan as an embodiment of the complex interweaving of language, biology, community, and time out of which the human subject emerges. The use of a varied modern theoretical apparatus affords a concrete if ever-shifting approach to slippery medieval literary imaginings of unrecorded and unrecordable speech. More than a complement to the historical research on childhood—though I have perhaps made some small contribution thereto—these critical readings attend to how literary representations of infant discourse "speak" to philosophical questions whose import stretches far beyond their immediate sociocultural context.

Centering my study on the epistemic problems to which imagined infant voices offer access, rather than on the cultural history of childhood, has called for different kind of chronology. This book follows the life course of the notional child, rather than the trajectory of a notion of child*hood*. In other words, I have eschewed a chronological ordering of textual materials in favor of building this book around successive moments in *child development*, each associated with its own set of questions. Exploring the imagined child voice as a prism through which other forms of knowledge are enabled, I consider in turn the particular kinds of knowledge that medieval writers imaginatively access through the voice of the fetus, then the newborn, then the nursing infant, then the newly verbal toddler, and finally the mute child whose miraculous healing overwrites normative expectations of child development. Each of these moments in infant life presents its own configuration of experience, perception, and socialization, and thus, each of these moments offers insight into a different set of epistemic problems:

• *What is a person, and when does personhood begin?* Chapter 1, "Voices from the Womb," focuses on literary representations of fetuses in utero, and especially of fetuses who mediate between the spiritual and the terrestrial as they speak from the womb. These moments expose the rather significant gaps that exist between seemingly contiguous concepts such as "age," "life," "humanity," "personhood," and "subjectivity"; the fetal voice expresses how these useful fictions come apart at the seams. In their literal acts of ventriloquism (with fetuses speaking from the maternal *ventre*, the Old French term for both "belly" and "womb"), talking fetuses constitute the womb as an experimental space knowable only from without, allowing theorization of the unknowable interior through sound. In this chapter I use key concepts in sound studies—especially the work of theorists who have elucidated the tensions between sounds and the structures from which they emanate—to show that numerous medieval writers use the sound of the fetal voice as a tool with which to expose the otherwise invisible mechanisms by which personhood emerges: as a relational tension between maternal and fetal autonomy, resolved through the conceptual effacement of the maternal body.

◆ *What elevates voice to speech, and sound to discourse? Can language capture the fundamental truths of the human condition?* Chapter 2, "Signs of Life," considers medieval representations of human newborns and their cries as a site where linguistic theory, religious doctrine and popular religious practice, and collective modes of reading and (inter) textuality overlap—positing infant vocalizations as the ultimate sign revealing hidden truths about the human condition. In this chapter I engage with two contemporary theorists of the voice, Mladen Dolar and Adriana Cavarero: building on their insights into voice's role in the production of meaning (Dolar) and of relationality (Cavarero), I show how medieval authors use the animal-like cry of the neonate as the basis of a thought experiment testing the limits of both *humanity* and *signification*. As medieval interpretations of newborns' cries tie the precariousness of the cognitive processes underlying human language to a more generalized precariousness of all human existence, the paradox of neonatal speech becomes, through its very irresolvability, a means of tapping into and communicating a "core humanity" that is otherwise difficult to access and express.

◆ *What roles do nature and nurture play in the formation of identity? How do interactions with female caregivers reinforce the universal alterity of the infant?* In chapter 3, "Nurture, the Domestic, and the Foreign," I interrogate the "nature" of the language with which women and infants communicate with each other, and the place of that "baby talk" in broader culture. The frequent assignment of the task of instruction in the "mother tongue" to the wet nurse, a domestic servant who functions as a proxy for the biological mother, highlights the relationality and the cultural constructedness of the supposedly natural maternal role—a construct I tease out by reading medieval representations of women's language-teaching duties in light of both feminist theory and sociolinguistic studies of language socialization. These reflections on language teaching as a gendered domestic chore lead me to consider the complicated relation of the domestic and the *foreign*, especially in the multilingual environments of late medieval courts. The chapter culminates with readings of poems by Christine de Pizan and Charles d'Orléans, which use two different kinds of baby talk to raise larger questions about alienation, domesticity, and foreignness. Placing the two poems in conversation with Susan Fraiman's notions of "extreme domesticity" and of migrant homemaking practices that "map domesticity from the margins,"[46] I argue that both Christine de Pizan and Charles d'Orléans exploit the interstice between the domestic as *home space* and the domestic *in opposition to the foreign*, at once invoking child language as an idiom of alienation and of innovation. When baby talk is taken seriously as a language, the mother-child dyad is revealed to be a remarkably fungible, even artificial relation establishing universal alterity within the home.

✦ *Is innocence enough to protect us from injustice? Who can speak truth to epistemic power?* In chapter 4, "Interrogating Innocence," I examine narratives in which truth-telling toddlers aid in the administration of adult justice. These include the future prophet Daniel's exculpation of Susanna, as depicted in secular romances and behavioral manuals; Merlin's legal defense of his mother in Robert de Boron's prose *Merlin*; and a group of fabliaux in which toddlers reveal maternal infidelity to their fathers. The words of these supposedly voiceless legal nonentities can carry serious weight—but discourses surrounding the role that "innocent" children can play in these fictional legal proceedings, all of which center on allegations of adult women's unchastity, also destabilize the very notion of innocence. Reading the medieval narratives through the lens of feminist epistemology, and especially Miranda Fricker's concept of epistemic injustice, I will demonstrate that child witnesses and advocates exploit but do not correct misogynistic epistemic injustice, underscoring that innocence plays only a limited role in resiliently unjust human systems of justice.

✦ *Is infancy a state of disability? How does child disability disrupt normative temporality and the forms of knowledge it enables? Do people unable to advocate for themselves remain in a state of perpetual infancy?* In the final chapter, "Mute Children in the Time of Miracle," I consider literary narratives of the miraculous healing of mute children, exploring the discursive overlap between childhood and disability and its implications for the kinds of knowledge infant language can enable—and the kinds of children whose stories can grant access to such knowledge. As mute children (and mute orphans in particular) gain or regain the faculty of speech, their social environments and even the temporalities of their stories are altered to accommodate their new abilities and needs. Thus, while offering new perspectives on what it means to acquire language, these stories also enable marvelous rewritings of the human life cycle, troubling notions about the relationship of language and experience to knowledge. Reading miracle narratives in conjunction with notions of "crip time" adapted from contemporary disability studies, I will show that the epistemic utility of infants' universal alterity is a function of time, and that disabled children, who inhabit nonnormative timelines, test the limits of infant universality and lay bare the contradictions inherent to the building of knowledge through narration—and thus to literary representation itself.

Studies of medieval childhood, even in the literary disciplines, have for the most part been firmly inscribed in a larger project of cultural history. Thinking of the literary representation of children as something other than an element of cultural history, however—that is, thinking of literary infants as something other than a possible reflection of the lived experience of the infants of the Middle Ages—invites new understandings of medieval literature as an instrument of critical and even philosophical reflection on unobservable and nearly ineffable parts of human experience. Ultimately this study reveals the extent to which infancy was, itself, a medieval theoretical apparatus: a way of distilling complex questions about the varieties of human experience without oversimplifying them. In other words, as this book will show, the infant is a familiar figure that serves, in many medieval literary texts, to advance abstract inquiry while structuring it into a recognizable and narratable form. Infants are familiar, but the discourses they enable—from even before birth—are far from simple.

CHAPTER ONE

VOICES FROM THE WOMB

In medieval French, the word *enfant* refers to humans both before and after birth. Modern studies of medieval childhood tend, unsurprisingly, to talk about their subjects only after they have been born; Claude Thomasset has even argued that children become available as literary subjects only at the moment of birth.[1] And yet, in a number of medieval French texts, fetal characters do speak—and the sound of these voices renders the intrauterine environment, and a fetal perspective on that environment, accessible to the outside world. These medieval discussions of the prenatal experience tend to confirm Barbara Johnson's argument that "the issue of 'fetal personhood' [brings] to a state of explicit uncertainty the fundamental difficulty of defining personhood in general."[2] In this chapter I will argue that the imagined voices of fetuses reveal personhood to be conceived as the product of a relational tension between maternal and fetal autonomy.

In considering the imagined fetal vocalizations and experiences through which medieval writers explore the ways that constructs of the "person" are made and unmade, I will draw on key insights from sound studies, particularly the work of three authors who have each, in his own way, elucidated the tensions between sounds and the structures from which they emanate. From Steven Connor's literary and cultural study of ventriloquism (*Dumbstruck*, 2000), I have derived a conceptual framework for understanding how displaced voices trouble boundaries between bodies and between differential states of aliveness; from the music theorist Brian Kane (*Sound Unseen*, 2014), I have gained insight into the various ways in which sounds emanating from an unseen source exist between bodies and thus pose a physical as well as an epistemic problem; and from the philosopher of science Michel Serres (*Le parasite*, 1980), I take the idea that the incongruous sound of the "parasite" (a beneficiary of a one-way relationship, or the static or bug in a system) is constitutive of relationality. With these guiding propositions in mind, I will show that medieval imaginings of the fetal voice constitute the womb as an experimental space knowable only from without, and that the "two-body problem" of the emergence of a new person is resolved through the effacement of the maternal body as the boundary between states of being unborn and born—and that this effacement is in part a sonic phenomenon.

Personhood, in medieval Europe, tends to be bound up with the problem of animation. A fetus becomes a living *enfant* at the moment it is endowed with a rational soul—the soul being an entity that, in Western art, itself comes to be represented in the form of an *enfant*.[3] Taking as my point of departure the basic medieval definition of a person as a composite of body and soul,[4] I will show how, for a number of medieval French writers, moments of fetal vocalization reveal the remarkable degree to which personhood is a notion reliant on sound and speech. Not just because of the putative etymology of the word *persona*—from *per sonare*, making one's voice heard across a barrier such as a mask[5]—but because audible and meaningful speech sounds emerge as the first conceivable indicator that both soul and body have developed sufficiently to form a new *person*. Medieval representations of talking fetuses in utero establish personhood as both a discursive category (constructed through language) and a discursive capacity (expressing itself through language).

In medieval canon law, the human fetus is typically called the *conceptus*, that which has been conceived[6]—a term at once evocative of a developing human and of an idea yet to be fully expressed. Speech proves to be one of the primary mechanisms by which the *conceptus* develops from a near abstraction to an entity that not only can be represented, but can be represented as expressing *itself*. Gestation is, in this view, constructed as a gradual process over the course of which an initial concept eventually emerges as someone who "end[s] up speaking to you," as the philosopher Jean-Paul Galibert puts it.[7]

Fetal speech offers medieval writers a compelling instrument with which to examine the emergence of the "person," from a vantage point that is both rational and at least partly pre- or nonhuman. But fetal speech, when perceived and reported by an external narrator, is also a very particular *sonic* phenomenon: it is experienced as an acousmatic voice, that is, a voice produced by a speaker concealed from sight. For Mladen Dolar, "the acousmatic voice *par excellence*" is the maternal voice ("the mother of all acousmatic voices") as experienced by the fetus in utero.[8] Indeed, as Brian Kane points out, the acousmatic "experience of sound in the mother's womb [. . .] is claimed to play a central role in the formation of the subject."[9] Medieval texts, however, suggest a reversal of this formulation: the sound that gives outsiders access to the earliest moments in the human experience, the "acousmatic voice *par excellence*," is the fetal voice emanating from within.

Medieval literary efforts to represent the *conceptus*, and to query the continuities that may exist between it and the later stages of human development, typically involve both the voicing of a fetal perspective and an alteration of the matrix from which it emanates. Often adopting a fetus-centered point of view, writers envision the interior of the maternal body as an *exterior* space that can then be penetrated, made transparent, through fetal speech.[10] Like ultrasound technology, the fictional fetal voice "reveals the interior" of the body, and in this case the womb, "without the necessity of physical invasion."[11] As auditory stimuli pass from the fetus's mouth to the listener's ear they create a vocalic space,[12] that is, a social space that encompasses and exceeds the maternal body. Literally ventriloquistic, the fetal voice expresses an unmediated *conceptus*, transforming the *ventre* (the medieval French word for both the belly and the womb) into a mask across which the fetal voice resounds.

Talking fetuses illustrate the universal alterity of the infant in its most extreme form: they foreground uncertainties about how a soul is joined to a body in gestational time, and thus they test the boundaries between the terrestrial and the spiritual, between the physical and the metaphysical. This is all the more so because the speaking fetuses that appear in medieval French texts are almost exclusively either divine or demonic entities. And yet, perhaps counterintuitively, the not-quite-human-ness of these fetal characters makes them particularly effective illustrations of the ways in which personhood is constructed as a vocalic phenomenon. These are extreme test cases that allow us to tease out a more general interdependence of soul and speech. A person is a composite of body and soul that can signal its own existence by making its voice heard; when that person exists in utero, its voice presents a potential bug in another person's system (to adopt Serres's terms).[13] Whether originating from the incarnate Word or a more ordinary *conceptus*, fetal speech and the meanings it produces emanate from a woman's body without being *of* that body. Texts that depict a supernatural fetus developing within a human mother only make clearer the complicated questions about identity that arise when one person serves as a spatial matrix through which a voice not her own expresses a subjectivity not her own.

Instances of fetal speech in medieval French literature effect peculiar physiological and spatial manipulations on the maternal body, suggesting that personhood emerges from a tension between two contiguous and nonautonomous bodies. These manipulations are effected by means of an acousmatic voice, a kind of sound object that brings with it questions about the body from which it might emanate and highlights the gaps between what we perceive and what we know. In Kane's memorable formulation, "the *being* of acousmatic sound *is* to be a gap."[14] And the acousmatic fetal voices in medieval French literature expose the rather significant gaps that exist between seemingly contiguous concepts such as age, life, childhood, humanity, personhood, and subjectivity. As outlined in the introduction, medieval French thinkers construct the human life span as a series of ages—but a closer look at literary representations of fetuses in utero shows that for these same writers, life, age, and personhood do not begin at the same time. Nor does a fetal voice necessarily express a state of mind that is continuous with the same "person's" consciousness after birth. It turns out that for medieval writers, the beginnings of *personhood*, thorny as the question may be, are somewhat simpler to define than are the beginnings of *childhood*. Nevertheless I will explore the beginnings of life and of the age of childhood first, as a necessary preface to any conclusions about the emergence of personhood, because the staggered starts of "life" and "age" create an indeterminacy *within* the maternal body that is requisite for emerging personhood—and they inaugurate a sequence of changes over time that cannot be seen but sometimes can be heard.

Across the ages-of-man schemas of the Middle Ages, the first age is consistently called *infantia*. The moment when this stage begins, however, is harder to pinpoint than one might suspect. Embryos and fetuses occupy a peculiar and uneasy position in medieval schematizations of the human life cycle. The fetus is and yet is not a child. Witness the discussion of childhood in encyclopedias such as Bartholomaeus Anglicus's *De proprietatibus rerum*, translated into French by Jean Corbechon in 1372. The text opens its discussion of the ages of man at the start of book 6 by stating that age begins at conception, but childhood begins at birth:

> Selon Ysidore aage est l'espace de la vie de la beste ou de la personne qui commance des sa concepcion et faut apres sa viellesce et a la mort. Ilz sont pluseurs divers aages selon Constantin et Ysidore. Le premier aage est enfance qui plante les denz, et commance cest aage quant l'enfant est [né]¹⁵ et dure iusques a vii ans, et en cest aage ce qui est né est appellé enfant qui vault autant a dire comme non parlant pour ce que en tel aage il ne puet pas bien parler ne parfaictement former les paroles, car il n'a pas encore les dens bien ordonnees ne affermees sicomme dit Ysidore et Constantin. (BnF MS fr. 16993, fol. 74r)

> According to Isidore, age is the part of the life of a beast or a person that begins at its conception and ends after its old age and death. There are many different ages, according to Constantine and Isidore. The first age is early childhood [*enfance*], which introduces the teeth, and this age begins when the child is [born] and lasts until age seven. In this age the one who is born is called *enfant*, which means "non-speaking," because in this age he can neither speak properly nor form

words perfectly, for he does not yet have well-arranged and firmly set teeth, as Isidore and Constantine say.

The status of the fetus is far from clear, for a number of reasons. The omission of the participle *né* from a number of manuscripts—including BnF MS fr. 16993, which is considered to be one of the earliest and most authoritative manuscripts of Corbechon's translation[16]—renders explicit the underlying question: when does a child begin to exist? But even in manuscripts that are free from this slip, the passage is self-contradictory, as Isidore, whom Bartholomaeus cites when he says that age begins at conception, in fact states that age begins at birth: "Prima aetas infantia est pueri nascentis ad lucem, quae porrigitur in septem annis" (The first age, the infancy [*infantia*] of a newborn child, lasts seven years).[17] Besides, if age begins at conception but infancy (the first age of man) begins at birth, what is the status of a fetus?

The ambiguity surrounding the beginning of *infantia* is reflected in the iconographic tradition as well. Corbechon's encyclopedia survives in many richly illustrated copies.[18] In these, book 6 usually opens with an illustration of the ages of man. Such images, as Elizabeth Sears points out, "provide a kind of commentary on the text in their own right" and often resolve the encyclopedia's refusal to state just how many ages there are.[19] It is quite rare, however, for as many as seven ages to be illustrated; often just a few are represented, though there is almost always at least one child. Some images portray multiple children, including BnF MS fr. 218, made in Poitiers in the late fifteenth century, whose seven figures on fol. 95r include a swaddled infant, a toddler in a walker, and a bigger child on a hobbyhorse. Most astonishingly, the mid-fifteenth-century BnF MS fr. 135 includes on fol. 193r a pregnant woman at the far left of its ages-of-man illustration, just next to a nursing woman and a small child (fig. 1.1). The implication is that the fetus in utero participates in the first age.

Bartholomaeus Anglicus's widely read encyclopedia is not the only medieval text to divide human life into ages that raise the question of the degree to which fetuses participate in the human

FIGURE 1.1 The ages of man (mid-fifteenth-century).
From *Livre des propriétés des choses* (BnF MS fr. 135, fol. 193r).
Photograph: Bibliothèque nationale de France.

experience. Another example is the passage from Jean Froissart's *Joli buisson de Jonece* (1373), in which Jonece (Youth) explains cosmology and the influence of the planets on human development:

> La lune coustumierement
> Gouverne tout premierement
> L'enfant et par .IIII. ans le garde,
> Et sus sa nourechon regarde.
> Tres qu'il est ou ventre sa mere,
> Le prent. (vv. 1616–21)[20]

The Moon customarily
Governs the infant right from the beginning
And protects him for four years,
And looks after his education.
As soon as he is in his mother's belly,
She takes to him.[21]

The "enfant" is under the Moon's influence for its first four years, beginning when it is still "ou ventre sa mere" (in its mother's womb).[22] The use of the ambiguous word *nourechon* to characterize the moon's tutelage of the infant could indicate the nourishment of a fetus in utero, but it primarily calls to mind the care and feeding of a born child.[23]

In languages such as Old and Middle French that use much of the same vocabulary to refer to humans both before and after they are born, it can be extremely difficult to sort out whether the act of calling a fetus an *enfant* reflects any particular attitude about its ontological status. More technical embryological terms are rare in the vernacular, though *fete* (from *foetus*) does appear in the Middle French translation of Guy de Chauliac's *Chirurgia magna*,[24] and Nicole Oresme appears to coin the French *embryon* when he discusses the vegetative soul in his translation of Aristotle's *Ethics*.[25] This latter term is identified as belonging strictly to the medical domain in the anonymous *Histoire de la première destruction de Troie* (probably dating from the 1470s), which includes the following observation in the description of a statue of Mercury:

> Mercure, selon les poethes, a puissance de revocquer les ames qui sont aux enfers, et luy est cest office atribuee, pource que la planete de son nom preside sur la masce qui est au ventre de la mere, que les phisiciens appellent "embrio," et que par son influence organize et dispose le corps a recevoir l'ame raisonnable.[26]

> Mercury, according to the poets, has the power to bring back souls that are in hell, and this function is attributed to him because the planet named after him presides over the mass in a mother's womb that the physicians call an "embryo," and because through its influence he organizes and prepares the body to receive the rational soul.

The Latin *infans* is quite frequently used to refer to fetuses in medical and legal texts alike,[27] and "in descriptions of the physiology of gestation, the term *foetus* often refers not just to the fetus but also to the newborn. The scholastics spoke of the nourishment of the fetus 'before and after birth,' or 'inside and outside' it mother's body."[28] Similarly, the only widely used term in the French vernacular, *enfant*, encompasses development both before and after birth.[29] It is often paired with the adjective *vif* or *bougeant* to denote a pregnancy that has progressed beyond the earliest stages. These locutions are telling, as they appear to pin infancy to aliveness, which may be felt to equate, in a woman's lived experience, with her perception of fetal movement—though, of course, fetal movement is not perceptible until long after conception. Indeed, such language hints that an embryo might not be an *enfant* from the moment of its conception but rather acquires this status later in its development.

At what point, precisely, is a fetus sufficiently developed to be considered an *enfant*? The terminology most often used in medieval texts (both medical and theological) is "formation": a fetus is fully "formed" when it has all of its major organs and has begun to take on a distinctly human shape. It is then human enough to receive a rational soul, for the rational soul can be present only in a body with advanced enough cognitive and sensory capabilities to make use of it.[30] This notion of formation underpins the *Livre des proprietez des choses*'s treatment of the thorny matter of when life and childhood begin. In chapter VI.3, "De la creation de l'enfant" (*De creacione infantis*), the period from conception to the full formation of the fetus is fixed at forty-six days—a duration that is based on the number of years it took for the Temple to be constructed in Jerusalem. It is roughly consistent with the calendar of fetal development laid out in more specialized embryological texts, which typically pinpoint the formation of a male fetus at anywhere between thirty and forty-five days' gestation. (Female fetuses, they assert, take up to twice as long to form.)[31] The fetus passes through four "degrees" of development and then, upon its formation, becomes a child:

> Le dernier degré si est quant touz les membres sont formez et separez l'un de l'autre. Et adonc c'est un enfant selon Ypocras car il

est souffisamment disposé a recevoir l'ame et la vie et se commance ja a mouvoir et a hurter des piez et des mains [. . .] . Il y a donc xlvi jours de la conception de l'enfant iusques a tant qu'il a vie et qu'il est du tout formé quant au fait de generacion de nature. (BnF MS fr. 16993, fol. 75r)

The last degree is when all of the members are formed and distinct from one another. And then it is a child according to Hippocrates, for it is sufficiently disposed to receive soul and life and it already begins to move and strike with its feet and hands [. . .] . There are therefore 46 days from the conception of the child until it has life and until it is fully formed with regard to natural generation.

After forty-six days, a fetus has become a living child—an entity that by definition cannot speak properly, but that is capable of vocalization, movement, and rational thought. Indeed, the *Livre des proprietez des choses* later attributes fetal movement to sensory observation and a rational cognitive process: "Quant l'ame entre ou corps de l'enfant il a vie et sent par nature qu'est avironnée d'une pel et se muet pour la rompre et par tel mouvement de l'enfant le corps et le ventre de la mere si est grevé" (When the soul enters the child's body he becomes alive and naturally senses that he is surrounded by a membrane, and he moves himself to break it, and the body and womb of the mother are caused pain by such movement on the child's part; fol. 75v).[32] This explanation of fetal movement reinforces the proposition, implicit in the widely used idiom *vif enfant*, that movement is the perceptible manifestation of the *conceptus*'s having become a fully ensouled child. So, while *aage* starts at conception, the *conceptus* becomes an *enfant*— and its *vie* begins—once it is sufficiently developed to receive a rational soul.[33] Physiologically, spiritually, and linguistically, this moment marks the transition from potential to actual humanity.[34]

Thus far much of this discussion has hinged on the vernacular vocabulary of the *enfant* as applied to a fetus. It should be noted, though, that the different terms used in Latin, including in medical and legal discourses, reveal a range of attitudes toward the question of fetal personhood. A number of the Latin terms for a fetus in utero suggest a state somewhere between human and animal. Ana Isabel

Martín Ferreira even reports instances in which a fetus is referred to as *animal*,[35] a vocabulary consistent with the Aristotelian embryological tradition, exemplified by Giles of Rome, whereby the embryo "lives an animal life" before the infusion of the soul.[36] Faint echoes of the fetus as animal are occasionally found in the vernacular, as in the *Livre des proprietez des choses*, which discusses both human and animal fetuses under the rubric "Du faon" (book 18, chapter 52) — in the book devoted to animals. As for legal codes, which "distinguished among many classes of natural persons, whose legal rights depended on social valuation,"[37] fetuses are described with various terms that sometimes underscore their continuity with born children but sometimes suggest a more indeterminate status. The unborn are most often referred to as *conceptus* in canon law and as *qui in utero* in civil codes, according to Anne Lefebvre-Teillard; but she notes that the legal language used to designate the unborn is highly unsystematic, citing disparate phrases such as *pueri qui sunt in utero, filius qui nascitur*, and *existens in utero* in the writings of thirteenth- and fourteenth-century jurists.[38] Thus, while medical language sometimes suggests the fetus is an essentially animal-like being, legal discourses fluctuate between seeing the unborn as a child (*pueri, filius*) and seeing it as an indeterminate and deliberately vague presence (*qui, existens*). In their own ways, the indeterminate vocabularies of these encyclopedic, medical, philosophical, and legal texts lead toward the same set of questions: Is a fetus alive? Is it a child? Is it a person? What does it even mean to *be* a person? For some medieval writers, the beings possessed of the necessary epistemic privilege to address these questions are fetuses themselves.

THE PHYSIOLOGY AND THEOLOGY
OF THE FETAL VOICE

While fetal vocalization might seem fanciful or even marvelous, according to medieval medical discourses it is a mundane occurrence; *every* human fetus laughs while in the womb. So, although fetal vocalization audible outside of the womb is extraordinary, the acquisition of a voice in utero is a fundamental marker of emergent personhood.

Medieval embryology, as Romana Martorelli Vico expertly demonstrates, is a dynamic area of inquiry situated at the shifting intersection of theological, metaphysical, and medical discourses.[39] More specifically, the metaphysical question—when does a human become a subject, or a person?—is resolved by placing biological conclusions (a determination of when the fetus develops the anatomical structures necessary to reason and self-expression) in dialogue with theological ones (when the fetus acquires a rational soul). As Robert Pasnau points out, conventional wisdom—as expressed by Aquinas, among many others—holds that "even though [...] the mind is an immaterial power that operates without any corporeal organ, [...] there are constraints on the sort of body that a human mind can inform."[40] In other words, a fetus must attain a significant degree of physiological development before it is adequately equipped to receive a rational soul. While such a notion of "delayed hominization" was not universally accepted in the Middle Ages, Pasnau has argued forcefully that it was a dominant viewpoint.[41] Following Albert the Great's influential mid-thirteenth-century commentary *De animalibus* (c. 1256–63), the anatomical structures presrequisite to ensoulment are generally accepted as being housed in the brain.[42]

According to received medieval wisdom, then, a fetus can only acquire its rational soul once its brain and its sense organs are sufficiently developed for it to be capable of perception and thought. When it is capable of these, its first action is a vocal expression: the ensouled fetus laughs. As Giles of Rome writes in chapter XVII of *De formatione humani corporis in utero* (c. 1285–95), the most important embryological treatise produced in the medieval West:

> Dicit autem Avicenna in IX *De animalibus*, quod puer in utero ridet post XL dies et ista est prima operatio quam habet anima rationalis, ut ait, in suo corpore. Sompniat autem, ut ait, post duos menses.[43]

> Moreover, Avicenna says in *De animalibus* IX that a child in utero laughs after forty days, and that is his first act once he has a rational soul, it is said, in his body. He also dreams, it is said, after two months.

This is a close paraphrase of Avicenna, who, in *De animalibus* IX, 5 (via Michael Scot's Latin translation), had considered at greater length the intellectual activities of fetuses.

> et ridet puer post .40. dies: et hec est prima actio quam operat anima rationalis in suo corpore: et somniat post duos menses: et ut putatur tradit oblivioni: et dico ego quod est: quia discernuntur in illo tempore res sensibiles: et remanent impressiones in virtute memorativa et anterior pars capitis est mollior: et non est ita in aliis animalibus.[44]

> And the child laughs after 40 days, and this is the first act that the rational soul operates in his body. He dreams after two months, and forgets [his dreams], it is believed. And I myself say that this is because things perceptible to the senses are discerned at that time, and impressions remain in the memorative faculty, and the front of the brain is rather soft. But it is not so in other animals.

Avicenna's description of fetal sensation is noteworthy for its emphasis on sense perception and on continuity of experience, as well as its affirmation of human exceptionalism. Laughter is a sign of a specifically human intellect. From this point on the fetus can sense and imagine: it has volition, rationality, a point of view—though the softness of the developing brain prevents its thoughts from enduring. The expression of such ideas is not limited to arcane scientific discourses; it also occurs in widely diffused encyclopedic texts, such as the above-cited passage from Corbechon's encyclopedia, wherein the first fetal movement is interpreted as a response to the surrounding membrane that the newly developed rational soul has allowed the fetus to perceive for the first time.

Ensoulment allows for a fetal perception of, and reaction to, its own surroundings. Yet Avicenna has also to acknowledge the unknowability of fetal intellectual activity: its perceptions, the impressions that result from them, and the oblivion that subsequently erases them are all acknowledged to be only putative.[45] The postulated oblivion allows for a reconciliation between different notions of the beginnings of life: bridging the gap between theological or scientific models that would situate the origins of personhood or *vie* at forty days' gestation, and the competing popular belief that life begins later, after fetal movements become perceptible to the mother.[46] But the unknowability and imperceptibility of the fetal laugh also mark this vocalization as nonspeech. Speech cannot exist in a nonsocial vacuum; unlike the "first invoking cry of the [newborn] infant," which according to Adriana Cavarero establishes the essential "relationality of the vocalic,"[47] the fetal laugh is imperceptible, non-relational, vocalic but unspoken. If a fetus laughs in the womb and no one else is able to hear it, has anything been communicated at all?

The idea that fetuses laugh at the moment of their ensoulment is not universally accepted in the Middle Ages.[48] Indeed, if taken literally the laugh at ensoulment would, according to the few medieval embryological texts that give any consideration to the physiology of speech, be impossible. The pseudo-Albertus's *De secretis mulierum* (*Women's Secrets*), for instance, fixes the formation of "the instrument of the voice" in the sixth month of gestation, long after the forty- or forty-six- or even ninety-day infusion of the soul:

> Sexto tempore influencia et regimen Mercurii instrumenta vocis for-mat, supercilia componit, oculos fabricat, pupillos crescere facit, capil-los et ungulas producit. Et huic operacioni sextus mensis attribuitur.[49]

> In the sixth month the influence and reign of Mercury form the instrument of the voice, compose the eyebrows and eyes, and make hair and nails grow. From this operation of the sixth month arises the verse: "Nine instruments to every child belong / Two lips, four teeth, one palate, throat and tongue."[50]

Other texts that specify which parts of the fetus develop in each month configure the developmental calendar differently: for instance, the *Liber de sinthomatibus mulierum* (Book on the conditions of women), by "Trotula," places the development of hair and nails in the third month but says nothing about the voice.[51] Medical accounts disagree, and evidence of what ordinary medieval people might have thought of this matter is scant. But the physiological possibility of prenatal speech is raised in a fascinating early fourteenth-century exchange recorded in the Fournier Register and described by Emmanuel Le Roy Ladurie: Raymond Roussel tells the pregnant Béatrice de Planissoles that a soul can transmigrate to a fetus via any orifice of the mother's body, as he himself seeks to gain private access to Béatrice's orifices; she asks him why, if babies are born with old souls, they can't already speak by the time they are born; and Raymond replies that babies do not speak because God does not want them to.[52] Leaving aside the question of metempsychosis, what's interesting for the present discussion is that the barrier to fetal speech is neither physiological or spiritual but a matter of divine will. There is no other reason for formed fetuses *not* to talk.

Other vernacular texts offer some evidence for a general associa-tion of sound—which may or may not manifest as speech—and the soul. In the late thirteenth-century prose dialogue *Placides et Timéo*, for instance, the teacher Timéo explains to his student Placides that a fetus is molded and formed like a cast metal bell:

> Et je vous di que on fait cloques et campanes pour sonner, et a ce faire couvient .II. coses: le metail dont on les fait et si couvient qu'il y ait son; ainsi couvient a homme et a femme faire et a toutes autres crea-tures deux coses: le matere au corps faire, ce est li spermes, et l'ame qui ou corps s'estent. Et tout aussi comme le cloque ou le campane, quant il sont fais, li sons est fais avec et en faisant li est li sons fais, tout ainsi est il d'omme ou de bestes, car, si comme je vous ay dit, en enfondant le sperme est l'ame creé et en creant l'ame est li sperme espandus.[53]

> And I tell you that bells and chimes are made to ring, and to do this two things are needed: the metal from which they are made is required, but it is also necessary that there be sound. Likewise to make a man or a woman or any other creature two things are needed: the matter of which the body is made, which is sperm, and the soul, which extends itself to the body. And just as when the bell or chime is made the sound is made with it—and in making it sound is also made—thus is it with man or beasts, for, as I told you, in casting the sperm the soul is made, and in creating the soul the sperm is poured.

The analogy between the soul and the sound of a bell establishes a connection between that which can reason and that which can make a sound—and be heard.[54] It reflects, albeit indirectly, a view similar to that expressed by Avicenna and Giles of Rome: that gestation is a period during which the developing human goes from having a potential voice to having an actual one. Though Timéo declares the soul present from the moment of casting (conception), the bell-founding analogy reminds us of the gap between casting and ringing, or between conception and a capacity for reason and speech. Just as a bell must cool and solidify, a fetus must gestate, and its voice can only ring out once that process is complete.[55]

Scientific texts and their vulgarizations present fetal experience as an enigma. Unavailable to language, the "germinal phases of a life" can hardly be termed "fully historical" (as J. Allan Mitchell calls them[56]); rather, the peal of the unborn *enfant*'s soul might provide the best approximation of what Giorgio Agamben describes as the *experimentum linguae* of infancy, testing the limits of language in a purely self-referential expression.[57] Along these lines, it is important to note that for the author of *Placides et Timéo*, the bell analogy applies equally well to *omme* and to *bestes*. What distinguishes the emerging human person from the nonhuman *faon* is not just sound, but speech.

Fetal development and the acquisition of a rational soul are bound up with speech in the most famous medieval literary vulgarization of embryology, from canto 25 of Dante's *Purgatorio*.[58] Here embryology serves to illustrate the relationship between soul and body: when Dante asks why the penitent souls of Purgatory have bodies that can be made to suffer, Statius replies with an explanation of fetal development, stating that the same organizing principle that forms the fetus also forms the aerial body.[59] Statius famously describes gestation as the process by which a fetus "d'animal divegna fante" (from animal, this thing becomes a child; v. 61).[60] We must note that here the developing fetus has become not an *infans* but a *fante*, a speaking subject,[61] and the "conceptual antinomy" between the mute beast and the speaking child underlines the importance of verbal capacity to the definition of humanity itself.[62]

There is no indisputable evidence of any medieval French person having read *Purgatorio*, though Philippe de Mézières alludes to Dante in the *Songe du vieil pèlerin* I.39,[63] and Christine de Pizan not only refers to Dante but models her *Chemin de long estude* on the *Commedia*.[64] Regardless of whether it was known in late medieval France, *Purgatorio*'s embryological canto is significant to the present discussion because it shows how the matter of embryology can inform poetic efforts to define what it means to be human, and how "the passage from animality to rationality" (as Bruno Nardi puts it[65]) can be portrayed as being fundamentally a function of *speech*. After all, the medieval French *raisonner*, like the modern Italian *ragionare*, means both "to reason" and "to speak." Like Avicenna's and Giles of Rome's idea that the first rational act of the ensouled fetus is to laugh, and like *Placides et Timéo*'s assimilation of soul to sound, Dante's description of the newly formed future infant as *fante* underscores just how strong the link is between reason, speech, and the human experience.

"LA DEMEURE DE L'ENFANT
OU VENTRE DE SA MERE"

Whereas scientific texts and their vulgarizations clearly present fetal experience as an enigma, it is to nonscientific, literary narratives that we must turn to find creative approaches to its resolution— for while both scientific and poetic imaginings of fetal existence are necessarily speculative, it is the literary texts that attempt both the visualization of the fetus and the representation (or even the adoption) of its perspective and voice. Vocal communication is commonly described by voice theorists as an "interior to interior" phenomenon. Produced in the utterer's mouth and larynx and perceived within the listener's ears, speech sounds are "a special sensory key to interiority";[66] they offer special access to the "interior 'real' body" or even the *person*, "the most interior of interiors."[67] Fetal voices emanating from the maternal body obviously compound and magnify the usual dynamics by which any voice "comes from the inside of a body and radiates through a space which is exterior to and extends beyond that body," thereby rendering perceptible "the co-operation of bodies and the environments in which they have their being":[68] these voices' trajectory from interior to exterior takes them through a first exterior that is actually the inside of another person's body. The creation of fictional acousmatic fetal voices resolves the enigma of fetal experience by introducing a new enigma, one that can only be resolved with further fictions; the acousmatic voice "encourages imaginative supplementation" through its very underdetermination, a deliberately created underdetermination that these texts will now supplement.[69] And they will supplement it by recasting the veil that conceals the voice's source from the auditor's view. Through imagined fetal discourse, the "interior to interior" phenomenon of vocal communication can transform a mother's womb into different kinds of space and open it to new modes of observation. A fetus cannot become a speaking person without fundamentally altering the maternal *persona* across which it resounds.

In examining how medieval writers imagine fetal subjectivity, I am struck, first of all, by their approaches to the womb as a setting in which speech occurs: how is one to observe a fetus within an utterly inaccessible place? One evident possibility might be to open the female body and expose its secrets—and this strategy is indeed employed across multiple medieval media, from the Shrine Madonnas most recently studied by Elina Gertsman,[70] to writers' and illuminators' portrayals of Nero directing the dissection of his mother, Agrippina,[71] to the illustrations in fourteenth-century manuscripts of Albert the Great's *De animalibus*. However, a number of writers instead attempt a less intrusive and more radically experimental approach, adopting language that configures the womb less as a female organ than as the object of the fetus's (putative) subjective experience. These poetic slippages into a quasi-fetal perspective enable what Jonathan Morton has recently (and stimulatingly) called "medieval thought experiments": "a range of imaginative procedures that allow for a kind of thinking not limited to the strictly empirical, the strictly possible, or even the strictly logical."[72] The pregnant woman's womb becomes, in this sense, an experimental space: one that is constituted through both fetal perception and fetal voice.

Experimental though it might be, the womb space is decidedly not an "indifferent prepersonal materiality,"[73] as J. Allan Mitchell calls it in an otherwise perceptive study of medieval gestation that somehow neglects to acknowledge that fetuses have mothers at all. Quite the contrary: in the medieval French texts I have encountered, the fetal environment is still, even when described or accessed metaphorically, conceived of as a part of a woman's body.

Because scientific accounts of the fetus's laugh describe it as inaudible, this sound is insufficient to let us "see" through the womb and into the developing person. Unlike the unheard laughter described by Avicenna and Giles of Rome, some fetal voices in literary narratives are indeed audible to outside listeners. This means that the fetuses and their listeners—who may include human characters, supernatural entities, and/or the reading and listening public—must "inhabit" a shared "acoustic space," to adopt Walter Ong's terms.[74] The fetus dwells in a space from which it can speak, and the listener, though not occupying that same womb, inhabits an adjacent space where the *vox clamantis in utero* is audible. I echo Ong's vocabulary of "inhabiting" deliberately, as medieval writers frequently imagine the gravid uterus as an inhabited, *domestic* space. The physician Evrart de Conty, in a prose gloss on the *Echecs amoureux* (before 1405), characterizes gestation as "la demeure de l'enfant ou ventre de sa mere," an extended stay (*demeure*) in a dwelling place (*demeure*): the equivocal pun on the "demeure de l'enfant" stages the maternal body as a setting for fetal action.[75] Such domestic spatialization of the inside of the mother's body is even more overt in other texts, wherein the womb is replete with its own architecture and even furnishings.[76] Fetal speech can render these domestic and anatomical interiors perceptible from the outside, and when the opaque maternal body becomes transparent, it opens itself to judgments of cleanliness and putridity.

When an ordinary woman becomes pregnant, her fetus, thought to be nourished by diverted menstrual blood, is typically described as dwelling in filth. This common misogynistic discourse is related to Aristotelian ideas but is widely disseminated in a number of non-scientific literary sources, especially *De miseria condicionis humane* (On the misery of the human condition), written in 1195 by Lotario dei Segni, the future Pope Innocent III. Lotario's tropes about the "detestable" gestational environment are projected into a uterine home space in the second book of the *Roman de Fauvel* (1314), in which the goddess Fortune describes Fauvel's mother's womb as a dirty room in order to demonstrate that Fauvel's inferiority is not just innate, but antenatal:

> Engendrez fus horriblement
> Et nourris en ventre ordement
> De la plus vilaine matere
> Que Nature pout onques faire;
> Et quant dedens le ventre estoies,
> Envelopez en ordes toies,
> Chambre avoies a grant destrece[77]

> You were engendered in horrible fashion
> And nourished foully in the womb
> With the most vile matter
> That Nature could ever make;
> And when you were within the womb,
> Swaddled in filthy membranes,
> You had a most distressing chamber

The passage is noteworthy for its emphasis on Fauvel's lived experience, as a fetus, within his mother's body. Dwelling in this soiled domestic space, Fauvel is a parasite in Michel Serres's sense of the term: a disruptor, both biological and sonic ("tantosts coummanças a braire" [right away you began to bray]; v. 3839). The reader is reminded that as with other parasites, fetal Fauvel's "outside is an inside"[78] — and, conversely, that the inside of the mother's body is exterior to someone else. The domestic interior is a private space, but one that can be opened to the outside. Indeed, Fauvel's one-time "chamber" is more accessible from the perspective of the outside observer (Fortune) than that of its former inhabitant, who, like Avicenna's sleeping fetuses, "tretout ce as omblié" (you have forgotten all about this; v. 3843). The expression of embryological discourse in the second person underlines the counterintuitive idea that fetal experience is knowable only from without.

Fortune's speech implies a thorough continuity of experience even during the profound transformations that occur from conception, throughout fetal development, to life outside the womb. The uterine narrative is, in a sense, a microcosm of *Fauvel* as a whole: "a story of transformation and metamorphosis," as Michael Camille puts it, with Fauvel passing through "a host of stages between the fully animal and the fully human (which he never is)."[79] And indeed—in case the point wasn't clear enough—the dialogue between Fortune and Fauvel takes place in a city called Macrocosm.[80] But while the adult Fauvel aspires to the riches of Fortune, he comes from a place that the goddess portrays as a perverse, soiled domestic space. In her account of Fauvel's fetal existence, Fortune implies that fetuses are sentient—they have an inner life, albeit one that they forget after birth. To render more effective her exhortation to humility, Fortune tries to make Fauvel retrieve his forgotten fetal subjectivity: she inverts the uterine space, opening it to the exterior so that Fauvel must relive the abjection and distress of life *in utero*.[81]

Another, somewhat less overt example of "fetal fiction" is to be found in the *Roman de Silence*, in which the process of gestation plays an unusually prominent role. The narrative lingers on the details of the process by which Nature molds "fruit en figure" (fruit into human shape; pp. 78–79, l. 1680).[82] The extended description of how Nature "vint a l'enfant" (came to the child; pp. 84–85, l. 1806) presumably describes events that took place during gestation, perhaps in utero—for the child Nature forms already exists but has not yet been born. This is far from a naturalistic description of a fetus, as the figure that Nature accords to Silence is described in the same terms usually afforded a perfect *adult* female form. The romance is considerably more realistic in its description of fetal movement and the discomfort it causes the mother: "L'enfes l'angoissce, et point, et broce" (The child pressed upon her and kicked her and jabbed her; pp. 84–85, l. 1777). This activity is juxtaposed to the passive receipt of Nature's gifts: prenatal Silence is described almost as a clay statue being molded. As she will be in her later life, fetal Silence is active but voiceless.

Movement is also linked to ensoulment in *Placides et Timéo*: Timéo tells his student that "quant l'ame du corps sent que le corps est assés roides par raison, si s'esjoïst et plus s'efforce, et commenche li enfes ou li faons de la beste a soy mouvoir" (when the soul of the body senses that the body is sufficiently firm with reason, it rejoices and makes greater effort, and the child or the baby animal begins to move; p. 143, para. 308). Timéo couches his explanation in terms of fetal affect: the soul is happy (*s'esjoïst*), and this feeling translates into movement. A nearly identical interpretation of fetal movement as a manifestation of happiness—right down to the typical use of the verb *s'esjoïr*—is characteristic of accounts of John the Baptist's movement during the Visitation, which will be discussed below.

Human beings may all laugh when we first receive a rational soul, but in medieval French literature, fetal voices typically cannot be heard *outside* the womb. On rare occasions typical human fetuses are co-opted by a higher power, speaking in a marvelous way, as "prodiges moult merveilleuses."[83] More often, fetal voices are manifestations of souls that are somehow non- or superhuman: those of saints, the offspring of incubi, or the son of God. In the remainder of this chapter I will turn to several such instances of "divine embryology," to use Maaike van der Lugt's evocative turn of phrase.[84] In these texts the phenomenon of audible fetal speech is a way of marking an exceptional soul, but in many cases the emergence of the fetal voice diminishes the agency, or even silences the voice, of the fully human expectant mother. These fetuses speak *for* the adults in their life, and especially for the adult in whom their life is taking shape. Whereas the examples discussed above tend to stake fetal subjectivity in terms of analogies with external reality—a filthy bedroom, the sound of a bell, a response to current events—divine and diabolical fetuses use their voice to alter maternal embodiment and even human history, offering a unique perspective on the creative destruction required to become a person.

LISTENING IN AT THE VISITATION

The ability of a fetus to speak from its mother's womb is, in all of the remaining examples to be discussed, granted through divine grace.

This is most notably the case in discussions of Jesus's prenatal development: this fetus was exceptional from the start because, unlike any other human, Jesus Christ was held to have been formed instantaneously.[85] In other words, his body was already fully developed (though presumably very tiny) at the moment of his conception. As I have already discussed, medieval Christian conventional wisdom held that a human fetus could only be ensouled once its organs were prepared to fulfill intellectual functions; but since it is impossible that Jesus might ever have existed without a rational soul, he must present an exception to the embryological rule. This doctrine is remarkable enough that the *Livre des propriétés des choses* mentions it twice: to clarify that the embryological explanations in VI.3, *De la creation de l'enfant*, apply to all human bodies "excepté le corps de ihucrist qui fut par l'euvre du saint esperit fait et formé parfaictement en sa conception" (except the body of Jesus Christ, which was by the works of the Holy Spirit perfectly made and formed at His conception; BnF MS fr. 16993, fol. 75v); and to repeat the assertion in VI.4, *De l'enfant*, with an added appeal to the authority of Saint Augustine ("le corps ihucrist tout seul fut formé tout ensemble et soudainement le premier instant de sa conception selon saint Augustin" [the body of Jesus Christ alone was completely and instantaneously formed at the first moment of his conception, according to Saint Augustine]; BnF MS fr. 16993, fol. 75v). Christ is different from other humans, body and soul—a difference that manifests in his powers of prenatal speech.

For medieval thinkers, as Jacqueline Tasioulas has shown, the perceived realities of the human fetal experience prove particularly difficult to reconcile with the divinity of holy figures—such as John the Baptist and, especially, Christ—whose prenatal existence becomes a frequent object of artistic and literary representation.[86] A number of vernacular narratives based on the Gospels present Saint Elizabeth's and the Holy Virgin's wombs as domestic interiors, but these, unlike that of Fauvel's mother, are sparklingly clean. The writers of these popular texts generate a remarkable vision of fetal subjectivity by altering, rendering transparent, the matrix in which the holy person develops. The contents of these wombs then become an observational space, perceptible to the reader through sight and especially—when the holy fetuses speak, as they often do—through sound. In other words, these *ventres* thereby become the sort of "public space" that only "language creates."[87]

The Visitation, the meeting of Mary and her cousin Elizabeth during both women's miraculous pregnancies (Luke 1:39–56), is surely the most widely known story of fetal expression in medieval Europe: the unborn John the Baptist, hearing Mary's voice and sensing the presence of the unborn Christ, is filled with the Holy Spirit and dances for joy. The Visitation is situated within a broader set of episodes centering on miraculous muteness, voice, and speech. The Gospel of Luke begins with the angel Gabriel announcing the future birth of John the Baptist to John's aged father, Zachariah; when Zachariah expresses doubt, Gabriel announces that the old man will be struck mute until his son is born (1:20). Next Luke narrates the Annunciation and Incarnation of Christ, then the Visitation, which includes John's manifestations of joy within his mother's womb, followed by Mary's singing of the Magnificat. At the end of Mary's visit to her cousin, John is born and Zachariah regains his powers of speech at his son's bris.

In standard accounts of the Visitation, John reacts to his unborn cousin's presence *only* through movement. According to the Gospel, as rendered in the late thirteenth-century *Bible historiale*, the Virgin

> entra en la maison Zacharie et salua Elizabeth, et Elizabeth l'oï. L'enfant se elieesca ou ventre de sa mere, et Elizabeth fu raemplie du saint esperit et cria a haulte vois et dist, tu es benoyte sur toutes femmes et beneuree. Et le fant de ton ventre est benoyt. Et ou ay ie desservi que la mere monseigneur veigne a moy. Quant la vois de ton salu m'entra es oreilles l'enfant qui est en mon ventre se elieesca en ioye, et tu es benoyte qui as creu. Ce qui t'a esté dit de par Dieu sera fayt.[88]

> entered the house of Zachariah and greeted Elizabeth, and Elizabeth heard her. The child [John the Baptist] rejoiced in his mother's womb, and Elizabeth was filled with the Holy Spirit and cried aloud, "You are happy and blessed above all women. And the child [*fant*] in your

womb is blessed. And how have I deserved that the mother of Our Lord should come to me? When the sound of your greeting entered my ears, the child in my womb rejoiced, and you who have believed are blessed. That which God told you will be done."

It is perhaps significant that while the above-cited passage twice refers to John the Baptist as an *enfant*, Elizabeth calls Mary's unborn offspring a *fant*.[89] This term, reminiscent both of Dante's *fante* and of the animalistic *faon*, underscores the indeterminate status of fetuses in general and the unique status of the Word made fetal flesh.

The episodes surrounding the conception, gestation, and birth of John the Baptist are permeated with questions of speech and voice. But it should also be noted that the Visitation, in particular, is an episode of *female*-dominated discourse. The time of John's gestation corresponds almost exactly to the time of Zachariah's muteness; the women, alone, meet and speak and sing; John communicates his joy with movement, not with words. A man loses speech, word is made flesh, women speak while a fetus communicates nonverbally, the man regains speech only after the male child is born and named. As Jean Gerson describes it, this is a scene whose real protagonist is the Virgin Mary: the nonverbal fetal communication responds to *her voice*.[90] Just as the Virgin is the great mediatress, the fetal communication occurring during the Visitation is mediated by maternal bodies: mothers nourish fetuses in their wombs, and they also serve as conduits for fetal sense perception.

The Visitation enjoys a substantial presence in medieval religious and visual culture, especially in the late Middle Ages. The Feast of the Visitation was established in 1389, in hopes that Mary would reunify the Church.[91] Even before that date, the Visitation is a popular theme in the visual arts across medieval Europe.[92] In addition to their theological significance, pictorial and sculptural representations of the Visitation are of interest to social historians, as they offer one of the rare contexts in which visibly (and unambiguously) pregnant women are depicted. There is ample evidence that the visibility of the pregnancy was often seen as an essential element of this iconographic tradition: for example, Anne Marie Velu cites a now-destroyed Visitation sculpture, commissioned in 1444, for which the

contract specified that the two female figures should be "grosses d'en-
fens" (great with child).[93] Such images constitute a tacit reminder
that in many representations of the Visitation, the scene is about the
holy children (and about the incarnation of the Word) much more
than it is about the women who carry them.

The effect by which the fetuses hidden within their mothers' bodies are brought to the forefront is equally pronounced in vernacular
literary retellings of the gospels, many of which assign speaking roles
to the fetal participants in the Visitation. I will consider examples
from three "pious fictions":[94] the *Histoire de Marie et de Jésus* (first
half of the thirteenth century), Jean d'Outremeuse's *Myreur des histors* (late fourteenth century), and Guillaume de Deguileville's *Pèlerinage de Jhesucrist* (1358). In these literary renderings of the Visitation,
the maternal figures are made "transparent," visible less on their own
terms than as vessels that serve to amplify fetal voices. The authors
of these texts resolve the two-body problem of personhood by making the source of the ventriloquized fetal voice both audible and visible; as in Gerson's description of John hearing through Elizabeth's
ears, they thereby reconfigure the perceptual pathways of mother
and child alike.

The *Histoire de Marie et de Jésus*,[95] part of the larger sequence
published by Camille Chabaneau in the late nineteenth century as
Le romanz de saint Fanuel, was one of the most widely diffused pious
fictions in the *langue d'oïl*.[96] The author adds new layers to John
the Baptist's fetal subjectivity, imagining a more direct link between
the Visitation's two fetal participants as a direct impetus for John's
movement—and giving John a speech that will have a long afterlife
in the next century. John's novel reaction seems to literalize Augustine's reading of John as the voice that spreads the Word (*logos*),
of which Christ is the embodiment.[97] This literalizing vocalization
occurs within a womb space that is defined above all by the fetal
activity it can accommodate. In the longer of the two versions of
the text, as transcribed from BnF MS fr. 1533 by Maureen Boulton:

> Saint Jehen, qui estoit a nestre,
> Conut son seignor et son mestre.
> Il se dreça sor ses .ii. piez

Et puis si s'est agenoilliez;
Ses .ii. manetes, qu'il avoit
Dedenz le ventre ou il estoit,
Vers son seignor les estendi
Et puis si lor cria merci.
"Sire," dist il, "bien viegnes tu
Qui m'as doné tant de vertu
Que je me puis ceeins drecier
Et retorner et aiesier.
Or sai je bien certenement
Dedens mon cuer parfitement
Que es venuz ta gent saver
Et des granz penes delivrer." (fol. 5vb)[98]

Saint John, who was yet to be born,
Recognized his lord and his master.
He stood up on his two feet
And then he knelt down;
His two little hands, which he had
Inside the womb where he was,
Toward his lord he stretched them
And then cried out for mercy.
"Lord," he said, "you are welcome,
You who have given me so much strength
That I can stand up in here
And turn around and get comfortable.
Now I know most certainly
Within my heart, perfectly,
That you have come to save your people
And deliver them from great suffering."

The fetal Christ doesn't just inspire but actually enables his cousin's movement and speech. And what that speech reveals is an interest in Saint Elizabeth's body, not as her own body but as the setting for John's lived experience. Elizabeth's womb, to which John rather casually refers as "ceeins" (in here), is a space defined by his presence

within it ("le ventre ou il estoit"). The passage's focus on John's full
capacities of sensory perception,[99] verbal expression, and, a bit com-
ically, his desire for physical comfort ("aiesier") promotes a view
of the "ventre" primarily as the unborn saint's home environment.
And the reader sees it this way because the fetus himself is telling
us that this is how *he* experiences his surroundings.

In comparing this passage to other aforementioned references
to fetal movement causing maternal discomfort, in texts such as
Silence and the *Livre des propriétés des choses*, it is evident that this
theological romance is interested in pregnancy as a fetal rather than
a maternal experience: whereas the fetus verbalizes his own sensa-
tions of comfort, the question of maternal comfort or sensation has
been dropped completely. The degree to which Elizabeth is written
out of the passage in question, and her response to the presence of
Christ supplanted by her fetus's reaction, is quite extraordinary. In
this regard the *Histoire de Marie et de Jésus* differs substantially from
the account of the Visitation contained in the widely transmitted
and roughly contemporaneous *Legenda aurea* of Jacobus de Voragine. The *Legenda aurea* states explicitly, in its accounts both of the
Annunciation and of the birth of John the Baptist, that John leapt
within his mother's womb precisely *because he could not speak* ("motu
salutauit quem uoce non potuit").[100] This affirmation of John's
inability to speak is retained in the later Middle French translation
("salua celui par esmouvement qu'il ne povoit saluer par voix"[101]).
The *Legenda aurea* is clearly not the source for the *Histoire de Marie
et de Jésus*'s prenatal speech: to the Golden Legend's more biblically
faithful account of meaningful, communicative movement the *Histoire de Marie et de Jésus* has added just the sort of voice that the
Legenda aurea declares unavailable. And this intervention has a significant influence in later medieval French-language pious fictions.

Jean d'Outremeuse's *Myreur des histors*, likely composed in the
last two decades of the fourteenth century, is a universal chronicle
recounting all of human history from the book of Genesis to the
author's own fourteenth-century Liège.[102] Pierre Courroux compares
the *Myreur* to a medieval Wikipedia: "Jean d'Outremeuse tries to say
everything about every subject, the true and the not-so-true, and he

only haphazardly mentions his sources."[103] One of the unmentioned sources is the *Histoire de Marie et de Jésus*, on which Jean d'Outremeuse relies for his account of the life of Christ in book 1.[104] D'Outremeuse faithfully replicates John's speech in utero, and in at least one manuscript of the *Myreur des histors* the fetal John the Baptist takes over his mother's body in an even more remarkable way than he does in the source material:[105]

> Sains Johans, qui encor astoit en ventre sa mere, cognuit son Saingnour, si soy drechat sour ses dois piés, et puis s'engenulhat et jondit ses doois mains vers son Sangnour, et li priat merchi et dest: "Sires, bien vengniés tu qui m'as tant de vertus donneit que je me puy drecher chaens; or sai-ge bien que tu es venus por tes gens salver." Et commenchat sains Johans à dire le *Magnificat anima mea Dominum*; et si hault disoit tout chu que la vois en venoit fours de la bouche Elisabeth sa mere. Chu fut en la citeit Juda, en la maison Zacharie, le promier an del incarnation Jhesu-Crist, le XXIIIIe jour de mois de junne.—En cel propre jour fut saint Johans neis.[106]

> Saint John, who was still in his mother's womb, recognized his Lord, and stood up on his two feet, then knelt down and clasped his hands in his Lord's direction, and begged him mercy and said: "Lord, you are welcome, you who have given me so much strength that I can stand up in here; now I know truly that you came to save your people." And Saint John began to recite the *Magnificat anima mea Dominum*; and he said all of this so loudly that his voice came forth from the mouth of his mother, Elizabeth. This was in the city of Judah, in Zachariah's house, the first year of the incarnation of Jesus Christ, the twenty-fourth day of the month of June. On this very day Saint John was born.

This account is notable for its divergences from the Gospel of Luke—in the Bible it is Mary who sings the Magnificat, and the Visitation occurs in the sixth month of Elizabeth's pregnancy—as well as from the other manuscript on which Borgnet based his edition.[107] In a remarkable instance of prenatal ventriloquism, both adult female voices are subsumed to that of the unborn male saint. The Holy Spirit is channeled through the fetus, the *ventre*, and the mouth of a saintly woman who loses her own voice in the process.

This hijacking of the maternal womb *and* mouth relates to the more extended account of the Visitation given in the most significant literary example of speaking fetuses, Guillaume de Deguileville's *Pèlerinage de Jhesucrist* (hereafter *PJC*) of 1358. In this final installment in Deguileville's very popular pilgrimage trilogy, the life of Christ serves to complete the two previous volumes' story of man's journey through life and death. Like the *Histoire de Marie et de Jésus*, the *PJC* is heavily reliant on dialogue.[108] The portion of the *PJC* recounting the Incarnation and the Visitation includes multiple prenatal vignettes, speeches, and dialogues, including a "Dialogue contemplatif de iesucrist et sainct iehan estans es ventres de leurs meres" (Contemplative dialogue of Jesus Christ and Saint John, standing in their mothers' wombs).[109] Before his Incarnation, Christ is addressed by the angel Gabriel, who offers a series of metaphors to describe the womb that Jesus is about to inhabit; he is then conceived, and the narrator has a vision of him within his mother's transparent, glasslike body; the fetal Christ then addresses the assembled angels; during the Visitation he and his cousin undertake a lengthy dialogue from within their respective mothers' wombs; and finally, Christ speaks to his mother from within, asking her to sing to him and thus inspiring the Magnificat. The notion of Mary's transparency, made literal in the narrator's vision of the Incarnation, is key to all of these episodes. She recedes from view even while remaining present.

In his speech to the not-yet-incarnated soul of Christ, the angel Gabriel urges Jesus to *look* at his future mother and to *see* her. She is not yet transparent; rather, she is presented as an object for contemplation:

> Voiz la la Virge, voiz la la!
> Regarde la! Tant est belle
> Que tout le ciel s'esmervelle
> De sa biauté, de sa bonté
> Et tres plaisant humilité.[110]

See the Virgin there, see her there!
Look at her! She is so beautiful
That all of heaven marvels
At her beauty, her goodness
And her very pleasing humility.

Gabriel insists on Mary's visibility, especially in the line "Voiz la la Virge, voiz la la." While there is no evidence to substantiate a claim that Deguileville might here be punning on *voiz* and *voix*, this is the beginning of an extended series of set pieces that will play on the relationship of sensation and voice. This one verse, "Voiz la la Virge, voiz la la," perfectly illustrates the double mechanism whereby the Virgin is made both ultra-visible and transparent, fading away even as she remains emphatically present. The line is dominated by the repeated consonants /v/ and /l/, and by the vowel /a/; the only word to break this pattern is *Virge*, with its /i/ and /ʒ/, rendering the Virgin highly *audible* within the verse. She is highly visible, too, for *Virge* appears at the very center of the line, and the first four words' chiastic repetition v-l-l-v sets up a direct connection between the words *Voiz* (see) and *Virge* (Virgin). But the line also illustrates, quite literally, her apparent erasure: for the first half of the verse is repeated after the caesura, but with the critical omission of the word *Virge*. The first and the second *voiz la la* look and sound the same as one another, but in fact a critical transformation has occurred, as the meanings of the homophonous pronoun, article, and adverb *la* have been shifted.[111] The Virgin is still present, but she will soon be fundamentally changed, her transformation taking place beneath a crystalline surface.

The angel Gabriel then describes the womb that Christ is about to occupy as, in turn, a house, a bed, a pilgrimage station—in short, as a *place* defined by the ways in which Christ will inhabit it. The womb is a changing room of sorts, where Mary will clothe Jesus in human flesh and harbor him until it is time for him to proceed on his journey. While she is Christ's "hostel" (p. 53, v. 1575), she is also his host. Her womb becomes visible to mortal humans, the narrator and by extension his reader, precisely at the moment when it is first inhabited by the being that is not only already capable of speech, but is the embodied Word. At the moment of Incarnation, the narrator sees Christ glow: "par mi la Virge luisoit / Et comme cristal la moustroit / Tresparant" (shone within the Virgin, and showed her to be like crystal, transparent; 49, vv. 1439–41). This phenomenon allows him to witness the Incarnation, directly, through Mary's crystalline body: "je le vi tout a plain / En la fourme de cors humain [. . .] a mon semblant / Petit estoit et com enfant (I saw him completely in the form of a human body [. . .] it seemed to me he was small and like a child; pp. 49, vv. 1449–50 and 1453–54). This language picks up on the famous trope of the Virgin's conceiving as analogous to the penetration of glass by a ray of light—but directs our attention not to the glass itself, but to the "form of a human body" on which it offers a window. It allows the narrator to examine Christ's fetal body without disrupting Mary's intact body, and thereby to confirm the doctrine of Christ's immediate hominization. The narrator demonstrates quite plainly that Christ is fully formed (and thus already in possession of a rational soul) at the moment of conception. He has "la fourme de cors humain" and, though "petit," he is "com enfant." Already endowed with the power of speech, he addresses the angels from within "ma mere où je fas sejour" (my mother where I am staying for a while; p. 50, v. 1474).

The Incarnation, the act by which the embodied Word is implanted in the Virgin's womb, seems to establish divine presence among men as a form of ventriloquism, as it places the *logos* in the *ventre*. Indeed, Mary Hayes has argued that "Christ's Incarnation is itself, strictly speaking, a ventriloquial act, as he emanates as the Word from the body of the Virgin Mary."[112] Such use of the language of ventriloquism is helpful in recentering the Incarnation as an aural phenomenon: as Walter Ong declares, "The Incarnation itself is an event not only in the objective world but also in the history of communication, in the mystery of sound."[113] However, such vocabulary also obscures some of the particular ways in which Deguileville's text offers its reader a "view" of Mary's womb. The transparency of the crystalline Virgin body obviates the "disruption of seen space" that elsewhere stands as a hallmark of ventriloquism.[114]

Jesus's prenatal voice, unlike that of any other human fetus, is non-acousmatic: its source has been seen. With all visual obstructions out of the way, the author attends more to aural stimuli: in the *Pèle-rinage*, this manifests in a careful attention to who can hear which voices at which times.

Next, Mary visits her cousin, whose name is withheld in dramatic fashion: she is identified merely as "Une fame [. . .] Qui estoit encainte d'enfant" (A woman who was pregnant with a child; p. 50, vv. 1482–83). The conversation between Mary and Elizabeth is presented less as a meaningful encounter in its own right than as the means by which two far more significant persons, Jesus and John the Baptist, can be introduced to one another. Elizabeth's greetings are interrupted by those of her son, who hears the women's conversation, senses his divine cousin's presence, and exerts himself to ensure that he will be heard:

> Et afin que parler ouï
> L'enfant de la fame que di
> Qui tex paroles haut disoit
> A cil que la Virge portoit (p. 50, vv. 1487–90)

> And so that his speech would be heard
> The child of the woman I am talking about
> Said these words aloud
> To him whom the Virgin was carrying

What follows is a seventy-six-line dialogue between the two holy fetuses, a long interpolation into the Gospel narrative that serves to defer, if not supplant, the maternal speech related by Luke. John the Baptist's wordless joy, interpreted and verbalized by his mother in the original narrative, is now translated into a strategy session between "ces .ii. enfans qui pas né / N'estoient" (these two children who were not yet born; p. 53, vv. 1568–69). John promises to announce Jesus's coming and to "dir en'apert" (speak openly, i.e., literally; p. 52, v. 1551). Yet one cannot forget that the promise to speak "en'apert" is made under cover of the mother's womb. This fetal dialogue, biologically

impossible though it may be, aims to render the truth more accessible to even the least sophisticated people. It does so by placing that
truth in the mouth of a not-yet-babe.

Jesus responds positively to John's offer, and the dialogue ends.
Meanwhile Mary and Elizabeth have been carrying on their own
unrecorded conversations ("autres pluseurs / Que les meres dirent
entr'euz" [many other (discourses) that the mothers spoke among
themselves]]; p. 53, vv. 1569–70), apparently oblivious to the con-
current dialogue taking place within and between their bodies. The
latter is a very different sort of interior-to-interior communication,
one that bypasses the exterior entirely: the fetal words are audible
at their points of enunciation and reception, within their respective
mothers' bodies, without creating *any* vocalic space in between. But
later, Christ does make himself heard to his mother, expressing his
own desire to hear her voice:

> Si te pri que tu me dies
> Une chançon, et des lïes
> Ta douce voiz que dë ouïr
> J'ai grant volenté et desir.
> [. . .]
> Si te pri: or en commence!
> Aprestee est l'audience. (pp. 53–54, vv. 1581–84, 1593–94)

> I beg of you to recite me
> A song, and unleash
> Your sweet voice that
> I have great will and desire to hear.
> [. . .]
> So I beg of you: begin it now!
> The audience is ready.

The song she sings is, of course, the Magnificat, though the *PJC*
does not reproduce the canticle's lyrics; the audience that eagerly
awaits her performance consists at once of Jesus, the *PJC* narrator, and the book's real-world readership. Pamela Sheingorn reads

this reference to the audience, combined with the elision of the lyrics themselves, as an invitation to readerly participation.[115] Jesus's prenatal speech and the song it prompts thus underscore the performative and even theatrical quality that many modern scholars have identified in the *PJC*.[116] Here the Magnificat is not ventriloquized, as in the variant *Myreur des histors* manuscript, but is sung at Jesus's request, prompted by his sense perception (*ouïr*) and his will (*desir*).

The question of audience takes on added significance after Mary sings the Magnificat, for someone else has overheard the song: Joseph, who presumes that Mary was singing for an unknown third party, perhaps the biological father of her unborn child. Spurred on by suspicion and hurt feelings, Joseph sulks until an angel sets him straight. In the end, though Mary sings the song, it tells us little about her. Mary has a voice, but it serves mainly to illuminate the state of mind of the men in her life (and in her womb). So, while the more biblically literal position (as fleshed out in Gerson's sermon *Multi in nativitate ejus gaudebunt*) is that any fetal communication occurring during the Visitation is mediated and experienced through the maternal body, other vernacular texts create a direct connection between the fetuses and in various ways subsume Mary's and Elizabeth's voices to their own. The fully formed but unborn Christ, in particular, has the seeming ability to transmit his voice across different vocal channels, not only tailoring his speech to different audiences, but using it to configure relationships within their own, distinct vocalic spaces. In so doing, he continually recasts the maternal womb: now a domestic space, now an invisible barrier, now a *persona* across which the divine Word can resonate.

"LA VOIX D'UN ENFFANT EN SON CORPS S'ESCRÏA"

My final example of imagined fetal speech is the most overtly acousmatic, and the text in which it appears, the late epic *Tristan de Nanteuil*, is the one that comes closest to constructing an "imaginary world that disclose[s] the precise logic of acousmatic sound."[117] In the episode I will discuss, a key character is saved (and many less important people are lost) through the speech of a demonic fetus. Like the holy fetuses at the Visitation, *Tristan de Nanteuil's* unborn speaker addresses an external audience, reinforcing Maaike van der Lugt's observations about incubus lore as a "perverted analogy" to the Incarnation of Christ.[118] But *Tristan de Nanteuil's* nonhuman fetal voice tells more than a titillating story: it positions itself between life and death, doing and undoing, in a way that highlights some of the contradictions inherent to personhood in general and to fetal personhood in particular. Ultimately, the only way to silence it is to destroy its dwelling place.

Tristan de Nanteuil is a confoundingly complicated fourteenth-century *chanson de geste* of more than 23,000 lines. The instance of fetal speech comes at the dramatic climax of a longer episode that takes place during the youth of the future Saint Giles (laisses CDXV–CDXXIV). Marie, the niece of the bishop who is educating the orphaned Giles, falls in love with the youth and tries in vain to seduce him. Frustrated, she sleeps with an incubus, who impregnates her; when her uncle discovers the pregnancy, she maliciously accuses Giles of rape. Giles is condemned to death. As the future saint is about to be burned, Marie renews her accusation, but the fetus audibly proclaims itself the devil's child. Marie throws herself on the fire and dies, and the devil flies out of her body, causing a roof collapse that kills forty-two onlookers. The holy man is thus saved from the slanderous accusations of a spurned admirer—an unmarried pregnant "anti-Virgin"[119]—through the truthful speech of a demonic fetus. Giles, along with the bishop, becomes a hermit and goes on to become the confessor of Charlemagne; indeed, the incubus episode anticipates Giles's legendary role as Charlemagne's confessor, as the emperor's crime, too, is one of sex, lineage, speech, and silence.[120] *Tristan de Nanteuil's* episode of fetal speech is imbricated in a larger thematic thread that explores the relationships between speech crimes, sexual transgression, and confession. The emergence of the fetal voice as an unexpected agent of divine justice strongly echoes Robert de Boron's prose *Merlin*, continuing the earlier text's exploration of the fine line between saintly and demonic lineage. *Tristan de Nanteuil's* speaking fetus also resonates with the *chanson*'s unique construction of idiosyncratic genealogies that reflect nonnormative ways of inhabiting the gendered human body.[121]

Beyond Marie's lies, the episode from the youth of Saint Giles is filled, from start to finish, with sins of the tongue[122]—to which Giles's quiet forbearance, and the demonic fetus's ironic truthfulness, stand in stark contrast. First of all, we may note that despite the fact that he is fifteen years old, Giles is called an "enffes" throughout these laisses: though he is an adolescent at the cusp of young adulthood, the vocabulary used to designate him establishes an "age expectation" of purity and silence.[123] As she tries to resist her lustful impulses, Marie, too, holds her tongue: she loves Giles "An et demy l'ama sans parolle noncie" (In silence for a year and a half; CDXVI.19840[124]). When she bears false witness, she claims that Giles seduced her with words ("de paroles vo corps sy me donna / Que ne m'em sceus garder" [you gave me your body with such words that I could not protect myself from you]; CDXXIV.20110–11). Yet Giles remains silent when a priest is brought to him, as he has no sins to confess ("Et Gilles lui a dit que rien il ne dira, / Car il ne sot que dire. Adoncques s'acoysa" [And Giles told him he will say nothing, for he knew not what to say, so he was quiet]; CDXXI.20054–55). Giles primly expresses his offense at the crude language of the men who come to arrest him, admonishing them, "Parlés courtoisement ne jamés ne jurés" (Speak courteously and never swear; CDXIX.19981). Together, these instances of virtuous silence and intemperate speech construct a narrative world in which silence is holy, and speech rarely is—all inscribed within a passage wherein the narrator repeatedly announces the fetal speech to come while exhorting his listeners to silence.

The vocal dynamics in this episode are especially complex. Like other representations of fetuses in utero, this story calls forth a set of nested images, a body within a body. Here the externally audible fetal voice is clearly both ventriloquistic and acousmatic. Such apparently disembodied voices tend to bear "a communicated meaning of considerable import" that can be experienced by the listener as "a subjection to overmastering power";[125] "the hidden voice structurally produces 'divine effects.'"[126] Such is evidently the case in *Tristan de Nanteuil*, and yet, this episode also presents several reversals of the more typical ways in which acousmatic voices are produced and received. Instead of lacking an apparent source, this acousmatic voice has altogether too many. By virtue of emanating from a fetus, the voice emanates from Marie's *ventre* as well, contradicting and ultimately occluding the maternal voice; and the divine origin of the fetal voice (endowed by God) is a mismatch to the diabolical origin of the body (engendered by an incubus) from which it projects. All of this occurs within a text that self-consciously presents itself as an oral performance: the fetal voice emanates from within one adult body even as it is embodied, in performance, by another.

Brief narratorial interventions, especially those marking a transition from one interlaced subplot to another, are a hallmark of the *chanson de geste*—but *Tristan de Nanteuil* takes this tendency to the extreme, with an abundant metadiscourse suggestive of oral performance.[127] The demonic fetus, in particular, becomes a disruptive vocal presence even before its speech, as the narrator repeatedly interrupts his storytelling in order to hype the novel episode to come. The talking fetus is announced, for example, at the end of laisse CDXVII: "ly ennemis volt a lui abiter, / Et volt en celle dame ung enffant engendrer, / C'on oÿ ens ou corps de la dame parler, / Ainsy que vous pourrés oïr et escouter" (the devil wanted to lie carnally with her and engender a child in this woman, which was heard speaking from within the woman's body, as you will be able to hear and listen; CDXVII.19894–97). It is announced again at the beginning of laisse CDXVIII: "Seigneurs, ly ennemis a la dame abita, / Et vous di pour certain, ung dïable engendra / Qui ou corps de la dame parfaittement parla, / Ainsy que vous orrés, qui taire se vourra" (Lords, the devil lay carnally with the woman and, I tell you truly, he engendered a devil that spoke perfectly within the lady's body, as you will hear, those of you who will kindly be quiet; CDXVIII.19898–901). This second time, the listeners are urged to silence so that their own voices might give way to that of the fetus. The preternatural voice preempts adult, human speech—and also, as the anticipatory build-up is inserted at earlier points in the story, it disrupts linear narrative time.

When at last the fetus does speak, it produces a strange vocalic space that it traverses from exterior to interior and back again:

la voix d'un enffant en son corps s'escrïa.
Mais je croy, se fut voix que Dieu y envoya,
Car la voix tout en haut a la dame parla,
Qu'aussy tost qu'elle ot dit: "Sire, ardés cestuy la!
Car c'est cil qui le fruit de mon corps engendra,"
Dont dist la voix d'enffant que Dieu y ottroya:
"Sire, evesque, dist il, ja ne vous avenra
Que vous ardés Gillon, vraiment coupe n'y a,
Car oncques en sa vie vo niepce n'adeza,
Ne ne fus engendrés de lui, ne doubtés ja.
Filz suy de l'ennemi et cil engendré m'a.
Ma mere s'y rendi et son corps obliga,
Dont vint ly anemis et a lui abita.
Il fera grant aumosne qui tous deux nous ardera;
Sy lessés le proudome, oncques ne le pensa."
　　(CDXXIV.20118 – 32)

the voice of a child cried out within her body.
But I believe it was a voice that God sent there,
Because the voice spoke out loud to the lady,
So that as soon as she had said: "Lord, burn him!
For it is he who engendered the fruit of my body,"
The child's voice that God provided said this about it:
"Lord bishop," said he, "Never will it occur
That you will burn Giles, truly he has no fault,
For never in his life did he make advances toward your niece,
Nor was I engendered by him, have no doubt.
I am the son of the devil and he engendered me.
My mother surrendered herself to him and pledged her body to
　　him,
So the devil came and lay carnally with her.
Whoever burns us both will do a good deed:
So leave the good man alone, he never thought of [committing
　　this sin]."

The voice is localized "en son corps" (within the maternal body) even as it is assigned an external origin ("que Dieu y envoya"): the divinely ordained voice has penetrated Marie's body from without, only to traverse her body again on its way back to the external space where it will be heard "tout en haut." The devil has lain with this body ("a lui abita"; literally, inhabited it) in order to create the inhabited, vocalic womb space from which the fetal voice will call out. Neither the speaker nor the addressee is who he seems to be, however. The narrator had previously hyped this episode by promising a talking devil-fetus, but here he takes great pains to specify that what the onlookers actually hear is "la voix d'enffant que Dieu y ottroya" (the child's voice that God provided), a voice without a person; yet, when the direct reported speech begins, the fetus announces, "Filz suy de l'ennemi" (I am the son of the devil). The spectator is faced with an act of double or triple ventriloquism, as God speaks through the devil that speaks through Marie's body (as reported by the narrator). As for the addressee, the narrator tells us the voice spoke "a la dame," but the voice itself calls out to "Sire evesque." The shift is small but perhaps significant. The unworldly voice seems to speak to the mother, but actually speaks across her—to the bishop, and also to the rest of the assembled crowd.

The group of diegetic listeners gathered in the fetus's vocalic space includes the ".xlii. persones" who will be killed in the building collapse. The disaster appears to confirm Serres's observation that "the introduction of a parasite in [the] system" (in this case, the fetus who disrupts sonic and social order) produces the inevitable result that "the system crumbles and everything dies."[128] The victims of the roof collapse are, incidentally, the only characters in this section explicitly called "persons" at all—up to this point both the demonic fetus and the teenaged Giles have consistently been called "enffes"—and the doomed listeners are only identified as "persons" at the moment of their undoing, at the separation of body from soul. These *persones* are killed at the very moment when Marie, the fleshly mask across which the fetal voice has resounded, silences the voice by destroying herself. Cutting off a voice has, explicitly and perversely, brought about a loss of personhood.

The truth-speaking, divine-justice-administering fetus in utero echoes a not-uncommon folk motif.[129] In numerous religious exempla from across Europe, newborns and small children affirm the innocence of men wrongfully accused of having engendered them.[130] But such a story does not appear in the life of Saint Giles that the *Tristan de Nanteuil* author explicitly cites as his source—even though the portion devoted to Saint Giles is the most "documented" and source-dependent part of *Tristan de Nanteuil*.[131] Instead the author weaves in another intertext, making a very specific allusion to Robert de Boron's thirteenth-century prose *Roman de Merlin*.[132] *Merlin* begins by recounting the title character's demonic origins and his virtuous mother's entrapment by the incubus that sired him; unable to name her child's father, Merlin's mother is condemned to death at the stake but is saved by her toddler son's precocious speech to the judge. The *Tristan de Nanteuil* narrator's supposition that God must have granted a voice to the demonic fetus recalls Robert de Boron's romance, in which Merlin explains, quite explicitly, that while a devil engendered his body, it was God who gave him powers of speech and prophecy.[133] And when the diabolical fetus of *Tristan de Nanteuil* predicts that "ja ne vous avenra / Que vous ardés Gillon," it uses language that recalls the words Merlin uses to reassure his mother when she is in danger of being burned at the stake: "ja ne sera, tant com je vive, qui vos osse ardoir ne mestre a juise de mort dors Diex" (never will it be, as long as I live, that anyone dare burn you or condemn you to death but God).[134] But in *Tristan de Nanteuil*, in an ironic intertextual twist, the fetal voice urges his addressees to burn his mother. This is a demonic directive with which the mother herself rapidly complies.

Also noteworthy is the density of negations in the fetus's speech, especially in lines 20124–27 of laisse CDXXIV. On its face, this is hardly surprising, as the fetus's purpose is to refute its mother's public testimony. But the focus in this speech on *that which did not happen* and *that which will not happen* also highlights the peculiar position of this unborn speaker. All fetuses are, in a sense, suspended between the past moments of conception and ensoulment and the future moment of birth, in a present that is inaccessible to the rest of the world and bound for oblivion. Marie's fetus is suspended between a contrafactual past and an impossible future: a misrepresented conception, an unconventional ensoulment, and a birth that will never transpire. And this is just one of many instances in *Tristan de Nanteuil* in which a constellation of negating structures is deployed to communicate the curious status of this unborn and not-fully-human entity: an entity whose voice makes it (to adopt Steven Connor's terms) "a less-than-presence which is also a more-than-presence,"[135] or (in Serres's formulation) "being and nonbeing at the same time."[136] This same contradiction is bound up in language itself, for in medieval as in modern French, *personne* designates both a person and a negation of human presence.

Tristan de Nanteuil, however, uses other negations to render the fetus's humanity even more precarious. The initial confrontation between Giles and the bishop (laisse CDXX), for instance, includes some clever wordplay on the idiomatic negation *rien nee,* which means "nothing" or "no one" but derives literally from birth imagery ("nothing born"). The Bishop tells Giles his denials are worthless: "tout ce n'y vault rien nee" (all of that is worth nothing; CDXX.20008). Not only are Giles's words without value, they are outweighed by the "rien nee," the corporeal evidence of the not-yet-born entity known to be growing inside of Marie. Giles reiterates his denial, this time asserting himself more strongly, and in the bishop's own terms: "oncques n'en fis rien nee" (l. 20019). He never did anything; he never made an unborn thing. And as the denouement of this episode reveals, the "rien nee" never will be born.[137] Speaking from a perspective beyond human time, but having adopted the human form that is most associated with rapid and consistent development over time—that of a fetus—the incubus is a *rien* that plays with the limits of the *personne* through a consistent disruption of linearities: epic genealogies, narrative strategies, and the continuous progress of fetal development.

PER-SONARE: SPEAKING ACROSS THE WOMB

The ability to reason and to speak is constitutive of medieval understandings of what it is to be human. In early gestation there are many resemblances between "la beste [and] la personne" (to take up the binary from Corbechon), but it is fundamentally *human* to be able to speak—across a mask or, in this case, across a womb. The talking fetuses examined in this chapter, though, are all situated at the limits of humanity: they are creatures of extreme sanctity, offspring of incubi, or the incarnation of the Word. Even though speech is proper to humans, a speaking human fetus is fundamentally *unnatural*. The "prodige" of fetal speech lends great weight to what is being said; little wonder that such scenes appear as a dramatic device in performed or performative texts such as the *Pèlerinage de Jhesucrist* and *Tristan de Nanteuil*. These "extreme" cases, which imagine a definitive human activity exercised by a human entity that ought not yet to be able to exercise it, become a tool for drawing difficult distinctions between that which is alive, that which can feel, and that which can think.

What little study has been devoted to these talking fetuses has focused primarily on the folkloric: reduced to a decontextualized, transcultural motif, episodes of fetal speech have been deemed more picturesque than significant. But when placed back in an intellectual context, they show us much more. Given the medieval debates and uncertainties surrounding fetal development and ensoulment, a literary depiction of a fetus in utero is not merely colorful. Reading these disparate texts in light of both embryological ideas and the simultaneous ubiquity and instability of medieval ages-of-man schemas, we see that they expose deep uncertainties as to what constitutes a child, a living person, or a lineage. Talking fetuses raise the possibility of life without age, of a form of existence both before and outside of infancy. They speak in response to anxieties about paternity, signaling the inadequacy of their mother's word, whether her account of paternity is true (Mary in *PJC*) or false (Marie in *Tristan de Nanteuil*). Indeed, when fetuses enter into dialogues, they display a remarkable ability to alter, eclipse, or enhance adult (especially maternal) voices. Fetuses are sometimes discussed with a language that marks them as something less than human, but talking fetuses are also something more.

If voice can play such an important role in the constitution of medieval fetal personhood, it is perhaps because the fetal experience, like sound itself, embodies a state of constant change. Simply put, sound is—even before the advent of ultrasound technology—the sensory stimulus best suited to conveying a fetal perspective. Just as medieval embryology "create[s] vital distinctions over time and space," as Mitchell has shown,[138] sound creates an ever-changing social space contingent on time. Unlike the objects of the other senses, sound progresses through time; it "implies movement and thus implies change."[139] Or, as Angela Leighton puts it in her recent study of sound in literature, "the sound we hear is already *in medias res*, a passenger through time, cut off from its cause and quickly lost as it fades."[140] In this regard it is not unlike the fetus as understood in the medieval West: an indeterminate being suspended between a point of origin and a future emergence in a new form, a future in which its present subjectivity will have been forgotten. Nor is such a notion of sound inconsistent with medieval perspectives; Isidore of Seville opens his *Etymologiarum* (*Etymologies*), after all, with the famous declaration that writing is necessary to preserve speech sounds that otherwise would "slip away into oblivion" (*Etymologiarum*, bk. 1, chap. 3; *Etymologies*, p. 39). Writing freezes discourse in time; when medieval writers transcribe imagined fetal vocalizations, then, they pin down an entity that, from an embryological point of view, cannot be "identified as one identifiable thing."[141] The new identifiability that the voice affords is key to the establishment of human social relationships, marking the development of the ensouled body into a full-fledged person. And because the fetus is experiencing a phase of existence the memory of which will inevitably disappear, it is an epistemically privileged witness to the way humanity emerges at the beginning of life.

My reading of medieval literary texts also highlights an important question that is less easily addressed when thinking just about embryology or just about sound: texts such as *Placides et Timéo* and the *Pèlerinage de Jhesucrist* indicate that speech is an essential component of personhood, but also remind their reader that speech sounds must travel through a medium—and that, in the case of a speaking fetus, the medium is the mother. These texts force us to grapple with what it might mean for one person to supply, give way to, or even become the *persona* for another, emerging being. Representations of the fetus that invite reflection on its differentiation from the mother, such as we see in several of the texts discussed above, cast the "universal alterity" of the infant in a different light, as an alterity that originates within. Reconciling the "other within," and allowing it to communicate its universal yet universally inaccessible experiential knowledge, requires that the developmental matrix become permeable to sight or sound. Continuity in the *infans*'s prenatal and postnatal experience requires disruption not just to maternal embodiment but to the maternal voice that emerges from it. Instances of literal ventriloquism give new meaning to Connor's ideas about acousmatic voices producing a vocalic body that is a "body-in-invention,"[142] raising the possibility that when an imagined medieval fetus speaks, its voice serves to constitute not just a developing body, but a developing conception of what it means to be a person, and a definition of the person as one who cannot be brought into being without a disruption of another's embodied experience.

CHAPTER TWO

SIGNS OF LIFE

A. a. a. ie ne scay parler
Enfant suis: iay la langue mue.

A a a, I don't know how to speak,
I am an infant: I have a mute tongue.

(DANSE MACABRE, 1485)

At the moment of their birth and first vocalization, infants already expose and surmount the challenges of linguistic sign systems: their cries are both affective and semantic, conveying feelings and also, as numerous medieval writers argue, signifying deeper truths. In this chapter I will consider the vocalizations of babies, and especially of newborns, in light of both medieval and twenty-first-century theories of the voice. "Medieval ideologies," as Rachel May Golden and Katherine Kong remark, "placed voice at the very core of humanity."[1] Although medieval grammarians and philosophers of language articulate a robust and systematic theory of *vox* (voice) and *sermo* (speech), the phenomenon of infant crying and babbling, as that which "hovers between meaningful language and a perturbing nonlinguistic sonority,"[2] constitutes a test case revelatory of otherwise easily elided disjunctures between voice, language, and reason. Medieval literary imaginings of the infant's cry tend to treat it as a site of paradox (as in this chapter's epigraph, from the Infant's speech in the *Danse macabre*) but also of universal truth. The newborn's cry, typically written as a vocalic *A*, *E*, or *A-a-a*, expresses many ideas, including original sin, animality, and intellectual beginnings. Using the infant *A* to express the essence of the human condition, the authors of poetic and devotional texts engage in a sustained reflection on the mechanisms of linguistic signification, and on the process by which sound might become discourse. Just as a baby's babbling is her first, presymbolic experiment with language,[3] these adult authors' representations of infant cries serve as a thought experiment, one that ends up defining language through the animal-like cry of the neonate.[4] Acceding to its status as spokesbaby for undistilled humanity, the infant produces the quintessentially animal phenomenon of *voice* in the form of utterances interpretable as the quintessentially human rational faculty of *speech*, both undermining and confirming claims to human exceptionalism.

Because the spontaneous and sub-intellectual character of newborns' cries is seemingly at odds with the forms of signification that many medieval writers assign to them, infant voices invite the elaboration of a nonlogocentric model of speech. For medieval writers voice is not an excess, a surplus, or a "leftover" of speech; sound and voice must exist within language, as well as outside of it.[5] In experimental medieval literary spaces, child language development can be accelerated, or it can be made to signify in ways that confound even the most basic received ideas about semiosis. These infant cries are a voice and something more.

In this chapter I propose to read medieval representations of human newborns and their cries as a site where linguistic theory, religious doctrine and popular religious practice, and collective modes of reading and (inter)textuality overlap—positing infant vocalizations as the ultimate *sign* revealing hidden truths about the human condition. Two distinct but complementary theoretical reevaluations of voice—those of Mladen Dolar (*A Voice and Nothing More*, 2006) and Adriana Cavarero (*For More than One Voice*, first published in Italian as *A più voci: Per una filosofia dell'espressione vocale* [Milan: Feltrinelli, 2003])—help frame the discussion of the epistemic work that newborns' voices can do. From Dolar I adopt the idea of voice as a "lever of thought" negotiating between body and language; from Cavarero, the idea that the embodied relationality of maternal and infant vocal exchanges can serve as an antilogocentric tool. By inverting Cavarero's relational proposition to focus on the infant rather than the maternal voice and taking up Dolar's invitation to sift voice from meaning in order to examine how voice *produces* meaning, I will show how medieval interpretations of newborns' cries tie the precariousness of the cognitive processes underlying human language to a more generalized precariousness of even mainstream human existence. I begin by sketching the distinctions made in medieval philosophies of language between sound, voice, and speech, showing how infant cries test the boundaries between the latter two categories. These categorizations have direct implications for the various ways in which infant voices are treated as interpretable signs, and especially as what I term "signs of life": those vocalizations that establish that a live birth has occurred or save the life of a threatened child; those that animate a newborn human character in order to give voice to a meditation on the brevity or animality of human life; and those interpreted as *E* and *A* sounds that combine to compose the name Eva, a name itself meaning "life." In all of these examples, the paradox of neonatal speech becomes, through its very irresolvability, a means of tapping into and communicating a "core humanity" that is otherwise difficult to access and express. Infant voices call for the adult reader to identify with the bare humanity of the newborn, in a way that requires him, I will conclude, to *disidentify* with the cultural trappings that have instilled in him an unfounded sense of human superiority. Human nature is most clearly visible in those people whose condition is most readily compared to that of an animal; the most profound truths are voiced by those who cannot yet speak.

SOUND, VOICE, SPEECH

The interrelated phenomena of sound, voice, and speech occupy a prominent place in medieval philosophies of language. Specifically, language theorists evince an interest in developing classificatory schemas to define what differentiates these categories. Natural philosophers, as well as encyclopedists and other vulgarizers, tend to have no trouble defining *sermo* (speech) in opposition to *sonus* (sound); but *vox* (voice) is more difficult. Voice can be considered a subset of sound or a phenomenon opposed to sound; it may be conceived as a component of speech, or speech may be thought of as a type of voice. It is evident to medieval thinkers that *sermo* signifies and that *sonus* does not, but the question of whether and how voices signify is very much subject to debate.[6]

What follows is a brief overview of medieval received ideas about voice, specifically as it is distinguished from speech in debates on language and grammar.[7] I will begin with encyclopedias before moving into more technical discourses. Isidore's highly influential seventh-century *Etymologiarum*, an encyclopedia that uses language as the structuring principle for human understanding of the world, starts with a book on grammar. And the discussion of grammar begins as a meditation on the relationship between speech and voice—and on written language as *speech without voice*. Isidore writes in book I, chapter 3 that "letters are tokens of things, the signs of words, and they have so much force that the utterances of those who are absent speak to us without a voice, for they present words through the eyes, not through the ears."[8] In other words, while voice is writeable, writing is what enables one to see clearly the difference between voice and speech. Indeed, in other grammatical discussions, especially those debating the status of interjections, writability or transcribability is dispositive to the question of sound versus voice.[9]

Most of Isidore's explicit reflection on voice comes in his chapters on music; the same is true of Bartholomaeus Anglicus's thirteenth-century *De proprietatibus rerum*, a widely diffused encyclopedia that was translated into French by Jean Corbechon in 1372. It is in the chapters on music that the distinction between *vox* and *sonus*, rather than that between *vox* and *sermo*, becomes a central question. For Isidore, "Properly, voice is a human characteristic, or a characteristic of unreasoning animals" (*Etymologiarum*, bk. 3, chap. 19, sent. 2); but efforts to understand it are complicated, he says, by the improper tendency to misuse *vox* to refer to sounds.[10] Bartholomaeus builds on Isidore, expounding at length on the fact that every voice is a sound but not every sound is a manifestation of voice. The question is so important that Corbechon translates the rubric to Bartholomaeus's chapter "De musica" (On music) as "Des voix et des sons" (On voices and sounds; BnF MS fr. 16993, fol. 341va):

Et a difference entre vois et son car toute voix est son, mais tout son n'est pas voix. Car la voix est un son qui vient de la bouche d'omme ou de beste, mais le son vient de toutes choses corporelles comme de arbres briser, de pierres tailler ou de hurter, de bestes courir, et de telles choses. La voix est un air tres delié qui est touchié de la langue pour donner cognoissance des penssees du cuer car la parole est par l'entendement premierement conceue dedenz la penssee et puis portée hors par la voix. Et pour ce dit Ysidore que la voix est la charrette qui porte la parole. (BnF MS fr. 16993, fol. 324vb)

And there is a difference between voice and sound, for every voice is a sound, but every sound is not a voice. For the voice is a sound that comes from the mouth of a human or a beast, but sound comes from anything in the physical world, such as trees breaking, stones being cut or striking things, animals running, and so forth. The voice is a very fine [flow of] air that is touched by the tongue to make known one's inner thoughts, for words are first conceived in thought by the intellect, and then carried outward by the voice. And for this reason Isidore says that the voice is the vehicle [literally, the cart] that carries the word.

Corbechon thus foregrounds the problem but also streamlines its resolution; whereas he is normally a fairly faithful translator, here he has greatly pared down the source text. Most notably, he has cut out the examples of sounds that come from the mouth of a human or beast: Bartholomaeus followed the examples of trees and stones with "garritus avium, mugitus animalium, voces, clamores & clangores hominum" (the chattering of birds, the lowing of animals, the voices, shouts, and crying out of men).[11] Instead Corbechon has substituted "de bestes courir" (the *footfalls* of beasts), keeping the categories of voice and sound more distinct.

Like other fields of medieval natural-scientific knowledge, linguistic theory is structured as a tree of ever more specific categories and subcategories, allowing individual sounds, voices, and utterances to be distinguished from one another according to binaries such as confused/distinct, complex/simple, or natural/conventional.[12] As with many things, perhaps the most creative and cogent treatment of the question of sound, speech, and voice is laid out by Albert the Great. He articulates the distinctions between the three categories most explicitly when meditating on the difference between human and animal vocalizations, "in an effort to preserve the qualitative distinction between the human and other animals with respect to the capacity for language."[13] For Albert, the three categories are nested. *Sonus* can be produced either by animals or by inanimate objects. *Vox* is a type of sound produced by animals that breathe and have blood (*De anima* II.3.22). Following Aristotle (*De anima* II.8), Albert emphasizes that voice cannot occur in the absence of an imaginative faculty; rather, it must actually express something: "vox est diversa a sono, eo quod vox est sonus cum ymaginatione ab ore animalis ad aliquem affectum demonstrandum prolatus" (voice is different from sound, in that voice is a sound together with a mental image, brought forth from the mouth of an animal, expressing a feeling to someone else; *De animalibus* IV.2.2).[14] Lastly, *sermo* is an exclusively human type of voice produced through a rational intellectual process: "Est enim sermo vox articulata et literata, conceptum mentis hominis denuntians, et hic non competit nisi homini" (For speech is an articulate and writable voice, expressing a concept in the mind of man, and this pertains only to humans; *De animalibus* IV.2.2).[15] Albert goes on to describe the physiology of vocalization, in great detail; but it is the presence of a transcribable *conceptum mentis*, rather than the shape of the tongue and epiglottis, that distinguishes *sermo* from *vox*. Still, medieval *vox* is also a meaningful product of the imagination, and so it does not correspond to what Dolar characterizes as the modern view of voice, as "what does not contribute to making sense."[16] Rather, the medieval idea of *vox* as a sound corresponding to a mental image dovetails neatly with the view of language as a "lever of thought," albeit of a form of thought not restricted to the human. In the Middle Ages, voice differs from sound because it is necessarily produced by a living creature in an effort to communicate some affective state; speech is the deliberate vocalization of the only truly rational animal.

Even this brief overview has made it clear that medieval efforts to understand *vox* typically hinge on the key concepts of animacy, purposefulness, imagination, reason, and transcribability. For a sound to signify, there must be intention.[17] In order to judge whether this intentional expression rises to the level of discourse, one must assess whether the vocalizer is capable of reason, and which utterances are and are not rooted in this highest order of sense. As Umberto Eco, Roberto Lambertini, Costantino Marmo, and Andrea Tabarroni have demonstrated, medieval efforts to tease out distinctions between sound, voice, and speech often test the integrity of the *sermo* category from its margins, basing their thought experiments on animal vocalizations (especially the bark of a dog) and the wails of sick people.[18] As Julie Orlemanski puts it, "The medieval utterances that stand closest to voicelessness [...] generate especially sustained inquiry into processes of expression."[19] The cry of the human infant is not typically adduced as one of these "test cases." However, as I will show, medieval written representations of babies' cries often liken them to the vocalizations of the infirm or of beasts. Moreover, infant cries are often characterized in the literature as "interjections," which constitute, for medieval grammarians, a troubling grammatical category that straddles the line between voice and speech.[20] For Priscian, interjections are distinct from adverbs because they can "plenam motus animi significationem, etiamsi non addatur uerbum, demonstrare" (fully express a "movement of the soul," even without being explicitly linked to a verb)—but sometimes they merely "sonituum illiteratorum imitationes" (imitate inarticulate sounds).[21] Moreover, interjections can be mimetic or involuntary, like the spontaneous groan of a person in pain (which is *vox*)—or they can signify by convention, like the "ouch" of a person in pain (which is *sermo*).[22] As the similarity of these examples indicates, it can be difficult to determine whether a given interjection qualifies as speech.[23] The same language used to determine whether interjections are words (do they signify by convention?) is also used in debates on whether a particular *vox* counts as *sermo*: the interjection is where the categories of *vox* and *sermo* overlap. Isidore calls interjections *voces* that are "interposed between meaningful phrases," suggesting that they are themselves not meaningful in the same way; but he also points out that they are "specific to each language, and are not easily translated into another language," an observation that brings them closer to a writable *sermo* signifying by convention.[24] As an interjection, like the bark of a dog or the sickbed cry, a baby's bawl is uncomfortably situated at the crossing of nature and culture: it is the spontaneous voicing of an emotional state, but also a rule-bound and interpretable form of signification.

The cry of a newborn is, in several ways, the epitome of voice. It is the expression of a bodily and affective condition. As Adriana Cavarero points out, it is an invocation, destined to be heard by another, a call for care, a meaningful sound that precedes and exceeds the logic of the written word.[25] And in medieval texts, infant cries are transcribed as vowels (*vocalis*): voiced sounds, or, as Isidore calls them, a "complete and self-contained *vox*."[26] Indeed, Isidore goes on to declare that "A autem in omnibus gentibus ideo prior est litterarum, pro eo quod ipsa prior nascentibus vocem aperiat" (A is the first letter among all peoples, because it first initiates voice in babies as they are being born).[27] And Thomas of Cantimpré cites *A* and *E* (which happen to be the most frequent ways that medieval writers transcribe newborns' cries) as his two examples of the transcribable *vox articulata*.[28] Of course, the typical medieval transcription of babies' cries as *A* and *E* (rather than, say, *wah*) is conventional, not natural; unlike the lowing of cattle, infants' cries can be spelled with letters—and, as I will demonstrate below, for medieval audiences they signify by "nature" but also by convention. For medieval writers, an infant's scream is not always what it is for Cavarero, "a radically primal orality where the semantic order has not yet made its entrance."[29] Although it can be difficult to determine whether a given utterance is best understood as *vox* or *sermo*, any *vox* has the potential to be interpreted as speech, because any human utterance is "able to be imposed on a thing to be signified."[30] Even babies, therefore, must be taken seriously as potential producers of discourse and as epistemic agents. Their universal alterity focuses attention on the negotiations between body and experience from which vocalized discursive meaning is generated.

"INFANT SIGNS"

The modern reader sees infant communications as prelinguistic, but in the Middle Ages babies' vocalizations and movements often take on the status of *signs* that convey meaning by means of the symbolic logic of language. In many medieval French texts, as in our own lived experience, infants communicate primarily through nonlinguistic means: gestures, body language, smiles. This is notably the case in the German Dominican Henry Suso's *Horologium sapientiae* (c. 1339), which evokes scenes from the life of Christ as part of a meditation on divine love. Successive versions of the text, though, suggest different ways of "reading" infant gestures. In part I, chapter 16, the first-person narrator, in a vision-dialogue, exhorts Jesus (as divine Wisdom) to think of his mother:

> Reminiscere, quaeso, omnium servitiorum et exhibitionum, quae tuis in infantilibus annis ab ea recepisti, cum te in gremio infantem delicatum tenens, ocellos ridentes ad blandientem tibi matrem retorsisti, et brachiis delicatissimis tibi arridentem amplexatus fuisti, eamque prae cunctis tenerrime dilexesti.[31]

> Remember, I beg, all the care and the nurture that you received from her in your infant years, when she nursed you in her bosom as a tender babe, and you turned your laughing little eyes on the mother who smiled at you, and with your most tender arms embraced her, beaming on you, and loved her most dearly and before all others.[32]

This devotional treatise, exceptionally popular throughout Europe in the later Middle Ages, was translated into French in 1389.[33] The French translation transforms baby Jesus's cuddles into something more significant—that is, something more legible *as sign*:

> Si te prie qu'il te souviengne de tous les agreables services que tu as receu de par elle en ton enfance. Comment elle te portoit et appaisoit en son giron et entre les bras et tu la regardoies d'uns yeulx rians en retournant ta face vers lui et faisoies les signes infanciaulx que seulent

faire les petiz enfans pour monstrer l'amour qu'ilz ont a leur mere. (BnF MS fr. 461, fol. 56v)

I beg you to remember all of the pleasant ministrations you received from her in your childhood. How she held and comforted you in her lap and in her arms, and you looked at her with smiling eyes, turning your face to her, and you made the infant signs that small children usually make to show the love they have for their mother.

The Christ child's simple embrace has become "signes infanciaulx"— not speech, but a sort of pantomime "que seulent faire les petiz enfans" (commonly practiced by babies) and widely understood to communicate an affective state. Such *signes* are evocative not of a prelinguistic but of a paralinguistic order. They are in some regards a gestural equivalent to *vox*, inasmuch as they convey a message that must be interpreted in order to be received, but a message whose content is affective rather than semantic.

Infant cries, too, can manifest as signs, as a mode of communication that constitutes something more than *vox* but something less than *sermo*, nonverbally communicating content beyond the baby's emotional or physical discomfort. For most medieval writers who address the question, neonates' cries are revelatory of suffering *and* of the human state of sin: the cries are both emotional and, if not rational, at least prescient. William of Conches attributes newborns' cries to their discomfort at the sudden transition from the warm and wet uterine environment to the cold and dry earth;[34] during birth an infant also experiences discomfort at the narrowness of the vagina, according to the pseudo-Albertan *Women's Secrets*.[35] As Jean Corbechon puts it in his encyclopedic translation *Le livre des propriétés des choses*, "Quant il est né et il sent l'air trop froit ou trop chaut il conmance a plourer pour les miseres ou il entre" (When he is born and he feels the too-cold or too-hot air he begins to cry at the miseries into which he is entering).[36] The "miseres ou il entre" are, as I will show below, evocative of both physical discomfort and a more existential form of suffering.

Infant vocalizations function explicitly as "signs of life" in the domain of secular customary law. Robert Jacob has noted that the newborn's cries are taken as the ultimate sign of a live birth in medieval law codes across northwestern Europe.[37] The *Facet*, a mid-thirteenth-century law code from Saint-Amand en Pévèle, near Valenciennes, specifies that "Hoirs que oïs est de ausi loncq que du feu jusques a l'uis [. . .] de tel hoirs est on ahirtés" (An heir who is heard from a distance equal to the distance from a home's hearth to its front door, from such an heir one can inherit); here it is not just a cry, but a cry strong enough to be audible in the next room, that proves a live birth.[38] In French law codes the sound of a cry is generally preferred to baptism, which is the other criterion for live birth that is frequently mentioned. Philippe de Beaumanoir, in his *Coutumes de Beauvaisis* (1283), makes this particularly clear in his discussion of the tricky inheritance questions that arise if a posthumous only child, born after his father's death, dies just after his own birth:

> Se fame demeure grosse quant ses barons muert et n'i a autres enfans aparans, a li apartient la saisine des biens au pere, si comme nous avons dit dessus. Et après, s'ele porte tant l'enfant qu'il soit nes, si qu'il puist estre bien tesmoignié que l'en li ait oï crier et après muert, tout soit ce qu'il ne vive pas tant qu'il soit portés au moustier pour baptisier, nous creons que, puis qu'il i a eu oir né, que li mueble et li chateuse de la partie au pere eschieent a la mere comme a la plus prochiene. Et aucun pourroient cuidier que non fissent puis que l'enfes ne fu baptisiés, et nous creons que si doit fere; car, si tost comme oirs est nes, nous creons que li drois du pere et de la mere li soit descendus temporeument et par le baptesme l'eritages de paradis espirituelement.[39]

> If a woman is left pregnant when her husband dies and there are apparently no other children, the woman takes possession of the estate of the father, as we have said above. And afterwards, if she carries the child until it is born, so that it can be testified to that the child was heard to cry and afterwards it died, even though it did not live long enough to be taken to the church and be baptised, we believe that since there has been a live heir, the personal and purchased property of the deceased's estate go to the mother as the closest relative.

And some might believe they do not go to her, since the child had not been baptised, and we believe that they should; for as soon as an heir is born, we believe that the temporal estate of the father and mother passes to it by descent, and by baptism the spiritual inheritance of paradise passes to it.[40]

The baptism question has been raised only to be rejected: inheritance of property is a temporal question, not a spiritual one.[41] Beaumanoir's discussion of a specific and presumably rather rare scenario renders concrete the question, already encountered in discussions of fetal vocalization, of whether voice is a key attribute of the living person. Here, however, the question of aliveness is linked less to the child's personhood and rights than to those of his next of kin, because, as with later examples in this chapter, the newborn voice is a sign of life occurring at the moment of death. Property rights are to be decided by a judge on the basis of a reported infant cry; though Beaumanoir doesn't specify whose testimony would suffice to establish a live birth, presumably these witnesses would have to have been present at parturition, and might therefore include midwives, female domestics, or female relatives of the mother.[42] In other words, the entire operation rests on implicit female speech reporting the infant vocalization—but Beaumanoir does not say this outright; he does not treat the women's speech as quotable text.[43]

A newborn's cries can also function as a sign that *preserves* life, as the newborn's voice brings out adults' protective instincts. This is notably the case in textual traditions that feature narratives of averted infanticide. The most famous of these is the story of Oedipus. In the Old French *Roman de Thèbes* (c. 1150), the men who have been ordered to kill the infant Oedipus decide to expose him instead—suspending him from a tree so that wild beasts won't eat him—because he has laughed.[44] The infant's unexpected vocalization evokes the men's pity and saves Oedipus: it is a sign of their shared humanity. Similarly, in Jehan Maillart's early fourteenth-century *Roman du comte d'Anjou*, an infant's laughter preserves life and the family unit and solidifies social bonds. The countess of Bourges and her newborn son have been unjustly condemned to death, and four serfs have been promised their freedom in exchange for carrying out the deed. The countess pleads for her life, persuading two of the four would-be executioners. The two holdouts share their companions' doubts as to the countess's guilt, but they understandably value their own interest (emancipation) over the greater social good (justice). What changes their mind is the infant's vocalization: one serf, about to throw the baby in a well, stops when the infant "se prist a remüer / Et a rire mout doucement" (started wiggling and laughing very sweetly; vv. 4224–25); the other is stopped when he hears the infant who "Gazouille et rit et s'esjoïst" (Gurgles and laughs and rejoices; v. 4265), and "gazouillier / Et rire" (gurgles and laughs; vv. 4269–70). Both consider these vocalizations to be "miracles," for the baby is just a few days old, and they have never known such a young infant to laugh (vv. 4240–45, 4284).[45]

Presented in this manner, even relatively ordinary infant laughter can have marvelous effects. This is not unlike the miraculous manifestations of divine grace such as those described in Psalms 8:3: "Out of the mouth of infants and of sucklings thou hast perfected praise" ("en la bouche des enfans et des alaitans Dieu a parfaicte sa loenge," in Christine de Pizan's paraphrase[46]), or in Wisdom 10:21 ("For wisdom opened the mouth of the dumb, and made the tongues of infants eloquent").[47] Outside of a devotional context, speaking newborns—such as the granddaughter of the duke of Rome, who is born speaking Chaldean in the thirteenth-century *Roman de Cassidorus*—are, if not miraculous, at the very least marvelous.[48] One might reasonably expect that beyond miraculous and marvelous occurrences, behavioral "signs," laughs, and cries would be the only vocal communicative mode available to neonates. Upon closer examination, however, one finds a number of medieval textual traditions in which meaningful newborn speech is normal— universal, even—rather than exceptional.

"INTERJECTIONS EXPRESSING THE MAGNITUDE OF THE PAIN"

According to medieval tradition, newborn boys cry out *A*; newborn girls cry out *E*. These cries are meaningful in a way that is akin to language's symbolic logic, but that exposes the particular challenges of sign systems. An influential discussion of these vocalizations appears in Peter Comestor's widely disseminated compendium *Historia scholastica* (c. 1170), wherein the name Eve is presented as bearing a coincidental resemblance to newborns' cries:

> Imposuit ei et aliud nomen Eva, scilicet post peccatum, quod sonat *vita*, eo quod futura esset mater omnium viventium. Tamen quia hic non legitur imposuisse, sed infra, post maledictionem, forte quasi plangens hominis miseriam, dixit eam Evam, **quasi alludens eiulatui parvulorum**. Masculus enim recenter natus ejulande dicit, *a*, mulier vero *e*, quasi diceret: Omnes dicent *e*, vel *a* quotquot nascuntur ab Eva.[49] (emphasis added)

> He also assigned her the name Eve (after the Fall, of course), which means *life*, this because in the future she would be the mother of all living people. And yet, since he did not assign the name then, but later—after the curse—as luck would have it, as a man bewailing his misery, he called her Eve, **as if alluding to the vocalizations [*eiulatui*] of infants**. Indeed, a newborn boy crying out says *a*; a female newborn, however, [says] *e*, as if to say: Everyone will say *e* or *a*, however many will be born from Eve.

Adam named his partner Eva *after* the Fall, but *before* she gave birth to any of their children; this act of naming therefore occurred before any human infant had ever cried. Still, Eva's name somehow anticipates the *E* and *A* that will later prove to be characteristic of neonates' cries, as if the former were an allusion to the latter ("quasi alludens eiulati parvulorum"). Despite Comestor's careful attention to the temporality of these separate acts of naming and wailing, the result is difficult to interpret, and the name Eva can easily be read as an echo of infant cries despite the literal anachrony of such a reading. This effect is still more pronounced in Guiart des Moulins's translation of the passage in his *Bible historiale* (1291–95):

> Et si l'apela ausi Eve qui vaut autant comme vie pour chou qu'elle devoit estre mere de tous vivans. Et nequedent ne l'apela mie chi Adans Eve mais chy avant apres les maleichons dont il furent maldit

pour leur pechiet. De quoi on dist k'il l'apela ensi en plaignant leur misere et leur pleurs. Car quant li hons marles naist sour terre il crie en plourant et dist .a. et la feme crie et dist .e. (BnF MS fr. 152, fol. 15ra−b)

And he also called her Eve, which means the same as *life*, because she would be the mother of all living people. And yet Adam did not at all call her Eve then, only afterward, after the maledictions with which they were cursed because of their sin. Therefore it is said that he called her that while bewailing their misery and their tears. For when a male child is born into the world he cries out, wailing, and says *a*, and a female child cries and says *e*.

Gone is Comestor's careful hedging language, the *quasi* (as if), the *forte* (as luck would have it). Instead the reader faces a chain of chronological markers (*chi, chy avant, apres*) and causal expressions (*de quoi, car*): Adam named Eve after the Fall, and therefore he was crying when he named her, because newborn babies cry *E* and *A*. While the substance of the passage denies any direct significatory relationship between infants' cries and the name of Eve, its rhetorical structure encourages just such an interpretation.

Not long after the composition of Comestor's biblical paraphrase and commentary, a modified version of his explanation of Eve's name became the dominant interpretation of neonates' vocalizations. This tweak to Comestor's account, which will remain fundamental to discussions of infants' cries in later medieval French texts, is disseminated throughout the West in *De miseria humanae conditionis*. This best seller of the *contemptus mundi* tradition was written by Lotario dei Segni, the future Pope Innocent III, in 1195.[50] It enjoyed widespread and long-lived popularity in the Middle Ages, and was, according to Christine Martineau-Génieys, a primary vehicle for the transfer of monastic values to a lay readership.[51] Though the language in Lotario's account of the name Eva remains similar to Comestor's, the precise way in which newborns' cries are understood to echo the sin of their first mother changes profoundly: from phonic resemblance to deeper signification.

In chapter 6, "De dolore partus et eiulatu nascentis" (Of the pains of childbirth and the crying of the child), Lotario writes that all babies are born crying *E* or *A*, which he identifies as the two syllables of the name Eva.[52] Babies, in crying, speak her name; and her name is one with the painful postlapsarian human condition:

> Omnes nascimur eiulantes ut nature miseriam exprimamus. Masculus enim recenter natus dicit "A," femina "E." Dicentes "E" vel "A" quotquot nascuntur ab Eva. Quid est igitur Eva? Utrum dolentis est interiectio, doloris exprimens magnitudinem. (p. 103)

> All are born crying in order to express the misery of nature. For the newly born male says "Ah," the female "E." All are born of Eve saying "E" or "Ah." What is "Eve" therefore? Either syllable is the interjection of one in pain, expressing the magnitude of the pain. (trans. Lewis, p. 102)

Unlike the authors cited above, who identify newborns' cries as simple interjections expressive of physical discomfort, Lotario assigns these vowels a signification. But, like the word *eiulatu* that he and Comestor use to describe these cries, the *E* and the *A* straddle the line between *vox* and *sermo*, between sounds that are emitted involuntarily and those that signify by convention.[53] The problem of the interjection reveals itself here as a manifestation of a greater paradox: an utterance that is semantic without the semiotic, a discourse without words. *E* and *A* are involuntary interjections expressive of pain, but together, these phonemes form the name Eva, a name meaning "life."[54] The name Eva, through association with the Fall of man, gives deeper meaning to the interjections; and the interjections, through the pain they express, add meaning to the name Eva. *E* and *A* are not signs that point to any discrete meaning; they point, rather, to this broader discourse of life as sin and suffering. Moreover, no individual child utters the name Eva; each cries out only a part of it, jumping directly from a phoneme to a name that unlocks a fully developed discourse. The signifier Eva can only be reconstructed through a collaborative rational process that, like the conception of offspring, pieces together a male and a female contribution to

formulate a new whole.[55] The piecing together of *voces* to form meaning also evokes the medieval writerly process, the compilation of "an
assemblage of found texts ('*voces*') to communicate meaning."[56] And
the voice of the infant, as written by Lotario, indeed also becomes
a *vox* in the sense of a "quoted text" — for *De miseria*, and this passage
in particular, are endlessly cited, translated, adapted, and reworked
throughout the thirteenth, fourteenth, and fifteenth centuries.

This interpretation of newborns' cries is a construct that differentiates children by gender but that places male and female infants on
an equal footing: each utters half of Eve's name, and each expresses
the same misery. Furthermore, although most texts derived from
Lotario's manage to convey this idea no less clearly than he does, at
least one manuscript of a French translation of *De miseria humanae
conditionis* gives a most compelling misreading. Whereas most of
the French manuscripts I have examined offer some variant on the
phrase "l'un mot et l'autre est nez de douleurs" (both one word and
the other are born of pain; BnF MS fr. 916) or "l'un mot et l'autre
est vois de douleur" (both one word and the other are the voicing
of pain; BnF MS fr. 957), one deluxe fifteenth-century manuscript
(BnF MS fr. 461) differentiates between the linguistic status of *A* and
E: "Et **li ungs est motz et li autres est voix de douleur** demoustrans
et exprimans la grandesce de la douleur" (And **the one is a word and
the other is a vocalization of pain**, demonstrating and expressing
the greatness of the suffering; fol. 97r–97v; emphasis added).[57] This
variant, while more likely revelatory of scribal miscomprehension
than of a deliberate rewriting, nonetheless highlights the uneasy status of the interjection, which here is perhaps bound up with theological debates and with larger questions of gender and reason.[58]
For Lotario, a newborn's cry is clearly a type of speech — though one
whose exact signifying mechanisms don't quite correspond to those
of adult language — but in MS fr. 461 some infant interjections are
sermo and some are barely transcribable *vox*.

The problem of the interjection is again raised in another adaptation of Lotario's text, the *Miroir d'humilité*, attributed to Jacques
de Gruitrode, which is included in a beautiful manuscript copied by
David Aubert in the 1460s (Valenciennes BM MS 240):

nous naissons tous plourans et gemissans en quoy faisant nous exprimons la misere de notre nature et sommes prophetes de nostre calamité. Le malle nouueau né crie en plourant .A.a. et la fille crie .E.e. Certes tous dient en plourant .E. ou .a. qui naissent de notre mere Eva. Que vault a dire Eva sinon heu ha quy sont deux interrections exprimans magnitude de douleur. (fol. 5r)

We are all born crying and complaining; in so doing, we express the misery of our nature and we are prophets of our own calamity. The male newborn cries out sobbing A-a and the girl cries E-e. Certainly all those who are born of our mother Eve say E or a as they cry. Which means "Eva" or else "Heu, ha," which are two interjections expressing the magnitude of the pain.

This version interprets the utterance both ways. E and A could either add up to form the significant name Eva, or "if not" (*sinon*), they could just be two interjections expressive of pain. The additions of "complaining" (*gemissans*) and "prophets of our calamity" reinforce the sense that E and A are meaningful speech formed with intention and foresight, but the double interpretation of E and A leaves the question open.

Other French versions of Lotario's text, without explicitly raising the problem of interjections, call attention to the unusual ways in which newborns' cries might signify. One of the earliest, Guillaume le Clerc's *Besant de Dieu* (1226–27), appears to omit the A/E discussion entirely,[59] though it does repeatedly call attention to newborns' wails: the neonate "crie e brait" (cries and wails; v. 234), "plore et se guarmente" (weeps and complains;[60] vv. 235–36), "comence son plor" (begins his weeping; v. 244), and "Le premerain cri qu'il gette / Est de misere e de dolor" (the first cry he emits is one of misery and pain; vv. 1274–75). Other French writers, however, do take up the topic. Perhaps the most celebrated adaptation of *De miseria* is Eustache Deschamps's *Double lay de fragilité humaine*, a verse condensation and adaptation of Innocent's text that Deschamps presented to King Charles VI in 1383.[61] Deschamps takes considerably more creative liberties with his source material than do the authors of the other French versions—including the author of the French prose translation that, like Deschamps's poem, was held in the French royal library (Besançon MS 434, dated 1372).[62] Because Deschamps's poem is so much shorter than Innocent's treatise, he edits out a significant amount of material, though the *mise en page* of his bilingual presentation manuscript promotes the illusion of a continuous and faithful translation.[63] Even in this highly selective adaptation, Deschamps retains the passage on neonates' cries, writing, "En naissant le fil crie .A. / Et la femelle crie .E. [. . .] Cy nous est representé / Dolereusement Eva" (While being born the male cries *A* and the female cries *E* [. . .] here is represented for us, with pain, Eva).[64] The exact mechanism of signification is elided—Deschamps does not explain that *E* and *A* can be put together to form the name Eva—and the language of *representation* ("cy nous est representé") suggests rather a different logic, one that places the infant's utterance in a symbolic or performative rather than a semiotic register.

About a century later, the monk Guillaume Alexis (or Alecis) composed the *Passe temps de tout homme et de toute femme* (1480), a versified translation of *De miseria* in rhymed couplets.[65] He expands the discussion of neonates' cries:

Pour la misere de nature
Demonstrer, toute creature
Humaine crie a sa naissance:
C'est de douleur vraye congnoissance.
La fille dit E, le filz A,
De quoy est fait ce nom: EVA.
Ce fut nostre premiere mere.
En quoy de ceste vie amere
Verras signification,
Se tu, par aspiration,
Profferes les deux pars de EVA,
En disant par douleur: *eu, a.*
Nous devons bien noter cela. (pp. 118–19, vv. 231–45)

To demonstrate nature's misery, every human creature cries at its birth: it is a true recognition of pain. The daughter says E, the son A, from which is made this name: EVA. That was our first mother.

In which you will see the signification of this bitter life if you, aspi-
rating, utter the two parts of EVA, saying with pain: *eu, a*. We must
take proper note of that.

Like Deschamps's "representation," this cry is a demonstration, one
with *signification*. Alexis's insistence that the interjections must be
aspirated evinces a real attention to phonology before the letter.[66] It
also enhances the sense, already present in Deschamps, that these
cries are a performance: readers are invited to mimic the cry, to feel it
for themselves, to cry *with pain*. At least a part of the sounds' meaning comes from the manner in which they are voiced, and their true
meaning can be comprehended only through reenactment. The text
models this process of construction and deconstruction chiastically,
first presenting the cries *E* and *A*, then putting them together to
form *EVA*, and reminding the reader of *les deux pars de EVA* before
breaking the name down to its constituent *eu* and *a*. But *eu* and
a are not just artifacts of *vox*: the instructions for the adult reader's
reconstruction of the infant's *EVA* move these interjections beyond
the onomatopoeic, the emotional, or the reflex, showing them to be
both the product and the starting point of a deliberate signifying
process. These few letters pack in a great deal of meaning, meaning produced collaboratively by the crying neonate and the adult
reader.

Other linguistic interpretations for newborns' cries call even
greater attention to the gap between the semiotic and the semantic.
Michael Scot writes in his early thirteenth-century *Physionomia*, for
example, that an infant boy's first cry is "'Oa' signifying: 'O Adam,
quare peccasti, quia pro te patior miseriam infinitam?' and that of
an infant girl is 'Oe' or 'O Eva quare peccasti, man pro tuo peccato
sum passura miserabilem vitam in hoc mundo?'"[67] Quoted here from
a sixteenth-century French translation:

L'homme né, crye oa, mais la femme oe: si comme le masle die, o
Adam pour quoy as tu peché? car pour toy ie seuffre misere infinie, &
la femme die en son chant lamentable, o Eue pour quoy as tu peché:
car pour ton peché il me fault souffrir vie miserable en ce monde.[68]

The male, once born, cries *oa*, but the female *oe*: such that the male says, "O Adam, why did you sin? for because of you I suffer infinite misery," and the female says in her pitiful song, "O Eve, why did you sin: for because of your sin I must suffer a miserable life in this world."

The boy's cry is speech, the girl's is a *chant lamentable*, but both signify in a surprising new way: as an acronym, or an extreme apocope, with two vowels standing in for a longer (and highly meaningful) utterance. This signifying mechanism calls attention to the "gap from sign to sentence" that has preoccupied semioticians since Saussure and Benveniste.[69] And it illustrates that *sonus* can become *vox* and *vox* can become *sermo* not because of any audible change, but simply because of a change in the listener's way of imagining the mental process that must have given rise to the utterance. According to Michael Scot's model, newborns' signs (the cry phonemes) are no longer transformed into discourse through an accumulation of sounds and cultural associations (E + A = EVA = original sin and the source of human suffering). Rather, *Oe* and *Oa* appear to signify sememically, as meaningful linguistic units, or perhaps as statements.[70] Even more than with *E* and *A*, an interpretation is already built into the sign. The *vox*-as-vocalization is also a grammatical *vox*.[71] Michael Scot's reading of *Oe* and *Oa*—like any semantic interpretation of an infant cry—denies infancy as a limit of human language, and extends discourse all the way back to the first moment of extrauterine life. The appeal to both Adam and Eve, like the other infant cries of *E* and *A*, also suggests another sort of extension backward, to the beginnings of human existence. Both cries pinpoint the Fall as the origin of humanity's suffering and assimilate it to birth as the origin of each individual human's suffering.[72] But the invocation of Adam and Eve together also gestures back further, toward a pre-Babel and prelapsarian linguistic unity, toward a time not just before but *outside of* infancy.[73] For Adam and Eve are the only humans not born of woman; the only humans never to have been infants; the only humans endowed with language without ever having had to learn it; the only humans who did not come into the world crying *A* or *E*, *Oa* or *Oe*.[74]

UN AUTRE PETIT FEON: UNDISTILLED
HUMANITY, IN ANIMAL FORM

Up until now I have been exploring newborn cries as expressions of suffering, expressions that are binarily differentiated by gender. Even when infant cries are not construed as speech, babies' voices are construed as a sexually dimorphic trait. The gender distinction between male and female neonates' cries is maintained, for example, in the very popular *Women's Secrets*, by the pseudo-Albertus, but with a physiological rather than a linguistic explanation: "If a child is male he naturally cries 'Ah! Ah! Ah!' because 'A' makes a coarser sound than 'E,' and the opposite seems to be true of girls, for they have a thinner voice and cry 'Ay! Ay!'"[75] Female children's "thinner" voices, present from birth, are determined by biological difference— the distinctions between female and male infant vocalizations are natural rather than cultural.[76]

Despite these gender distinctions, which are written into the infant's voice, the newborn experience is also frequently cited in the Middle Ages as a time of equality: when all, even those who will become kings and nobles, are alike in their humility. This makes birth, like death, a moment of social leveling. These two moments at the extremes of the human life span offer somewhat different models of equality, however. Male and female humans are more strongly distinguished from each other at birth than they are at death, as evinced in their cries but also in the necessarily sexed maternal embodiment of gestation and parturition. On the other hand, the equalization inherent at birth, much more than that of the moment of death, conveys across social classes *and across animal species*. While "dominion over animals" was "one thing that every person [in medieval Europe] had in common," as Peggy McCracken notes, newborn humans share a universal inferiority to more mobile and self-sufficient newborn animals.[77]

The commonplace of equality at birth reaches perhaps its clearest, pithiest expression in a ballade by Eustache Deschamps bearing the refrain "Nous sommes tous d'une manière né" (We are all born in one way).[78] The second stanza paints this universal human condition in stark terms:

Fais et conçups de sang et pourreture
En povre lieu; vieultez est noz estaiges
Jusqu'a .IX. mois; naissons nus, plains d'ordure,
D'une orde pel est couvers noz visaiges,
Criant venons. Les bestes des boscaiges,
Elles nées, vont par bois et essart,
Et nous sommes jusqu'a .VII. ans poupart,
Vil, malostru, foible et mal ordonné;
Ne sçay qu'orgueil de noz cuers ne se part;
Nous sommes tous d'une manière né.

Made and conceived of blood and corruption
In a poor place; vileness is our dwelling place
Until nine months are up; we are born naked, full of filth,
Our face is covered with a filthy caul,
Crying we come. The beasts in the thickets,
Once born, traverse woods and fields,
And we are helpless babies for seven years,
Vile, miserable, feeble and disordered;
I don't know how pride could but depart our hearts;
We are all born in one way.

Deschamps recycles the familiar misogynist tropes of uterine filth. His favorable comparison of animal independence to human infants' helplessness, too, is thoroughly conventional. More interesting is the way in which he accords the neonate's voice a prominent place, with the rejet of "Criant venons" at a middle line of the middle stanza — just at the moment when he pivots from the human to the animal realm. Perhaps counterintuitively, it is through animal comparisons, including a likening of infants' cries to nonhuman animals' vocalizations, that the newborn emerges as an exemplar of undistilled humanity.

In exploring how animal comparisons are deployed to underline the fragility of the human neonate, we can start with the French vocabulary used to characterize babies' cries: after *crier*, the most frequently used verb (often paired with *crier*) is *braire* — which can characterize either a human or an animal sound. The comparison of babies' cries to animal noises is a cliché, one against which Philippe de Novare appears to push back in his mid-thirteenth-century treatise on the ages of man. Born in Lombardy, Philippe lived in Cyprus after a long legal and crusading career—he wrote *Des IIII tenz d'aage d'ome* at the age of seventy. Unusually for this period, he offers a vision of childhood that appears to be grounded at least as much in personal experience as in textual authority.[79] He admits that babies are so annoying and labor-intensive that no one would put in the work of caring for them were they not naturally so loving and lovable: "car, se ce ne fust, il sont si ort et si annieus en petitesce, et si mal et si divers, quant il sont .I. po grandet, que a painnes en norriroit on nul" (for, if it were not so, they are so dirty and annoying when they are tiny, and so naughty and ornery when they're a little bigger, that hardly anybody would want to raise one).[80] But he seems to rejects the animal comparison outright: God, he says, "ne vuet mie que li anfant soient paroils as faons des bestes ne as pijons des oisiaus, qui sont sanz loquance et sanz raison et vivent naturelment sanz plus" (does not by any means want children to be like young beasts or chicks, which are without speech and without reason and live according to nature without anything more).[81] Human children are different:

> Et li anfant en cui Dieus a mise loquance et raison, et qui ont san et entendement et quenoissance de trier le bien dou mal en plusors choses, au moins despuis qu'il ont passé .x. anz, il ont franc arbitre de faire bien ou mal.[82]

> And the children in whom God has put speech and reason, and who have the sense and intellect and knowledge to sort out the right and wrong of many things, at least once they have passed ten years of age, they have the free will to do right or wrong.

If children are unlike nonhuman animals by virtue of their ability to speak and reason after age ten, it follows that babies and very young children exist in a prelinguistic and prerational condition that perhaps *could* be assimilated to an animal state. This is consistent with Karl Steel's observation that "even the most mainstream medieval thinkers, in their attempts to separate humans from all other animals, recognized that claims to human reason rested on a shaky foundation."[83]

Nor is the animal state necessarily temporary: the newborn's weakness, in this view, is just the easiest way to *see* the generalized precarity of the human condition. This is another way to understand universal alterity: the newborn is man stripped of his pretensions to superiority. Returning to Deschamps's *Double lay de fragilité humaine*:

IX. De la foiblesse et nudité de l'enfant en sa nativité
Nous naissons povres et nus,
En plour, sanz nulles vertus;
Tous sommes en ce cas frere;
Plus que bestes sommes mus,
Courbés, petis et bossus.
A beste homs ne se compere,
Car elle quiert mere ou pere;
Elle née va dessus,
Et nous gisons confondus,
Plains de [tres] toute misere.[84]

IX. On the feebleness and the nudity of the child at its birth
We are born poor and naked,
Crying, devoid of all virtue;
In this we are all alike;
We are muter than beasts,
Curved, little, and hunched.
Man cannot compare to a beast,
For it [the beast] can seek out its mother or father;
It moves upright as soon as it is born,
And we lie helpless,
Full of utter misery.

A human newborn is not just *like* a "mute beast" (a very common turn of phrase in medieval French), but *muter* and *more helpless* than a beast; and unlike Lotario dei Segni, who speaks of babies in the third person, Deschamps includes himself among the poor, naked sub-animals.[85] This is but one of the small but significant departures from the source material that can be seen in this stanza of the *Double lay*.[86] Deschamps has eliminated Lotario dei Segni's fairly lengthy discussion of children born with impairments or deformities, retaining only the slightest hint of that discourse with his choice of the word *bossus* ("hunched" or "hunchbacked").[87] But he is rather more harsh in his animal comparison. The source text describes human neonates as "differing very little from beasts, in fact having less in many things," and then cites the differences in locomotion.[88] Deschamps, however, casts newborn humans as downright inferior to other animals. Lacking the upright posture associated with human reason, newborns challenge the human/animal binary on which discourses of human intellectual superiority depend.[89] Deschamps's further remark that animal newborns (unlike humans) can seek out their parents reveals not just the weakness of the neonate, but the fragility of human social bonds.[90]

The contrast is underscored in a remarkable illustration from the presentation manuscript of the *Double lay de fragilité humaine*, BnF fr. 20029, with images painted by Pierre Remiet.[91] The stanza in question is accompanied with a side-by-side representation of human and animal births (fig. 2.1) that Michael Camille has memorably called a "dual icon of human helplessness."[92] The human neonate, with a prominent umbilical cord, lies splayed on the chest of his exhausted mother, who looks away from him. The two are on a bed that stands on a floor strewn with straw, but otherwise there is nothing to place them in a familial or social setting. Nor is there a midwife, a father, a friend; the mother and child are completely alone. The child's nakedness and the visibility of his umbilical cord reinforce this isolation. Typically, according to Corbechon's nearly contemporary encyclopedia, a midwife immediately cuts the cord, then washes and swaddles the child:[93] "C'est chose naturele de coupper le nombril aux enfans quant ilz sont nouveaus nez" (It is a natural thing to cut infants' umbilical cord when they are newly born).[94] Remiet has colored the umbilical cord with the same brown used

FIGURE 2.1 Human and animal birthing scenes (1383).
From *Double lay de fragilité humaine* (BnF MS fr. 20029, fol. 8v).
Photograph: Bibliothèque nationale de France.

for the straw; as one of the few colored-in elements in the image, it stands out, and this cannot be accidental. The navel, the site of the first modification of the neonate's body, stands at the intersection of nature and nurture and marks an early postnatal divergence of the human infant from other animals.[95] But this infant's umbilicus remains uncut: in their isolation from social support, the newborn and his mother are in a sense denatured.

The odd unnaturalness of the bare human condition is even clearer when one compares the isolated human mother and child to the female ass at the right, in her woodland habitat.[96] One of her offspring already stands and suckles as the second one emerges; the family unit is functioning as it ought to, in the environment proper to it. The choice of a jenny to stand as counterpoint to the human mother is particularly rich, given the donkey's symbolic resonances in the literature of the medieval West. Asses are noted for their extreme lust, for their perhaps excessive love for their offspring, and as an emblem of humility.[97] All three are ideas that converge in this part of *De miseria* and of the *Double lay*: humans are sinful, conceived in parental lust, born in filth; we must remember this in order to remain humble. Moreover, the donkey is known in medieval lore for its "antimusical voice,"[98] another characteristic that makes for an especially rich comparison with the "braying" human infant. The choice of an ass may also conjure up a distant echo of monstrous or "unnatural" birth, for the jenny's young could be hinnies (the hybrid offspring of a female donkey and a male horse). Deschamps himself rails, in his *Miroir de mariage*, against "mules et mulès, / Qui sont contre nature fès" (mules and hinnies, which are made against nature).[99] Though the miniature seems to establish a simple contrast between the human and the animal, between weakness and strength, the interplay of the human and the asinine—like the distinction between that which is natural and that which is unnatural—is less starkly differentiated than it initially appears.

Pierre Remiet's dual image of childbirth is unsettling for the contrasts it establishes between human and donkey, but also because of the ways in which it upends representational conventions as well as received ideas about human parturition and maternity. This and the other illustrations in BnF MS fr. 20029 function as "anti-aesthetic objects," using thin washes of "ugly" colors to evoke misery and fragility.[100] The artist's iconographic choices are often idiosyncratic too, and nowhere is this clearer than in the childbirth scene. As discussed earlier, according to medieval literary and legal convention a human infant, if born alive, cries during and after its birth. The mother, too, must necessarily give voice to her pain: "Quant la mere enfante elle est contrainte de crier" (When the mother gives birth she is compelled to cry out), as Corbechon puts it (BnF MS fr. 16993, fol. 77rb). But the human mother in the image appears silent and still, in sharp contrast to the donkey mother, who offers a visible trace of an audible sign of life: she brays.

The jenny also, unlike the woman, fulfills the fundamental and definitive duty of the mother: she feeds her young; "La mere est ainsi appellee pour ce qu'elle baille les mamelles pour l'enfant nourir sicomme dit Ysidore" (A mother is so called because she offers her breasts to nourish her child, as Isidore says).[101] But the human mother remains inert; though she and her son are both inclined in a bed, their lack of interaction violates the expectation that the maternal present itself as "a primary instance of *care* for the *other*."[102] This absence of nurture only heightens the paradigmatic "congenital vulnerability" of the human infant.[103] This is a vulnerability that Lotario and Deschamps link to an inability to move, and that other adapters of Lotario connect more specifically to the inability to seek out food. So Jacques de Gruitrode adds to his chapter "De l'imbecilité des hommes" that because of our inability to move ourselves around at birth, "si ne scaurions nostre vie trouuer se nostre mere ne nous mettoit la mamelle en la bouche" (therefore we wouldn't know how to find our own life [sustenance] if our mother didn't put her breast in our mouth; Valenciennes BM MS 240, fol. 5r). Guillaume le Clerc had amplified this passage in the *Besant de Dieu* in a similar manner:

Qu'il n'a mie tant d'escïent
Come un autre petit feon
De une beste que nus veon.
[...]
E passera mult long termine
Ainz qu'il sache sa tettine
Prendre s'om ne li met a boche.[104]

That he doesn't even have as much knowledge
As another little fawn
Of a beast that we see.
[...]
A very long period of time will pass
Before he knows how to grab her nipple
Unless someone puts it in his mouth.

This image of the human as similar to but lower than "another fawn"—indeed, for that matter, the Middle French use of the word *faon* to refer to human young—signals a decentering, a becoming-minor of the human.[105] The inferiority of human newborns to their animal counterparts is a useful epistemic tool, inasmuch as it enables adults to meditate on the one way they *can* be superior to animals: by recognizing their own inferiority.

Such a move is unsurprising in penitential or *contemptus mundi* texts, but it also crops up in less expected places. Olivier de la Haye, in his 1426 medical poem on the Black Death known as "Poème sur la grande peste de 1348," introduces a "Digression on the feebleness, fragility, and great vulnerability to suffering of the human creature" that owes much to *De miseria*.[106] Noting that a human newborn

> n'a puissance, à dire voir,
> A soy drecier ne soy mouvoir,
> N'autre chose ne peut-il faire
> Fors peu crier, plorer et braire, (pp. 66–67, vv. 1306–9)

> doesn't have the strength, to tell the truth,
> To bring himself upright or move himself,
> Nor can he do anything else
> But cry a little, weep and wail,

Olivier de la Haye concludes that beasts, though imperfect, "nous sourmontent" (are superior to us; p. 68, v. 1338) in everything but our intellect and our free will. And it takes the tiniest, most minor people to make that point: the infant condition, because it is so weak and inconsequential and animal-like, is revelatory of deep truths about a purportedly universal *human* condition. The infant is less of a person, but (and therefore) more nakedly human.

BIRTH AS DEATH: THE *DANSE MACABRE* AND THE OFFICE OF THE DEAD

The fragility of the newborn experience and the baby's crying entry into the world are universal: "And being born I drew in the common air, and fell upon the earth, that is made alike, and the first voice which I uttered was crying, as all others do" (Wisdom 7:3). Because of this putative universality, medieval texts often pair the moment of birth with the only other point in the life cycle at which all humans are construed as equal: the moment of death. In this last section I will focus on the famous *Danse macabre* along with a briefer consideration of another multimedia assemblage, the Office of the Dead, which also collapses the moments of birth and death. The *Danse macabre* and the Office of the Dead encode modes of social performance that were culturally significant in the Middle Ages, available to a broad audience of men, women, and children. Moreover, both texts signify through a juxtaposition of word and image, and of infant and adult voices. Their concentrated use of the voice to communicate about and after death prompts me to a reflection inspired by Dolar's idea that "it *is precisely the voice that holds bodies and languages together*."[107] If so, what happens to voice and language—specifically, infant voice and language—when the body dies?

The phrase *danse macabre* is widely familiar today, in large part thanks to the popularity of Camille Saint-Saëns's jaunty 1874 tone poem of the same name. The common usage of the word *macabre* belies the mystery surrounding its origins, which remain hotly debated.[108] What was initially either a textual trope or a homiletic/performance tradition appears to have become a broader French cultural touchstone with the installation, in 1424–25, of a *Danse macabre* mural and poem in Paris's Cemetery of the Innocents.[109] Painted in the arcade beneath the charnel houses of the south side of the cemetery, the fresco included thirty living human figures, all male, each being led away by a dancing skeleton; beneath the figures were painted *huitains* (eight-line stanzas) in the voices of the cadavers and of those they are pulling away from the realm of the living. The "dancers" include both clerical and lay figures, from the pope to a humble hermit; the third-to-last is an infant. Like the adults, he too pronounces his own *huitain*.

The *Danse macabre* enjoyed a certain cultural ubiquity for most of the fifteenth century (and beyond), mainly in northwest Europe.[110] Many of the site-specific visual representations of the dance have disappeared, including both the iconic Parisian fresco and the London version, with verses translated from the French by John Lydgate, that was installed in Pardon Churchyard at St. Paul's just a couple of decades later.[111] There are tantalizing documentary traces of more deliberately ephemeral instantiations of the theme, too: sermons and dance performances, and even snow sculptures.[112] In a recent study of the *Danse macabre*, Seeta Chaganti has proposed that we understand this constellation of texts, artifacts, and practices as "installations," a term that restores the texts to their positions as parts of assemblages that also included paintings, architectural context, performance, and especially movement (both dance and the movement of the spectator within a social space).

The text of the Paris mural was copied in a number of manuscripts, but without images. The poem and an accompanying set of woodcut illustrations were famously printed by Guyot Marchant in 1485, and aside from the obvious updates to the figures' clothing, these illustrations are thought to reflect the general appearance of the Paris frescoes.[113] That first edition was quickly followed by an expanded edition (1486) that added other "macabre" texts including a *Danse macabre des femmes* supposedly authored by Martial d'Auvergne. Even though "very few of the [medieval] readers of the poem will have approached it as sheer text,"[114] it is in the format of the printed book that the *Danse macabre* has been available to scholars (indeed, to most postmedieval readers). Guyot Marchant's late fifteenth-century page design has thus had a formative effect on twentieth- and twenty-first-century scholarship on the *Danse*, as most studies have focused on the text-image relationship as laid out on the printed page. There have been far fewer considerations of the *Danse* in other, more sociable contexts, such as the cemetery, a lacuna that is beginning to be rectified in the recent work of Elina Gertsman and Seeta Chaganti.[115] With that in mind, I will start by discussing the poem—which, oddly, has also been neglected as a poem—but I will also consider the visual components and the architectural context. This multidimensional reading will draw out the embodied relationality that makes the *Danse macabre* infant such a potent figure of universal alterity.

The textual component of the *Danse macabre* consists of octosyllabic *huitains*, all constructed with the same rhyme scheme and ending with proverbial expressions. The symmetrical and repetitive structure of the poem, and the "squareness" of each stanza (eight lines of eight syllables each), has led to condemnations of the poem as flat and boring. In other words, if the poem *qua* poem has been neglected, it is because the accompanying images are ostensibly the only things that lend it any interest. It should be noted, however, that the sense of "flatness" is amplified when one encounters the text in a codex format, whether with images (as in Marchant's and other early print editions) or without (as in the majority of the manuscripts). Chaganti argues against such "flat" readings by proposing that the interaction of text, image, and spectatorly movement produces a dynamic multidimensional "virtuality"—an approach that does revalorize the artistic interest of the *Danse*, but still somewhat at the expense of the words. So, to her astute readings I will add that some of the individual stanzas are really quite interesting as poetry, too, and the speech of the infant, in particular, does not disappoint.

The child's *huitain* crystallizes some of the same problems of signification seen in the texts discussed above, but this infant's language quickly progresses beyond *E* or *A*. The cadaver has interpellated the "petit enfant na gueres nez" (little child just born), concluding with the proverbial statement "Qui plus vit plus a à souffrir" (He who lives more has more to suffer). The infant replies, beginning with an interjection that will by now be quite familiar:

A. a. a. ie ne scay parler
Enfant suis: iay la langue mue.
Hier nasquis huy men fault aler
Ie ne fais quentree et yssue
Rien nay meffait, mais de peur sue
Prendre en gre me fault cest le mieulx
Lordonnance dieu ne se mue.
Aussi tost meurt ieusne que vieux.[116]

A a a, I don't know how to speak,
I am an infant: I have a mute tongue.
Yesterday I was born, today I must go away.
I make nothing but an entry and an exit.
I've done nothing wrong, but I am sweating with fear.
Take it in stride is what I must do, it's for the best.
The commandment of God cannot be changed.
The young person dies just as readily as the old.

This speech furnishes a surprisingly sophisticated snapshot of a number of the issues at play both in the *Danse* and in the broader discourses around infant vocalization that I have discussed above. Unlike other characters—whose "last words" come at the end of a lifetime of talking—the infant is granted a preternatural power of speech only for that ability to be taken away; paradoxically, he speaks in order to proclaim his own inability to speak. This stanza enacts an accelerated linguistic development, from the initial *A a a* to the concluding proverb. It thus encapsulates the "temporal disorientation" that marks the *Danse* as a whole, especially in its reception as interactive "installation."

The baby's initial cry has been shown to derive from Jeremiah 1:6 ("Et dixi: A, a, a, Domine Deus, ecce nescio loqui, quia puer ego sum" [And I said: Ah, ah, ah, Lord God: behold, I cannot speak, for I am a child]).[117] The nonverbal *A a a* serves as evidence of the lack of speech that the following words will either belie or overcome. It is reasonable also to read this line as referring to the well-established tradition of infants crying either *E* or *A*. In this case, the *A a a* marks the speaker as male—which is hardly surprising, since all of the figures in Marchant's 1485 edition (and, apparently, in the Innocents fresco) are male. We may note, however, that this first line ends with a rhyme in *-er*: so the infant's first outcry takes us (phonetically) from *A* to *E*, encompassing the totality of the newborn's voice. The infant quickly gains the capacity to communicate in a more "adult" manner. While critics such as Gertsman and Oosterwijk have seen this stanza as being written in a particularly infantile style, this is true only of the beginning of the infant's speech.[118] The syntax grows progressively more complex over the course of the *huitain*, tracing a development from *vox* to *sermo*. The infant's expression soon comes to exceed mere vocalization. From the simple declarations "ie ne scay parler" (v. 1), "Enfant suis," and "iay la langue mue" (v. 2), the child quickly masters parallel clauses (v. 3), restrictive negation (v. 4),[119] and inversion and coordinating conjunctions (v. 5). Finally he achieves both wisdom and fluency: infinitive subjects, passive constructions, and value judgments tossed in as an aside, culminating in two impersonal, universalizing pronouncements. Baby has had to grow up fast!

For Chaganti, "what is terrifying and compelling about *danse macabre* is not simply its reminder of death's inevitability—it is, more comprehensively, the suggestion that confronting death involves an agglomeration of multiple rates and structures of temporal passage at once."[120] My reading of the infant's syntax supports this idea, as it portrays the passage of time as both accelerated and arrested. Nor is the syntax the only means by which this stanza highlights the peculiar temporalities of the infant suspended at the point of both birth and death. Quite literally, more stable expressions of time such as "hier" and "huy" (v. 3) give way to the relativism and immediacy of "aussi tost" (v. 8), and while "le mort" teasingly addresses the child with many verbs in the future tense, the child responds almost exclusively in the present tense, confirming our sense of this stanza as a snapshot of a being who exists only in the present. Nor is Death the only one who appears to be teasing. The child calls out with a stereotypical infant cry, which viewers will know as the sound of "an invoking life that knowingly entrusts itself to a voice that responds,"[121] but the one who is there to answer the call is Death.

The discomfiture of "dying before one's time" inherent to the scene of the infant is amplified by the rapidity of the change from *A a a* to the wisdom of the proverb. The child quickly passes from *vox* to *sermo* and then on to sermonizing. The proverb—that which is axiomatically familiar—becomes uncanny when voiced by a newborn, a creature who has not yet been acculturated but is nonetheless somehow able to tap into a cultural commonplace. Yet perhaps the proverb is not so different from *A-a-a* after all; Dolar has opined that proverbs, with their "strangely coercive quasi-automatism," generally "make more sound than sense."[122] In a perceptive study of the function of proverbial discourse in the *Danse macabre*, Jane H. M. Taylor observes that the proverbs have an explicitly extratemporal quality, and that the concluding of each stanza with this "toujours-déjà-dit-par-tous" is a way of facilitating readerly complicity and identification.[123] However, in its temporality the infant stanza is distinct from most of the others, since the infant has no past on which to reflect; the "articulation" that occurs in his *huitain* is one that bridges different modes of universality and untimeliness. The child's progression from free infant vocalization to the fixity of the proverb is an exaggerated form of the process of linguistic acculturation that all people who learn to speak must undergo, a process that Cavarero has likened to a form of death: "language ends up being a system whose 'rigor' depends on rigor mortis. The free vocalizations of the infant are replaced with a grave silence."[124] And if the proverb represents the always-already-said, the fragile newborn, exemplifying humankind's precarious mortality, is the always-already-dead.

Like proverbs, which express a broadly shared worldview, the *Danse* as a whole relies on a logic of identification. Viewers are supposed to "see themselves" in the dancing figures—hence Marchant's labeling of the *Danse* as a "mirror."[125] But the process of identification must occur differently with the infant than with other characters, and it unfolds differently in an architectural context than in a book. The *Danse*'s identificatory model appears simple: pick the character most similar to you and identify with his voice.[126] Where the infant is concerned, however, the viewer is obligated to identify with a voice that is not his own and cannot be. *A-a-a*: no viewer old enough to understand the *Danse*'s message speaks in that way, although every one of them *used to*. On top of the conventional macabre logic of *sum quod eris* (I am what you will be), the infant simultaneously conveys the message *sum quod eras* (I am what you were).[127] Or, rather, because he gets to exit this world before having experienced the full range of its miseries, the dying infant is what the adult viewer ought to wish he could have been.[128] The distinction between the infant and the adult dancers is also a matter of singular and plural social identities, for, while the others are differentiated by their "estate" (social status), the infant exists outside of the world of work and worship.[129] He is therefore of completely indeterminate status: he currently has no standing at all, but he is pluripotent: had he lived, he might have grown up to become anything. The infant at once occupies no social role and all of them.

As one moves beyond the text to think about image, movement, and space, other peculiarities of the *Danse macabre*'s infant figure come into focus. The infant is special not just because he can't speak (yet he does), but also because a one-day-old baby can't walk (and

still must dance).[130] The internal contradiction of the infant discourse, like the overarching contradiction that structures the *Danse*
(confrontations of the living and the dead), yields meaning even as it
highlights the real-world impossibility of the poem's entire premise.
Yet "impossible" does not mean "untrue." Reimagining the *Danse* in
its Parisian cemetery context enables us to recover other visual and
kinesthetic modes of reading the dance, and access other truths that
the text could reveal.

Recent studies have begun considering the *Danse macabre* more
seriously as an object that medieval viewers would have encountered within the very specific architectural setting for which it was
designed. Gertsman has remarked extensively on the horizontal
directionality of the painted procession;[131] to this horizontal axis
Chaganti introduces skew lines and verticality in her "virtual" pro-
jections.[132] These interventions, with their focus on embodied movement, counter the rigor mortis of the *Danse*'s fixity in print. If we add
yet more depth, we uncover other readings of the *Danse*. First, it is
essential to revisit the question of vertical axes of interpretation, for
the Parisian cemetery in which the French *Danse* was installed is an
environment very unlike the English church interior on which Chaganti focuses her discussion of verticality. The overall visual effect of
the *Danse* in the Cemetery of the Innocents would have come not
just from the frescoes' imagery and text, but also from the human
remains stacked above; the bones in the charnel houses must be considered a co-text, to be interpreted in conjunction with the painted
figures and words. Such a vertical reading is completely consistent
with late medieval iconographic conventions and habits of mind.[133]
However, this mode of reading the Parisian *Danse macabre* cannot
be construed as purely vertical in the same sense that a stained glass
window or a manuscript page might be read vertically, because the
different registers of the installation are legible to the viewer at different distances. Anyone close enough to read the text must himself
be standing under the arcade, that is, *beneath* the bones; he cannot
see them, but he must know they are there, and by standing beneath
them the viewer too participates in the *sum quod eris* assemblage.
Conversely, anyone standing far enough back to see both the bones

and the fresco probably cannot make out the words of the poem. Different parts of the complex come into focus from different vantage points.

As the viewer faces the painting, moving farther away or closer, he traverses the consecrated ground of the cemetery. This space, too, participates in the *Danse*'s complicated play of temporalities. Bodies were buried in this ground, of course; but once the flesh had decomposed, the bare bones were transferred to charnel houses, including the ones above the *Danse macabre* fresco, to make room for new bodies.[134] Moreover, a medieval cemetery, and the Parisian Cemetery of the Innocents in particular, was full of the living. As one of the largest open spaces within the city walls, it was the frequent site of sermons and other mass gatherings. The cemetery offered an especially effective backdrop for moralizing predication, because an audience standing in the cemetery was not just looking at the *Danse macabre*, but participating in a three-dimensional *sum quod eris* installation. Just as medieval macabre imagery typically shows bodies in multiple stages of decomposition, a visitor to the cemetery of the Innocents had to position her own flesh between bodies in the process of rotting (below her feet) and the already-bare bones above. Furthermore — and this is a state of affairs that should not be overlooked in a reading of the Infant stanza in particular — the viewer was standing in a cemetery devoted to the most famous set of dead infants in the medieval religious imaginary: the Holy Innocents massacred on Herod's order.[135] A viewer facing the *Danse macabre* would have stood near the cemetery's church, which contained, and had done since the time of Louis IX, the putative relics of a biblical Innocent.[136] The infant voice conceived in such a space would exemplify what Dolar punningly calls "*plus-de-corps*: both the surplus of a body, a bodily excess, and the no-more-body, the end of the corporeal."[137] But all of this context is missing from the print editions, which eliminate the text's social, sociable, architectural, and symbolic contexts.[138] Marchant's *Danse* stabilizes the legibility of the text but imposes an order of reading (based on the fresco's horizontal register) that not only segments the text image, but eliminates the possibility of bringing the rest of the assemblage into view. By reenvisioning the dimensionality of the assemblage, we can better understand the infant voice as call-ing *out* to a spectator whose own bodily position plays an important role in how the infant voice produces meaning.

Toward the end of Middle Ages, *danse macabre* imagery also begins to inflect the Office of the Dead. Included in just about every Book of Hours—personal prayer books that became very popular in the fourteenth and fifteenth centuries—the Office of the Dead consists of prayers that were meant to be sung the evening before and the morning of a funeral mass. They came to be recited by the laity more frequently, even daily, in the later Middle Ages.[139] In the ways it implicates and employs multiple voices, the Office of the Dead stands out from the rest of the prayers that typically appear in Books of Hours. Unlike the texts geared toward individual spoken recitation, the Office of the Dead may be sung communally.[140] As a worshipper reads or sings the Office of the Dead, she also occupies a number of first-person subject positions: different portions of the Office express the point of view of the person praying, of Job, of a deceased person, even of a newborn exiting the womb.

The Office of the Dead concludes with nine lessons for Matins from the book of Job, which became some of the most frequently recited prayers in late medieval France, and which came to be known as the *petit Job*.[141] This daily experience includes, as the ninth and final lesson, the "Quare de vulva" verses (Job 10:18–22), which begin: "Quare de vulva eduxisti me? qui utinam consumptus essem, ne oculus me videret. Fuissem quasi non essem, de utero translatus ad tumulum" (Why didst thou bring me forth out of the womb: O that I had been consumed that eye might not see me! I should have been as if I had not been, carried from the womb to the grave). Although voiced by the adult Job (and, when read aloud, by the adult wor-shipper), this passage, with its focus on the moment of birth, also prompts a reflection on newborn cries. These same words, "Quare de vulva eduxisti me," are inscribed in a phylactery just above the head of a newborn in the childbirth scene that illustrates Jacques de Gruitrode's *Miroir d'humilité* in Valenciennes MS 240 (fig. 2.2): Job's words have been repurposed as infant speech.[142]

The book of Job is a touchstone both for the conflation of birth

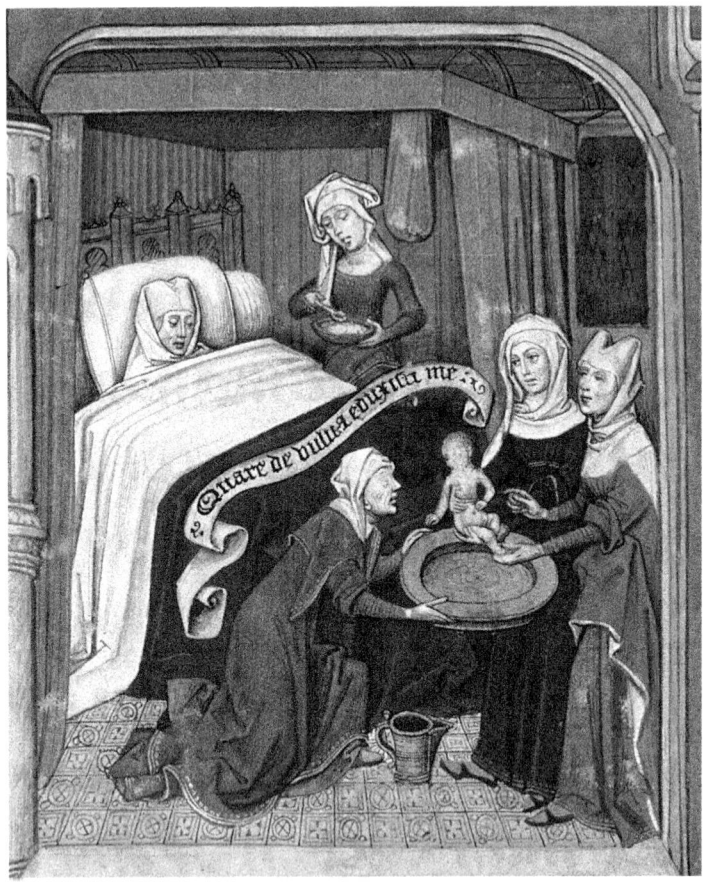

FIGURE 2.2 Newborn speech (1462–1463). From *Miroir d'humilité* (Valenciennes MS 240, fol. 1r). Médiathèque Simone Veil de Valenciennes. Photograph: © CNRS-IRHT.

and death characteristic of the *contemptus mundi* tradition and for the same sort of meditation on equality in death that the *danse macabre* inspires.[143] Given the convergence of these textual traditions around the figure of Job, it is little surprise that the makers of Books of Hours begin illustrating the *petit Job* with images alluding to the *danse macabre* and other related scenes such as the *accidents de l'homme*.[144] In fact, the earliest surviving visual representation of the *danse macabre* is in the margins of a Book of Hours from the workshop of the Bedford Master, made in Paris in the early 1430s.[145] This is not a one-off, but a lasting phenomenon; the use of the *danse macabre* to illustrate the Office of the Dead continued through the print era. As Books of Hours continued to reach an ever-larger audience, so, too, did the *danse macabre*'s voices of the dying and the dead.

Thinking about northern French Books of Hours as a vehicle for the dissemination of *danse macabre* imagery has renewed implications for our reading of the *Danse macabre* infant as preacher and as teacher. The audience of the Book of Hours quite explicitly includes children, as many such books contain images and/or texts designed for teaching the alphabet.[146] In the margins of Books of Hours the dead and the dying, including children, are calling out to a broad swath of book users, including other children: learning to read is part of the same lesson as learning to die. This reflection on the Book of Hours as a pedagogical tool, specifically one used to teach the alphabet, also offers a new resonance with the *Danse* infant's stanza, whose opening *A-a-a* also calls to mind medieval techniques in the teaching of the alphabet to very young children. Up to now I have likened the cry of the *Danse*'s dying infant to the traditional *A* of the male newborn. It is important to note, however, that a vocalized *A* is also a typical utterance of the mother, nurse, or schoolmaster who teaches a young child the beginning of the alphabet. In the European Middle Ages, as today, early reading texts (including objects that were used for infants and toddlers, such as covered baby-food bowls) often focus on the letter A.[147] Additionally, the same *A-a-a* spoken by the *Danse* infant is frequently placed into a schoolmaster's voice in comic texts and images, including those that depict futile attempts to teach human language to animals.[148]

One notable example from the period when Books of Hours proliferated is the "Ballade de l'A.B.C.," a poem probably composed in the fifteenth century that was printed in Antoine Vérard's *La chasse et le depart damours* (1509): "Quant mon maistre dit .a.a.a. / Je cuidois qu'il fust esbahy" (When my schoolmaster said *a-a-a* I thought he was in a panic; vv. 8–9).[149] The ballade's funny play on the misinterpretation of an apparently inarticulate cry recalls the particular interpretive challenges of the vowel-interjection, even as it ups the ante: constructing a joke not just around a *vox/sermo* divide, but through the reception of specifically pedagogical adult speech as a nonintellectual and infantile voice. This is a breezy bit of humor that, like the other examples examined above, gets to the heart of the paradox of infant speech.

LIVING PARADOX

A newborn infant lies at the threshold of life. We know which side of that threshold he occupies if he cries loudly enough to be heard at the threshold of his family home. He can remain on that side if, like Oedipus or the son of the countess of Bourges, his voice charms those who have been sent to harm him. But the same voice that proves and preserves life also stretches across the full span of human history, calling back to Adam and Eve, expressing present discomfort, anticipating future misery, speaking from a moment that sometimes marks the end of a lifetime not yet lived. The threshold of birth easily converges with other liminal spaces: a state between human and animal, between life and death.

From a modern perspective, most of these functions of the newborn voice appear fanciful, even fantastical. It seems self-evident that neonates' cries must signify little more than physical discomfort and surprise; any suggestions that they might be interpreted as equivalent to verbal utterances are typically made for comic effect, as in the 1989 comedy film *Look Who's Talking*, in which a newborn's first cries are memorably dubbed with the words, "Put me back in!" Medieval writers, however, build onto a different, existing set of cultural commonplaces—the womb as tomb, the newborn's cry as a reference to the Fall, the beastlike irrationality and sub-bestial incapacity of the human infant—and use them as a framework within which to address serious questions about the human condition. Though they are impossible in a literal sense, medieval infants' voices are still doing real intellectual work, and of the many paradoxes inherent in representations of newborn speech, this is the most meaningful of all.

The intellectual work performed by the newborn's voice, as presented in a broad range of texts, mainly of a popular-devotional bent—*contemptus mundi* treatises and poems, Books of Hours, *danse macabre* images—can perhaps best be summed up as follows: to imagine the speech of a neonate is to create a subject-position for the expression of a universal human voice through a universal language. These instances of infant speech offer the linguistic underpinnings with which lay readers and viewers can come to a fuller understanding of humanity, and of language itself. To situate a crying, speaking, signifying subject at a point that is both prelinguistic (infancy) and postlinguistic (death) makes possible the elaboration of a voice that is at once individual and generalizable, diachronic and utterly untimely.[150] Such a speaking subject can produce a singular yet universal language that no one else can: an utterance like *A* or *Oe*, a nonsignifier that comes to stand in for the signifier in general.[151] Any effort to determine whether this *vox* constitutes significant *sermo* requires the listener to lay bare the intellectual processes that underpin these cries—and all language. We all were once infants, and we all produced the same cries when we came into being; therefore, to seek meaning in a newborn's cries, to figure out whether they are a product of imagination and reason, requires us to reenter our own past state. And yet, the specific messages imputed to the medieval infant's cry—I am here, I exist, but I'd have been better off if I didn't; adult culture is a vain effort to cover the naked weakness of the human condition; birth is the beginning of death—mean that the listener's radical reidentification with the alterity of the infant self is ultimately envisioned as a tool with which he must deconstruct common cultural narratives of the (adult) self. I think of this as a process of disidentification: not in the sense in which the queer theorist José Esteban Muñoz popularized the term (that is, as a strategy by which the minoritized subject can "read oneself and one's own life narrative in a moment, object, or subject that is not culturally coded to 'connect' with the disidentifying subject"[152]), but inversely, as a means by which the adult, majoritarian subject can divest himself of the acculturated fictions of identity from which he derives his sense of privilege.

This effect of disidentification, whereby the reader is invited to take a dispassionate view of human nature and to find it wanting, is fundamentally a pedagogical tool. Thus, as is especially apparent in the *danse macabre* corpus, the neonate is a born teacher: his *A-a-a* begins a primer on human nature that requires its audience to abandon any conception of human superiority or exceptionality. More than an adult who has an acculturated investment in thinking himself made in God's image and thus superior to the animals, an infant subject is unfettered by either experience or aspiration. The newborn is better positioned, then, to give voice to necessary but unflattering truths about human vulnerability—and to assign rational speech to an *infans* is to suggest that we adults are all a bit less rational, a bit less differentiated from children and nonhuman animals, than we'd like to seem. The newborn's "signs of life" undoubtedly signify—but are the rest of us enlightened enough to read them?

CHAPTER THREE

NURTURE, THE DOMESTIC, AND THE FOREIGN

In this chapter I consider what medieval representations of infantile language can show us about broader debates on the interplay of nature and nurture. In the late medieval West these two influences are not conceived as a strict binary, nor do their definitions align with modern conceptions of these terms: nurture itself is constructed as natural, especially when women are doing the nurturing. Looking at textual instances where adults (usually women) adopt different forms of baby talk, I interrogate the nature of the language with which women and infants communicate with each other and the place of that language within broader cultural spheres. Can baby talk work outside of the home? I address these questions first by considering the role of the mother or wet nurse in domesticating the infant's experimental babbling by teaching him the mother tongue. Like the feminist philosophers whose work informs the framing of this chapter, notably Hélène Cixous and Adriana Cavarero, medieval writers typically liken language to milk. Both flow from mother to child—but the frequent assignment of this transmission to the wet nurse, a domestic servant functioning as a proxy for the biological mother, also highlights the relationality and the cultural constructedness of the natural maternal role. In short, the interchangeability of mothers and nurses as nourishers and language teachers reveals an interplay of nurture and nature, not a strict binary. Nor is the linguistic transfer of first-language teaching exclusively a one-way influence. Women, as they prepare infants to enter the world of adult language, are themselves likened to children—a phenomenon I will examine in light of sociolinguistic insights into "language socialization," that is, how caregiver speech helps children become "speakers of cultures."[1]

The alterity of women and the alterity of infants are not the same, but women and infants do come to speak the same language.

These reflections on the domestic labor of mother-tongue pedagogy will lead me to consider the complicated linguistic relation of the domestic to the foreign, especially in the multilingual environments of late medieval courts—environments in which linguistically displaced writers (foreign born, exiled, multilingual) occasionally adopt baby talk as an idiom of adult communication. The chapter culminates with readings of two fixed-form poems, a ballade by Christine de Pizan and a rondeau by Charles d'Orléans, which use two different kinds of baby talk as linguistic signifiers of alienation. In the former, an infant's point of view is domesticated and expressed through adult language; in the latter, an adult point of view is expressed through domestic but undomesticated infantile language. These two authors deploy the mixed idioms of adult vernacular and baby talk to very different ends. For Christine, *doulce nourriture* becomes a crucial tool with which to carve out a public space for the woman writer; for Charles, the "gnogno" of little children affords an opportunity for a virtuosic but mostly private display. However, when viewed through the lens of both poets' linguistic alienation— Christine as a nonnative speaker of French, Charles as a multilingual half-Lombard prince who spent much of his adult life as a prisoner in England—their choices in representing baby talk take on new meaning. Placing the two poems in conversation with the feminist literary theorist Susan Fraiman's notions of "extreme domesticity" and of migrant homemaking practices that "map domesticity from the margins," I argue that both Christine de Pizan and Charles d'Orléans exploit the universal alterity of infant speech to show that the language of the domestic sphere can be profoundly foreign: child language is an idiom of alienation and of innovation. These poems, like the less appreciative evocations of female caregivers' infantile speech, demonstrate that the more obvious *developmental* aspects of the infant's universal alterity are inseparable from gender- and class-based acculturation and are transferred to the maternal figure during the process of domestication. But these texts also elevate baby talk, prompting one to take *langage enfantin* more seriously *as language*.

MEDIEVAL MOTHERESE AS *LANGUELAIT*

Any inquiry into infant voices must of necessity attend also to the voices of those adults who are charged with speaking to babies, teaching them language, *and* listening to them: mothers and wet nurses. As obvious as this may seem, it is easier said than done, for the voices of infants are, in many respects, more audible in medieval French texts than are the voices of the women who care for them. Women's speech to children is sometimes described but rarely transcribed. The tone and register of their speech is an embodied and gendered phenomenon—one that is explicitly related to the sweetness of breast milk and the texture of baby food. The transmission of speech, like the flow of milk, is presented as a biological act and a biological fact; nurture comes naturally to women.

As a starting point for my analysis of medieval discourses around the nature of lacteal and linguistic nurture, I will refer to Hélène Cixous's formulations of *écriture féminine* as a milklike and vocal communicative mode, which show a certain overlap with medieval ideas about nurture: I claim no direct connection between these ideas, of course, but the unexpected similarities will provide an entrée to reflection on the varied kinds of linguistic creativity that emerge during the nurturing process of language socialization. Across her key writings from the 1970s, Cixous consistently thinks women's writing in relation to voice and to milk. The female voice is "inexhaustible milk,"[2] taking written form in and as the medium of "white ink."[3] This imagery, despite its homely comfort, also gestures toward a multiplicity, a foreignness, even a substitutability of maternal and other languages. The mother tongue is, in its vocality, alienated from semiotic linguistic systems ("less language than music");[4] meanwhile, the acquired nonmaternal language can nourish too, as is most audible in Cixous's punning reference to her third language, "Languelait" (*l'anglais*), that sustains her "at the intersection of the other languages."[5]

Medieval texts, too, characterize maternal language as nourishing sweetness, as *languelait*.[6] Indeed, in medieval descriptions of women's speech to babies, which we might today term "baby talk" or "motherese," the tone inspires greater interest than does the content.[7] This is particularly clear in the *Liber de sinthomatibus mulierum* and the *Trotula major*, a twelfth-century text attributed in the Middle Ages to a female Salernitan physician called Trota or Trotula. In the chapter "On the regimen for the infant," which is mainly derived from Rhazes,[8] preparing an infant for future speech is one of the midwife's first duties once a child has been born: "Et ut cicius loquatur, unge palatum cum melle et nares cum aqua calida, et unctionibus semper mundificetur, et muscillagines semper emungantur et emundentur" (And so that it might talk all the more quickly, anoint the palate with honey and the nose with warm water, and let it always be cleaned with unctions, and let the mucous secretions always be wiped off and cleaned; pp.106–7). The newborn's sensitive eyes ought to be covered after birth, but later on,

> Ante ipsum sint diuerse picture, panni diuersi coloris, margarite, cantilenis et facilibus uocibus utatur; ante eum non est asperis uocibus cantandum neque raucis, sicut lumbardis. Postquam hora loquendi appropinquauerit, nutrix eius linguam frequenter cum melle et butyro ungat, et hoc maxime faciendum est cum loquela tardatur. Ante eum frequenter est loquendum et facilia uerba dicenda sunt. (p. 108)

> There should be different kinds of pictures, cloths of diverse colors, and pearls placed in front of the child, and one should use nursery songs and simple words; neither rough nor harsh words (such as those of Lombards) should be used in singing in front of the child. After the hour of speech has approached, let the child's nurse anoint its tongue frequently with honey and butter, and this ought to be done especially when speech is delayed. One ought to talk in the child's presence frequently and easy words ought to be said. (p. 109)

While no precise examples are given, it is clear that women should both sing and speak with an "easy" vocabulary and a gentle tone. The contrast between the negative verbal counterexample (words that are *asperis* and *raucis*) and the positive recommendation of the oral application of honey and butter reinforces the advice that the nurse speak with a honeyed tone. These lexical choices establish a linguistic nursery space that bears a startling (though, of course, coincidental) resemblance to what Hélène Cixous calls "the language that women speak when no one is there to correct them."[9]

Similar instructions are given in Aldobrandino of Siena's mid-thirteenth-century *Le régime du corps*, a remarkable regimen written in the vernacular for a female dedicatee:[10]

> Et quant il commencent à parler si convient le norrice le bouce fro-ter de salse gemme, de miel, et puis laver le bouce d'ewe d'orge, espe-ciaument à celui qui targe trop à parler; et commence à dire paroles où il n'a lettres ki face le langue trop movoir, si com à dire maman, papa. (p. 78)[11]

> And when they begin to speak it is proper for the nurse to rub the mouth with crystalline salt, with honey, and then wash the mouth with barley water, especially for those whose speech is delayed; and begin saying words like *mama* and *papa*, in which there are no letters that require the tongue to move too much.

Like "Trotula," Aldobrandino adapts instructions from Rhazes's *Liber ad Almansorem*: tone and ease of pronunciation are again emphasized, but this time with concrete examples.[12] Now we know what makes words "easy": they demand less of the child's tongue.[13] Implicit in these instructions is a recognition of the physiology of speech. The examples themselves are unsurprising, though the inclusion of child-friendly vocabulary in a scientific work—one under-taken, unusually for the thirteenth century, in the vernacular—is exceptional. Dictionaries give these as the first written attestations of *maman* and *papa* in French, taking them as references to the female and male parent respectively. However, Michele Bellotti has demon-strated in a brilliant study that this text's *papa* more likely alludes to baby food, which is most often referred to in medieval French as *papin*.[14] The conversion of the more typical *papin* to *papa* could be an Italianism or Latinism,[15] or it could be an "infantilism," replac-ing a nasal vowel with a simple plosive-plus-vowel repetition typi-cal of baby talk.[16] Either way, the use of the dual examples *maman* and *papa/papin* suggests a convergence between that which is easy to say and that which is easy to swallow and digest; it posits feeding, not the father, as the mother's natural partner, and it establishes an analogy between what is happening in the mother's or nurse's mouth and what is happening in the infant's mouth. But whereas modern theorists such as Dolar have mused on the complementarity or mutual exclusivity of the incorporation of food and the emission of language,[17] medieval depictions of *nourreture* tend rather to stake the relationship between breast milk, language, and pedagogy as metonymic and simultaneous. The word *nourreture* can signify the nurturing, nourishment, tutelage, or guardianship of a child, but it can also designate the child him- or herself. We *are* the way we are raised, fed, spoken to, and taught.

The polyvalency of the word *Nourreture* highlights the human relationships at the heart of feeding and language-teaching as processes. Nurture creates a bond between the child and the woman feeding her, of course, but also between the adults responsible for the child's upbringing: mother, wet nurse, father. Numerous medieval texts offer advice about the choice of a wet nurse: these are sometimes addressed to fathers, as in Jean Petit's *Livre du champ d'or* (1389),[18] but more often to mothers, as in Aldobrandino's *Régime* or in Deschamps's *Miroir de mariage*. While medieval French texts often associate mother and wet nurse, with the former in an advisory role over the latter, they rarely stake this partnership in affective terms. One notable exception is Nicole Oresme, who uses mother and nurse as part of a highly original analogy in one of his glosses on Aristotle's *Ethics*. Trying to reconcile Aristotle's statement that the virtuous man loves himself (*phylautos*) with a Christian ideal of love for God, Oresme concludes that the virtuous man loves himself for God's sake, "aussi comme la mere qui aime la nourrice pour son filz, il s'ensuit que elle aime mieulx son filz" (just like the mother who loves the wet nurse for her son's sake, it follows that she loves her son more).[19] The two women enjoy an affectionate relationship, but only as a reflection (by association) of the mother's deeper love for her child—and only as an analogy for the virtuous *man's* self-image.

The process of language socialization is just as relational as the process of breastfeeding—this is a key insight in Adriana Cavarero's *For More than One Voice*, though she never phrases it in precisely this way—and the relationality of infant nurture establishes, if you'll pardon the pun, fluid relationships. Although medieval writers are nearly unanimous in preferring that mothers breastfeed their own children, they pragmatically acknowledge that this doesn't work for every family. As long as a nurse is healthy, abstinent, and of good moral character, her milk is a more than adequate substitute. This logic of substitution extends to the women themselves, as the word *mère* is often used to refer to the lactating caregiver regardless of whether she is in fact the nursing infant's biological mother. Of course, this substitution that adds to a family circle masks the less heartwarming substitution of the nursed child for the wet nurse's own, now-absent biological offspring.[20] And, more surprisingly, literary descriptions of a nurse's nurture can also conflate the mother figure and the child.

The nurse and the infant converge in surprising ways in an ancient image that was widely discussed in the medieval period: Paul's wet-nurse metaphors in 1 Thessalonians 2:7–8 ("we became little ones in the midst of you, as if a nurse should cherish her children. So desirous of you, we would gladly impart unto you not only the gospel of God, but also our own souls: because you were become most dear unto us") and in 1 Corinthians 3:1–2 ("As unto little ones in Christ I gave you milk to drink, not meat; for you were not able as yet"). The former has inspired much debate because of its philological ambiguity and because of the mixed metaphor that would result from the *lectio difficilior*:[21] the apostles become little children cared for by a nurse, *and* they become the nurse who patiently teaches the faithful.[22] As received in late medieval Christendom, however, these verses shared an unambiguous message. Paul is like a gentle nurse who nurtures new Christian communities, but also like the child who stands meekly among them, as both figures embody the values of humility, care, and community. The common repetition of Paul's wet-nurse comparison in medieval texts destined for laypeople suggests that medieval audiences did not deem the elision of child and nurse to be as discomfiting as modern scholars do; rather, they found in it a readily understandable shorthand for the apostolic mission.[23] It is also perfectly consistent with medieval Western discourses about nurses and the two types of *nourreture* that they provide: feeding, and fostering language production.

The image of Paul as a wet nurse appears to vivid effect in Jean Gerson's sermon for the feasts of Saints Peter and Paul, *Nimis honorati sunt amici tui, Deus*.[24] Here the analogy between Paul's teaching of doctrine and a nurse's teaching of speech is more overt. Gerson introduces the wet-nurse image in the same context in which Paul introduces it in 1 Thessalonians. Noting that Paul was criticized for wheedling or flattering discourse, Gerson defends him with a very concrete allusion to daily life:

> Pour tant disoit il que il avoit esté comme la nourrice qui gouverne ses enfants en toute doulceur et humilité en baillant doctrine selon leur capacité. Comme la nourrice parle aucune foys imparfaictement et en begueant pour condescendre a la parole de son enfant, puis masche sa viande, puis siet a terre, puis rit a luy, puis pleure, et briefment elle se fait enfant avec son enfant, pareillement lisons nous de vous, o tres piteux saint Pol. (p. 507)

> Therefore he said that he had been like the wet nurse who educates her children with complete gentleness and humility, teaching them doctrine according to their capabilities. Just as a nurse sometimes speaks imperfectly, stuttering in order to come down to her child's level of speech, then chews his food, then laughs with him, then cries, and in short becomes like a child with her child, likewise do we read of you, oh very compassionate Saint Paul.

In his defense of Paul, Gerson draws on both 1 Thessalonians and 1 Corinthians: the image of the gentle nurse comes from the former, but breastfeeding as a figure for knowing one's audience and tailoring one's speech to their needs owes more to the latter. The combined allusions justify a description of Paul as *piteux*, a word that can encompass multiple meanings in Middle French—pious, compassionate, pitiful—and thus captures the particular combination of love and humility that the nurse embodies for many late medieval writers. But whereas Paul alludes to the nurse as one who feeds a child, Gerson's vignette specifically presents her as one who feeds *and one who speaks.*

Gerson enriches Paul's appropriation of the feminine sphere by fleshing it out into a fully conceived domestic tableau. While he gives no examples of baby talk, as Aldobrandino had, he offers a vivid characterization of it and of a number of related behaviors. The description of the nurse as "begueant" (stuttering), for example, evokes baby talk's tendency toward doubling (*dodo, papa*).[25] This sketch of "la parole de son enfant" illustrates not just infant babbling but babbling *to* the infant, which Dolar has described, tongue partway in cheek, as "no doubt a more successful dialogue than most."[26] The vignette of the nurse made childlike through her speech beautifully illustrates what Cavarero calls the "duet" of "repetition, echo, and miming" that takes place between child and mother[27]—but Gerson's emphasis on this speech as *imperfect* and *stuttering* underscores that the echo effect is led by the child; it is generated not just from the give-and-take between conversation partners, but also from within the childlike words themselves. Returning to Dolar's idea of baby babbling as an "experimental" process, we can see "begueant" as a space of freedom, too: a place where the nurse or mother can assume a persona and share in an alternate communicative idiom.[28] Yet, in the process, the nurse adopts the same presocial expressive mode she is tasked with domesticating.

Just as in the Pauline metaphor that inspired it, in Gerson's vignette the nurse changes places (*condescendre*), straddling the lines between adult and child and between speech and mere vocalization.[29] Her first concession to the child, though imitative of the errors and reduplications of baby talk, is still unambiguously speech ("parle," "parole"), but by the end of the list she sits on the ground (a "condescension" both verbal and postural); she laughs and cries, emitting vocal expressions of emotion that are probably devoid of semantic content. And between his mentions of speech and of nonverbal vocalizations (laughter, crying) Gerson inserts a reference to food-chewing.[30] In this sequence we see a convergence of vocalization,

mastication, digestion, and comprehension.[31] All in a triply pedagogical context: Gerson teaches a Parisian congregation by preaching
about the apostle Paul, who explained his mission to the Christian
communities at Thessalonica and Corinth by comparing himself
both to a child and to a woman nurturing a child. However colorful
Gerson's evocation of nursely activities may be, however, these multiple allusive layers effectively serve to distance this discourse from
the maternal figure's natural nurturing, feeding, and teaching of language. Gerson is invoking a nurse's motherese specifically as an analogy for *male* teaching, and it is for this reason only that the nurse's
speech patterns are recorded in such detail. Moreover, while Gerson deploys the image of a stuttering wet nurse as part of a *defense*
of Paul, the same sort of image can figure in antifeminist attacks:
witness *Cité des dames* I.x, wherein Christine de Pizan responds to
the misogynistic slur that women, and female caregivers in particular, communicate well with children because they are themselves
simple: "un aucteur dit que femmes ont par nature chetif courage et
que elles sont comme l'enfant et pour ce conversent voulentiers les
enfans avecques elles et elles avec les enfans" (one authority says that
women naturally have a weak character and are like children, and for
this reason children converse willingly with them and they with children).[32] Reason replies by confirming that female caregivers *do* speak
differently than other people do, and that their speech, in its humility and its rhetorical sensibility, is superior to more mature (read:
male) linguistic modes. And yet, when not brought into conversation with male-centered communicative modes, mothers' and nurses'
communications with their infants—like the "unheard-of songs"
Cixous proclaims for and in the female body[33]—are quite difficult to
hear.

LOST LULLABIES

In Coudrette's verse retelling of the Mélusine legend (1401), the titular fairy, deprived of human form and forced out of her home by
her husband's transgression of her taboo, returns at night to nurse
her youngest son. A noteworthy illustration of the scene in BnF MS
fr. 12575 shows Mélusine's body—fully visible thanks to the unusual

FIGURE 3.1 Mélusine nursing her infant (first half of the fifteenth century). From *Roman de Mélusine* (BnF MS fr. 12575, fol. 89r). Photograph: Bibliothèque nationale de France.

standing posture from which she somehow nurses her son as he lies in his cradle behind her— displaying sirenlike features (a fishlike tail, no wings; fig. 3.1) rather than the more dragonlike or serpentine attributes that are typical of the woodcut illustrations in early print editions of Mélusine texts. The mermaidlike appearance of the mother, even as she carries out a human act of nurturing, combines two stock images of female vocalization: the siren song and the maternal cradle song. Mélusine, however, sings no lullaby; she remains completely silent ("Coyement mais mot ne sonnoit").[34] This silence is emblematic of the greater challenge of attending to women's voices, especially as used in domestic spaces, with small children. For, as Emma Dillon points out, any consideration of medieval music or soundscape implies "listening for something that cannot be recuperated,"[35] and traditional musicological methods are especially ill-suited to the study of medieval woman's song.[36] Even though "all cultures seem to have certain songs, rhymes, games and language routines that are used for interacting with babies,"[37] until recently very few of those cultures have made a point of writing or recording them—or any other textual or melodic products of the feminine domestic sphere.[38] John Haines puts it even more bluntly: "the medieval lullaby is anonymous, common, childish and lacking written codification. [. . .] In the traditional history of medieval music, the lullaby has no place."[39] The problem of the lullaby crystallizes, in their most extreme form, the difficulties inherent in any project seeking to investigate medieval soundscapes, popular song, and women's contributions thereto. If a woman sings to a child in the nursery and no man is present to transcribe what she sings, can she have generated meaningful language at all?

As suggested in chapter 2, singing can present an especially challenging sort of *vox*—and women's sung words are the most difficult to classify as speech.[40] Yet nurses, who teach babies to speak, are also expected to sing to them. One of the wet nurse's primary duties, as enumerated in Corbechon's *Livre des propriétés des choses*, is that she "esbat l'enfant par son chant pour lui faire dormir" (relaxes the infant with her singing to make him sleep; BnF fr. 221, fol. 79rb).[41] This encyclopedic mandate finds a charming analogue in the early fourteenth-century epic *Brun de la Montagne*, in which a fairy wet nurse unswaddles the titular infant, warms him by the fire, then cuddles him and sings him to sleep: ".IIII. foys le baissa, et toudis en chantant / Et moult courtoissement, si l'ala endormant" (Four times she kissed him, singing all the while, and she very gently put him to sleep; p. 69, vv. 2013–14).[42]

Unsurprisingly, many medieval texts associate feeding, rocking,

and singing as the preludes to an infant's sleep. Corbechon had earlier written in the chapter on infants that

> les enfans prannent moult de nourrissement, et pour ce ilz ont besoing
> de moult dormir pour rappeller la chaleur naturelle dedenz le corps
> pour faire la digestion de leur viande, et c'est la cause pour quoy on
> berce les enfans a celle fin que la chaleur esmeuve l'enfant a dormir par
> les fumees qui montent au chef. Les nourrices aussi doivent aucune
> fois chanter empres l'enfant pour donner plaisance et delit au sens de
> l'enfant par la douceur de la voiz. (BnF MS fr. 16993, fol. 76r)

> infants require much feeding, and therefore they require much sleep
> in order to restore to their bodies the natural heat needed to digest
> their food, and that is the reason why infants are rocked, so that the
> heat will prompt the infant to sleep because of the smoke that rises
> to the brain. Wet nurses should also sometimes sing near the infant
> in order to please and delight the infant's senses through the sweet-
> ness of her voice.

The combination of singing and rocking evokes a state of relaxed
comfort that ushers in an altered, less rational consciousness.[43] Here
again, as in the *Trotula*, weight is given to the nurse's voice as a tone
rather than as a conveyor of meaning. Unlike most human vocalizations, whose "essential destination" is speech,[44] the lullaby's essential
destination is oblivion. A lullaby's essence is not sung words, but
audible *sweetness*, an untranscribable "phonic [and] haptic caress"
designed to *curtail* waking thought.[45]

The lullaby is therefore, from the standpoint of medieval linguistic theory, a paradoxical vocal production. It can include words emitted with intention but is apparently devoid of concepts; it is writable but remains unwritten. The lullaby seems to exemplify what
Bruce Holsinger has called "the music of the body," that is, "the music
most completely divorced from the language, literature, and linguistic
ways of knowing that seek to describe and contain it."[46] But lullabies
are not divorced from language: they are "nonlinguistic" not because
they lack lyrics, but because they lack a higher concept—which is

in itself somewhat ironic, as the singing woman has already successfully brought another kind of *conceptus* (i.e., the fetus) to fruition. As Cavarero sums up the received wisdom: "To put it formu-
laically: woman sings, man thinks."[47] Still, the mother's or nurse's
singing voice (like her teaching voice) is one that carries heavy cultural freight.

The nurse's sweet provisions to her charge, lullabies and breast
milk, are imagined as a particularly efficacious vehicle for cultural
transmission. Nourishment is a form of teaching—as in Christine
de Pizan's binomial expression *nourriz et dotrinés*[48]—and even of
indoctrination. This becomes most explicit in discussions of mul-
ticonfessional households, when a servant or slave is employed by
a family of a different faith tradition. For instance, urban Jewish
women often hired Christian wet nurses, and the late twelfth- to
early thirteenth-century *Sefer Hasidim* specifies that a Christian
nurse should be asked not to sing to a Jewish charge.[49] Christian
songs can be dangerous "even if the child is already asleep and the
singing is intended only to prevent him from waking up again."[50]
Elisheva Baumgarten notes that despite this perceived risk, most
Jewish scholars do not argue that Christian wet nurses should not
be employed in Jewish homes, simply that their cultural influence
be mitigated as much as possible by the parents.[51] In a somewhat
similar vein, in the French romance *Floire et Blanchefleur* (c. 1150),
Blanchefleur's mother (a Christian slave at a Muslim court in Spain)
teaches French to the pagan queen but is not allowed to breastfeed
the Muslim prince Floire.[52] Confessional differences also limit nourishment in the chanson de geste *La bataille Loquifer* (early thirteenth
century), in which the abducted Christian infant Maillefer refuses
the milk of a Muslim nurse; she resorts to feeding him with a *cornette*
or horn, the forerunner of the baby bottle ("l'ai acorneté," she reports
in l. 4033), and because of his naughtiness he often goes hungry ("par
felonie a mainte fois juné"; l. 4036).[53]

These examples indicate not only that breast milk is a "nourriture spirituelle,"[54] but that milk (and perhaps also the lullaby) has a
cultural power that incorporates but also exceeds language. Milk is
a potential vehicle for the introduction of vice and corruption, because

ancient and medieval authorities maintain that breast milk transmits all sorts of physical and moral attributes—hence the importance of choosing a nurse with care. There is ample evidence for the cultural ubiquity of this idea, not just in medical texts or in the numerous manuals advising parents how to choose a nurse, but in a number of medieval urban legends about breastfeeding. These include the antisemitic slander, spread by Pope Innocent III, that Jewish parents obliged their Christian wet nurses to express their milk into a latrine for three days following their having taken the eucharist;[55] and the widespread story of a mother inducing her baby to vomit after he has been suckled by the "wrong" sort of woman.[56] Just as there is concern that lullabies can influence even a sleeping child, there is concern that breast milk, too, is an avenue for passively received corruption. This corruption does not appear to be a *linguistic* concern—nurses are feared for their potential to teach the wrong religion, the wrong values, more than the wrong mother tongue—and yet, just as there is song in women's speech,[57] there is speech in their song. Women's vocalized nurture communicates *languelait*, a mother tongue always already foreign, and therefore both nourishing and unsettling.

For all of the cultural work that they might do, medieval lullabies, especially those sung in French-speaking lands, have left frustratingly few traces. John Haines, author of the most penetrating study of medieval Romance lullabies to date, writes, "My initial round of investigation on lullabies in medieval literature [...] has proved frustrating, and I wish future researchers in this area the best of luck."[58] Despite Haines's best wishes, my luck, too, has been limited: and this lack of results may in itself be significant. The most lullaby-like text I have found appears in the fifteenth-century *Mistere de Saint Quentin*, possibly authored by Jean Molinet, in which the future saint's mother speaks or sings to her newborn in stanzaic verse.[59] Some of these lyrics, especially in the latter half of the poem, pick up on typical lullaby motifs:

Il faut que ton cry se taise,
Que je te baigne et solaise
Et complaise,

Que je te porte et alaitte.
En ta bouche vermillette,
Qui me rit et si oeullette,
Tant doulcette,
Filz, il fault que je te baise. (p. 11, ll. 629–36)

Your cry must be quieted,
I must wash and comfort
And humor you,
I must hold and nurse you.
On your little red mouth
That smiles at me brilliantly,
So sweet,
Son, I must kiss you.

The mother later enumerates all she has done for her son, including "je chantoye" (I sang; p. 55, l. 3414), which supports the notion that these "vers assez gracieux" could be a lullaby.[60]

Beyond this single literary example, I have found no medieval French lullabies—nor have I even been able to ascertain what the medieval French word(s) for "lullaby" might have been.[61] Tantalizing references to songs sung to infants tend to allude to them without naming them. The passage from the *Trotula* cited near the beginning of this chapter simply alludes to a *cantilena* (little song); likewise, Aldobrandino of Siena recommends that "a l'endormir de l'enfant doit chanter beles chanconnetes et douces" (to put him to sleep [she] should sing nice, sweet little songs).[62] Bartholomaeus Anglicus's statement that a nurse "Solet etiam cantus adhiberi" (Typically uses singing; VI.4, 238) to calm her charge is rendered in John Trevisa's English as "singe lullinge[s] and oþir cradil songis"[63]—but Corbechon's French just reads "chanter." Indeed, medieval French writers tend to use verbs such as *bercer* (to rock), *chanter*, or perhaps *niner*[64]—rather than nouns—to evoke the lullaby. Thus the lullaby is not a thing, a text, a linguistic object; it is more often a relation, something a mother or a nurse *does*. "Je chantoye," as Saint Quentin's mother reminds him in the *Mistere de Saint Quentin*'s classic maternal guilt trip. The French lexical evidence bears out Haines's beautiful characterization of the lullaby: "It is the simple and ephemeral voice of fragile human relationships."[65]

This apparently exclusive conceptualization of a lullaby as an unnamable und untranscribable relational act, rather than as a verbal and textual artifact, seems to set medieval French culture apart from other European cultures. French certainly displays no developed *written* tradition parallel to the Middle English lullaby carol, of which there are some twenty surviving examples,[66] nor even the far less well documented Italian *ninna nanna*;[67] no French writer created a text anything like the *Naeniae* of Giovanni Gioviano Pontano (1469–71). It has been supposed that many of the early, unrecorded medieval lullabies must have been religiously inspired;[68] both the English texts and the allusion in the Rhenish *Sefer Hasidim* confirm this to have been the case in regions contiguous to France. But philologically speaking, this is as far as I've been able to get. Because it embodies a relation that leaves no material trace—and because it hits the airwaves softly, in an explicitly feminine and infantile space—the medieval French lullaby is a lyrical mode whose words and whose very name now elude us. Despite the music that must have inhabited it, the medieval nursery has become, for us, what Jacques Rancière calls a "world of silent witnesses."[69] Unlike the newborn's *A-a-a*, which embodies the semantic without the semiotic, the maternal lullaby occupies the role that Dolar assigns to infant babbling: purely phonic, containing neither semiotic nor semantic meaning, and therefore leaving no intellectual trace. But if this sort of sonic nurturing leads to oblivion, mothers' other milklike communications to their children have a far more lasting intellectual impact.

TEACHING *FEMINAE*

Women, especially mothers and nurses, are identified in medieval literature as a child's first teachers. Their primary charge is to see that the child acquires language, then a basic moral education. This is construed as a pedagogical role, but a largely nonintellectual one.[70] Medieval discourses on the mother's role as the original language teacher are structured around two received ideas: that women are the natural teachers of languages (or of vernacular mother tongues, at least) and that domesticating and socializing processes should begin in early childhood. It is essential to begin language instruction early, for, as Giles of Rome explains (here cited in Henri de Gauchy's translation from 1282), those who do not begin learning a language when they are young can never attain near-native proficiency: "Nos veons que se li hons [n]a [apris] aucun langage en sa jennesce, il ne le puet parler bien et distincte(e)ment, ainz s'aparçoivent cil du païs qu'il n'est mie nez de cele terre et qu'il est estrange" (We see that if one did not learn a language in his youth, he cannot speak it well or distinctly, but rather, people from the country perceive that he is not native to that land and is a foreigner).[71]

The naturalness of maternal language-teaching does not mean that women are seen as superior instructors or that the language they convey is highly regarded. The mother is strongly associated with learning of the vernacular, which, when discussed in opposition to other languages, is construed as simplest and the most naturally acquired.[72] Thus, if women are babies' natural language teachers, it is not only because of the nature of the mother-child bond, but because of the quasi-infantile nature of the language women teach, too. In Italian language debates of the fourteenth century, "use of the vernacular is [derided as] a sort of 'babytalk,' while the use of Latin is the sign of the mature author"; Boccaccio, for instance, in his *Trattatello*, mocks unsophisticated readers who better comprehend the vernacular as "coloro che ancora il latte suggano" (those who still suck down milk).[73] I have not found any such explicit comparisons in French, but there *is* a common trope among clerical writers and early French humanists that Latin is inaccessible to women—this despite the fact it is in fact Latin that is referred to in the first attested use of the phrase *langage maternel* in French: Oresme uses it to point out, in his gloss on Aristotle's *Ethics*, that while Latin is a learned language in fourteenth-century France, for the ancient Romans it was Greek that was a learned language, and "le langage commun et maternel, c'estoit latin" (the common maternal language was Latin).[74]

This was a subtlety lost on many of Oresme's contemporaries.

Amusingly, Pierre Col writes, in a letter defending the *Roman de la Rose* (1402), that Ovid wrote his *Ars amatoria* in Latin precisely so that women could not read it—apparently forgetting that Latin was the ancient Romans' mother tongue.[75] A similar idea is implicit in the sixteenth-century comical dialogue *Le mirouer et exemple moralle des enfans ingratz*, wherein the father repeatedly peppers his speeches with the word "Nota"; at every repetition of "Nota" his wife, never engaging with the substance of his arguments, simply protests, "C'est ung mot de latin" (That is a Latin word).[76] What these examples share with the more elevated Italian discussions is the notion that there is a hierarchy of sophistication among languages, with men (Latin) at the top, infants (baby talk) at the bottom, and women rather closer to babies than to men.[77] And again, it is typically women, not men, who use baby talk (motherese) as a communicative idiom.[78] That the lower feminine and infantile linguistic forms are typically characterized as natural does not entirely obscure the uncomfortable fact that these, too, are cultural constructs; just as medieval interpretations of cries like *A* or *Oe* reveal the unsettling leap from sign to discourse, the frequent interchangeability of mothers and wet nurses highlights the "alienation" and the "ontological gap always already inherent in human language."[79] But unlike modern formulations of a nature-nurture binary (which Cixous rejects as a patriarchal formulation ultimately reducible to a male-female binary), the medieval discursive interchangeability of the mother and the nurse—like the personified battle between Nature and Norreture in the *Roman de Silence*—hints that nature and nurture are *both* female.[80]

The instrumental role of mothers and nurses in language teaching is a commonplace in medieval texts, extending even to allegorical depictions of exclusively male pedagogical institutions.[81] The blurring of nature and nurture that "teaching women" can signal is especially pronounced in two French-language instructional books, produced in England and sometimes known as the *Femina* (or *Tretiz de langage*) and the *Femina nova*.[82] The former, ostensibly written for a noblewoman by Walter of Bibbesworth in the thirteenth century, presents French vocabulary necessary for child-rearing and for agrarian and artisanal activities that a nobleman might need to discuss as part of the management of a rural estate. The latter, likely compiled shortly after 1415, reproduces most of the earlier *Tretiz* and adds to it Latin rubrics, a Middle English translation, a bilingual treatise on manners, and a three-column glossary of French words and their pronunciations in parallel with Middle English equivalents. While the *Tretiz* was written for a noblewoman who already had a command of French, as an aid to her instruction of her son, the *Femina nova* appears destined for young men of the rising administrative class.[83] Both, however, play into the cultural commonplace that vernacular language teaching was primarily women's work.[84] As the initial Latin rubric of the *Femina nova* puts it: "Lyber iste vocatur femina quia sicut femina docet infantem loqui maternam sic docet iste liber Iuvenes rethorice loqui gallicum prout infra patebit" (This book is called *Femina* [*Woman*] because just as a woman teaches a child the mother tongue, thus does this book teach youths rhetoric in the French language exactly as can be seen below).[85] Literally called "Woman," the text overwrites the "white ink" of maternal language teaching and replaces the woman as a functional but nonintellectual transmitter of language.

The at-times contradictory visions of a mother's role in language teaching that emerge from the two *Femina* texts are illustrative of broader medieval debates about the interplay of nature and nurture. Women have a special role in providing nurture as teaching, yet their pedagogical interventions are frequently characterized as being more natural than those of formal schooling.[86] The convergence of nature and nurture in the figure of the mother or nurse as language teacher is beautifully illustrated through the *mouvance* of Bibbesworth's *Tretiz*. Different versions of the prologue disagree as to whether nature or nurture dictates the book's contents: the Arundel manuscript (BL Arundel 220), edited by Thomas Wright in the nineteenth century, states that the *Tretiz* offers a mother the French vocabulary she will need "du primer temps ke homme nestra, oeweke trestut le langage pur saver *nurture* en sa juvente" (from when a child is first born, with absolutely all of the language needed to know how to *nurture* him in his youth; my emphasis);[87] the manuscript more recently edited by William Rothwell (Cambridge University Library MS Gg.i.i) reads, "de primere tens ke home neistra ou tut le langage par sa *nature* en sa juvente" (from when a child is first born, with all of the language through his *nature* in his youth; my emphasis).[88] In both versions of the *Tretiz*, nurture is guided by nature. The teaching calendar is dependent on biological development,[89] which is only appropriate since speech is the "naturele noise" of the human animal: "Home parle, ourse braie" (Humans speak, bears bellow; v. 248).[90] However, the teaching of this "natural" human sound is explicitly designed to facilitate the child's entry into culture, into society: the prologue cites the management of an estate as a rationale for learning French, and the first motivating factor mentioned in poem itself is "Qu'i[l] en parole seit meuz apris / E de nul autre escharnis" (That he have better mastery of the language and not be mocked by anyone else).[91] Even if speech is presented as a natural faculty, it is one that is inculcated through the tender attentions of a mother, for the purposes of social and economic integration.[92]

The imbrication of nature and nurture plays out rather differently in *Femina nova*, addressed as it is to youths rather than to mothers. From the beginning, the emphasis is firmly on language as a formally taught skill rather than as a natural or familially transmitted capacity. As early as the tenth line, shame appears as a motivator: "Hony est il qui nest norry" (translated two lines later as "Heny ys he þᵗ ys nat tauȝh" [Shamed is he who is not taught]).[93] Likewise, the section on manners, *De moribus infantis*, opens with the lines "Ore nurture ieo voile aprendre / A toteȝ qui sount dage tendre / Now nurture y wyl teche / To al þᵗ ben of age tendre" (Now I want to teach nurture to all who are of tender age).[94] Note the flexibility of the term *nurture*: teaching, feeding, speaking, and culture are all implied. But nature does still have its place, even in the *Femina nova*, as the student's goal is to speak "naturalment" ("kyndely").[95] Nature, or a convincing facsimile thereof, is cultivated through *nourreture*; it takes a lot of nurturing to learn to mimic nature.

As a nurturer who develops children's natural language abilities, the *femina* wields creative and potentially innovative linguistic tools.[96] The medieval distinction between speaking *litteraliter* (writably, in Latin) and speaking *maternaliter* (maternally, in the vernacular) points to a specifically *poetic* creative potential inherent in women's speech:[97] to speak maternally is to be unlettered, but it is also, if one chooses to read "litteraliter" against the grain, to speak nonliterally. Accordingly, though the language women and small children share "when no one is there to correct them" was broadly dismissed by medieval writers as intellectually inferior, a few poets did experiment with the expressive potential of baby talk. In the remainder of this chapter I will focus on poems in which Christine de Pizan and Charles d'Orléans use the "infantile" language of mother-child communications to open imaginative poetic spaces. For these multilingual poets whose "coming to language" was plural—those with no single home and no single home language, with "no permanent residence" and a "music in [them] from elsewhere"[98]—the universal alterity of infant language is a tool with which to linger "at the intersection of the other languages" that have marked their linguistic and authorial development. Both poets, I will show, use infantile poetic personas to tap into a profound "foreignness" that is (paradoxically) domestic yet undomesticable. Like the "lost lullabies" of medieval France, these poems prompt us to reconsider how nurture—which, in these poems, as in the *Femina* and *Femina nova*, is constructed as a gendered, relational cultivation of nature—contributes differently to the making of knowledge and identity *when no one else is there to listen.*

CHRISTINE DE PIZAN'S *DOULCE NOURRITURE* [99]

The language with which we talk about our first language—mother tongue, native speaker—is redolent of birth, early childhood, and the intimate domestic sphere.[100] But the domesticity of first-language learning can, in late medieval Europe, constitute what the feminist literary scholar Susan Fraiman terms an "extreme domesticity": fundamental to culture yet outside of its mainstream, and marginal to broader, public, male-dominated social structures. In this sense the heart of the home is also a site of the alien, the foreign. Indeed, as noted above, the Middle French vocabulary of the "langage maternel," though expressive of notions of inborn familiarity, is (perhaps coun-terintuitively) a neologistic product of a large-scale translation project: the language expressing that which should be quintessen-tially native is in fact a transplant from foreign soil.[101]

Christine de Pizan, widely heralded as the first self-supporting professional woman of letters in the French tradition, is herself a transplant from foreign soil—a biographical reality that becomes a cornerstone of her writerly persona.[102] Throughout her oeuvre, Christine combines references to her own coming into the French language with strategic poetic references to nurture, thus casting her own professional activity as a rebirth and reacculturation into a new poetic language.[103] Christine's language of nurture forms an interpre-tive thread that helps bind together disparate elements of Christine's oeuvre into a coherent case for a uniquely female claim to authority, one intimately linked to an exclusively feminine capacity for linguis-tic innovation. With an ever more expansive vision of the types of female body that can produce or can imbibe *doulce nourriture*, Chris-tine explores what it means to learn, to transmit, even to generate a mother tongue.

Christine first probes the connection between *nourriture*, lan-guage production, and coming to poetry in the fifteenth of her *Cent balades* (1394–99). Here, at the beginning of her literary career, she produces a fused infant-adult and male-female voice as the mark of her new relationship to language. This poem crystallizes the broader trajectory of *Cent balades*: creating a first-person voice that the reader may identify with the poet herself, then revealing the multiplicity and alterity of the lyric *je*, a rhetorical surprise that signals the writer's alienation as well as her virtuosity and generative power.

Bearing the refrain "Puis qu'ay perdu ma doulce nourriture" (Since I have lost my sweet nourishment), Ballade XV begins with an emphatic declaration of infancy: "Helas! helas! bien puis crier et braire, / Quant j'ay perdu ma mere et ma nourrice" (Alas! alas! I certainly can cry and wail, when I have lost my mother and my nurse; vv. 1–2).[104] The further reference to "doulz lait" (sweet milk; v. 5) and the speaker's characterization of himself as "foiblet" (a weak little [male] thing; v. 9) only confirm that the "sweet nourishment" of the ballade may, on the most literal level, refer to breast milk. As its refrain makes clear, this ballade is about mourning the loss of a nurturing bond, more than a natural one.[105] The mother/nurse (does it make a difference which?) is lamented, only to disappear from the poem even as the memory of her *doulce nourriture* looms much larger. This peculiar metonymic logic of substitution, by which the departed mother gives way to the also-gone but more verbally present nurture she used to provide, manifests in numerous ways. In the first stanza, mother, nurse, and milk are subtly equated with one another:

> Helas! helas! bien puis crier et braire,
> Quant j'ay perdu ma mere et ma nourrice,
> Qui doulcement me souloit faire taire.
> Or n'y a mais ame qui me nourrice,
> Ne qui ma faim de son doulz lait garisse.
> Jamais de moy nul ne prendra la cure,
> Puis qu'ay perdu ma doulce nourriture. (vv. 1–7)

> Alas! alas! I certainly can cry and wail,
> When I have lost my mother and my nurse,
> Who sweetly used to hush me.
> Now there's not a soul who might nourish me,
> Nor who might cure my hunger with her sweet milk.
> Never will anyone take care of me,
> Since I have lost my sweet nourishment.

The repetition of the phrase "ay perdu ma [...]" (I have lost my [...]), completed first by "mere et ma nourrice" and thrice in the refrain by "doulce nourriture," cements the substitution of milk for mother figure. The adjective *doulz/doulce* is used over the course of the ballade to modify (and thus, to establish a certain equivalence between) three nouns: milk (v. 5), nourishment (vv. 7, 14, and 21), and mother (v. 17). In this last instance, however, the syntax is reversed—"ma mere la doulce et debonnaire / Me nourrissoit" (my mother the sweet and noble [one] used to feed me, vv. 17–18)—which at once reinforces the mother's role as milk producer and alienates her from that function, through both an inverted word order and a line break. The words that are thus thrown into relief, "Me nourrissoit," consitute the ballade's only rejet.[106] Their verse establishes a stark contrast between past and present, placing the imperfect "nourrissoit" (used to feed) on one side of the caesura and the emphatically present "or fault que tout tarrisse" (now it is necessary that everything dry up) on the other. The same contrast is implicit in in the refrain's "ay perdu" (I have lost), a present-perfect form that depicts a current state conditioned by a past loss.[107] When the mother is gone, what remains is the absence of the nurture she consistently provided in an irretrievable past.

In Ballade XV breast milk is associated with sustenance and health—and also, consistent with the tradition of mother as language teacher, with voice and speech. Milk is presented as that which could "cure" (*garisse*) hunger; without it no one will care for the child ("prendra la cure"[108]) and he is doomed to languish ("Or convendra qu'en orphanté languisse"; v. 12) and perish ("or fault que [. . .] a doleur perisse"; vv. 18–19). The evocative rhymes *nourrice, garisse, languisse, tarisse, perisse* (nourish, cure, languish, dry up, perish), all verbs in the subjunctive mood, trace the undoing of a body in decline. This sequence culminates in the ballade's final two lines, placing the "malons" and "pouvre enfonture" with which the speaker must now suffer (ulcers and malnourishment; v. 20) in counterpoint to the "doulce nourriture" that could have prevented them.[109] However, while the maternal "nourriture" met the child's bodily needs, it does not initially appear to have fostered language production. The loss of "ma mere et ma nourrice" is first lamented not because she used her milk to feed the baby, but because she used her milk to quiet his cries ("doulcement me souloit faire taire"; v. 3). Nourishment tamped down the baby's vocal production rather than cultivating it. Having been weaned against his will, on the other hand, has led the child to language. Back when his mother nourished him, he used to please everyone ("a tous souloie plaire"; v. 15), and it is unclear whether he pleased them with speech or with nonverbal behaviors; but now he "can cry and wail," indeed he *must* complain and cry ("Plaindre et plourer je doy bien mon affaire"; v. 8).[110] But he does not cry out *to* his mother; rather, his poetic outcry becomes "a way of *being addressed.*"[111]

The child's newfound voice is established, in the first line of each stanza, as one that is not (or is no longer) pleasing. Why has the poet adopted this ostensibly anti-aesthetic choice? To address this question, it is helpful to consider the relationship between infant and adult speech as presented in Ballade XV, and what the creation of an idiom that floats in the air between a mature poet and an infant persona allows Christine to do. First, to state the obvious: the poem is written from a small *child's* point of view, but with strictly *adult* language. There is no infantile cry, no stilted or stuttering rhythm; even the interjection, *helas,* is written in its conventionally significant form. In other words, this child speaks about himself in the way adults speak *about* children—not in the way adults speak *to* children, and certainly not in the way a small child would himself speak. Christine's translation of an infant point of view, like any other "good translation," "domesticates" the other's language.[112] And while the poem *does* construct a sense of development, of linguistic maturation and the passage of time, relationships and chronology are layered, rather than appearing in either a linear or a lineal order. The lyric persona spends most of the poem talking about the recent past, the present, and the near future; only near the end does he arrive at a more distant past. On the one hand, this can be seen as a sign of growth: from the "non sachant" (know-nothing; v. 10) who is "jeune [. . .] de sens" (young in sense; v. 11), aware only of his immediate environment, to a more sophisticated thinker capable of abstract engagement with less proximate time frames. On the other hand, the evocation of a remembered "temps passé" (past time; v. 15) is hard to square with an infant persona. Despite the nominal infant subjectivity, this poetic voice clearly signals its adult origins.

In conceiving (of) a lyric baby, Christine "open[s] up the standard dialect and literary canons to what is foreign to themselves, to the substandard and the marginal."[113] This very specific gesture is a key part of Christine's larger project, in the *Cent balades,* of creating a poetic origin story. In Ballade XV she stages her initiation into public, literary life as analogous to a baby's more literal entry into life. She is, in a sense, giving birth to a writerly self and then abandoning that self to the world; she is both the creator and the orphaned creation. But she brings her baby alter ego into the world in the middle of her "story," not the beginning; this placement creates a synchronic layered effect and resists biographical reading, highlighting that Christine's poetic activity is an intentional creative process. The crying child might seem at odds with the other lyric persona developed in ballades V through XX, the widow, but in effect the two personae collaborate to satisfy the preconditions Christine must meet in order to establish her extraordinary career. The baby, like the widow, is a sexless poetic neophyte; both of these characteristics allow for the creation of a respectable, innocent, nonamorous, nonthreatening public image.[114] Even more than the widow lyrics, the baby ballade points toward two ideas that will become pillars of Christine's vision of female authorship, as elaborated in her major works of the first decade of the fifteenth century: one, that solitude (manifesting here as being weaned and orphaned) is a necessary precondition for coming into poetic language; the other, that a woman's capacity to conceive, bring forth, and nourish a baby directly supports her powers of literary creation and knowledge production.

After the *Cent ballades* Christine increasingly emphasizes not just her femaleness but her foreignness as an essential characteristic of her writerly persona, and this allows her to juxtapose notions of the foreign tongue and of the mother tongue in order to posit foreign femaleness as a special impetus to poetry. Thus, in the *Mutacion de Fortune* (1403), the first-person narrator includes in the story of her/his foreign birth the fact that she/he was breastfed by Mother Nature; and in the *Avision Christine* (1405), the narrator presents her migration and widowhood as linguistic and literary rebirths. Christine highlights the disjunctures between her multiple comings into language by offering parallel autobiographies (one metaphorical and one "factual") in the *Avision*. Metaphorically speaking, Christine's widowhood plunged her into a second childhood, an idea we saw expressed differently in Ballade XV: here, Lady Philosophy admonishes Christine that when she mourns her lot, she resembles "l'enfant trop mignot qui se deult du petit coup de la verge que son pere lui

donne, et ne scet congnoistre le bien qu'il lui fait" (the overly deli-
cate child who cries at the little spanking his father gives him, unable
to recognize the good it is doing him; p. 118, ll. 58–60).[115] This second childhood is not a dotage, however, but a developmental do-
over. Christine emerges as an author by retracing a new educational
path, as described in *Avision* III.10. Before she could become a writer,
she had to relearn how to read: "comme l'enfant que au premier on
met a l'a.b.c., me pris aux histoires anciennes des commencemens du
monde [. . .]" (like the child that one first sets to work on her ABCs,
I applied myself to ancient histories of the beginnings of the world;
p. 110, ll. 16–18). She quickly matures to the point where she can also
understand poetic language:

> Puis me pris aux livres des pouetes, et comme de plus en plus alast
> croissant le bien de ma congnoissance, adonc fus je aise quant j'oz
> **trouvé le stille a moy naturel**, me delictant en leurs soubtilles couver-
> tures et belles matieres mucees soubz fictions delictables et morales,
> et le bel stille de leurs mettres et proses deduites par belle et polie
> rethorique aournee de soubtil langage et proverbes **estranges**. (110, ll.
> 23–31; emphasis added)

> Then I applied myself to the poets' books, and as the balance of my
> knowledge was growing more and more, I was satisfied to have **found
> the style natural to me**, taking delight in their subtle figures and fine
> subjects concealed beneath pleasurable and moral fictions, and the
> beautiful style of their verse and prose executed through beautiful
> and refined rhetoric adorned with subtle language and **unfamiliar**
> proverbs.

At the time being described, Christine was a consumer of poetry,
not a producer; but the sophisticated syntax of the passage, with its
layered prepositional phrases illustrating the poetics of concealment,
demonstrates that she has since internalized the poets' stylistic lessons. Christine finds poetic language both strange and natural. It is
trouvé, found or invented, and then incorporated—but without los-
ing its foreignness. Nor should we overlook the fact that Christine

finds her natural voice through the reading and emulation of *male* authors' works. And unlike the Old French mother tongue, which the twelfth-century coiners of the phrase *lingua materna* define as a fluid oral idiom (in contrast to written Latin), Christine's new language exists first, and only, in written form.[116] Her new poetic vernacular is both *litteraliter* and *maternaliter*.

Nature is pleased with Christine's growing interpretive skills, but the budding reader wants more: "que par l'engendrement d'estude et des choses veues nasquissent de moy nouvelles lectures" (for new readings to be born from me, by means of the fertilization of study and things seen; p. 110, ll. 33–34). Christine's generative textual ambitions soon come to fruition. Proceeding in her internal dialogue with Nature, the latter declares:

> Ou temps que tu portoies les enfans en ton ventre, grant douleur a l'enfanter sentoies. Or vueil que de toy naissent nouveaulx volumes, lesquelz les temps a venir et perpetuelment au monde presenteront ta memoire devant les princes et par l'univers en toutes places, lesquelz en joie et delit tu enfanteras de ta memoire, non obstant le labour et traveil, lequel tout ainsi comme la femme qui a enfanté, si tost que elle ot le cry de son enfant oublie son mal, oublieras le traveil du labour oyant la voix de tes volumes. (p. 110, ll. 37–44)

> Back when you carried children in your womb, you felt great pain in giving birth. Now I want new volumes to be born, which will present your memory before princes and everywhere across the universe, in the future and forevermore; which you will birth from your memory with joy and pleasure, despite the labor and work. Just like the woman who has given birth and who forgets her pain as soon as she hears the cry of her baby, you will forget the travails of your labor upon hearing the voice of your volumes.

Here "the maternal [. . .] displaces the sexual" as Christine rewrites the *Rose*'s literary-generative metaphors of pens, hammers, and plows.[117] Still, a birth almost always implies a previous sexual experience, so there is something autoerotic in the engendering of her books through solitary study, and something untimely in the already-mature way they will call out to her and to her patrons when she brings them into the world. Comparing her book babies to her human ones, Christine expresses greater joy at the advent of the former; she rewrites the medieval commonplace that women forget the pain of childbirth upon first seeing and holding their offspring, instead finding delight in her books' "voice." But in what language will they cry? Has Christine the author been reborn into a different maternal tongue, and what tongue will she pass on to her biblio-children?

If one can even ask this question, it is because Christine presents her own "first" childhood and first mother as having conditioned a coming-into-language that was very different from the poetic acquisition of her adulthood. Her early years, as described in the *Avision*, were marked by a sense of profound linguistic dislocation. Leaving her native country when she was about four years old, her mother tongue was suddenly foreign, and she was not immediately able to acquire another: "Mais comme trop joeune encore fusse, ne me savoie appliquer ne mes a apprendre le langaige different d'icellui de mes parens" (But since I was still too young, I didn't know how to apply myself or to learn a language different from that of my parents; p. 15, ll. 22–24). Christine's time of migration falls in a gap between two moments of language acquisition, during the interval when the child, already weaned, is too young either for cultural learning or for a natural rebirth.

Christine's depiction of migration as engendering linguistic in-betweenness highlights that her poetic persona traces her origins more to her departure from Italy than to her emergence from the maternal womb. She has been born, and has acceded to language, three times: first biologically, then culturally, then authorially. Her foreignness, both natural and cultural, is a foundational aspect of her persona: a "femme ytalienne" who was "estrangement instituee" (strangely educated; *Mutacion*, p. 11, v. 128).[118] Christine's education was "strange" for a girl, but was also that of a stranger to France. Her declarations of linguistic and cultural alterity enable a self-portrayal "as the incarnation of the *translatio studii*," as Lori Walters has shown.[119]

The multiple narratives of Christine's origins suggest a subject cut off, geographically and linguistically, from both the old environment and the new—and thus uniquely able to refashion her own story. Christine's perpetual rewriting of her multiple comings to language highlights the "inventedness" of domestic nurture, an inventedness that is, as Susan Fraiman writes, "all the more urgent and explicit at the moment of reinvention in a foreign national context."[120] The alterity in the way Christine has acquired her languages, her "distance from her mother tongue,"[121] her multiplicity of linguistic rebirths, also means that Christine has enjoyed a unique, iterative, adult relationship with her own baby talk. Because she acquires her writerly language as an adult—a language "natural" to her that she both finds and invents ("oz trouvé le stille a moy naturel")—she is able to produce a metadiscourse on her own linguistic development, from a vantage point that is at once fresh and mature. Like other immigrant children, she "can draw upon linguistic and cultural resources from [her] homeland and host country to improvise genres that build [her] hybrid identit[y]" and "usher in alternative subjectivities."[122] Once she finds her own poetic voice, she can produce and consume her own *doulce nourriture*.

Returning to Ballade XV, then, we can hear the voice of the *foiblet* as that of a newly reborn writer acquiring a new, motherless native tongue. Just as the *foiblet*'s "orphanté" (v. 12) separates him from his mother or nurse, his gender separates him from the poet who conceived him—an alienation that is compounded by the foreignness of the word *foiblet* itself, the predilection for diminutive suffixes being one of the most "Italianizing" neologistic elements of Christine's poetic language.[123] His unwanted weaning has left him in the state of solitude that is a necessary condition for poetic creation. His "orphanté" leaves him homeless—excluding him from the domestic sphere as he once knew it, in "the exilic state of being without national, marital, or other social standing"[124]—but he has not yet fully entered the public either. It is in this interval between the domestic and the public, and between the domestic and the foreign, that Christine makes a different and more durable name for herself, one that is explicitly transcultural and unapologetically nonnative. Christine does not just become a writer, she is reborn as one; she does not just write books in her adoptive language, she births them. The migrant's linguistic dislocation, coupled with the mother's powers of linguistic generation and transmission, has yielded a tool with which to carve out a public space for the woman writer. This should be understood as not just a poetic but an epistemic tool: reflections on young children's *doulce nourriture* have facilitated consciousness of the unnaturalness of all language, even the supposedly natural mother tongue, and this consciousness enables the creation of new linguistic tools with which to understand a migrant experience. As the linguist Giulio Lepschy remarks, "No one is a native speaker of the language of poetry"—but this is precisely how Christine has remade herself, originating a new mother tongue that she can pass down through the "voix de [s]es volumes."

CHARLES D'ORLÉANS: *CHE GNOGNO*

Baby talk also plays a role in the poetics of the best-known transnational poet of the French fifteenth century, Charles d'Orléans (1394–1465). During twenty-five years of captivity in England (1415–40), the duke learned English and composed a lyric oeuvre that he would continue to develop upon his return to France. His writings ultimately comprised works in French, English, and a smattering of Latin.[125] He also composed a handful of works at least partially in Italian. As the son of the Milanese princess Valentina Visconti, in whose name he would unsuccessfully stake a claim to the commune of Asti, Charles's public persona was both superlatively French (prince of the blood, father of King Louis XII) and multicultural. Indeed, the last of his lyric manuscripts compiled under his supervision was a reorganized, bilingual French-Latin edition prepared by an Italian ducal secretary, Antonio Astesano.[126] Even by the cosmopolitan standards of the late medieval court, Charles's background and especially his years of exile make him an exceptionally international poet. I propose, therefore, to read Charles's linguistic play in light of Fraiman's contention that "the effect of considering migrant domesticity is to multiply the meaning of home."[127] Unlike Christine de Pizan, whose poetics of *doulce nourriture* highlight woman's creative potential to recenter her own linguistic experience, Charles plays overtly with language hierarchies and gender expectations in order to put forth a new vision of the "foreign" that reaches into the domestic, feminine sphere. In so doing, he signals some of the epistemic limitations inherent to the adult use of baby talk: infantile speech becomes an obstacle to effective communication, not because it is unable to convey a message, but because adult interlocutors may be unequipped to receive it.

Sometime after 1441 Charles d'Orléans authored a well-known baby-talk rondeau (Champion R170, Fox and Arn R138). This poem, one of relatively few premodern texts to incorporate so much infantile vocabulary, is best remembered today as the first written attestation of still-current expressions like *joujou* and *dodo*.[128] Despite the depth of the linguistic questions it raises, this poem is itself typically treated like a small child: patted on the head and told "aren't you cute," but not taken seriously on its own terms:[129]

Quant n'ont assez fait dodo,
Cez petitz enfanchonnés,
Ils portent soubz leurs bonnés
Visages plains de bobo.
C'est pitié s'il font jojo
Trop matin, lez doulcinés,
Quant n'ont assez fait dodo.
Mieulx amassent a gogo
Gesir sur molz coissinés,
Car il sont tant poupinés!
Helas! che gnogno, gnogno,
Quant n'ont assez fait dodo.

When they haven't gone beddy-bye,
These itty-bitty babies,
They wear, under their bonnets,
Boo-boo faces.
It's a shame if they get up and play
Too early in the morning, the little sweeties,

When they haven't gone beddy-bye.
They'd weally weally like it better
If they could lie on soft little pillows,
'Cause they're such coddled little dolls!
Too bad, what a *nyah nyah nyah*,
When they haven't gone beddy-bye.[130]

The depiction of early childhood is both sympathetic and mimetic, with a number of lexical features typical of traditional baby talk: duplications, diminutives, and a largely informal vocabulary. The syntax is not especially simple, but the poem is remarkable for its lack of the personifications and reifications that are characteristic of much of the duke's oeuvre.[131] As Claudio Galderisi notes, the baby talk, like other neologistic forms that appear in the duke's rondeaux, inscribes the poem within a concrete quotidian reality rather than the abstract topography of the poet's typical allegorical landscape.[132] But it should be noted that these baby-talk elements also resemble caregiver speech (motherese): they reflect the way an adult would speak to a young child, as much as the way the young child herself would speak. The exception is *gnogno*, which appears to be an ono-matopoeic evocation of a childish whine—in other words, a direct reporting of an infant's vocalization or speech.[133]

The phrase *che gnogno, gnogno* is also a significant outlier within the context of this poem, insofar as this phrase is marked as both non-adult and non-French. John Fox surmises that *gnogno* is likely related to the attested French *gnongnon*, meaning "scolding," but that the rhyme-ending *-o* and the preceding *che* mark the phrase as mor-phologically Italian, or at least Italianate.[134] On this basis, Fox clas-sifies this rondeau among Charles's dozen or so macaronic verses; I submit that the juxtaposition of baby talk and adult language already creates a sustained effect of linguistic admixture. Thus *Quant n'ont assez fait dodo* is doubly inscribed within the series of macaronic ron-deaux R135–R139, all copied by Charles himself into in the upper halves of pages 354–58 of his personal manuscript, BnF fr. 25458.[135]

Quant n'ont assez fait dodo is especially important among Charles's rondeaux because, as a linguistic and rhetorical outlier, it illustrates largely unexplored dimensions of Charles's creative flexibility. Charles is widely acknowledged to have been, as Mary-Jo Arn puts it, "a transcultural figure with vast linguistic resources" and "a poet of progressive adaptability, unfettered by literary requirements, with an extensive bicultural background."[136] If we take a closer look at that "bicultural" background, however, it proves to be deceptively complex. What *was* Charles's native language? Were his native language and his mother tongue one and the same? Alice Planche posits that Lombard was not Charles's mother tongue but his *mother's* mother tongue.[137] But this may not be accurate. Charles's mother, Valentina Visconti, though the daughter of the duke of Milan, was raised under the supervision of her French mother and then, after the age of two, under the supervision of her paternal grandmother—who was a French-speaking Savoyarde.[138] Valentina appears to have been multilingual, or at least multiliterate: her library included books in Latin, French, and German.[139] In short, to call Charles's mother "Italian" or Charles's background "bicultural" is an oversimplification that does little to reflect the complicated intertwining of elite fourteenth-century Europeans' family trees. In any case, as with most children of the elite classes, Charles's linguistic formation would probably have been less the purview of his mother than of his nurse.

In a virelai he wrote for Valentina Visconti while she was pregnant, Eustache Deschamps exhorted her,

> Et pour vostre enffant nourrir,
> Faictes nourrice querir
> Qui soit nette, simple et coye,
> Dont tresbon lait puist yssir[140]

> And to nourish your child,
> Have a nurse sought
> Who would be clean, plain, and quiet,
> From whom very good milk could come forth

But what mother tongue did the "clean, plain and quiet" nurse teach Charles in his nursery? Fortunately for us, an unusual amount of

documentation of the Orléans' household expenses has survived—
but the name of Charles's nurse is unknown. It is recorded that
Charles had a cradle rocker (*berceresse*) known as Jeanne la Brune,
and that Jeanne d'Ierville, Lady of Maucouvent, was charged with
his care.[141] These would appear to be French names, suggesting that
while it isn't impossible that at least some of the female servants caring for Charles were among the Lombard women who accompanied
Valentina to France at the time of her marriage, the common language of his nursery was likely French.

It is tempting to speculate that the young Charles would have had
some exposure to Lombard speech, especially following his mother's expulsion from court in 1396, which resulted in Charles's spend-
ing most of his childhood in what we might term "domestic exile,"
moving among a number of homes with his mother and a smaller
household staff. It is perhaps also worth interrogating the specific
combination of French and Lombard influences Charles might have
experienced in his formative years. This is the same combination
evoked by Christine de Pizan, whose narratorial persona in the
Mutacion de Fortune situates her or his origins "near Lombardy";
and we may recall that medieval infant-care guides specifically mention Lombard as the language whose sounds are the worst suited
for inducing babies to speak. For the later medieval French, Lom-
bards represent a "familiar enemy,"[142] a linguistically and geographically proximate neighbor seen as hostile to domestic values—and
Charles d'Orléans is the son of the most abjectly Lombard woman in
France.[143] The partially Lombard origins of this French prince of the
blood could thus be construed as an element of the foreign within.

The Lombard or Italian, then, might have emerged as a crucial
counterpoint to the French in Charles's multilingual poetic repertory.
However, with the exception of Fox's brief discussion in "Glanures,"
almost all discussion of the duke's macaronic poetry, his translations,
and his multilingualism has centered on his use of Latin or of English.[144] But the unique linguistic combinations of *Quant n'ont assez
fait dodo* reveal it to be the most deceptively complex of all. Its placement in a sequence of macaronic verses invites the novel inference
that baby talk is its own idiom; its unique combination of Italian,

standard French, and infantile French posits baby talk as a site where distinct adult vernaculars converge. Thus, even if the charming, joyful evocation of the domestic (feminine) sphere has led to the trivialization of this poem and its neglect in scholarship, its manipulations of child language call forth more serious subtexts. *Quant n'ont assez fait dodo* also provides a representative snapshot of a particular moment in Charles's poetic career *and*, with its implicit juxtaposition of early childhood and old age, a distillation of the knotty diachronic dynamics of the duke's manuscript itself.

The lyrics of Charles d'Orléans, especially most of those composed after his return to Blois in 1441, are notoriously difficult to date with any precision. In her rigorous codicological study of the duke's personal manuscript, Arn has placed *Quant n'ont assez fait dodo* within Charles's "third stint" of copying, which she situates from the mid-1440s to the mid-1450s. The poem was written far closer to the end of Charles's poetic career than to the beginning. This is a period in which rondeaux become the duke's preferred form, and in them, he undertook a vast thematic and linguistic expansion. While other writers' poems had previously been copied into the duke's manuscript on occasion, the "third stint" marks an explosion in the number of lyrics authored by others: this is the period of the misnamed "Concours de Blois" and other poetic dialogues or collaborative games. The macaronic poems engage in these ludic exchanges in multiple ways—sometimes as elicitors of replies from poetic interlocutors, but also as self-contained dialogues between multiple idioms and/or registers.

The baby-talk rondeau was written in the poet's old age, but also, and perhaps more important, about two-thirds of the way through a manuscript that itself changes with age and time. As Arn has painstakingly demonstrated in *The Poet's Notebook*, Charles began work on his personal manuscript during his long captivity in England, then brought the book back with him to France. He continued to have new poems copied into it (sometimes writing them himself), and after filling all of the blank pages brought from England, he added more quires on multiple occasions. Poems continued to be added until the early 1460s.

Quant n'ont assez fait dodo appears in quire CC, in a particularly interesting portion of the manuscript. During an earlier stint, short poems had been copied onto the lower halves of pages 235–392 (quires T–EE), with their forms (*Chancon, Rondel,* or *Carole*) labeled at the top of the page. These are identified in modern citations, with page number, as *infra* poems. The reason for leaving this unusual blank space above the lyrics remains unknown.[145] In any event, the space was (re)used later as a series of mostly third-stint poems, including *Quant n'ont assez fait dodo*, were fitted into the gaps between the form labels and the *infra* poems; these are identified as the *supra* poems. Because of this peculiar layout, opening the book to any pair of pages in this section produces a diachronic story. Given what we think we know about the production of the duke's personal manuscript, the two adjacent *infra* poems were likely composed at around the same time as one another, and likewise the two *supra* poems, but the *supra* poems are a good bit later than the *infra* poems with which they share their pages. The *mise en page* places the later poems beneath the not-always-accurate form labels initially intended for other, earlier poems and obscures the actual order of composition and copying.

Because of this section's idiosyncratic layout, the lyrics can be read either horizontally or vertically—that is, in a direction that either replicates or jumbles the order of copying. When read horizontally with the other *supra* poems, *Quant n'ont assez fait dodo* is revealed to be part of an extraordinarily creative series of linguistic experiments in which (to borrow Cixous's characterization of a multilingual coming to writing) languages "call to one another, touch and alter one another":[146] two rondeaux in English, then a *carole* in Latin, then five macaronic Latin and French rondeaux in the midst of which appear two rondeaux playing on grammatical terms, then *Quant n'ont assez fait dodo*, then another French-Latin rondeau.[147] *Quant n'ont assez fait dodo*'s clearest "horizontal" interlocutor is *Gardez-vous de mergo*, which appears on the upper register of the facing page (356s) and is the only other of Charles's rondeaux to feature a rhyme in -*o*.[148] On a purely thematic level, these two rondeaux could scarcely be more different; it is a common spirit of linguistic play and a multilingual rhyming echo that unites them, rather than any coherent story they might allow the reader to imagine.

Read vertically, however, *Quant n'ont assez fait dodo* participates in a quasi-narrative on-page drama. Both of the lyrics on page 357 are written in Charles's own hand (as are the two poems on the facing p. 356). The *infra* companion to *Quant n'ont assez fait dodo* is *Avoglé et assourdy* (Fox & Arn R36, Champion Ch85[149]), a rondeau denying the possibility of joy to the aged subject, now disabused of love's folly. The later poem—composed in the poet's old age, but encountered first by the top-to-bottom reader—represents extreme youth, while the earlier poem expresses the melancholy of age through an explicit contrast to a schoolboy's confidence. The first-person subject of *Avoglé et assourdy* refers to the time when he was "nourry" (v. 8), a reference to child development that creates a sense of continuity with the nursery setting of *Quant n'ont assez fait dodo*. He then ends his poem by declaring himself "rassoty" (v. 11): become foolish *again*, a descriptor often reserved for aged people in their "second childhood." In other words, the addition of *Quant n'ont assez fait dodo* to this particular page amplifies the past-versus-present dynamic already present within *Avoglé et assourdy*, creating a quick sketch of the ages of man. I make no claim that the juxtaposition of the two rondeaux is deliberate; I cannot contest Arn's interpretation of the rondeau series as indicative of "a book owner more interested in the recording of the poetic material than in the precise placement of it."[150] Even if their proximity is purely serendipitous, the contents of page 357 nonetheless encapsulate the broader tendencies of Charles's later poems, creating what Galderisi calls a "mask" revealing only contradictions.[151] More than most of the other rondeaux, *Quant n'ont assez fait dodo* and *Avoglé et assourdy* toy with the reader's desire for an autobiographical metanarrative, allowing the voice of many ages—from young childhood to dotage—to resonate across the poetic persona's mask. In a way, this is consistent with the well-attested play-function of baby talk itself. Together these two lyrics *font jojo*.

In another, important way, though, *Quant n'ont assez fait dodo* is denied its chance to play. As much as it may resonate with its neighbors in the duke's personal manuscript, the baby-talk rondeau does not participate in the ludic collaborations that are characteristic of this period in Charles's poetic career: it does not elicit any direct responses from other poets and thus remains on the sidelines of the lyric games for which the court of Blois is known.[152] Its *mise en page* does "allow rich cross-readings" *within* the duke's own oeuvre; but unlike many of the third-stint poems, including some of the other macaronic verse, the rondeau does not readily admit such cross-readings as "can permit the recovery of social *relationships*" between poets.[153] There is a certain irony in the fact that the rondeau containing baby talk and motherese—an idiom "modulated on the play of echo and resonance," a "reciprocal invocation"[154]—is excluded from the poetic games of the duke's circle, games that are themselves a play of echoes. The same register that is so well suited to fostering linguistic production among small children apparently proves stifling to linguistic play among adults. Why? Perhaps the very linguistic freedom that Christine de Pizan celebrates, the freedom of linguistic (re)acculturation and the opportunities for self-fashioning that come along with it, would have been too threatening to the ludic but more or less rigidly defined social order of Charles's lyric interlocutors. As the linguist Charles Ferguson points out, baby talk can and does appear in "conventionalized adult word-play,"[155] the key term being *conventionalized*: in the absence of clear convention, the use of baby talk tends to stifle rather than promote dialogue.[156] And as Planche contends, there are *no* conventional uses of early childhood in medieval French poetry.[157] The lack of written response to this poem, along with its placement within the macaronic series, leads me to ask whether baby talk, the accessible domestic idiom par excellence, is simply too alien to Charles's fellow poets, steeped as they are in courtly conventions.[158] Appearing in the midst of a poetic oeuvre that largely unrolls in an allegorical landscape, the nursery space of *Quant n'ont assez fait dodo* ends up feeling further away, on some level less real, than the allegorical landscape of the *forêt de longue attente*.

I propose, therefore, that baby talk functions as a foreign language for Charles and his circle. If so, we are led to an innovative redefinition of the foreign, one that situates it not in opposition to the domestic but at the very heart of the domestic sphere. All infants are, in this respect, foreigners whose "free vocalization" must be sac-rificed,[159] via the maternal teaching that domesticates their wild babbling and shapes it into the basic idiom of the domestic sphere. When reported through a man's voice, baby talk is a foreign sound, sort of like Italian but not quite, *gnogno*. By deciding not to translate infantile words into an adult idiom, Charles has left them undomes-ticated and thus, despite their homely familiarity, unintelligible to his circle of readers.[160] The mother tongue passes to an infant naturally, as easily as milk, but in the mouth of an adult man it becomes a self-conscious linguistic artifice; authentic baby talk produces a dialogue based on imitation, as caregiver and child repeat each other's sounds, but Charles whispers *gnogno* to an audience that cannot or will not repeat it, leaving his rondeau stranded alone. The rondeau, like its creator, is a perpetual exile, occupying domestic spaces but never fully at home. "Would that the gods could make all exile a birth," as Michel Serres writes in *The Parasite*[161]—but even if Charles's poetics are largely born out of exile, and even if Charles d'Orléans's successive exiles continually expanded his linguistic horizons, they did not lead him, like Christine, to imagine rebirths into new native tongues. In his baby-talk rondeau, the infant is frozen in a perpetual present in which it remains dependent, incapable of articulate expression, inca-pable of ever maturing; and because it speaks a composite language it shares with no adults, it remains perpetually foreign.

Another fifteenth-century text that makes use of the infantile expression *dodo* offers further evidence that baby talk could indeed combine with adult language to produce a singularly macaronic effect: this is the farce *Le savetier Calbain* (Calbain the shoemaker), which likely dates from the last third of the century. Calbain, a char-acter who sings nonsense songs throughout the play, has just been drugged by his wife: she is doctoring his drink so that he will fall into a deep sleep, during which she plans to steal his purse and buy herself some new clothes. As he drinks, Calbain says:

Donnez moy donc encores à boire.
Il est bon. Terraminus minatores
Alabastra pillatores.

Je suis saoul de vin, m'amye.
Je suis auprès de vous, m'amye.
Je vous pry, couvrez moy le dos,
Car, par ma foy, je veulx dodos.
Couvrez moy bien.[162]

Give me some more to drink already.
That's good. *Terraminus minatores*
Alabastra pillatores.
I'm drunk on wine, my girl.
I'm close to you, my girl.
Please, cover my back,
'Cause upon my word, I want to go beddy-bye.
Cover me well.

Once again we see a deliberate juxtaposition of macaronic French-Latin and an element of baby talk, as the speaker craves *dodos* and asks to be tucked in. While Calbain's Latin is apparently meaningless,[163] its contrast with what follows highlights the babyishness of his succeeding utterances. As in the duke's notebook, a move from macaronic Latin to French baby talk *could* be read as an illustration of a descent from adulthood to (second) childhood, from reason to impulse: "a nostalgic regression toward nonsense," as Cavarero puts it, where — just as with the neonate's cry — "the infant and the animal coincide."[164] Baby babble, as "biologically conditioned linguistic delirium,"[165] also stands in for inebriation even as, like other forms of delirious speech, it "calls for attention."[166] Or, both the Latin and the baby talk could just be variations on the same fundamental nonsense that has defined Calbain's speech since his first lines. As (mis)communicative modes, Latin and baby talk bear analogous relationships to adult French: one its venerable ancestor, one its immature offspring, neither currently capable of conveying meaningful messages to the common man.

These cases are noteworthy because they feature an adult male writer voicing baby talk through the "mask" of an adult male persona, communicating with other adults. Or, in the case of comic theater, *mis*communicating with other adults, creating a comic effect with a reversion to "second childhood" as a sign of drunkenness or foolishness.[167] And indeed, the *fun* of using this vocabulary should not be overlooked: baby talk, lying somewhere between simple vocalization and fully developed speech, offers "a musical pleasure that the semantic order both exploits and limits, and yet still fails to control."[168] Like motherese, which "has been described as both 'spoken music' and 'musical speech,'"[169] macaronic male-voiced baby talk nestles comfortably between sound and sense, between consciousness and sleep, between dialogue and solitude.

Ultimately, the key to understanding late medieval constructs of nature and nurture, especially as they pertain to the development of human language, may lie in a renewed understanding of the lyric imagination—and vice versa; for while this chapter has touched on a broad variety of materials—baby-care and language-instruction manuals, sermons, satires—it is the lyric that best encapsulates the affective mechanisms by which baby talk can convey meaning without containing any meaning at all.[170] From *chansonetes* sung but never written (the lullaby) to those written but perhaps not successfully shared (Charles d'Orléans), the lyrics of infant speech tap into an underlying but well-concealed artificiality at the heart of maternal nurture—an artificiality that is also embodied in the substitution of nurse for mother. When the mother figure does not fully domesticate the wild vocalizations of the infant, when *doulce nourriture* is lost or a cry of "gnogno" goes unanswered, the uneasy overlap between nature and nurture becomes ultra-perceptible. Medieval constructs of the naturalness of feminine nurture depend on erasures of the cultural traces of women's work: erasures that have resulted, for example, in the inaccessibility of medieval lullabies. But Christine de Pizan and Charles d'Orléans, in denaturing the domestic and placing the foreign at the heart of the home, create a lyric language out of the *relation* between caregiver speech and the written word: lyric built on both voicing and voice.[171] The reader, imagining the vocalizations of the lyric infant, does not slip into a caregiver's role—but she enters an imagined space that focuses attention on otherwise inaudible feminine and infantile voices. In other words, the imagined infant voice becomes a means of attaining the otherwise unknowable truth of what mothers, nurses, and infants experience "when no one is there to correct them." With these poems, "between the silence of the page which greets us, and the sounds we recall or imagine and for which we might still listen at the end, literature happens."[172] That this literature in the *maternaliter* mode should be rarely written and barely writable underscores the paradoxical epistemic value of infant speech. Those who value solely the knowledge that is conveyed *litteraliter* can only puzzle over the inscrutable relation of nature to nurture; meanwhile, the domestic yet alien baby talk and cradle song hold a unique power to express the essence of nurture, and they do so thanks to the poetic plasticity of the humblest of vernaculars.

CHAPTER FOUR

INTERROGATING
INNOCENCE

Il est impossible d'établir son innocence, en soi. Elle est un néant.

It is impossible to establish one's innocence, in and of itself. It is a
nothingness.[1]

The idea that young children embody innocence, and therefore
tend to tell the sorts of truths that rational adults might attempt
to conceal, has deep cultural roots. It is a commonplace by the end
of the Middle Ages.[2] Jean Daudin's late fourteenth-century translation of Vincent of Beauvais's educational tract *De eruditione filiorum
nobilium* names innocence as the defining characteristic of "puericie" (childhood)—which is fitting, as the seventh-century encyclo-
pedist Isidore of Seville had proposed that the word *puer* (child)
derived from *puritas* (purity).[3] "Innocent" is even used as a synonym
for "small child," most famously in the case of the Holy Innocents
(the children under the age of two who were massacred at Herod's
command, according to the Gospel of Matthew). The vocabulary
of innocence can also be used more precisely to refer to the virginal asexuality of childhood.[4] Childish innocence, in this context,
aligns with a modern political fiction Lee Edelman has described:
the imaginary of the Child "unmarked by the adult's adulterating
implication in desire itself."[5] In medieval literature, innocence as an
age expectation for childhood overlaps strongly with innocence as a
bodily and moral state; but when these types of innocence are put
into dialogue with innocence as a political or juridical concept, children's voices emerge as a crucial site of both ethical and epistemic
interrogation. Because of "the deeply *relational* quality of children's

capacities, competencies and, in turn, agency,"[6] the truths they tell are bound up with a knowledge of the adult world as they cannot yet have experienced it. Unlike the modern discourses of childhood that Edelman explores—those that "spirit away the naked truth of heterosexual sex" by inscribing it not in desire but in collective political futurity[7]—the speaking toddlers in medieval literature function as a present, vocal, embodied reminder and product of sexual activity.

In this chapter I examine textual episodes in which truth-telling toddlers aid in the administration of adult justice. My primary focus will be on French vernacular versions of two culturally pervasive narratives—the biblical story of Daniel and Susanna and the romance story of Merlin—followed by a briefer analysis of child witnesses in three fabliaux. Daniel and Merlin are very young children who intervene in order to exonerate adult women accused of sexual transgressions; the fabliau children innocently (or not so innocently) reveal their mother's infidelity. The entanglement of tiny children in tales of adult sexuality situates them at the nexus of multiple varieties of sexual innocence: asexuality, virginity, chastity, involuntary sexual contact, fidelity. In medieval French literature, the words of these paradigmatically voiceless legal nonentities can carry serious weight; but the discourses surrounding the role that "innocent children" can play in these fictional proceedings also destabilize the very notion of innocence. Particularly when a child is defending the virtue of his own mother—as does Robert de Boron's Merlin—the child can speak the truth, but a child also *embodies* the not-so-innocent truth, inasmuch as he is the result and the living proof of a prior sexual encounter.[8]

The trial scenes in which children intervene tend to be highly dramatic, in both the theatrical and the colloquial sense, as well as in their prominent deployment of the *persona*, the mask. The children who speak on women's behalf become conduits for divine voices and divine knowledge, and by extension, for a divine justice not expressible in adult human language; they provide the human form across which truth can be heard. Which does make a certain poetic sense: if all literary testimony stands "between the historical and the imagined," as Jamie K. Taylor has argued, then testimony can perhaps achieve its purest form in the mouth of a character who is himself situated between the historical and the imagined, namely the speaking *infans*.[9]

I will examine these cases of infant speech through the lens of feminist epistemology, and especially the philosopher Miranda Fricker's influential theorization of "epistemic injustice." The kinds of injustice Fricker has explicated—testimonial injustice, which "occurs when prejudice causes a hearer to give a deflated level of credibility to a speaker's word," and hermeneutical injustice, which occurs "when a gap in collective interpretive resources puts someone at an unfair disadvantage when it comes to making sense of their social experiences"[10]—are exploited and circumvented, but not resolved, by child agents such as Daniel and Merlin. The proceedings in which these children intervene underline that epistemic oppression, which Kristie Dotson defines as "persistent epistemic exclusion that hinders one's contribution to knowledge production,"[11] is an important but undertheorized element in medieval misogyny. Women, especially, "suffer when hermeneutical resources that could articulate and illuminate important aspects of their social experiences are generally unavailable."[12] The result is a silencing of the marginalized knower.[13] In its linkage of injustice to the suppression of language, this recent epistemological work shares important ground with the postmodernist philosopher Jean-François Lyotard's theorization of the *différend*, a linguistic failure wherein harms cannot be expressed within dominant legal or political discursive regimes, and therefore justice cannot be achieved. Despite Fricker's critiques of postmodernism's failure to account for the situatedness or intersectionality of those to whom these harms are done,[14] Lyotard's insights into the unprovability of innocence do dovetail with more recent notions of "epistemic injustice": he too explores injustice as a silencing of other parties' ways of knowing.

Speaking toddlers are able to resolve the paradoxical legal-epistemic situations in which accused women are entangled, situations akin to Lyotard's differend: in an exclusively male legal-discursive system to which they have limited access, a system increasingly built around the "science of the fact,"[15] women can present no "proof" of their own experiences. This inability stems from both testimonial and hermeneutical injustice: female defendants are disbelieved simply because they are women (as in Susanna's case) and may be further disadvantaged by a lack of language with which to understand and explain their own experiences (as with Merlin's mother). The accused women therefore can only defend themselves through an eloquent silence that cries out for interpretation — interpretation provided in the voice of a small child.[16] Young children such as Daniel and Merlin serve as an effective instrument for redressing legal wrongs *without* restoring or valorizing a female victim's voice. This occurs precisely because these children's divinely endowed speech imbues them with a unique epistemic independence,[17] even as they embody the same paradox later pointed out by Lyotard: the unprovability of innocence. To confirm innocence requires a standard of proof that it is not humanly possible to achieve, for even the most paradigmatically innocent humans, small children, have been born in a state of sin — a sin they recall and lament with their first audible cries of E and A. And so, as marvelous as they may be, courtroom fictions featuring speaking toddlers raise some crucial real-world questions. Like the crying neonates, they expose adult vulnerability (in this case, their epistemic dependency on sometimes unreliable testimony) and testify that in the face of epistemic violence, "innocence" doesn't factor into human systems of justice at all.

Small children's universal alterity marks them as marginalized knowers — and this makes them potent figures with which to point out epistemic injustice, since "it is from marginalized situatedness that the inadequacy of our epistemic resources for making sense of parts of the experienced world is noticed."[18] In my readings of literary treatments of the stories of Daniel and Merlin I will demonstrate that theirs is a "subversive lucidity" they can only attain thanks to their marginal position: not because they "have experiences that from the point of view of the dominant ideology or hegemonic perspective are considered *alien*" (which is how José Medina says members of subordinate groups can achieve such lucidity), but because of their very lack of experience.[19] Even as they nudge adult judges away from practices of epistemic injustice, though, they leave intact the discursive regime that silences other innocents.

SI JEUNE ENFANT QUI PARLOIT: DANIEL'S INNOCENCE AND SUSANNA'S VIRTUE

Of the numerous narratives in which justice is done through a child's intervention, the one with the broadest cultural reach in medieval Europe is the tale of Susanna and the Elders, as told in Daniel 13. The biblical story was familiar to a broad public thanks to its frequent representation in the visual arts,[20] vernacular literature,[21] theater,[22] healing charms,[23] and sermons, and especially through its use as a reading for the third Saturday of Lent.[24] Portraying Daniel as a child, this chapter serves as a prequel of sorts to the twelve that precede it. The story is simple: two elders, overcome with lust for the virtuous married woman Susanna, surprise her as she bathes. They threaten to accuse her of adultery if she does not comply with their desires. She refuses, the elders testify against her, and Susanna is sentenced to be stoned to death. The child Daniel arrives and cross-examines the elders, tricking them into revealing their own deception, and the elders are executed in Susanna's stead.

Daniel's youth is key to this story, for it highlights his status as a vessel through which the divine will is channeled and voiced. Biblical, patristic, and devotional texts define Daniel's age somewhat imprecisely, though they are consistent in situating the judgment of Susanna in Daniel's late childhood.[25] This makes it all the more striking that late medieval French literary imaginings of Daniel almost all portray him as a very young child. Daniel's precise age is far from an incidental detail in these late medieval texts, and a consideration of the various ways Daniel's "youth" is imagined will begin to remedy what Jonathan Stavsky has called "the largely uncharted reception history of Susanna and the Elders in the late Middle Ages"[26]—and will show that Daniel is imagined at his youngest in the texts that most overtly grapple with justice, rather than female chastity, as their central problem.

Susanna's function as an exemplar of chastity, as a model whom modern women should emulate, is the more familiar and perhaps the more intuitive spin on her story. She appears as such in the two best-known didactic manuals produced for women in late fourteenth-century France: the *Livre du chevalier de la Tour Landry pour l'enseignement de ses filles* (1371–72) and *Le mesnagier de Paris* (1393).[27] In these conduct books, the young female inscribed reader is meant to identify with Susanna and to avoid any actions that would damage her own (or her husband's) reputation. So, despite their differences in tone,[28] both works use the tale of Susanna to similar ends, and both narratives are invested in upholding the general righteousness of the system that would have wrongly condemned her. In chapter 98 of the *Livre du chevalier*, as well as in part I, chapter 4 of the *Mesnagier*, Susanna is presented as a paradigmatically chaste woman.[29] In the *Livre du chevalier*, the intervention of five-year-old Daniel saves Susanna from public condemnation: glossing the story with a moral appropriate to a "culture of shame,"[30] the *chevalier* warns that other people's speech is a major threat to women and that the best remedy is usually for women to remain silent.[31] In *Le mesnagier de Paris*, Susanna's defender is a "jenne et petit enfant" (young and small child); though Daniel saves Susanna from punishment, the *Mesnagier* takes pains to point out that the punishment itself, the stoning of adulterous women, is just ("c'est bonne loy"; I.iv.8, p. 140) when it is applied fairly.

On the basis of these two versions, Lynn Staley has argued that late medieval French writers put the Susanna story to less "political" uses than do their English contemporaries.[32] However, the conduct books' upholding of an ideology of injustice is undeniably political[33] — and when the French corpus is extended beyond comportment manuals for women, we see that French writers also use Susanna to interrogate systems of justice more overtly. Intriguingly, these texts devoted to the thorny problem of justice tend to depict Daniel as an infant or a toddler. The Daniel who exposes epistemic injustice, in other words, is younger than the Daniel who merely confirms Susanna's sexual purity. The introduction of an infant Daniel brings the small child's universal alterity to bear, allowing for critique from a perspective that is both human and external to human juridical systems. Daniel's age also deepens these accounts' focus on the concept of *innocence*, showing just how small a role the protection of innocence actually plays in human systems of justice.

Daniel is portrayed as a very young child, but one with a great deal to say about justice, in the works of the most significant French writers of the latter half of the fourteenth century and the beginning of the fifteenth: Guillaume de Machaut, Eustache Deschamps, and Christine de Pizan. Machaut tells the story of Susanna at the beginning of his *Confort d'ami* (1357), a consolatory poem written for the imprisoned King Charles ("the Bad") of Navarre. The male narrator speaks to his imprisoned lord, recounting a long series of exempla designed to offer consolation and, in many cases, to show that the arc of the moral universe bends toward justice. These exempla rely, for their efficacy, on the noble male addressee's ability to identify with the persecuted protagonists.[34] The first of these exempla is the story of Daniel 13, in which the narrator encourages his interlocutor to identify with Susanna. Machaut remains quite faithful to the Vulgate and its commentaries—until Daniel appears:

> En la tourbe avoit une fame
> Dont le nom ne say ne la fame,
> Qui un juene enfançon portoit,
> Et au porter se deportoit,
> Qu'aler ne parler ne savoit
> Pour la juenesse qu'il avoit.
> Daniel ot nom l'enfançon,
> Si com tesmongne la leçon. (ll. 285–92)

> And in that crowd was a woman,
> Whose name or history I do not know,
> And she was carrying a young little child,
> Who took much joy in being held
> Since he could not walk or speak,
> So young was he at the time.
> The little child's name was Daniel,
> As Scripture tells us.[35]

The youth is now a cuddly baby in his mother's arms, not yet able to walk or speak, and therefore probably not much more than a year old. That he is introduced through his mother, rather than on his own terms—first we are told there was a woman, and then we learn that she held a child—reinforces the sense that Daniel is a vessel rather than an autonomous subject. It also establishes a subtle parallel with Susanna, who had been introduced to the reader via her relationship to her husband. Susanna and Daniel occupy analogous positions of dependency that will permit their use as illustrations of and channels for divine justice. The infant can speak for the woman because his "universal alterity" allows him to identify with this *other* "dependent rational animal."[36]

Machaut's Susanna is at first far more vocal than her biblical model. When accosted by the elders, she "Fort pleure, gemist, fort se plaint / Et dist, en gettant un grant plaint" (Wept bitterly, sighing, bemoaning her lot, and then said, after letting out a great cry; pp. 163–64). She gives a brief speech, then resists vocally: "Adont a haute vois s'escrie / Susanne: 'Aïe! Aïe! Aïe!'" (Right then Susannah cried out in a loud voice: "Help! Help! Help!"; pp. 175–76), creating a "clamour" (uproar; p. 182) that brings others running.[37] And when she receives her death sentence she prays aloud, "A haute vois, sans detrier, / Les mains jointes, prist a crier" (She began to cry out in a loud voice, her hands joined, not hesitating at all; pp. 255–56). That is the last time Susanna speaks. Daniel soon arrives, and while it is possible to interpret his voice as eclipsing Susanna's—"as if he were taking over for her," as Marie-Louise Fabre observes[38]—this discursive relay represents less a usurpation of Susanna's voice than an enactment of advocacy in its purest form. Still, though Daniel speaks in order to mitigate the epistemic violence being done to Susanna, he does not address the practices of silencing inherent to the system against which he speaks.

God grants Daniel the tools he will need to advocate for Susanna: a voice, reason, *and* the ability to walk ahead of his time:

> Mais Dieus li donna la puissance
> D'aler et de parler, science,

Congnoissance et entendement
De prophetisier tellement
Que la verité fut sceüe
Des faus prestres et cogneüe. (ll. 293–98)

Now God granted him the power
To speak and walk, intelligence,
Discernment, and understanding
To preach a prophecy
That would reveal the truth
About the false priests and make it acknowledged.

Machaut's enumeration implies that the two developmental leaps
are not unrelated. "La puissance d'aler" is vital because an upright
posture signals reason and self-sufficiency (as discussed in chapter 2). Furthermore, locomotion, speech, and knowledge together
are required so that Daniel can stand in for Susanna, in order to
resist—to stand against—injustice.[39] From his very first words,
Daniel prioritizes his own innocence and underlines his own marginality by denying complicity in an unjust judgment that, were he
to participate in it, would sully him:

Lors cria haut a sa vois clere
L'enfant entre les bras sa mere,
Si que li pueples et li mundes
L'entendi: "Je suis purs et mundes
Dou sanc de ceste creature." (ll. 299–303)

Just at that moment, he cried out in a clear voice,
This child held in his mother's arms,
So that all the people and the crowd
Could hear, saying: "I am innocent and clean
Of this person's blood."

His words, with their insistence on purity, hew closely to the Vulgate.[40] But in Machaut's retelling, this story's emphasis on innocence

and justice is even more overt. Susanna has already referred to herself as "de pechié pure" (pure from vice; l. 172) as she expressed her
resolve to resist the elders' proposition; Daniel's characterization of
himself as "purs et mundes" suggests again a similarity between the
two. Daniel explicitly appeals to the crowd's sense of justice when
he accuses them of having condemned Susanna without regard for
"verité, / Raison, justice n'équité" (either truth or reason, either justice or fairness; p. 12, ll. 313–14). When he interrogates the first of
the elders, Daniel lights into him precisely for his unjust oppression
of the innocent:

> Car les innocens opprimoies
> Et les courpables delivroies,
> Et Dieus dit qu'on n'ocie mie
> L'innocent et juste de vie. (p. 13, ll. 343–46)

> For you would oppress the innocent
> While setting free the guilty,
> And God says one doesn't kill
> The innocent, those who live justly.

The implication is that justice demands that the innocent be pro-
tected. But when considered in the broader context of *Confort*, the
relationship between innocence and justice becomes far less clear.

The *Confort d'ami* is a *dit* that, as R. Barton Palmer puts it, "develops irreconcilable (perhaps contradictory) approaches to the problem of justice."[41] The contradictions stem from this text's particular
consolatory practices, and also from the identity of the person being
consoled. Comforting an imprisoned patron, Machaut tells of characters (mostly biblical) who have endured punishment, even though
few have deserved their suffering; these exempla therefore tend to
portray a "disproportion between man's actions and his rewards in
the secular world."[42] However, as Martha Wallen points out, not all
of the exemplary sufferers are innocent—nor is Charles of Navarre's
innocence at all certain. So, while the patron is meant to take comfort in the promise of a just outcome, it is not at all clear what the

most just outcome might be. This ambiguity points to a larger ethical and political problem, as signaled by Giorgio Agamben in his reflections on the Shoah and the problem of witnessing: the conflation
of legal and moral conceptions of "innocence" and "justice" obscures
the true function of the law: "Almost all the categories that we use in
moral and religious judgments are in some way contaminated by law:
guilt, responsibility, innocence, judgment, pardon [...] . This makes
it difficult to invoke them without particular caution. As jurists well
know, law is not directed toward the establishment of justice. Nor
is it directed toward the verification of truth. Law is solely directed
toward judgment, independent of truth and justice."[43] Earthly justice does not necessarily bear any relation to the question of innocence or guilt. Because they were created by man, legal systems—as
Nicole Oresme points out in his gloss on Aristotle's *Ethiques*—are
all too fallible.[44] And yet, Daniel's cross-examination of the elders
also demonstrates the possibility of gleaning true knowledge from
false testimony.[45]

Moreover, the retelling of Susanna's story for a diegetic male
addressee who is meant to identify with her alters the ethical stakes
of her and Daniel's speech practices. This is, after all, the first exemplum in a book that raises—indirectly through its consolatory genre
and directly in some of the exempla themselves—the question of
who can speak for whom. The gesture of consolation, and indeed the
presentation of a book to a patron, can serve as occasions for contes-
tations of authority.[46] As Sarah Kay points out, "Many of the biblical exempla at the beginning of the *Confort* imply a parallel between
Machaut and the prophet Daniel that is more gratifying to the poet
than the king."[47] The poet, a repository of wisdom, communicates a
message to his temporarily immobilized and powerless patron. But,
were Charles to adopt Susanna's prayer, he might be able to enter
a different system of power, one in which he could access the sort
of divine justice that Daniel exercised on Susanna's behalf. If we
accept Alexandre Leupin's reading of *Confort* as "a mirror in which
the prince sees himself fall because language is the Law from which
his power abusively originates,"[48] then perhaps the emulation of
Susanna—a woman who can only be saved when she relinquishes

any claim to language, and when a child with God-given verbal abilities tricks Susanna's accusers into self-incriminating speech— offers
the opportunity to submit to a completely different law. Abandoning
epistemic power, Charles can perhaps attain the lucidity of a marginalized subject. Susanna cannot win in the elders' system; then again,
they cannot win in hers.

In this space between human and divine law, the voice of the
infant and the voice of the poet come to the fore, not least because
of the way the story of Daniel and Susanna foregrounds the problems of witnessing and testimony. Susanna is a wronged woman,
in exactly the sense of *tort* that Lyotard puts forth: "This is what
a wrong [*tort*] would be: a damage [*dommage*] accompanied by the
loss of the means to prove the damage. This is the case if the victim
is deprived of life, or of all his or her liberties, or of the right to make
his or her ideas or opinions public, or simply of the right to testify
to the damage, or even more simply if the testifying phrase is itself
deprived of authority."[49] Her accusers think they have committed
the perfect epistemic crime, which would consist in "obtaining the
silence of the witnesses, the deafness of the judges, and the inconsistency (insanity) of the testimony."[50] Susanna cannot bear witness
on her own behalf, and Daniel, a baby, shouldn't be able to either.
Indeed, Daniel embodies Agamben's paradox of testimony, "situating
the subject in the disjunction between a possibility and an impossibility of speech."[51] The infant interrogator ends up producing exactly
the "inconsistency [...] of the testimony" that might have facilitated
the "perfect crime" but has instead allowed divine justice to override
a flawed judicial proceeding. Daniel is the quintessential premodern
witness, as Andrea Frisch has defined that role: an "intersubjective
I" whose persuasive power is rooted in a nexus of "ethical relations
with his juridical interlocutors."[52] He manages to ascertain true facts
from false testimony by playing the role of interrogator, witness, and
detective. His clever speech rewrites Susanna's destiny.

The same biblical material is reframed as a story that is princi-
pally about the judges in another fourteenth-century narrative that
focuses on troubling injustice under the law: Eustache Deschamps's
lengthy retelling of the Susanna story in his antifeminist satire *Le*

miroir du mariage (c. 1381–89).[53] Composed some three decades after
the *Confort d'ami*, the unfinished *Miroir du mariage* is an expansive
dialogue on marriage and on the moral, ethical, and social questions
bound up with it. Susanna's story is presented in the character Repertoire de Science's long antifeminist letter to Franc Vouloir, in which
he argues against marriage. The tale of Susanna serves above all as
a warning about the societal danger of iniquitous judges, and about
the vices into which beautiful women tempt men. Indeed, the story
is framed in such a way that, from beginning to end, its protagonists
are the elders, "Ardens en la conupiscence / De Suzanne et son innocence" (Burning with desire for Susanna and her innocence; p. 146,
ll. 4407–8). While innocence is obviously in play, including as an
object of desire, the story is ultimately used to impart lessons about
judgment—especially judgment about women's innocence—to
men. It thus provides a striking illustration of epistemic power and
oppression.

Why is Daniel explicitly identified as a toddler in this version as
well? Like other iterations of the character, Deschamps's young Daniel puts his new verbal abilities to use by separating, interrogating,
and proving the dishonesty of Susanna's accusers. He also takes this
opportunity to preach to the dissembling elders, condemning their
"jugemens inutiles / Contre droit et les innocens" (useless judgments
against right and the innocent; p. 148, ll. 4476–77). The distinction
between "droit et les innocens" reinforces the notion that the law is
an abstraction (that which is right), whereas innocence is a human
quality, one that defines those people who possess it; innocence is
relational rather than absolute. When the interests of law stand in
direct conflict with the protection of innocence, it is the latter that
must be maintained, as Daniel argues by quoting from Scripture:
the accusers' behavior is "contre l'Escripture / Qui dit: 'L'ignocent
creature / Ne le juste aussi n'occiras'" (against Scripture, which says:
"The innocent and just person thou shalt not put to death"; p. 148,
ll. 4479–81).[54] Eventually the two false witnesses are "Condemp-
nez par bouche d'enfent" (condemned by the mouth of a child; p.
149, l. 4503) and "Ainsi fut le sang innocent / Sauvé ce jour, Dieu
congnoiscent" (thus was innocent blood saved that day, by God's

will; p. 149, ll. 4513–14). However, what might have seemed to be a story about the vindication of innocence is completely recast in the final moral, which pivots away from Susanna and back to the judges:

> Veoir puez que la manterie
> Fut en ces deux juges perie,
> Et que verité au derrain
> Par le vray juge souverain
> Obtint encontre le mentir.
> Juges, vueillez ci advertir:
> Ne faictes mie com l'yraingne
> Qui ses fix tent, afin que praingne
> Mouches pour souler son venin:
> Les petis mouches met a fin
> Si tost qu'ilz viennent en sa toile,
> Mais, quant gros mouche hurte au voile,
> Tost a toute sa toile route:
> Adonc en son trou se reboute
> L'yraingne: pas n'iert si hardie
> Qu'elle au gros mouche contredie.
> Ainsi est il, si com je luy,
> De justice au monde au jour d'ui:
> Justice pugnist petis cas;
> Petites gens prant a ses las,
> [. . .]
> Mais, quant il vient une fort mouche
> A la toile, cil fait le louche
> Qui la deust prandre et happer
> [. . .]
> Ainsis n'est justice c'un ombre (pp. 149–50, ll. 4529–58)

> You can see that lying speech
> Was the downfall of these two judges,
> And that finally truth,
> Through the true sovereign judge,

Won out over lies.
Judges, be warned of this:
Do not emulate the spider
Who hangs his threads, so as to capture
Flies to satisfy his venom:
He finishes off the little flies
As soon as they come to his web,
But when a big fly collides with his web,
Soon the whole tissue is broken:
Then the spider rushes back to
His hole: it wouldn't be so rash
As to contradict the big fly.
So it is, as I have read,
With justice in the world today:
The justice system punishes the small cases,
Catches the little people in its snares,
[…]
But, when a strong fly comes along
To the web, he looks away
Who ought to have taken and seized him
[…]
Thus, justice is but a shadow.

Repertoire de Science argues that justice is hollow and illusory, not because human systems of law do not adequately protect innocence, but because they are applied unfairly, according to the accused's social clout.[55] The judges are condemned less for their iniquity (attempting to condemn a person they know to be innocent) than for their inequity (leveraging their social capital to persecute a powerless person). Moreover, to put it in epistemological terms, the judges are leveraging their epistemic power in service of epistemic vice.[56] Daniel's young age is therefore less important as a signal of innocence than as a confirmation that Susanna is the "little guy" in this story—at least, until God intervenes and breaks the elders' web of lies. Susanna's innocence is merely incidental to this "moral" interpretation, as is the moral gravity of bearing false witness. When Susanna is alluded to again, later in the *Miroir*, it is as a warning—addressed again to a male audience—against allowing feminine beauty to cause irrational behavior (pp. 173–74). In other words, the lying elders are used as an identificatory cautionary tale about the dangers of womanly allure.[57] This allusion to Susanna as the passive object (or, worse, the active instigator) of men's disruptive concupiscence deprives Susanna of her heroic potential.

In French narratives produced around the turn of the fifteenth century, Susanna can serve either as an exemplar of heroic resistance or as an emblem of justice achieved, but seldom is she conceived in both roles. The most notable exception to this trend is in the works of Christine de Pizan. Susanna is allowed to "do" more in Christine's allusions to her story, which, brief though they are, focus more on Susanna's righteousness than on the wonder of the child's interrogation of the elders. In the *Cité des dames*, Susanna regains her voice and Daniel loses his; in the *Livre de paix*, Daniel's youth serves a specific political purpose, sending a pointed message about the essential role that women and children must play if there is to be peace in Christine's time. In both of these texts, the child and the woman collaboratively exploit their marginal situation to create new epistemic resources.[58]

Christine de Pizan's only full retelling of the Susanna story occurs in the *Cité des dames*, part 2, chapter 37, wherein Droiture (Rectitude) cites Susanna as an exemplar of chastity. The fact that Susanna's story is told by Droiture—a figure who bridges the legal and the moral forms of justice[59]—suggests that the question of her innocence will be weighted differently than it was in Machaut's and Deschamps's texts, with their more specifically administrative critiques of legal institutions. Droiture's primary responsibilities, as she herself enumerates them in *Cité* I.v, include "porter le droit des povres et des ignocens" (uphold the rights of the poor and innocent) and "soustenir la renommee des accusez sanz cause" (defend the reputation of the wrongly accused).[60] Susanna is therefore exemplary of her own virtues, but also of Droiture's unique powers. Droiture's account manages to put the spotlight squarely back on Susanna, both in the narrative itself but also, crucially, in its framing.

Droiture's version of Daniel 13 is noteworthy for its depiction of Susanna as a heroic figure. Susanna is introduced as being one of the "vaillans dames chastes" (worthy chaste women) of Scripture (318): *vaillans* in this context clearly means not just "worthy," but "courageous," "valiant." The emphasis on Susanna and other chaste women "avant eslissent la mort que enfraindre leur chasteté et netteté de corps et de pensee" (having chosen death before licentiousness) elevates them from exempla to genuine heroines.[61] And this Susanna is a heroine with a voice of her own. Despite the brevity of her account, Droiture conveys Susanna's own words in a relatively lengthy instance of direct discourse:

> Angoisses m'avironnent de toutes pars, car se je ne fais ce que ces hommes me requierent, j'encourray mort corporelle. Et se je le fais, je offense devant la face de mon createur. Mais non pourtant trop mieulx m'est innocent soustenir la mort corporelle que cheoir par pechié en l'ire de mon Dieu. (p. 318)

> Anguish assails me from every direction, for if I do not do what these men demand, I will risk corporeal death. And if I do it, I offend in the face of my creator. But nonetheless, it is far better for me to go, innocent, to my physical death than to fall through sin into the anger of my God.

Susanna clearly posits her own innocence in opposition to the "justice" with which the elders menace her. Her mind made up, she cries out.

Having allowed Susanna to explain her reasoning in her own words, Christine (via Droiture) makes quick work of the parts of the story where Susanna is deprived of her voice: the trial scenes. The initial trial and condemnation are summed up in a single sentence: "Et, a brief dire, tant firent les faulx prestres par leur desloyal tesmoignage que Susanne fu condampnee a mort" (And, to make a long story short, the false priests did so much with their disloyal testimony that Susanna was condemned to death; p. 318). Then along comes Daniel, mouthpiece of God:

Mais Dieux, qui tousjours pourvoit a ses amis, ouvre la bouche du prophete Daniel qui estoit petit enfant entre les bras de sa mere, lequel, quant on menoit Susanne a la justice a grant procession de gent qui apres elle pleuroient, s'escria que a grant tort estoit condampnee l'innocent Susanne. Si fu ramenee et les faulx prestres mieulx examinez et trouvez par leur mesmes confession coulpables et Susanne, innocent, fu delivree et eulx justiciez. (pp. 318–20)

But God, who always provides for those who love Him, opened the mouth of the prophet Daniel, who was a little child in his mother's arms, who, when Susanna was being led to her punishment at the head of a great procession of people weeping for her, cried out that it was a great wrong for the innocent Susanna to be condemned. So she was brought back and the false priests were examined more thoroughly and were found guilty through their own confession, and Susanna, innocent, was delivered and they were punished.

Daniel's age is not precisely given, but his position in his mother's arms creates an image similar to those of Machaut and Deschamps. What is most striking in Christine's version, though, is that while allusion is made to Daniel's God-given speech and his cross-examination of the witnesses, his words are not cited, nor is the substance of his speech outlined in any detail. Daniel's cross-examination of the accusers is described in the passive voice, minimizing Daniel's role in the reversal of the wrongful conviction. Indeed, all of Susanna's trial and her vindication are narrated in the passive voice: she *fu condampnee*, *fu ramenee*, and *fu delivree*. Christine's corrective grammar can be construed as an act of testimonial justice: grammatically as well as thematically, Susanna is restored as the subject of this narrative.

The framing of the tale, too, recenters Susanna's voice and sidelines Daniel's. Used as a rebuttal to those men who would charge all women with unchastity—participating, that is, in a debate between men and women—the direct discourse at the heart of this story allows Susanna to "talk back" to her accusers. *Cité* II.37 begins with Christine establishing a contrast between her own observations, which are aligned with Droiture's previous teachings, versus the accusations of "ces hommes" (those men) who "dient qu'il en soit si pou de chastes" (say that there are very few of them [women] who are chaste; p. 318). Droiture's telling of Susanna's story is a response both to Christine and to the male critics to whom Christine refers. This heroic Susanna can finally advocate for herself: thinking aloud in the garden, she also speaks to the modern men who would defame her and all women. Just as the elders' and Daniel's words are mentioned by Droiture but not cited verbatim, the misogynists' accusations are reported by Christine but not cited. Droiture presents her counternarrative to Christine, rather than to a male audience, as this time it is Christine who plays the role of judge.[62] Collectively, the participants in this judicial proceeding[63]—Droiture, Christine, and the narrated characters of Susanna and Daniel—create a new epistemic resource by which women's virtue can be properly understood. While the infant Daniel certainly plays a role in this process by preventing a grave injustice, it is the women who take the next step and pave the way for a new and more just knowledge of womanhood.

In a later treatise, Christine offers an alternate telling of Susanna's story that refocuses attention on the joint political power and political voice of women and children. This occurs in her *Livre de paix*, which Christine began composing in the fall of 1412, shortly after the fifteen-year-old dauphin, Louis of Guyenne, helped negotiate the peace of Auxerre between Charles d'Orléans and Jean sans Peur. The book opens with combined references to Psalm 8 and Daniel 13, creating a biblical mash-up that pronounces the power of the infant voice:

> De la bouche des enfans et des alectans voirement, Notre Seigneur Dieu roy celestre tout puissant qui deffaces et ostes quant il te plaist la misere du monde, est ton plaisir d'avoir parfaicte louenge si qu'il est par maintes foiz apparu si comme lorsque tu ouvris les enfantines levres de Daniel pour la bonne Susanne, accusee a tort, respiter de mort quant il dit: "Je suis net au sang de ceste, etc.," pour laquelle chose tu fus beneys de tout peuple. (p. 201)

> Our Lord God, almighty heavenly King who overcomes and takes away, when you wish to, the suffering of the world, indeed you are

pleased to receive perfect praise out of the mouth of babes and sucklings. This has been seen many times, as when you opened the lips of
the young Daniel, to reprieve the chaste and falsely accused Susanna
from sentence of death, when he said: 'I am clear from the blood
of this woman,' etc., for which you were blessed by every nation.
(pp. 59–60)[64]

The "enfantines levres" (infant lips) of Daniel thus fulfill the promise
of Psalm 8: "Out of the mouth of infants and of sucklings thou hast
perfected praise." This is a psalm that Christine has already put to
political use at the beginning of another treatise: the *Livre du corps
de policie* (1406–7), which, like the *Livre de paix*, was composed for
the young Louis of Guyenne.[65] Christine's dedicatee, who lived from
1397 to 1415, was a young boy at the composition of the *Corps de policie* and an adolescent at the composition of *Paix*; Christine's comparison of him to even more youthful "infants and sucklings" affirms the
often underestimated potential of the young. Simply put, the dauphin is to be taken seriously—despite his youth,[66] but also *because*
his youth (which Christine exaggerates for heightened effect) makes
him a potential agent of change. The dauphin's intervention in the
Orléans-Burgundy feud is, as Christine presents it, just the most
recent example of God's long-standing practice of "demonster par
enfans innocens et simples tes divines graces et vertus" (reveal[ing
his] divine grace and boundless virtues through innocent children;
p. 202, l. 60). The young dauphin is the child whose divinely inspired
speech has brought peace—but Christine, in singing his praises, is
also doing her part.

The introduction of the infant Daniel in the opening sentences of
the *Livre de paix* has complicated the political implications of Psalm 8.
As Machaut does in the *Confort d'ami*, Christine "effectively likens
herself to Daniel, prophesying in a situation of political danger."[67]
But if Christine is analogous to one of the babies cited in the opening
sentence of this book, is she also analogous to the other? That is to
say: is the "babe" offering "perfect praise" the dauphin, as one might
originally have thought (based on both an intertextual recollection of
the *Corps de policie* and the youth of the dauphin), or is it Christine
herself? The conflation of the two and the assimilation of both to

babies indicates that, as she did in the ballade discussed in chapter 3, Christine is continuing her productive reimagination of the affinity of woman and infant—this time, specifically as peacemakers and as interdependent epistemic agents who can testify to divine truth.[68]

The responsibility of elite women to foster peace is a recurring theme in Christine's works. Her most notable discussions of queens and princesses as peacemakers occur in the *Livre des trois vertus* (1405), which devotes its ninth chapter to the princess's peacemaking duties,[69] and the *Epistre a la reine* (1405).[70] As both Tracy Adams and Nathalie Nabert have argued, in these texts Christine links proclivities for peacemaking with a set of virtues that are explicitly marked as feminine and that are enhanced through maternity.[71] Indeed, peacemaking is an important component of what Karen Green has characterized as Christine's "original maternalist image of Queenship."[72] Even when the female peacemaker is not a queen, Christine sometimes represents her as the mother of very young child, as in the *Lamentacions sur les maux de la France* (1410),[73] with its exemplary portrait of the Sabine women rushing onto the battlefield with their babies in their arms. Through such imagery, those who would seem to hold the least political power—women with/and their children—are exhorted to take "non-violent direct action."[74]

The example of the Sabine women resonates with the story of Daniel, *when Daniel is presented as a baby*, in this key respect: Daniel is able to restore justice only because his mother has carried him in her arms to a field of (figurative) battle. Depictions of Daniel as a very young child, such as those we have seen in the works of Machaut, Deschamps, and Christine, introduce Daniel as part of a mother-child dyad. Psalm 8 implicitly does the same, for its reference to *alectans* (babies still being breastfed) defines the authors of "perfect praise" as existing within a relation to a nourishing woman, a relation between two marginally situated subjects from which the infants' language will emerge through a process underpinned by complete epistemic trust. When a baby uses his voice to restore or reinforce a just order, he does so from within that unit: a unit comprising two weak and powerless second-class citizens with an exceptional power to make peace. However, when these two unlikely heroes join forces to overcome injustice, it is the speaking baby and not his usually silent mother who does the heavy lifting. This can happen specifically because, in speaking, he embodies the strengths and weaknesses of both participants in the dyad. Susan Sered and Samuel Cooper have pointed out, for instance, that because Daniel is young and structurally powerless, but also male and articulate, he "obfuscates gender expectations" and thus "embodies a transformative role."[75] As spokesperson for an entity that is both infant and adult, both male and female, the infant Daniel speaking from his mother's arms exemplifies the very "liminality" that (according to Christine's political vision) can bring about reconciliation.[76]

Women and children are exemplary peacemakers, but mothers' peacemaking activities tend to confirm gender expectations (epitomizing feminine moderation and gentleness), while children's peacemaking defies cultural constructs around both gender and age. Christine de Pizan frequently calls upon women to make peace; when that fails, Christine appeals to a child (*Livre de la paix*), exaggerating his youth in a manner that suggests a heightened ability to counter a *tort*. Thanks to their divinely enabled speech voiced from a position beyond the reach of human law, talking babies have access to an ideal of justice that women on their own (not to mention men on their own) cannot attain. Without restoration of that more fundamental balance of justice, women's efforts at peacemaking will remain futile—as the story of Daniel and Susanna makes especially clear. Even though Susanna's sentence is reversed, Daniel's actions leave intact the resilient epistemological system that initially condemned her.[77] And while (as Paul Ricoeur points out) legal judgments serve in the short term to decide an individual case, their long-term purpose is to contribute to public peace.[78] A society in which *torts* against women can never be rectified is a fundamentally unstable society. Or, in the pithier contemporary formulation: *No justice, no peace.*

MA MERE N'A COLPES EN MOI: EQUITY THROUGH IMPURITY IN ROBERT DE BORON'S MERLIN

In the story of Susanna and Daniel, God speaks through an innocent child to ensure a just outcome for an innocent but not virginal woman. I am now turning my attention to a story that uses superficially similar characters to achieve a superficially similar outcome—but in a way that upends "justice" and sets aside the question of innocence entirely. This is the infancy of Merlin as recounted in the celebrated *Estoire de Merlin* of the Arthurian Vulgate Cycle, an early thirteenth-century *mise en prose* of Robert de Boron's mostly lost verse romance. Like Daniel, the precociously verbal toddler Merlin intervenes in a judicial proceeding and overturns a woman's death sentence (that of his own mother, whose inability to explain what has happened to her offers a paradigmatic example of hermeneutical injustice). However, Merlin exonerates his mother not by proving her innocence, but by proving another woman's guilt.[79] Thanks to his unique abilities to know the past and the future—a set of abilities resulting from a concession between opposing authorities, divine and diabolical—Merlin succeeds in proving his case. Yet this proof is only possible when the truth is divorced from any value judgment, when it is conceded that there is no "right" to be upheld. Ultimately, Merlin shows that justice itself, as much as innocence, is a "nothingness," a *néant*, as Lyotard characterizes the impossibility of verbal proof.

The prose *Merlin* opens with a council of devils debating how best to wreak havoc on earth. They settle on the persecution of a wealthy family, all of whose members eventually succumb to the fiends' depredations, save one daughter who remains virtuous thanks to the spiritual guidance of her confessor, Blaise. One night the young woman forgets to cross herself before going to bed; an incubus takes advantage of this momentary vulnerability and impregnates her. Once her pregnancy becomes visible, she is interrogated, first by other women, then by judges. Her inability to identify the man who impregnated her is interpreted as a willful cover-up, and she is imprisoned, with the expectation that she will be executed once her child has been born and weaned.

That child, of course, is Merlin. Horrifyingly hairy at birth, he grows quickly and speaks precociously. He is, as Anne Berthelot calls him, the "*puer senex* par excellence" whose alinear development confounds the traditional ages of man.[80] Because of his mother's faith (and because the baby has been baptized), God grants Merlin the ability to know the future;[81] but because God will not take away that which rightfully belongs to Satan, the demonically fathered Merlin also retains the devilish gift of perfect knowledge of the past.[82] Merlin intervenes in his mother's trial, securing clemency by proving that the head judge's own mother has been an unfaithful wife, and that the judge himself was conceived from her adulterous affair with a priest. He makes the accusation through his knowledge of the past and is able to prove it thanks to his ability to predict the future: thus, his diabolical and divine gifts together allow him to achieve his desired outcome. Merlin not only knows the past and the future, but he is endowed with what epistemologist José Medina calls *meta-lucidity*: a "capacity to see the limitations of dominant ways of seeing" (in this case, an awareness of judicial (im)partiality as an exploitable loophole).[83] Unwilling to punish his own mother, but cognizant of the hypocrisy of punishing Merlin's mother while sparing his own, the judge frees the prisoner. Thus has Merlin ensured equal injustice under the law.

The episode hinges on novel modes of interrogation, accusation, and proof. Robert de Boron fully exploits these discursive forms, producing a detailed and "realistic" rendering of a trial.[84] However, the interrogations, accusations, and testimonies are largely voiced by atypical actors—women, a toddler—whose speech is configured in a "vast polyphonic structure" that denies the possibility of a single, simple truth.[85] What's more, the words of Merlin and his mother illustrate what Agamben calls "the very aporia of historical knowledge: a non-coincidence between facts and truth."[86] The fact of Merlin's mother's pregnancy is misaligned with the truth of her innocence, and the gap can only be bridged with Merlin's peculiar historical, future, and meta-lucid knowledge: forms of knowledge that give him complete mastery of the situation. The noncoincidence between facts and truth underlies the trial episode's broader noncoincidence between innocence and justice. The outcome of the trial shows that although the truth can be used to establish the facts, the facts don't add up to the truth; and while the punishment of the innocent is surely unjust, the punishment of the guilty may not represent a just outcome either.

Merlin's mother is first subjected to an informal interrogation by other women.[87] The conversation is remarkable for its circularity: the interrogation is useless for the establishment of a factual narrative because Merlin's mother can only repeat her utter inability to identify the father:

> Et eles demandent: "Iestes vous grosse?" Et ele respont: "Oïl, ce m'est avis." — "Et de cui?" Et ele dit: "Si me doint Diex a estre delivre a joie, com je ne sai a esciant de cui." Et eles respondent: "Ont le vos dont tant home fait que vos ne savez assener au quel?" Et ele respont: "Ja Dieu ne place que je en soie delivre, se onques hom a mon veu ne a mon seu a moi ot afaire en meniere que ce me deust avenir." Et celes qui ce oïrent si se seingnierent et distrent: "Bele amie, ce ne porroit estre, ne il ne fu onques ne de vos ne d'autrui. Mais vos amez plus espoir celui qui ce vos a fait que vos ne faites vos meismes: si nel volez encuser. Mes certes granz damaiges est de vos, car si tost com la justice et li juge le savront, ausis tost vos covendra morir." Quant cele l'oï, s'en fu molt espoantee et dist: "Einsis face Diex l'ame de moi sauve, com je onques ne vi ne conui celui qui ce m'a fait." (pp. 44–45)

And they [the other women] ask: "Are you pregnant?" And she replies: "Yes, I think so." — "And by whom?" And she says: "May God save my soul, for I don't know by whom." And they reply: "Did so many men do it with you that you don't know which one it is?" And she replies: "May it never please God that I be saved, if ever any man, within my sight or to my knowledge, had such dealings with me that this could have happened." And those who heard this crossed themselves and said: "Fair friend, this cannot be, nor was it ever so, for you or for anyone else. But you'd rather back the man who did this to you than stand up for yourself, so you don't want to accuse him. But this will surely do you great harm, for as soon as justice and the judges find out, you will have to die." When she heard this, she was very afraid and said: "Well, may God save my soul, because I never saw nor knew the one who did this to me."[88]

This is a clear instance of hermeneutical injustice, which occurs when a situation is "ill-understood by the subject herself, because collectively ill-understood":[89] her own experience is culturally and

therefore communicatively unintelligible. Merlin's mother, unaided
by interlocutors who tell her that what she has testified "ne porroit
estre," finds herself unable to prove an unsayable truth that she does
not fully grasp herself. She is restricted to repetitively negative discourse (**Ja** Dieu **ne** place que je en soie delivre, se **onques** hom a mon
veu **ne** a mon seu a moi ot afaire; je **onques ne** vi **ne** conui)—not
reduced to total silence, but limited in her repetitive inability (interpreted as a refusal) to *accuse*. The only defense that could be available to her is an offense that she cannot execute. She cannot name
her rapist, nor can she even be named herself.[90] She does name her
son, however, in a fashion that doubly inscribes him in *her* lineage:
she gives him her father's name, which, as Francis Dubost observes,
sonically inscribes him in the maternal line (*Mer-lin*).[91]

At her trial Merlin's mother is allowed to speak, but she can say
little because she does not know what has happened to her. When
asked directly who the child's father is, she can only reply: "Sire, je voi
bien que je sui livree a torment, et ja Diex n'ait pitié ne merci de moi,
se je onques le pere vi ne conui ne se onques vers home terrien fui tant
abandonnee que il me deust enfant faire ne que jel deusse par lui retenir" (p. 58 [My lords, I see clearly that I am doomed. May God show
me no mercy if I ever saw the father or ever even let a man come close
enough to make me pregnant; p. 311]). Her response is almost exactly
the same as the one she gave to the ladies, many months before. Interrogations, a trial, and repeated calls for testimony have gotten us no
closer to the truth. In a convergence of hermeneutical and testimonial
injustices, her words are neither understood nor believed.

As did the ladies before them, the judges then shift the focus of
their investigation. Once again it becomes apparent that the unwed
mother's chief crime is not having conceived out of wedlock, but
refusing to accuse the man who impregnated her. In the interrogation's first iteration, the other ladies spelled this out for Merlin's
mother; now the judge is telling Merlin himself, after the baby asks
why his mother has been condemned:

> Li enfes [. . .] vient tot droit as piez de la jostise et dist: "Je vos pri, se
> vos le savez, que vos me dites por quoi vos volez ma mere ardoir." Et cil

respont:"Je le sai bien et je le te dirai: por ce qu'ele t'a eu en mauvaistié de son cors et qu'ele ne viaut encuser celui qui en son cors t'engendra. Et nos tenons encores tant de la viez loi que nos fesons de tel femme jostise, et por ce la volons faire de ta mere." (p. 60)

The child comes straight to the judge's feet and says: "I beg of you, if you know it, to tell me why you want to burn my mother." And he replies: "I know it perfectly well and I will tell you: because she bore you in bodily wickedness and because she does not want to accuse the one who engendered you in her body. And we still hold so firmly to the old law that we execute such women, and therefore we want to execute your mother."

Merlin asks judge to explain the reason *if he knows it*. The suggestion that a judge might not be aware of the reasoning behind his own judgment underscores an unsettling lack of connection between knowledge, truth, and justice. Yet the judgment is based entirely in fact: Merlin's mother *did* bear a child outside of marriage, she has *not* named the father, and the law *does* dictate a death sentence for such action. Still, these clear-cut facts fail to reflect the murkier truth. This is a case in which the same evidence can substantiate multiple interpretations: the "disagreement of judgement in response to the same evidence entails difference of meaning" and therefore "there can be no learning from testimony."[92] The noncoincidence between facts and truth is in this instance highly gendered: the juridical "science of the fact" refuses to admit the evidentiary value of a woman's knowledge of her own body.

The noncoincidence between facts and truth also points to an unsettling gap between speech and knowledge, one that is present throughout *Merlin* but is particularly salient in the trial episode. The purpose of a trial is to arrive at a just verdict by hearing and assessing verbal testimony. The process is reliant on knowledgeable and truthful witnesses—that is, people who know and speak the truth—just as the institution more generally, the system of justice, relies on its participants' confidence in what Paul Ricoeur calls the "rule of sincerity," the expectation that "each will *mean what he or she says*."[93] This critical "fiduciary base" is missing from the trial even before Merlin's intervention. Instead, this trial is built on the presumption that Merlin's mother *means what she does not say* (the name of Merlin's father). The process is inherently unstable because those who control it lack faith in the rule of sincerity. The failure of the multiple interrogators to elicit the truth *seems to them* to signal the unreliability of women's testimony, especially as regards paternity.[94] In effect it exposes the precariousness of a more fundamental rule—that words can be used to establish the truth—on which the rule of sincerity and the epistemology of testimony are founded. The presumption of veracity on which institutions of justice rely has broken down *because the relationship between knowledge and speech is illusory*, such that justice can only be served through the intervention of a diabolical offspring who uses superhuman verbal abilities to generate his own truth. No other talking infant makes as clear an argument for the universal alterity of childhood as an epistemic tool.

"Merlin's truth," E. Jane Burns writes, "is that of the artificer, a truth that underscores difference and demonstrates how things do not ever match their appearance."[95] Another way to think about it is that the precociously verbal toddler's speech both accentuates and fills the gaps between facts and truth. Informed by his uncanny knowledge of both past and future, the child speaks as a supplement to the unsatisfactorily factual speech of his unnamed mother. Merlin is, as R. Howard Bloch put it, "the representation of that which cannot be said and of everything that can be said."[96] Merlin utters his very first words in order to reassure his mother, to overcome her doubts as to her own fate with his certain foretelling of her eventual vindication. It is significant to note that Merlin's speech coincides with his weaning and with his mother's condemnation for the crime of which he constitutes the physical proof. We have already considered the moment of weaning as an impetus for acquisition and creative use of language (chapter 3); in *Merlin*, weaning is also what allows the administration of justice—though not in the way the judges expect.

Breastfeeding is a life-giving act, and in *Merlin* it is one whose mode of delivery is determined by the infant's diabolical nature.

Because Merlin has such a frightening appearance, "autre femme ne l'osast norrir ne alaitier" (no woman [but his own mother] dared feed or suckle him; p. 52). And it is precisely because she is still nursing her son that Merlin's mother is spared as long as she is: on Blaise's recommendation, the judges resolve to defer their judgment of the baby's mother "tant [. . .] qu'il porra mengier par soi et demander ses estouvoirs" (until he can eat on his own and ask for what he needs; p. 48).[97] Here weaning is tied to the acquisition of language, and to notions of responsibility. Once the infant can be held responsible for his own sustenance—and for the verbalization of the needs that his mother has until now anticipated and satisfied—only then can the mother be held responsible for her criminal act.[98] That is the judges' plan, anyway. Ultimately Merlin's weaning and his acquisition of language lead to a redistribution of responsibility, severing ties between guilt and punishment.

As soon as he has demonstrated his ability to speak, Merlin steps forward to supplement his mother's speech and her knowledge. The first verbal strategies Merlin applies to his mother's defense are largely grounded in deflection and redirection: he speaks only to contradict others or to accuse his mother's accusers. While Merlin defends his mother against direct accusations, he answers no other questions. Instead, he strategically withholds his speech. When Merlin finally wriggles out of his mother's arms and speaks directly to the judges, he challenges the epistemic order, placing knowledge itself on trial.[99] He creates and deforms truths, for he is "an embodiment of the principle of fiction itself."[100]

The purpose of a trial, it has been argued, is the production of truth and "the rendering of justice based upon the oral testimonies of defendant and plaintiff"[101]—but Merlin makes us question whether that is the essential function of the process at all. For in exposing one truth (the judge's parentage), Merlin forecloses the trial's search for another truth (the extramarital activities of Merlin's mother). Merlin does not need to prove that his mother is innocent: he merely needs to prove that she is less culpable than another woman who has gone unpunished. The desired outcome—what Merlin calls "droite jostice" (p. 63)—isn't acquittal, but dismissal. Or, more precisely, the desired outcome is the avoidance of punishment: as Merlin predicted in the very first words he uttered, "Bele mere, n'aiez pas paor, que vos ne morroiz por pechié qui de moi vos soit avenuz" (p. 53 [Dear mother, do not be afraid; you will never die on my account; p. 309]). And while the link between guilt and punishment might seem transparent—as Nicole Oresme will write in a gloss on his *Livre de Ethiques de Aristote*, "par pugnicion est declaré qui avoit droit ou tort" (through punishment it is declared who was right or wrong; book 5, chapter 14[102])—the fact that the trial in *Merlin* doesn't culminate in a punishment does *not* mean that no one did wrong. Rather, it suggests there is so much wrong in this world that "punishment" is a meaningless tool with which to attempt to establish justice. And if there were any such thing as justice, innocence would have little to do with it.

For all his resistance, Merlin is complicit in the judges' system, exercising a divinely and diabolically endowed epistemic privilege. In the end, he gains his mother's freedom by colluding with the judge, exploiting the latter's "willful hermeneutic ignorance" (his refusal to lend credence to the female defendant's description of her own experience) and getting him to invest in a different variety of ignorance (willfully ignoring both women's apparent indiscretions).[103] Merlin's meta-lucidity disturbs but does not redefine paradigms of justice; as in the Daniel narratives, his untimely speech frees one woman but leaves judicial power intact, confirming the resilience of the unjust epistemic system.

When divine and diabolical influences are removed from the equation, however—when we attend instead to the imagined naturally acquired speech of fully human children—a different balance between knowledge, innocence, and justice will emerge. In the final section of this chapter I will consider truth-telling children in fabliaux whose words testify to their own mother's guilt. In such stories, careful attention must be paid to the intentions of the marginally situated child informant: these children, speaking in accordance with a child's mentality rather than a divine intellect, can be witting or unwitting *perpetrators* of epistemic violence. At the same time, their speech, and the willful misinterpretation thereof, can nevertheless serve as an instrument of justice.

ISSI FOUT L'ON: CHILD WITNESSES
TO MATERNAL GUILT

Pourquoy pleurent les enfans nouveaulz nez?
Pour tant que leur mere n'est plus pucelle.[104]

Why do newborn babies cry?
Because their mother is no longer a virgin.

In comic literature, the problems of innocence, punishment, and extrajudicial forms of justice are often expressed through a small child's voice. According to a medieval French proverb, *folz, yvres et enfans ont de coustume de vray dire* (madmen, drunkards, and children tend to tell the truth).[105] The proverb is illustrated to humorous effect in fabliaux such as *Celui qui bota la pierre* and *Baillet le savetier*, in each of which a small child reveals his or her mother's infidelity. In these remarkable stories, some of the few fabliaux in which children play a major role,[106] children's speech not only provides the narrative impetus, it also reinforces patriarchal norms of female behavior on which the stability of the nuclear family unit is constructed. The product of the marriage becomes its "enforcer" and its greatest test: the child's marginal perspective serves to reinforce rather than challenge the (adult male) epistemic order, in apparent contradiction to the ethos of "reversal"—with reversals often enabled by differential knowledge[107]—that is so central to fabliau humor. Yet these stories do conform to the fabliaux's broader "truth-seeking compulsion."[108] Though *Celui qui bota la pierre* and *Baillet le savetier* do not figure among the thirty or so fabliaux culminating in a judicial scene,[109] they nonetheless concern themselves with testimony, fact-finding, and justice. As the children confirm their mothers' unchastity, their speech, revealing that which ought to have remained hidden, also hints at the children's *own* lack of innocence. The fabliau children's disingenuous speech makes them appear guileless, but children's innocent appearances can be deceiving, especially because their speech is so unpredictable, even when their intentions seem transparent.[110]

Rather than obscuring or denying "the constant threat to the social order of meaning inherent in the structure of Symbolic desire," as Edelman argues that the figure of the child can do,[111] these children render hidden adult desires visible, becoming agents of comedic familial disorder even as they reinforce the underlying epistemic order.

The most conventional fabliau that stages the revelation of female infidelity through a child's speech is *Celui qui bota la pierre*, which exists in two distinct versions: a longer version (114 lines) datable to the first half of the fourteenth century, and a shorter one (62 lines) dated to the second half of the century. In both versions a boy watches his mother banter with a priest. As the woman kicks at a loose stone, the priest flirtatiously tells her she'd better stop kicking the stone or else he will have to ravish her, at which point she of course kicks the stone again and the priest follows through on his threat. When the boy's father returns home, the boy warns him not to kick the stone, lest the priest come back and do the same thing to him. Hilarity ensues: a sound wife-beating in the long version and a vague threat of revenge in the short one. Both end with the same moral: one should never engage in illicit activities under a child's watchful eye.

The differences between the two versions of *Celui qui bota la pierre* center chiefly on the paired questions of the child's innocence and the mother's punishment. In the longer version, the child—who is, significantly, the first character to be introduced—straddles a line between innocence and guile, prerational infancy and more responsible childhood. The boy, we are told in just the second line, is "uns enfes mout medisans" (a bad-mouthing child); we soon learn the age of the child, "Qui n'avoit pas set ans, non sis;/ Mes mout fu sages" (Who wasn't seven years old, nor even six, but was very wise; p. 142, ll. 15–16).[112] It is significant that the age we are told he has not yet attained is the traditional age of reason—and yet we are also told he is wise beyond his years, and the characterization of him as "medisans" suggests a certain degree of willfulness, if not full responsibility for his intemperate speech.[113] This allusion to the child's specifically verbal form of ill intent alerts us to the possibility that the child could become a perpetrator of epistemic violence: as Dotson reminds us, verbal but prerational children can be agents of epistemic injustice too.[114]

In subsequent allusions to the child's speech, his "wisdom" takes on distinctly juridical overtones. When the boy witnesses his mother's extramarital activities with the priest, he doesn't just remain silent: he "n'en tint parole ne plait" (made neither word nor plea;[115] p. 143, ll. 67–68). Similarly, when he describes the priest's "thrashing" of his mother, he declares "Ce ne sai ge s'ele i ot coupe, / Car ainz point ne se desfendi" (I don't know if she was at fault, for she did not defend herself at all; p. 144, ll. 94–95). The child's report is thus concerned not just with a narration of events, but with a judgment of the mother's culpability, a judgment enabled by the child's privileged status as eyewitness: "Ge le vi bien dou feu ou g'ere" (I saw it well from the hearth where I was; p. 144, l. 92). His marginal status, as a child observing from outside of the husband-wife-lover triad, gives him as much of a privileged point of view as does the position at the edge of the room from which he can observe the entire scene: in any event, his age does not prevent his eyewitness testimony from being heard and taken seriously as a source of knowledge.

It is that eyewitnessing that presents the real problem, as the fabliaux's final six lines attest:

Par ceste fable moustrer voilg
Que l'en se gart dou petit eulg
Autresint bien comme del grant.
De fol et de petit effant
Se fait touz jors mout bon garder,
Car il ne sevent riens celer! (p. 144, ll. 109–14)

Through this fabliau I want to show
That one should watch out for little eyes
Just as carefully as one does for big ones.
From fools and from little children
It is always very good to guard oneself,
For they don't know how to hide anything!

The shorter version reaches a similar conclusion—"Que l'en se gart do petit oil" (Watch out for little eyes; p. 141, l. 56)—with some notable plot differences that tend to create a greater impression of childish innocence. Whereas the long version's child is introduced first, setting him up as major character, the short version does not mention the child, hidden in plain sight, until the sex scene has already begun:

> Un enfançon seoit au feu,
> Qui bien les vit el lit chaoir
> Et au prestre les rains movoir.
> "En moie foi, dist l'enfançon,
> Je cuit bien que issi fout l'on."
> L'enfes se tot et ne dist plus. (p. 141, ll. 34–39)

> A small child was sitting by the fire,
> Who clearly saw them fall into bed
> And saw the priest pumping his lower back.
> "My word," said the small child,
> "I do believe someone is fucking here."
> The child hushed and said no more.

The child's age is never specified, though the diminutive suffix -çon does suggest he is quite young. In the words of one so small, the salty language produces a considerable comic effect. But the meaningful rhyme of *enfançon* and *issi fout l'on* also cements the child's status as witness to, and proof of, his mother's sexual activity. As in the longer version, the problem isn't adultery, but witnessing and reporting, as is made explicit in final three lines:

> Se l'enfançon n'eüst veü
> Lo prestre joer a sa mere,
> Il nel deïst pas a son pere. (p. 141, 60–62)

> If the little child had not seen
> The priest sporting with his mother,
> He could not have told his father.

The child's speech is disruptive precisely because it is *not* deceptive. Whether the disruption is intentional (as appears to be the case with the *enfes mout medisans*) or unintentional (as the *enfançon*'s may be), the outcome is the same.[116] Linked as he is with the *fol* in the long version's moral, the *petit effant* comes to resemble an adult fabliau archetype, the ignorant naïf.[117] The addition of this type to the stock triangle of husband, wife, and clerical lover, even in infantile form, destabilizes the calculus of blame. As in the story of Merlin's mother, this fabliau portrays a disconnect between guilt and punishment: who deserves punishment, and who receives it.[118] The long *Celui qui bota la pierre* is the only version in which any punishment is carried out ("la bat et la lesdenge" [he beats and insults her]; p. 144, l. 106)—though the futility of this action is noted:

Mes por chasti ne por ses cous
Ne remaindra qu'il ne soit cous! (p. 144, ll. 107–8)

But neither punishment nor his blows
Will make it so that he's not a cuckold!

The shorter version, on the other hand, makes it clear that only vengeance will be possible—vengeance, a mere "simulation of justice"[119]—and even that is deferred ("Mais il s'en venja bien aprés"; p. 141, l. 53). The moral, which immediately follows the "vengeance" or "punishment," further obscures the matter of culpability: the woman, it is implied, is more to blame for her indiscretion than for her adultery; and even if a child is not punished for blabbing in the way that comes naturally to him, he certainly can be blamed.

The similar morals that conclude the two versions of *Celui qui bota la pierre* present dissimulation as an ideal, and untimely (and honest) child speech as a problem. They thus confirm Jürgen Beyer's argument that in many fabliaux, "the moral actually documents the unfitness of the fabliau for moralization" as it "plays with the form of morality, primarily by exposing it to laughter."[120] Fabliau morals, like proverbs, may express "communal judgments" that purport to express a truth *déjà-toujours-dit-par-tous*,[121] but they also raise the question of whose knowledge is being expressed, in whose voice—and the perspective from which *Celui qui bota la pierre*'s lessons are imparted is both morally and epistemically dubious. If *Celui qui bota la pierre* is a story about the danger of truthful but ill-intentioned testimony, it is also a call for concealment of truth. Child witnesses' lucidity can be subversive, but only if they are *allowed* to become witnesses in the first place.

Another moral about peeping children is conveyed in the formally and codicologically eccentric *Baillet le savetier* (also known as *Le prestre qui fut mis au lardier*), a *fabliau chanté* preserved only in the fourteenth-century *Rosarius* manuscript.[122] The eponymous cobbler discovers his wife's infidelity (with the priest, of course) when his three-year-old daughter innocently remarks that her mother serves much nicer food when Daddy leaves for work and the priest comes over. Baillet announces his departure, then comes home early to catch the lovers in the act; perceiving that the priest is hidden in the larder, Baillet proclaims that he has decided to sell the larder. As Baillet begins to move the cabinet, the priest audibly prays in Latin, and Baillet chortles that he'll be able to fetch an even better price for Latin-speaking furniture. He eventually sells the larder to the trapped priest's brother, having maximized both the amusement and the financial profit he could gain at the adulterers' expense; aside from whatever anxiety and embarrassment she might have suffered during the ordeal, the wife goes unpunished. Though its stanzaic form sets it apart from other fabliaux, *Baillet le savetier* unites what Per Nykrog argues are that genre's two most characteristic preoccupations: erotic affairs and juridical or pseudo-juridical ones.[123] These converge in the words of a child, one who, in comparison with the boys in *Celui qui bota la pierre*, is younger and seemingly more innocent.[124] Her innocence, like the boys' *médisance*, is played for laughs.[125]

In *Baillet le savetier*, as in the shorter version of *Celui qui bota la pierre*, the young child is introduced only after the adult triangle of husband, wife, and priest has been established. She enters the story, of course, as a mechanism for the revelation of the wife's secret—though she is initially named not as the adulterous couple's daughter, but as Baillet's:

Le savetier frans
Une fille avoit
D'environ trois ans,
Qui molt bien parloit (p. 90, ll. 17–20)

The worthy shoemaker
Had a daughter
Of about three years,
Who spoke very well.

The child's salient features, her extreme youth and her capacity for speech that exceeds age expectations, are presented in their own pentasyllabic quatrain. When the child later speaks to her father, she refers to "my mother" ("ma mere"; ll. 22 and 30). This oddly indirect sketch of family relations—"Baillet's daughter" referring to "my mother" in conversation with Baillet—preempts questions about the girl's paternity even as it suggests how attenuated the marital bond has become, the two parents connected to each other only through their child.

Baillet's daughter may speak well, but she speaks according to a thoroughly childlike logic: she wishes her father would go away because she prefers the fancy and plentiful food set out when the priest visits. The girl's speech is not thoroughly innocent (she displays a rather naturalistic early-childhood gluttony), but it certainly constitutes neither *médisance* nor *plet*. Indeed, the child's gluttony serves here as a signal of the sincerity of her testimony, and thus of her epistemic reliability: the truth her father gleans from her testimony is not the message she meant to communicate, but it is true nonetheless. This certainly is a case in which "the significations of the body exceed the intentions of the subject,"[126] but with a twist, as the child's truthful words gain their excess meaning through the sexual engagement of the *mother's* body—the body (and the type of activity) from which the child herself originated. The toddler's words thus couple together the infantile and adult versions of *lècherie*.

Despite the superficial similarities between the fabliaux, the child's speech is also central to a significant structural divergence between *Celui qui bota la pierre* and *Baillet le savetier*. In the latter the child's speech serves not just as a plot mechanism but as a framing device, for the story's second act—Baillet's revenge—centers on another form of unexpected speech. From a toddler to a large piece of furniture (with a guilty priest inside), from tot-talk to Latin, from a gluttonous girl to a larder with no food inside, the little girl's guileless speech is but the first of two different verbal proofs of the mother's guilt emerging from "marvelous" quarters. Baillet responds to the two proofs quite differently, as he correctly interprets his daughter's words but willfully misinterprets the priest's speech by attributing it to the larder. This misinterpretation constitutes a joking interpretive injustice that, by the logic of the fabliau, serves a "just" end (the punishment of the unfaithful spouse).[127]

The wife has no defense—yet this *is* a trial of sorts, as the narrator makes clear in the story's moral:

> Par ceste chançon vous puis tesmoignier
> Que du petit weil se fait bon guetier:
> *Ex oculo pueri noli tua facta tueri,*
> Quar par la fillete
> Fu le fait sceü,
> Qui estoit jonete. (p. 98, ll. 167–71)

> With this song I can testify
> That a little eye makes a good lookout:
> Don't try to hide your deeds from a child's eye,
> For through the little girl
> Was the deed known,
> Who was a young little thing.

The narrator's choice of the verb *tesmoignier* calls our attention to the epistemic status of the narrator, the source of his knowledge and the position from which he communicates that knowledge to the audience. If Baillet's daughter can unwittingly testify to her mother's guilt simply by remarking on what she has seen (and tasted), the narrator must rely on a completely different process, as his source of knowledge is an imagined story whose conflict is sparked by the fictional child's speech: the moral issues from a meta-narrative, but not meta-lucid, vantage point. The moral-as-testimony brings back into view the story's core informant, the little girl, who had long since disappeared from the story, again emphasizing her very young age (*petit weil, fillete, jonete*). As in the main body of the fabliau, the girl's words have a Latinate pendant: the same moral is repeated in the girl's idiom (*du petit weil se fait bon guetier*) and in the language of the larder (*Ex oculo pueri noli tua facta tueri*). Both the larder and the child are treated as vessels of sorts, as is evident in the narrator's statement that the truth came to be known *through* the little girl (*par la fillete*)—and if there had been enough food in either one of them, the plot wouldn't have unfolded as it did. But in the end, the girl is assimilated less to the larder than to the song itself: note the repeating near-parallel structures of "par ceste chançon vous puis tesmoignier que" and "par la fillete fu le fait sceü qui." Like the song itself, the girl is an artistic creation. Neither lucid nor meta-lucid in her own right, the toddler is little more than an instrument used to convey the fabliau narrator's "truth" about women—which is that children's innocence compels them to reveal that their mothers can never be innocent.

Testifying toddlers, when read through the lens of feminist epistemology, become powerful mouthpieces for illustrations and critiques of the epistemic injustices to which women in particular are subject. They thus shed new light on the perennial topic of cultural expressions of medieval misogyny: child voices emphasize that in the Middle Ages, too, misogyny was not only an ethical but an epistemic problem. As José Medina points out, "Social injustices breed epistemic injustices; or rather, these two kinds of injustice are two sides of the same coin, always going together, being mutually supportive and reinforcing each other."[128] Both mother and child are marginal participants in the dominant epistemic systems portrayed in medieval narratives (and trial narratives in particular); but in literature, at least, children are nonetheless well positioned to contribute to their mothers' liberation—or condemnation. The children discussed in this chapter possess a unique *cognitive* innocence that allows them to express knowledge unencumbered by experience, providing a lucid account of personal iniquities and systemic inequities—even if the child speaker herself does not understand that this is what she's attesting to. Yet the children's innocence, contrary to the etymological sense of the word, also has the capacity to do significant harm. Even if we accept Lyotard's contention that innocence cannot be established through discourse, in medieval narratives innocents can perpetrate epistemic justice or injustice through discourse: innocence can establish infant alterity as a powerful instrument not only for knowing "human nature" but for participating in epistemological systems and the injustices inherent to them.

CHAPTER FIVE

MUTE CHILDREN IN
THE TIME OF MIRACLE

The infant's inability to speak is the rule and not the exception; it represents a norm (not that this exact concept existed in the Middle Ages[1]) rather than a deviation, and thus can hardly be construed as a disability. Yet the discursive overlap between childhood and disability cannot be denied. Indeed, this was already the case well before the Middle Ages. Cicero writes in *De senectute* 10.33, for instance, that "Nature has only a single path and that path is run but once, and to each stage of existence has been allotted its own appropriate quality"—and that quality, for childhood, is *infirmitas*.[2] In the Middle Ages, too, childhood remains "the quintessential state of weakness."[3] Medieval children are largely excluded from participation in the social institutions that structure adult life, on the grounds of their physical and cognitive deficiencies. In this respect they are treated much like mute or mentally ill adults:[4] a grouping that is hinted at not just in law codes, but in popular wisdom too, such as the proverb about "folz, yvres et enfans" cited in chapter 4. But this assimilation to grown people with disabilities does not mean children were conceived of as little adults, disabled or otherwise. Unlike other categories of not-quite-full-persons to whom they were often compared, children's degree of exclusion was expected to wane over time, with adolescents and youths taking on increased responsibility. If childhood was (like) a disability, it was one the survivors were expected to outgrow.

A child's putative inability to speak properly might yield behaviors similar to those of a person with a speech disorder or disability—yet there is an evident gap between the commonplace of the speechless *infans* and the realities of lived experience, as chatty children clearly existed in medieval Europe just as they do today. In this chapter I propose to explore the meanings hidden in the space between the notional speechlessness of the *infans* and the "typical" reality of child speech by focusing on one class of "atypical" child: mute children whose powers of speech are restored in miracle narratives. In their early years, even normate children are axiomatically weak and speechless;[5] each child acquires language on her own schedule. And yet, a child who is mute as part of a healthy developmental process is not the same as a child who is mute because of a disability. At some point, the muteness of an *infans* ceases to be an expectation and becomes a perceived problem.[6] In other words, the divide between "typical" and "atypical" childhood embodiment is situated not just in the body, but in time.

Tales of mute *miraculés* introduce anomalous developmental timelines and therefore can be productively understood through the lens of disability studies (though they also exceed this critical framework). After all, disability studies, too, depends on structuring discourses of temporality, as Alison Kafer has forcefully demonstrated;[7] and though miracle narratives seem inscribed in precisely the sort of "curative time" with which disability scholars and activists contend, the particular developmental arcs of mute *miraculés* also confound these temporalities, in a manner that can enter a productive dialogue with contemporary theoretical formulations of "crip time." Crip time, recently defined as "the way disability disrupts normative understandings of time and the life course,"[8] will emerge as a key concept in this chapter as I consider the ways that the miracles effected upon mute children can short-circuit the life course, producing a child whose now-normate physiology is out of sync with his developmental progress. The acquisition (through processes of socialization) of mature speech—more than any other developmental change—is the vehicle through which children "age out" of their natural disability and become social actors. When such "aging out" occurs at the "wrong" age, however, and when the late language-learner has no mother (as is the case of nearly every *miraculé* discussed here), the resultant narratives must confront competing models of alterity, truth-telling, and the emergence of personhood from communal interactions. Once-mute *miraculés'* defiance of developmental expectations indicates, I argue, that even infant alterity is fundamentally a normate state; but disabled children who "exist in tension with the expected timeline of progress and development" are another potent figure with whom to think through their own set of epistemic problems,[9] particularly problems surrounding the biographical disjuncture of past and present that is effected through miracle.

Because it is a period marked by the slow acquisition of adult capabilities, childhood can blur the distinctions between ability and disability; and because it is a liminal phase of life less subject to reason and less susceptible to control, childhood is often considered to be the age most open to miracle.[10] But when the logic of the miracle—a phenomenon conceptually opposed to nature[11]—confronts the raw human nature of childhood, normative expectations about human development are scrambled in manners that can expose deeply unsettling obstacles to the construction of reliable knowledge. In this chapter I will read miracle stories representing the coming to language of mute children, highlighting what I see as some of the most intriguing interpretive problems posed by the miracle-narrative genre.

As I have sought to demonstrate, children are used in medieval fictions to typify a number of fundamental human characteristics. My readings in this chapter will show that medieval miracle narratives further the image of normate childhood as unfolding within an intact family unit, using speech as a primary tool for family and community integration. The mute child, especially when she lacks the socializing support of a family, is doubly voiceless: not only is she physically unable to narrate her own experience, but even if her capacity to speak is restored, she may lack the social skills and the social capital to bear witness to her own embodied change.[12] Miracle recipients are endowed with physical capabilities, but not necessarily with the know-how required to act on that new potential. When the power of speech is given, for instance, does language still need to be learned? Miracle narratives offer an underexplored tool with which to test medieval perceptions of the biological and cultural underpinnings of language learning: on those occasions when child *miraculés* do speak about their own experience, their words provide rare insights into the interplay, and the separation, of language and voice. After all, the miracle is a seen phenomenon (*mirari*, to look on with wonder), but also one that must be vocally reported; verbal testimony becomes ever more important with the increasing bureaucratization of the canonization process over the course of the thirteenth century.[13] However, though receipt of a miracle makes a child observable and worthy of narration, it does not lend her the authority or credibility that is conventionally denied to her age cohort; and though the miraculous healing of muteness physically enables the *miraculé* to speak, it also erases the very condition (speechlessness) whose former presence must be established in order to prove that a miracle has occurred. In other words, the very fact that a (putatively) formerly mute person can provide spoken testimony both constitutes evidence that a miracle has occurred and casts doubt on the authenticity of the miracle by making it difficult to prove whether the *miraculé* was ever mute at all. The reported speech of and about once-mute *miraculés*, especially those mute since childhood, thus points to a discomfiting insufficiency of testimony to establish truth even within a testimony-dependent system. In an age of belief, what constitutes evidence?[14]

When an older *miraculé* has to learn language as an infant would, his restoration disrupts linear time and reconfigures the normative life cycle, highlighting the underlying tension between nature and socialization that makes the universal alterity of the infant such a potent literary tool. In other words, like fictions of fetuses and infants who speak "before their time," narratives of mute *miraculés* gaining the power of speech and learning language "after their time" trouble notions about the relationship of language and experience to knowledge.

Such revisions to the life cycle, moreover, allow a reconsideration of the degree of alterity within which infancy remains an efficacious instrument of knowledge: does the often inhumane treatment of mute children prior to their healing dehumanize them, and if so, are they nonetheless treated as sufficiently human to give insight into "the human condition" and its narration? These accounts of the socialization of children with disabilities oblige us to question whether *all* children can embody the epistemic privilege of universal alterity.

My overarching claim in this chapter is that miraculous healings of muteness reveal the epistemic utility of infants' universal alterity—like the distinction between typical and atypical muteness—to be a function of time. The speaking infants discussed thus far are already dislocated from the normative time frame of the ages of man, talking out of turn in a way that concentrates the reader's attention on truths that are obscured rather than clarified by experience. However, representations of disabled children—more specifically, of mute children who miraculously (re)gain the ability to speak—pose even more insistent questions about time. Ultimately, tales of muteness healed, and the developmental do-overs that sometimes follow, indicate that just as fetal personhood emerges from the relation with the mother as sounding environment, the normate subject emerges through a communicative blurring of the boundaries between person and community; a normate subject is formed when the biographical time in which such communication is undertaken synchronizes with the developmental time inscribed in his body.

QUE JAMÉS PARLER NE PEÜST: GUILLOT OF CHARTRES

Muteness is conceived in the Middle Ages, in medical and nontechnical writing alike, as stemming most commonly from an absence or deficiency of the tongue.[15] Not only do tales of the healing of muteness involve a physical healing of the tongue, but they also shed new light on debates about the "mother tongue": whether speech is innate or learned, whether the formerly mute *miraculé* will acquire the language of his own mother or that of the Mother of God, and what it is that miracles cannot do when they confront the limits of human physiology or culture.

These are especially salient questions with regard to mute children. Children constitute a significant proportion of *miraculés* in general, and of deaf and mute healing recipients in particular: they represent 50 percent of mutes and 60 percent of deaf-mutes in the miracle corpora examined by Pierre-André Sigal.[16] Most of these *miraculés* never had the chance to learn to speak properly—they were never socialized into spoken language—so when they are miraculously granted the ability to speak, their new vocal production tests the boundaries of nature, culture, and miracle. In this chapter I will consider these questions with a particular focus on two stories: one from Jean le Marchant's *Miracles de Notre-Dame de Chartres*, the other from Guillaume de Saint-Pathus's *Miracles de saint Louis*. In these, the physiology of speech is tied to questions of family and community (re)integration, as different forms of communication—gesture, signs, dialects, and "bon françoys"—speak volumes about the ineffability of faith and miracle.

These problems come to the fore at the very beginning of a significant collection of vernacular miracle narratives in French: Jean le Marchant's *Miracles de Notre-Dame de Chartres*, completed in 1262. The vernacular verse adaptation of a Latin text composed some fifty years earlier, this collection focuses on miracles that occurred while Chartres Cathedral was being rebuilt following the fire of 1194.[17] The fourth chapter in Jean le Marchant's collection—and the second in his Latin source—relates the first miracle story, "De l'enfant a cui Nostre Dame rendi la parole et la langue" (Of the child to whom Our Lady restored speech and tongue).[18] This is the tale of "uns enfans de petit aage" (a child of a young age; p. 79, l. 2) who witnesses the dalliance of a knight and a young woman. For fear of their affair's being discovered, the knight, at his lover's behest, cuts out the child's tongue. The child comes to Chartres, where he lives as a beggar. On Easter he prays to the Virgin and she restores his ability to speak, though without restoring his tongue; then, on Pentecost, she endows him with a new tongue. As Our Lady goes on to perform further miracles, Chartres becomes an ever more important pilgrimage site.

The story is propelled by age expectations, and in this case, expectations of typical child speech. The child is talkative precisely because he is so young:

Parliers et enjoëz estoit,
Si com l'aage l'aportoit;
Ce que voyeit ne savoit taire:
Ce pöeit a pluseur despleire. (p. 79, ll. 3–6)

He was talkative and lighthearted,
As his age made him to be;
He did not know how to keep quiet about what he saw:
This could upset many people.

The child is, in other words, a "jangleeur" (as he is repeatedly called).[19] Though he does not talk about the sexual activity he has witnessed, the prospect that he will do so is threat enough. The risk stems from an ability not just to speak but to narrate: a social capacity, learned through interactions with caregivers, that underlines the boy's personhood.[20] Like the "enfes mout medisans" (bad-mouthing child) in the fabliau *Celui qui bota la pierre*, this "janglieres mesdisans" (bad-mouthing chatterbox; p. 80, l. 37) has witnessed an illicit encounter: but despite the fabliau-like setup, Jean le Marchant's narrative veers toward the tragic before ending in redemption.[21] Unlike the speaking toddlers of chapter 4, Guillot ultimately affirms not the sexual activity of a human mother—Guillot appears to have no mother— but rather, the miraculous power of the Virgin.

If his boyish loquacity is what singles out the future *miraculé* for mutilation, another typical childhood characteristic ensures the knight's success: the boy is so "geune et nice" (young and foolish; p. 80, l. 50) that he follows his attacker to an isolated location. Thus, it is because of his childlike innocence that he can be made unchildishly silent, "Que jamés parler ne peüst / Si de Dieu vertu n'i eüst" (Such that he could never speak unless he gained that power from God; p. 80, ll. 63–64). Once "amuï" (rendered mute; 81, l. 71), he goes straight to Chartres and thenceforth is not treated like a child at all: his muteness arouses the townspeople's curiosity, but not any particular forms of care. Nor does the boy behave like a child: formerly "enjoëz" (lighthearted), he is now "de corrouz plein" (full of anger) as he goes "d(e)'huis en huis querant son pain / Comme povre et comme orphelin" (from door to door, begging for his bread as a poor orphan; p. 81, ll. 73–75).

His behaving "comme orphelin" highlights the social dislocation that was already implicit in the child's backstory. The child's family is never mentioned at all; he witnesses the hanky-panky in "l'outel ou l'enfant ert" (the house where the child was; p. 79, l. 8), but there is no allusion to the child's own home; the only character with a family is the young woman, the daughter of the lord of the manor (p. 79, l. 12). Indeed, the young woman fears two things: "Son pere qui crüel estoit / Et l'enfant qui ert jangleeur" (Her father, who was cruel, and the child, who was a chatterbox; p. 80, ll. 29–31). The boy's pairing with the father as twinned sources of fear brings the child into this unhappy family circle while also establishing him as a disruptive outsider and an antagonist. Despite his "petit aage," this boy does not elicit caring impulses.

Though it lacks a mother-child pair—a relationship many of the *Miracles de Notre Dame de Chartres* do feature[22]—this initial miracle packs an emotional punch. The utter motherlessness of the child enhances the pathos and the miraculousness of the Mother of God's re-formation of the child's body. Though he is not "reborn" through the Virgin the way certain of Gautier de Coinci's child *miraculés* are,[23] this is nonetheless a story in which the generation of a child's flesh is linked to the "woman's work" of teaching the "mother tongue." In this interpretation I differ from Didier Lett, who uses the lack of family ties as evidence for reading the child as noncorporeal.[24] On the contrary, this is a story that consistently draws its audience's attention to the corporeality of everyday communication. Throughout the tale, the young *miraculé* makes his body speak. First, and most literally:

> Mes de sa langue ot retenu
> La partie qui fu trenchiee,
> Qu'il moult avoit bien estoiee;
> A cels la monstreit en espiart
> Qui demandoient dom il iart
> Et comment il estoit müet. (p. 81, ll. 80–85)

> But of his tongue he had held onto
> The part that was cut off,
> Which he had brought along;
> He showed it openly to those
> Who asked him where he was from
> And how he had come to be mute.

Agata Sobczyk has argued convincingly that the eighth panel of the *Miracles de Notre-Dame* window at Chartres Cathedral depicts this miracle, and that the object represented in the child's hand in that window is his severed tongue.[25] If so, this iconographic choice highlights that the tongue serves not just as an object or attribute, but as a signifier that can still "speak for itself" even when separated from the rest of the body.

Later, as is conventional in narratives of miraculous healings of mute people, the boy's body speaks in another way: as he silently prays, his body language reflects the inner state of his soul:

Devant l'autel s'egenoilla,
De lermes sa face moilla;
Dou cuer avoit contrictïon
Et en orer devocïon (p. 81, ll. 99–102)

Before the altar he kneeled,
His face wetted with tears;
In his heart he had contrition
And in his prayer, devotion

This poses the important question of the efficacy of unspoken and unheard prayer, for, as Lett points out, in this period prayer is generally held to be a necessarily *spoken* activity.[26] Guillot's prayer is instead inscribed in his body but decoupled from speech—just as, in this story, the progressive nature of the miracle will ultimately distinguish the act of speech from the body that performs it.

The decoupling of speech from the body is already implied in the title rubric "De l'enfant a cui Nostre Dame rendi la parole et la langue" (Our Lady restores the child's speech *and* his tongue). The same is underlined again at the moment of disabling: "La parole ot einsint perdue / Li enfent et la langue mue" (Thus the child had lost speech and had a mute tongue; p. 81, ll. 69–70). The ability is lost when the body is muted, but tongue and speech are not one and the same. Lest the distinction wasn't clear enough, the child's *parole* and *langue* are restored months apart—and the word returns *before* the flesh.

The boy regains the power of speech on Easter, when he prays devoutly. Others, pilgrims and locals alike, hear him praying, and these witnesses confirm that the boy's speech cannot be a trick (ll. 117–22)—even though he continues to lack a tongue. Our Lady decides to restore the physiological basis of speech only on Pentecost, the day God made the apostles'"langues renouvelees [. . .] parler en noveax langages" (renewed tongues [. . .] speak in new languages; p. 83, ll. 166–67). At this time his tongue"rentheringnee / Fu de char novelle et entiere" (was restored with new, intact flesh; p. 84, ll. 176–77). While Lett has read the Easter-Pentecost calendar as indicative of this story's symbolic resonances,[27] it is also important to think about what is ostensibly happening in and to the boy's body. The first phase of healing is explicitly described as"contre reison et contre droit" (against reason and against right; p. 83, l. 148), so much so that it can only be captured with a counterfactual: the boy speaks *as if he had a tongue*:

> Ce fut oeuvre contre nature
> Et vertu, c'est verité pure,
> Qu'i parla ausint droitement
> Com s'eut entier son estrument. (p. 82, 113–16)

> It was a work against nature
> And against bodily ability, it is the pure truth,
> That he spoke so correctly
> As if he had his whole instrument [i.e., his tongue].

The repeated emphasis on the first phase of the miracle as contrary to nature, reason, and the physiology of speech is a reminder of this tale's fundamental divide between language and speech; it draws the reader into the circle of astonished witnesses so that they might share in the public consensus on the child's miraculous speech. But it also underlines that what makes this miracle especially marvelous is the way it has unyoked ability from anatomy, thus upending the stories we tell about the way bodies are supposed to work.

Taking place early in the cathedral's rebuilding and featuring a child who miraculously talks and thus gives others something to talk about, this miracle plays an especially important role in the propagation of the *Miracles de Notre-Dame de Chartres*, as word of mouth is crucial to the emerging prestige of Chartres as a pilgrimage site.[28] The vernacular retelling also allows the *miraculé's* fuller emergence as a speaking subject. The child with no apparent mother and with no tongue acquires a tongue from the Mother of God; and it is in the vernacular version of his story, not the Latin one, that he acquires a name:

> En livre ne truis pas son non,
> Mes j'oï dire a tel qui l'ot
> Veü, qu'il avoit non Guillot;
> A tous reconta s'aventure
> Si comme el est en escripture. (p. 84, ll. 196–200)

> In [the] book I do not find his name,
> But I heard it said by one who had
> Seen him, that he was named Guillot.
> He recounted his adventure to all
> Just as it appears in writing.

Remarkably, at this moment in the written French translation of a written Latin account, the spoken word takes priority. Writing a half century after the events, Jean le Marchant still has access to oral channels of knowledge about the *miraculé*, and these provide him with information unavailable in writing; even the supposedly authoritative Latin text offers only an incomplete echo of the original tale as recounted by the protagonist himself. Yet this alternate vernacular authority does not extend directly to the *miraculé* himself: whereas Guillot has regained the power of speech, his words are reported only indirectly, and the supplemental vernacular details of the story are furnished instead by an eyewitness.

Guillot's story is followed by an allusion to a string of other miracles. Word of them spreads far and wide (ll. 223–26), prompting throngs to come bearing offerings that support the rebuilding of the cathedral. The narrative draws a direct line from the miracle to the shrine's growing fame to the rebuilding of the cathedral to the confirmation of faith through the eyewitnessing of miracles—and it all begins not just with Guillot's story, but with Guillot's telling of his own story ("A tous reconta s'aventure"). The knight cut out Guillot's tongue so that the boy could never speak, but the knight and his lover soon disappear from the narrative, while Guillot's capacity to narrate remains intact—and it is Guillot's tongue that brings the faithful to Chartres to witness new miracles.

Guillot's miraculous ability to speak, regained before he reacquires the requisite bodily structure, would seem to mirror and amplify the marvelous dimensions of the infant speech examined in previous chapters. In many respects, his story encapsulates the mute child's potential as an embodiment of infants' linguistic alterity, differing from other infants only in physical size and degree of dependency. Guillot displays qualities that will recur in other miracle narratives of the same type: the child lacks a mother, but his story privileges the mother tongue; his nonverbal prayer is heartfelt and therefore efficacious; his muteness is an obstacle to truth-telling (i.e., conveying knowledge), but a miraculous intervention enables a return to full linguistic capacity. And yet, his is ultimately a story that does not trouble the apparent linearity of human development, nor does it disrupt any cultural script according to which "disabled people long for a lost whole, pre-illness, pre-disability body."[29] This is a child who is sent to infancy and back again, dipping into and out of crip time without disrupting normate temporality. Other mute *miraculés*, however, pose a more significant challenge to the kinds of knowledge that infant voices can construct and convey and, indeed, to the epistemic status of infancy itself.

RESTORATION AND ACCULTURATION

As Guillot's story makes clear, the importance of speech to the propagation of miracle tales and miracle shrines' reputations, in combination with the high emotional charge of child *miraculés*, makes the otherwise invisible condition of childhood muteness highly visible in miracle collections. This condition, in turn, brings to light further questions about disability and the acquisition of language. Some of the mute children healed in medieval narratives, like Guillot, are able to hear and have already been acculturated into spoken language either as speakers or as listeners. Others, however, are congenitally deaf and mute: a category of person typically held by medieval writers to be unteachable and/or mentally deficient.[30] In miracle accounts, mute children display a range of different abilities in the wake of their healings. Sometimes the cognitive process of language acquisition can occur simultaneously with the anatomical restoration of the tongue (or even prior to it, as in Guillot's case); but sometimes speech-restoring miracles are progressive, as the miraculous physiological cure must be followed by the hard work of language teaching and learning.

Immediate language acquisition, such as that experienced by Guillot, is the most typical outcome, and the outcome most analogous to the sort of instantaneous healing that occurs in accounts of the miraculous cures of other conditions. Jenni Kuuliala, for instance, explicitly compares mute people who immediately regain the power of speech to paralytics who immediately get up and walk, showing no signs of the muscle degeneration that might be expected to have occurred during a long period of immobility.[31] These are the stories that perhaps hew closest to modern readers' expectations of a miracle tale. For instance, Abbot Suger of Saint-Denis reports in his mid-twelfth-century *Gesta Suggerii abbatis* that a twelve-year-old girl named Lancendis, who had never spoken, went to a holy place with a charitable lady and there had a vision of a heavenly queen. The queen called her by name and the girl replied, with a voice that was clear but had evidently not been exercised before ("audiente tam prefata matrona quam aliis multis, clara voce, lingua inusitata, 'Domina' respondit"). From then on she spoke as if she had always done so—she experienced no learning curve at all ("Nec deinceps minus loqui aut scivit aut potuit quam si toto tempore vitae suae locuta fuisset").[32] Language acquisition is also instantaneous in a miracle of Saint Josse recounted by Jean Miélot.[33] Miélot's fifteenth-century *Vie et miracles de saint Josse* is a prose narrative preceded by

a verse summary of unknown authorship.[34] The verse outlines the
story as follows:

> En Engleterre ung enfant y avoit
> Né sans langue, fors que ung noiel n'avoit.
> Quatorze ans eut. Saint Josse vint aourer,
> Et bon piccard le saint le fist parler.[35]

> In England there was a child
> Born without a tongue, he had nothing but a nub.
> He was fourteen. He came to pray to Saint Josse,
> And the saint made him speak good Picard.

The English boy gains the ability to speak for the first time, but
not in English, the language he would presumably have heard in
his home community; instead, he acquires the saint's tongue, or the
tongue of the community surrounding the shrine—the author's own
language.[36]

Miélot's prose omits the mention of the child's nationality; it does
retain the attention to the language the *miraculé* was able to speak,
but this has become French, not Picard. Miélot reports that the child
was "né du ventre de sa mere sans langue" (born from his mother's
womb without a tongue; p. 71)—but since the child's nationality is
not revealed, we know only that he came from his mother tongue-
less, without knowing what his mother tongue ought to have been.
The youth prays, and like Guillot, he manages to display his sincerity without language: he "fist ses pryeres et oroisons plaines de pleurs
et cryoit feablement en son cuer" (made his prayers and orisons full
of tears, and cried out sincerely in his heart) and "il besguoit en la
bouche pour la nouvelle parfection de ce noble instrument que luy
failloit" (he stammered with his mouth, [asking] for the new completion of that noble instrument he lacked; p. 71). When he miraculously speaks, he does so "non mie angelicquement mais en bon
françois" (not at all angelically, but in good French; p. 71). The language he acquires is emphatically not divine but human—and it
is neither that of the Angles nor that of the angels, but that of the

country in which he gained the ability to speak. The *miraculé*'s acquisition of language occurs out of time and out of place.

Not all mute *miraculés* are immediately able to speak perfectly, be it the local vernacular or any other language; sometimes they initially struggle to articulate (like Lancendis), and sometimes, regardless of their age at the time of the miracle, they must learn language as a very young child does. At times both models, instantaneous fluency and gradual learning, appear side by side in the same saint's miracles. Such is notably the case in book 6 of William of Canterbury's miracles of Thomas Becket, composed in the 1170s.[37] Unlike his fellow hagiographer Benedict of Peterborough, William of Canterbury groups his miracles thematically rather than chronologically[38] — which yields a fascinating cluster of mute and speech-impaired *miraculés*. Miracles 115, 116, and 117 tell of three mute youths: the former two are French and without a family, while the third is a young Norman noble who has been deprived of his rightful property owing to his inability to speak.[39] The third mute *miraculé*, Henri, is something of an outlier, both because of his socioeconomic status and because of the stylistic peculiarity of his miracle narrative, which is written in a more elevated register and is addressed to the *miraculé*, in the second person.[40] I will set Henri's story aside for now and proceed to a comparison of the first two youths, which will highlight some of the larger questions at stake in the details of how *miraculés* are endowed with the faculty of speech.

Miracle 115 concerns Garin, a deaf and mute adolescent from the Maine region of western France, who makes the pilgrimage to Canterbury with other people from his village ("cum convicaneis suis"; p. 505). Like the boy visitor to the shrine of Saint Josse, he has been in this state "ab utero matris" (from his mother's womb; p. 505); like Guillot's, his healing is progressive. He first gains the capacity to hear ("ante paucos dies auditu recepto"; p. 505), at which point he finds himself in an intermediate state, neither fully disabled nor fully able-bodied ("nec aeger ex toto nec valens erat"; p. 505). Soon afterward, when Garin cries out the name of someone he has seen in a dream, he is stunned to hear himself speaking readily ("stupens interrogabat utrum loquendi facultatem recipisset, audiensque quia loqueretur

expedite"; p. 506). What he speaks is his "lingua materna" (p. 506)—
which he has only just begun to hear, surrounded by neighbors but
far from his mother and his home.[41]

The next miracle tells of an adolescent from Provins in the Île-
de-France, who was also congenitally deaf and mute; even after the
saint has corrected his lingual impediment ("vinculam linguae sol-
vit"; p. 506), this *miraculé* cannot immediately speak:[42]

> Nam cum possibilitate loquendi etiam actum loquendi non acceperat,
> sed erat rudis, nescius linguae quam non audierat, et tanquam bimus
> aut trimus prima rudimenta docendus infantiae. (p. 506)

> With the possibility of speech he had not also received the act of
> speech, but he was uneducated, not knowing a language that he had
> not heard, and he will have to be taught, as the first rudiments of lan-
> guage are taught to a two- or three-year-old child.

The saint has resolved the physiological impairment but has not
compensated for the youth's lack of previous sensory experience. The
miracle has thus altered his physical condition without addressing its
cognitive effects. The resultant noncorrespondence of chronological
age and speaking ability will have to be remedied through human
pedagogy—with the noteworthy irruption of the future into the
series of miracles otherwise narrated in past tenses.

The pairing of these consecutive miracles of Thomas Becket
shows the extent to which the recovery of hearing and speech, perhaps more than other types of miracle healings, must be supple-
mented by an engaged community network. Neighbors will be
called upon to help the formerly mute boys through different kinds
of developmental do-over: a resocialization in the former case, and
a return to toddler language acquisition in the latter. The story of
Garin from Maine focuses on who *hears* the boy's miraculous speech.
As for the unnamed boy from Provins, his story directs the reader's attention to what will follow the miracle: intensive work on the
part of the *miraculé* as well as the unidentified people who will teach
him how to speak. In both cases, special consideration is given to

the maternal language despite the absence of a mother from each story. Garin speaks his *lingua materna* following only a brief period of language exposure, during which he remained suspended between disability and ability; the other boy has never been exposed to language and therefore cannot talk—is this why he has no name?—but he will have to learn as toddlers do. And toddlers, as we recall, are expected to learn language from their mother.

In both cases, the *miraculé* requires the support of a newly expanded language community to supplement the miraculous intervention. Learning through the forging of social bonds is not a part of the miracle proper, but it is a necessary follow-up, without which the miraculous endowment of physical ability cannot be enacted. The supplemental function of language-learning, whether it occurs in a brief interval or as a longer process, disrupts the temporality of miracle. Successful healing miracles ostensibly consist of a straightforward "before" and "after," but for a previously mute person who still needs to be taught language, the "after" remains a time of major change, still situated before the language acquisition required for full social reintegration; it is an experience of time without the words to express time. "Incomplete" miracles such as these—incomplete because they require a social supplement, not because they have failed—occupy a time frame between the "epiphanic moment" of miracle and the "chronicity" of rehabilitation.[43] As such, they are a useful tool with which to reconsider the disability studies concept of "curative time," that is, the controlling narrative of progress through cure, which has the effect of eliding a disabled subject's present between a "healthier" past and a projected post-cure future.[44] The stories of Garin and of the youth from Provins show that, as Eunjung Kim has argued with respect to a very different geohistorical context, disability temporalities admit a space between future and past where "cure and disability coexist as a process."[45] Unlike the "temporal folding" Kim posits as a variant on "curative time," however—in which the present tends to disappear beneath an encroaching normative past and future—the "incomplete" cures of deaf and mute youths gather past developmental states and future proficiencies into an ongoing, richly textured present. When a *miraculé* like the adolescent from Provins is restored to the condition of a hearing but prelingual child, he partially returns to the dependency of a two- or three-year-old, occupying a position out of sync with his calendar age. Far from representing a memory of a normative past, this infantile state is a progressive present incorporating the receptivity of early childhood—and an acknowledgment of the infantile alterity that remains present within us as we grow. These observations about the temporalities of pedagogy, miracle, and community support are further amplified in the story of the best-known deaf and mute *miraculé* of the Middle Ages: a youth known to us only as Loÿs.

RESTORING LOÿS

Around 1257 a deaf and mute eight-year-old boy was abandoned at the castle of Orgelet, northeast of Lyon, having been led there by a child slightly bigger than he ("un jovencel un pou greigneur que li diz Loÿs l'amena a Orgelet et le lessa ilecques"; p. 50).[46] The child stayed at Orgelet for twelve years, first with someone named Aymon, then in the home of the smith Gauchier, to whom he served as an assistant. He was considered by all in the castle to be genuinely mute and deaf ("il estoit tenu pour sourt et muet communement, et estoit pour tel tenu en tout le dit chastel"; p. 51)—a conclusion they reached following a series of harsh physical tests.[47] He later served the Countess of Auxerre in Lyon. Unhappy at not being supplied with new footwear by his employer, he began to follow the cortege of Philippe III, who was then passing through Lyon as he accompanied Louis IX's bones from Tunis to Saint-Denis. At Saint-Denis the youth imitated the motions of other people who were praying and suddenly regained his hearing. He fled the basilica for fear of the unfamiliar noises, ultimately making his way back to Orgelet, where he was taught how to speak and given the name Loÿs.

There are a great many written versions of this story. The above summary is derived from the story's fullest telling: that of Guillaume de Saint-Pathus, a Franciscan who served as confessor to Louis IX's widow Marguerite of Provence and to Louis's and Marguerite's daughter Blanche, for whom he wrote the *Vie et miracles de saint Louis* in 1302–3.[48] The text survives in a famous illustrated manuscript from the 1330s (BnF fr. 5716).[49] The *miracles* section is a narrativization of inquest transcripts from the king's canonization proceedings of 1282–83, offering a tantalizing trace of the otherwise lost testimonies.

The story of Loÿs, in particular, has attracted much critical attention in the last decade. For Sharon Farmer, it offers "an insider's view of what it was like to be deaf";[50] for Irina Metzler, it serves as a caution against reading miracle tales as transparent sources of information about disabled people's lived reality, rather than as carefully constructed texts shaped by "hagiographic and legalistic conventions";[51] for Jenni Kuuliala, it documents a disabled child's socialization and integration in a household.[52] Building on these previous readings, I aim to focus specifically on the evidentiary and epistemic problems this tale raises, examining how the *miraculé*'s presumably congenital muteness crystallizes the tale's more general problematization of knowledge. What did the *miraculé* know at the time of the miracle? What has he learned since the miracle? What can the investigators learn from his and other witnesses' testimony? Which elements of the story can never be established as fact? Within the inquisitorial framework, the story's subtle undermining of received ideas about muteness, pedagogy, and age yields a unique view of language learning as an embodied social process, and of spoken testimony as an inadequate instrument with which to convey miraculous truths.

Miracle narratives, as noted above with respect to the *Miracles de Notre Dame de Chartres*, contribute to a process that occurs largely by word of mouth: the propagation of a saint's legend and the building of public consensus as to the miracle worker's sanctity.[53] The emergence of such consensus typically occurs independently of any written text, as Thomas J. Heffernan argues.[54] The cult of Saint Louis, however, emerged with an abundance of texts: biographies of the king by those who knew him, as well as miracle collections, composed in service of the push for rapid canonization. Across the various written versions of Loÿs's story, we witness a process of textualization as word of the miracle spreads, weaving together evidence from the distant past (when Loÿs was mute) and more recent events (as a result of which Loÿs can now testify). Guillaume de Saint-Pathus in particular blends the dual processes of popular consensus-building and official fact-finding into a single narrative, one that occasionally reveals traces of the collaborative process through which truth has been established. In the moments that betray the difficulty of this process, the problem of knowledge is written into the very grammar of the narrative.

As a youth who had been deaf and mute for as long as any miracle witness had known him—and possibly from birth[55]—Loÿs was (prior to his miracle) ignorant of even the most rudimentary linguistic, political, or religious structures. He did not know how to speak. He joined the royal funeral procession without knowing what the people he followed were doing:

> Adoncques il ne savoit que l'en fesoit. Ne ne vint pas la pour saint Loÿs ne pour devocion que il eust vers lui, ne pour ce que il eust esperance en riens du monde d'estre ilecques gueri ne delivré, car il ne connoissoit ne ne savoit riens de Dieu ne de ses sainz. (pp. 51–52, ll. 55–60)

> At that time he didn't know what they were doing. Nor did he go there because of Saint Louis or any devotion he might have had toward him, nor because he had any hope in the world of being healed or cured there, for he knew nothing of God or of his saints.

In this passage dense with negation and imperfect subjunctives, Loÿs denies either experiential ("ne connoissoit") or factual ("ne savoit") knowledge. The same phenomenon recurs in the enumeration of other things the still deaf and mute youth did not know prior to his miraculous cure. He follows the king and his entourage without knowing which one is the king ("ne ne savoit le quel estoit le roi ou les barons ne ne connoissoit plus l'un que l'autre"; p. 52, ll. 83–84). As a child in Gauchier's home he had gone to church because the rest of the household did, not out of any knowledge of what a church was ("non pas por ce que il seust qu'estoit eglise ne devocion"; p. 52, ll. 65–55), and he had prayed in imitation of the others, "non pas pour nule devocion" (not out of any devotion; p. 52, l. 69). In fact, he wasn't even aware that the other worshippers *did* know what they were doing: "ne ne savoit pas ne ne pensoit que les autres hommes seussent plus que il savoit" (nor did he know nor think that other people knew more than he knew; p. 52, ll. 70–72). Similarly, at Louis's tomb in the basilica of Saint-Denis, he prays "non pas par aucune devocion que il eust a ce ne par aucune entencion, fors por ce tant seulement que il veoit les autres einsi fere" (not out of any devotion he felt toward it [the tomb], nor with any intent, but simply because he saw the others doing so; p. 53, ll. 94–97). Despite his lack of intent, it is at this moment that he miraculously begins to hear.

Loÿs's mimicry of the gestures of prayer, divorced from any devotion or intention, has been one of the most commented elements of his story. Even more than the accounts of other mute children like Guillot, this story tests medieval ideas about the necessity of speech for the act of prayer. It is perhaps worth noting that Saint Louis's own prayer practices were regarded, in his time, as excessively gestural:[56] thus, though Loÿs is not able to pray "par bouche ou par panser" (with mouth or with thought)—as Saint Louis counseled his son to do in the *Enseignements à son fils*[57]—he does partially echo the characteristic behavior of the man for whom he will eventually be named. Loÿs's unintentional prayer has been read as evidence that in the late thirteenth century the gestures of prayer were highly prescribed,[58] or even that gestures could sometimes substitute for faith.[59] The mimicry of others' actions, without any understanding of the meaning that underlies those actions, can also be understood as characteristically childlike: not only is Loÿs incapable of articulating a verbal prayer—which makes him like an infant, as Maria Wittmer-Butsch and Constanze Rendtel point out[60]—but also, like a child playing dress-up, he is "trying on" behavior he has not yet grown into or even understood. Remaining in the infant stage of language development, Loÿs retains some of his universal alterity even as he goes through the motions of adult life.

The narrative continues to feature abundant negation to capture Loÿs's ignorance, even after his miracle. Loÿs feels intense fear and confusion as he first experiences everyday sounds:

Il aperçut la noise des hommes et le marcheis de ceus qui aloient et
qui se movoient et le son des cloches, et nonporquant il ne savoit que
tout ce estoit, ainçois fu si esbahi et si espoenté que il ne savoit que il
deust fere, et doutoit mout que les genz que il ooit parler ne li corus-
sent sus. (p. 53, ll. 97–102)

He heard the sound of the men, and the footsteps of those who were
walking and moving, and the sound of the bells. Yet he didn't know
what all that was, on the contrary he was so amazed and so frightened
that he didn't know what he should do, and he was very scared that
the people he heard talking might attack him.

He hears without understanding; his subsequent panicked flight
marks Loÿs's final "fall" into disability, a moment of public failure
that confirms his otherwise invisible infirmity.[61] Crucially, though,
this fall occurs *after* his physical impairment has been healed, in a
way that reflects the tricky temporality of proof in the canonization
trial. Loÿs's prior deafness makes its most directly observable impact
once he has begun to hear; likewise, a miracle can only begin to be
confirmed once the direct experience of a disability—the evidence
that would prove a miracle took place—has ceased.

Saint-Pathus goes on to explain that the youth's uncomprehend-
ing fear is not a sign of intellectual incapacity:

Mes il n'entendoit pas ne ne savoit jugier que c'estoit, que il n'avoit
onques mes riens oÿ. Ne il ne parloit pas, car il ne savoit parler ne ses
paroles former, et nonpourquant des cel tens eust il bien parlé se il fust
aucun qui li eust enseignié. (p. 53, ll. 114–18)

But he neither understood nor knew what it was, for he had never yet
heard anything. Nor did he speak, for he did not know how to speak
or to form his words; and nonetheless from that time on he could have
spoken well if there had been anyone who would have taught him.

The emphasis on the youth's ability to learn continues. Loÿs narrates facts of which he was unaware at the time being recounted,
but of which he has learned by the time of recounting. For example,

after receiving the miracle Loÿs follows a circuitous path from Paris to Lyon to Orgelet, even though there is a far more direct route ("tout soit ce qu'il ait entre Paris et Orgelet trop plus courte voie"; pp. 53–54, ll. 122–24). At that time Loÿs did not know any other way home—but *now*, at the time of testimony, Loÿs knows the more direct route ("la quele il set orendroit bien"; p. 54, l. 124). The narrative contains several different versions of Loÿs: a "before" and an "after," one deaf and mute, the other speaking and narrating, as well as the hearing but not speaking or understanding Loÿs in between. Only the last iteration is named, as is brought to the reader's attention from the very beginning: "Loÿs," as he is identified in the first word of the story, used to be "cil qui ore est apelé Loÿs" (he who is now named Loÿs; p. 50, l. 14).

The unnamed boy becomes Loÿs because he is able to learn; given the received ideas about the teachability of the deaf in this period, that doesn't go without saying. In fact, hints at his teachability are embedded in the story even before the account of the miracle. Just after the initial description of Loÿs's prayer made at Saint-Denis "por nule devocion," the narrative jumps back to the boy's time with Gauchier, the smith:

> Et nonporquant quant il estoit avecques le dit fevre et il fesoit aucune chose malvesement ou contre la volenté de son seigneur, que l'en li mostroit par signes, et il estoit por ce batu aucune foiz de son seigneur, il se gardoit une autre foiz de fere chose semblable. (p. 52, ll. 77–81)

> And nonetheless when he was with the aforementioned smith and he did something poorly or against his lord's desire, if they showed it to him by signs, and he was beaten for it a few times by his lord, he restrained himself from doing the like again.

As soon as we are informed that he prayed without understanding, it is specified that even before he could hear, Loÿs was capable of learning—when appropriately taught. This affirmation of the boy's intellect somewhat diffuses the discomfort occasioned by the inexplicable efficacy of his unintentional prayer.

The capacity to learn takes center stage in the final phase of Guillaume de Saint-Pathus's version of the story. When he first returns to Orgelet, Loÿs goes straight to Gauchier's house, where he uses gestures to indicate that he can now hear: "leur donna a entendre par les meilleurs signes que il leur sot mostrer que il ooit" (he made them understand, with the best signs he knew how to show them, that he could hear; p. 54, ll. 129–30). He must gesture because, though he is now physically capable of speech, no one has taught him language; and it is clear that the "signes" he uses do not rise to the level of language, for Loÿs is not able to remember or reenact them before the inquisitors ("ce ne sot il pas bien desploier ou recorder devant les inquisiteurs"; p. 54, ll. 131–21).

Once they have confirmed that the youth can now hear, the members of Gauchier's family begin teaching him to speak as one would teach an infant or train a bird:

> Le commencierent a enseignier ausi comme les enfanz sont enseigniez de leur premier aage, ou tout ausi comme l'en enseigneroit les oisiax, et disoient au dit Loÿs: "Di pain." Et il disoit: "Pain." Et si li disoient: "Di vin." Et il disoit: "Vin." Et tot ausi des autres moz que li enseignoient. (p. 54, ll. 136–42)

> They began to teach him just as children are taught in their first age [infancy], or just like birds would be taught, and they said to Louis: "Say bread." And he said: "Bread." And they said to him: "Say wine." And he said: "Wine." And just the same with the other words they taught him.

A few days later, the countess hears of the miracle and sends for Loÿs, placing him in her kitchens so that he will be immersed in conversation with more interlocutors ("ele le mist en sa cuisine, por ce que il fust avec pluseurs"; p. 54, l. 148). She also orders that he be taught to speak ("commanda que il fust enseignié a parler"; p. 54, l. 149). The kitchen workers carry out this task, not as one would do with an infant, but as one would do with a pupil in the second age of childhood (pueritia):

De quoi cil de la cuisine l'enseignierent en nommant li certaines choses chascun jour, et se il ne les seust nommer l'endemain, il estoit batu, ausi comme les enfanz sont batus as escoles quant il ne sevent leur leçons. (p. 54, ll. 149–53).

So the kitchen workers taught him by naming certain things to him each day, and if he did not know their names the next day he was beaten, just as children are beaten at school when they don't know their lessons.

Lastly, he is sent to learn the paternoster and the Ave Maria under the tutelage of the bailiff Jehan de Maynet; as proof of this learning, he recites those prayers before the inquisitors and their notaries, "ausi comme feist un autre lai homme" (just as any other layperson would; p. 55, ll. 160–61). The youth finally learns an even more fundamental lesson, namely his own origins: "entendi il du dit Gauchier et de sa femme et de sa mesniee que il l'avoient trouvé el dit chastel et en cel aage" (he heard from Gauchier and his wife and his household that they had found him at the castle and at what age; p. 55, ll. 163–65).

In the course of this education Loÿs proceeds rapidly from animality to *infantia* to *pueritia*; from behavioral training to immersion to corporal punishment; from an intimate home environment to a more school-like, quasi-institutional one. In a notable divergence from established practice, the youth learns his prayers from a man, rather than from his mother: this fact highlights the unusual age at which Loÿs (now a man and not a boy) is learning this lesson, but it also underscores his lack of a family and specifically of a mother. The youth's motherlessness distinguishes him from other youthful *miraculés* in the same collection: as Lorcin has observed, as in the *Miracles de Notre Dame de Chartres*, most of the children in the *Miracles de saint Louis* recounted by Saint-Pathus live in two-parent homes.[62] The lack of a family prevents the establishment of one key fact: whether Loÿs was congenitally deaf and mute, which is to say, whether he ever had a mother tongue at all.

Though Loÿs has no known biological family,[63] he does grow up in a household that socializes him, first into work and then into language. This socialization, however, occurs only after an abusive testing regime of loud noises and hot coals—one through which the people of Orgelet also socialize the boy into disability itself, thus building the consensus about his condition that will eventually constitute the essential proof of miracle.[64] But that proof of childhood deafness, like his socialization into language and religion, only comes long after the end of biological childhood.[65] And it is only after emerging from his extended infancy that the youth can learn, retrospectively, about his own past. Apparently nameless throughout his first stay at Orgelet and Lyon, he is now named, at Gauchier's suggestion. After he recovers *l'ouïe* he becomes Loÿs.[66]

The preoccupation with the limits of knowledge is not restricted to the time of Loÿs's deafness and muteness, nor to the deaf and mute subject: Guillaume de Saint-Pathus's text reveals deep anxieties about the knowledge of hearing people, too. This is a story that stages the epistemic uncertainties at play in this and other miracle stories, some related to the life and experiences of an apparently deaf and mute foundling, others related to the process of consensus-building and fact-finding that underlies the compilation of the dossier on which Saint-Pathus's narrative is based; all of these unknowables ultimately point toward the deep puzzle of evidence and faith. And while Loÿs's newfound ability to speak provides just as much evidence of a miracle as does the content of the story he tells, his untimely jump from an extended period of universal alterity to the full mastery of speech troubles the evidentiary value of experience.

The crisis of knowledge grows especially clear when it comes to proving the genuineness of the boy's invisible disability. At the time when he still appears to be deaf and mute, the people of Orgelet actively test his disability: making loud noises in his ear to see if he would react, throwing hot coals on his belly to see if he would cry out. These tests cannot produce an affirmative proof of disability, only a lack of evidence of ability. The testimony to Loÿs's former condition illustrates, in exaggerated form, a paradox of evidence:

> Et de tout le tens que il fu premierement trouvé ilecques et tout le tens que il i demora, il fesoit signes de sourt et de muet, et jusques au tens

que il revint de Saint Denis en France ou il disoit que il avoit recouvré
parole et oïe, ne en tout le tens devant, il ne pot onques estre aperceu
de nule persone par aucune maniere ou par aucun signe que il oïst
nule voiz ne nul son ne que il parlast. (p. 51, ll. 26–33)

And in all the time from when he was first found there and throughout all of the time when he stayed there, he made the signs of a deaf-
mute; and until the time when he came back from Saint Denis in the
Île-de-France, where he said he had recovered his speech and his hearing, and never in all the time before that, it could never be perceived
by anyone in any way or by any sign that he heard any voice or any
sound, nor that he spoke.

The only thing that can be established through direct observation is
that the boy made the same sorts of signs that deaf and mute people
make. The rest must be "proven" with nonobservation (he was never
perceived to do anything that would indicate he could hear or speak)
and with a grammatical shift from affirmation to hypernegation.
Absence of evidence does not constitute evidence of absence, as the
modern aphorism goes: but *ne, onques, nul,* and *aucun* are the only
words with which the witnesses can testify to the authenticity of
a no-longer-extant invisible disability.

Of course, this all occurs during a canonization inquiry, and
therefore these small evidentiary problems only serve to underscore a major one: how to prove that a candidate for sainthood
has worked a miracle. The unknowability of so much of Loÿs's
past poses a considerable challenge, as does the disruption of his
life cycle: the boy with no past, in many respects treated like a
mute beast, becomes a man who must still develop like a child.
The extent of the narrative disturbance that this disrupted life
cycle brings about becomes abundantly clear at the very end of the
story, when the underlying interrogation—mostly smoothed out of
the rest of the narration by Saint-Pathus, who has shown himself
more than capable of weaving multiple testimonies together into
a seamless narrative—erupts into the foreground. Here disability
troubles discursive structure, in an instance of the phenomenon

Ato Quayson calls "aesthetic nervousness."[67] We are explicitly told that the information given at the close of the narrative derives from Loÿs's own testimony: "le dit Loÿs fust enquis et demandé des diz inquisiteurs" (the aforementioned Loÿs was examined and asked by the aforementioned inquisitors; p. 55, ll. 167–68). Both of the questions to which Loÿs's responses are recorded *as responses* require Loÿs to discuss key moments of communication. First the inquisitors ask why he is called Loÿs, and he replies by describing a postmiracle conversation he had with Gauchier, and even citing Gauchier's words to him: "Je voil que tu soies apelé Loÿs a l'enneur de Loÿs le roi de France qui t'a delivré" (I want you to be named Louis in honor of Louis the king of France who has cured you; p. 55, ll. 171–73). Next the inquisitors ask if he believes it was through the prayers and the merits of the blessed Louis that he was healed, and he says yes; asked why he thinks he was healed despite his lack of devotion or even knowledge of God, Loÿs offers a remarkable response:

> Il respondi que il ne set nule autre cause de sa creance fors que tant que il avoit besoing de ce bienfet. De quoi il croit que pour sa miseri- corde le benoiet mon seigneur saint Loÿs proia Dieu por lui, et einsi reçut l'oïe, si comme il croit. (p. 55, ll. 179–83)

> He replied that he knows of no other reason for his belief [i.e., that Saint Louis brought about his cure] except that he had such great need of this beneficence. For which reason he believes that in his mercy my blessed lord Saint Louis prayed to God for him, and thus he received his hearing, so he believes.

When the youth was unable to pray, his future namesake must have done so on his behalf. In this testimony, Loÿs's initial (and grammati- cally negative) lack of knowledge ("ne set nule autre cause") gives way to an affirmation of belief ("si comme il croit"). Loÿs thereby moves the inquisition beyond any need for further "evidence of things not seen" (as Paul defines faith in Hebrews 11:1), giving the firmest proof yet of the efficacy of his linguistic and religious education. Even as the inquisitors question Loÿs, he uses his newfound voice to test the depth of their, and the reader's, faith.

THE MANY LIVES OF LOŸS

Loÿs's story occupies an important place even in the most stream-lined accounts of the miracles of Saint Louis, not only because it was one of the first to have occurred, but also, I contend, because of the way the deaf-mute's recovery dramatizes the miraculous as a multi-sensory experience. Shorter versions of the tale tend to gloss over some of the mysteries of Loÿs's origins and of his miracle; they also tend to endow him with immediate speech and, curiously, stream-line his generalized fear of ambient sounds into a specific terror of church bells. These patterns remain remarkably consistent across two hundred years' worth of narrative and theatrical retellings, with just two notable outliers: the prose narrative by Guillaume de Saint-Pathus, and the late fifteenth-century *Livre des faiz de monseigneur saint Loys*, with which I will conclude.

The earliest written account of Loÿs's miracle is to be found in Guillaume de Chartres's *Life and Miracles of Saint Louis*: the first col-lection of Louis IX's miracles, composed by the king's former chap-lain in the late 1270s.[68] This narrative, written in Latin, contains the germ of what will become the standard abbreviated account of this miracle. The *miraculé* is identified from the outset as "quidam ado-lescens circiter xxv annorum" (a young man aged about twenty-five), from Burgundy, who is "surdus et mutus a nativitate" (congenitally deaf and mute).[69] He uses signs to communicate with his family, and—in a significant departure from the testimony on which Guil-laume de Saint-Pathus will base his narrative—Guillaume de Char-tres states that when he left for Saint-Denis he knew exactly where he was going and why:

Non audiens nec loquens, sed solummodo signis utens, ita quod fere tota familia signa ejus noverat, et per signa suam voluntatem et motum animi tam ipse aliis, quam alii sibi totaliter ostendebant: com-perto per signa, quod apud sepulcrum gloriosi regis Franciae Ludovici

fiebant miracula, virtute operante divina, adjunxit se quibusdam pedi-
tibus venientibus Parisius.

> Not hearing or speaking, but only using signs, he could thus com-
> municate with signs the whole family recognized, and with signs [he
> could communicate] his will and the very movements of his soul to the
> others, such that they understood each other completely. It was ascer-
> tained through signs that at the tomb of the glorious king of France,
> Louis, miracles were taking place, performing divine works; he joined
> some people going to Paris on foot.

Guillaume de Chartres has exaggerated the communicative sophistication of Loÿs's sign system, an exaggeration that allows him to omit
the unsettling questions raised by the story of a *miraculé* unaware of
the very existence of saints or even of religious belief. In this version
the youth's prayer, too, is volitional: he prays "non oris, sed cordis, cum
gemitibus et suspiriis" (not with his mouth, but with his heart, with
groans and sighs). The miracle itself is characterized with the same
conventional language as that used by William of Canterbury with
regard to mute youths: "solutum est vinculum linguae ejus" (the chain
of his tongue is dissolved). The youth's speech is restored instantaneously, "non lingua materna, sed recte gallicana, ac si fuisset natus
in ipsa villa S. Dionysii et continue conversatus" (not the mother
tongue [dialect], but proper French, as if he had been born there in
Saint-Denis and had lived there ever since); the emphatic linkage of
language to place, along with an alternate and counterfactual origin
narrative (as if he had been born there), is notable. The instantaneous acquisition of French as spoken in the Île-de-France (rather
than in Loÿs's native Burgundy) will recur in most versions of the
miracle: Guillaume de Saint-Pathus's remarkable focus on language
socialization, apparently derived from witness testimony, is absent
from the "standard" version. Loÿs's voice does still come through in
Guillaume de Chartres's account, however, as his "proper French" is
not just described but reproduced as direct discourse. When one of
his companions asks if he knows his (the companion's) name, the
miraculé's reply is cited in the text "in gallico": "Vous aves non mes

amis. Quar daultre non ne sai-je riens" (you are named my friend, for I know nothing of any other name). Again, an awareness of a lack of names precedes the socializing interactions that will grant the once-mute *miraculé* access to fuller social personhood.

Even when language acquisition is instantaneous, there are limits to what the *miraculé* can know: in this case, while the sophistication of his signed language has perhaps enabled the smooth transfer of his prior knowledge to the spoken idiom, he does not know the names of those close to him. (No word here on whether he knows his own name, or even if he has one.) Nor does he understand the sources of everyday sounds. But while Saint-Pathus's longer narrative will enumerate many noises that frighten Loÿs, this account names only one: the sound of church bells, which, according to Guillaume de Chartres, the youth interprets as an indication that the building is about to collapse. He feels a "terror" not at a perceived human threat, but at an everyday sound; his ignorance of religion is transformed into a less troubling ignorance of the *sounds* of devotional practice.

The story of Loÿs remains well-known through the rest of the Middle Ages, if we are to judge by the sheer number of versions of the tale that have survived in written form. Even accounts of the life of Saint Louis that include just a handful of miracles almost always retain this particular miracle.[70] These include Primat de Saint Denis's chronicle, completed in 1274, a text known through Jean de Vignay's French translation;[71] the *Beati Ludovici vita* that Bernard Gui included in his *Sanctorale* (1329);[72] and some early print editions of the updated vernacular *Legenda aurea*.[73] Through these, the bones of the most widespread version of the story take shape: a narrative framework which will then be used, to comic effect, in the fifteenth-century *Mystère de saint Louis*.[74]

Not much is known about the *Mystère de saint Louis*, though the manuscript (BnF MS fr. 24331) bears a possessor's note of 1472 (old style), providing a firm *terminus ante quem*. A character clearly based on Loÿs is one of a few *miraculés* depicted at the end of the play. Just after the dead king's body has been deposited in the basilica, the prior of Saint-Denis sees a man (identified only as "Le muet," the mute) who appears out of place.

Que vient ce fol que voy ycy,
Qui regarde les gens aincy?
Est-il yvre ou hors du sens?
Il ne parle ne dit aux gens:
Fait-il le fol ou le lourt?
—Parlez, mon amy. Il est sourt,
Il n'ot goute: velà le point. (p. 391)

Why is this madman I see coming here,
Who is looking at people like that?
Is he drunk or out of his mind?
He neither speaks nor talks to anyone:
Is he mad or dim-witted?
—Speak, my friend. He is deaf,
He hears nothing: that's what it is.

The prior shows us how the deaf-mute is seen by others: he is visually distinctive owing to his abnormal interactions with others, not his physical appearance. A person possessed of an adult body but lacking normal language socialization is interpreted as mentally ill, intoxicated, or intellectually impaired. Or all at the same time: *fol, yvre et enfant.*

As the prior speaks these lines, the mute character evidently comes onstage and kneels, for again his actions are mirrored in the prior's remarks: "Que fait-il cy sy longue espace / Agenoillé en ceste place? / Il ne fait qu'empescher le lieu" (What is he doing here for so long, kneeling in this place? He's not doing anything but blocking the way; p. 392). In other words, the prior does not recognize the mute man's actions as prayer. Unlike the narrative by Guillaume de Chartres and the other brief miracle accounts written in its wake, this play shows a character casting doubt on whether the gestures of prayer are meaningful on their own.

In the play we never learn whether the mute man is genuinely praying "in his heart," but we see that his prayer is efficacious, for immediately after the prior complains that he is blocking the way, he begins to speak:

Très-glorieux amy de Dieu,
Je te mercy à jointes mains.
A! digne, precieux corps sains,
Humblement je te remercye:
Maintenant m'as rendu l'oye,
Et rendu la parole aussy
Et donné en ce lieu ycy.
Onques mais je n'avoye parlé. (p. 392)

Most glorious friend of God,
I thank you with clasped hands.
Ah! worthy, precious holy body,
Humbly I thank you:
Now you have restored my hearing
And restored my speech too
And given it to me in this place.
Never before had I spoken.

The statement that he has never spoken suggests a congenital
condition—as the *miraculé* confirms in his later speech, when he
swears, "Onques mais je n'avoye ouy, / Par ma foy! ne parlé aussy"
(Never had I heard, by my faith, nor spoken either) and calls himself "Sourt et muet tout de nature" (deaf and mute completely from
birth). The man later expresses gratitude for his newfound speech
and hearing, "ce que n'avoye eu en ma vie" (which I had not had in all
my life). The presence of the disability from birth is repeated multiple times, so that the audience cannot miss it. And once again,
though the *miraculé* is "né et natif [. . .] de Bourgogne" (a born native
of Burgundy; p. 392), he is speaking the French of the Île-de-France.
    The man's speech of thanksgiving continues, only to be inter-
rupted by the ringing of bells (indicated in the marginal note "on
sonne des cloches"; fol. 246v). The terror alluded to in the brief miracle narratives takes on a life of its own as the *miraculé* exclaims, "Hay!
qu'est-ce que j'oy marteller? / Onques mais ne fus à tels nopces"
(Yikes! what's that hammering I hear? I've never been at a party like
this; p. 392). A comic dialogue ensues:

LE PRIEUR
Qu'avez-vous, compains? Ce sont cloches.
Comment estes-vous esbay?
LE MUET
Cloches, cloches, cloches.
LE PRIEUR
     Oy,
N'en oys-tu onques parler?
LE MUET
Nennin. Qu'en fait-on?
LE PRIEUR
     Pour aler
Les gens tous lez jours à l'eglise.

THE PRIOR
What's wrong with you, pal? Those are bells.
Why are you astonished?
THE MUTE
Bells, bells, bells.
THE PRIOR
     Yes,
Haven't you heard tell of them?
THE MUTE
Not at all. What are they for?
THE PRIOR
     To get people going
To church every day.

The "dialogue de sourds" is amusing, but it is revealing, too. Church bells served as an important structuring element in medieval towns and cities, as Reinhard Strohm has shown,[75] and they "shaped the habitus of a community."[76] A failure to understand these signals is not just a misunderstanding, then, but a sign that one is out of sync with one's community. The reaction to "cloches, cloches, cloches" cements the *miraculé*'s status as an outsider, even after the miracle: what will make him whole again is not the bodily cure, but a

human-led process of acculturation. This is, however, an acculturation that cannot be carried out in quite the usual way, as Loÿs, like
the other mute people discussed in this chapter, must find a way
to synchronize with his community in the absence of the expected
agent of language socialization: his mother.

In a play like the *Mystère de saint Louis* the sound of the bell
would have provided the opportunity for a vivid stage effect, under-
lining that the theater is a multisensory phenomenon. This, plus
the theater's characteristic retelling of a story through dialogue—a
process inverse to Saint-Pathus's smoothing of multiple testimonies
into a single narrative voice—makes the story of Loÿs more *audible*.
Now, in the final adaptation I will discuss, the story is made *visually legible* through some remarkable representative strategies: most
notably, with a depiction of the *miraculé* as a much younger child.

MIRACLES PAR YSTOYRE

The *Livre des faiz monseigneur saint Loys* (BnF MS fr. 2829) is a
richly illustrated account of the life and miracles of Louis IX, commissioned by the Cardinal de Bourbon as a gift for an unidentified
duchess of Bourbon in the 1480s. In 1488 it came into the possession of Anne of France, and she presented it to her teenaged brother,
Charles VIII, for whom she was serving as regent. The book has
attracted limited attention from modern scholars.[77] It has been cited
primarily for its ownership history and for its beautiful illumina-
tions, but not for its text, whose author, like the artists, remains
anonymous.[78] But the *Livre des faiz monseigneur saint Loys* is far
more than an exquisite object: it is noteworthy for the conception
of its historiographic project, and especially for the role the images
play in that project. The *Livre des faiz* translates Guillaume de Saint-
Pathus's early fourteenth-century account of the life and miracles of
Louis IX into a modern linguistic *and visual* idiom. The complex-
ity increases in the latter half of the book, which presents a series
of *miracles par ystoyre* (miracles in images). Here the creators of the
book experiment overtly with multiple narrative and representational modes, creating a multimedia object.

In the book's prologue, the unknown author situates himself in a long line of "historiographes" whose writing has preserved memory of great men of the past (fol. 3va).[79] The writer defines his project as an effort to

> vaquier et recueillir les faiz de mon dit seigneur saint Loys pour les envoier a maditte dame pour sa consolation. Je me suis aucunement occuppé a extraire par l'aide et grace de dieu ce que a fait ycelui glorieux saint en sa vie et aucuns miracles apres la mort et l'ay en ce present livre ordonné et composé en xlii chappitres reiectees le plus que j'ay peu toutes choses superflues. (fol. 5r)

> rework and collect the deeds of my aforementioned lord Saint Louis in order to send them to my aforementioned lady, for her consolation. I have spent some time extracting, with God's grace and aid, that which that glorious saint did during his life, and some miracles after his death. I have ordered and composed it in forty-two chapters in this book, rejecting, as much as I could, all superfluous things.

The process of revision, composition, and rejection of the superfluous consists of streamlining the text and accompanying it with a rich iconographic program; together, the simplified text and the elaborate images will tell the saint's story to everyone "qui verront ou lyront" (who will see or read [the book]; fol. 5rb). *Histoire* as historiography and *histoire* as image cooperate throughout the book, but the transition from the life to the miracles marks a very visible shift from text-based to image-based storytelling, as the miracle narratives are vastly more condensed than the biography and are fitted into small decorative spaces framed by complex multipart illustrations that depict both the miracles and the testimonies confirming them (fig. 5.1). In this way, both the miracles and their recording are reinterpreted as visual phenomena. Offering a historiated yet nonhistorical resequencing of miraculous events, the *miracles par ystoyre* proffer a complex visualization of the temporal disruption effected by miracle.[80]

The *miracles par ystoyre* format enables the placement of multiple

FIGURE 5.1 "Le premier miracle par ystoyre" (ca. 1480–88).
From *Livre des faiz monseigneur saint Loys* (BnF MS fr. 2829, fol. 83v).
Photograph: Bibliothèque nationale de France.

time frames in relation to one another. The before-and-after of the miracle itself, as well as the moments of testimony and investigation, converge to form a richly layered framework within which the modern text is set. In the specific case of Loÿs, the format gives rise to a set of representational choices that cast new light on the story's configurations of muteness, nonverbal communication, and language socialization. The story is reduced and altered in ways that will make the miracle more visible, more legible as image. The text mentions the healed youth's "good French" and his panicked reaction to the pealing of bells, as do other condensed versions; but the images literally and metaphorically reframe the story within a master narrative about child disability, representing Loÿs as a young boy and integrating him in a family unit.[81]

The choice to represent Loÿs as a child seeks to conform Loÿs's experience to normative developmental and familial models—and yet, this reorientation ends up introducing new temporal wrinkles. I therefore find it helpful to read the visual retelling of Loÿs's story in light of theorizations of the particular configurations of temporality, disabled embodiment, and power structures that contemporary disability studies scholars have dubbed "crip time."[82] People with impaired mobility often require more time to get from place to place; people with intellectual or cognitive impairments may not keep pace in some kinds of social interactions; people with impaired speech may communicate at a tempo out of sync with "clock time."[83] Accounting for these and other embodied temporalities, disability activists have claimed crip time as a way of expressing a disabled subject's reorientation toward time. In the case of Loÿs, the concept of crip time can help grasp the complex ways that the miraculé's depiction as a child further complicates the temporal dislocations already effected in Saint-Pathus's version of the story.

The *Livre des faiz* alters Loÿs's story in both image and text, but not in precisely the same manner. Since the image clearly takes priority over the text, I will begin my analysis with the visual narrative of the *ystoyre* (fig. 5.2). The miracle story is told in two registers, each divided into multiple scenes and read from left to right. At the top left, a boy enters the basilica of Saint-Denis. At the top right, the boy

FIGURE 5.2 "Autre miracle" (ca. 1480–88). From *Livre
des faiz monseigneur saint Loys* (BnF MS fr. 2829, fol. 84r).
Photograph: Bibliothèque nationale de France.

prays atop the saint's shrine; just below the scene of prayer, but still in the upper register, the boy communicates with the adult couple who accompanied him into the basilica, as a group of both monastic and lay witnesses looks on. In the bottom register, at left, the boy bursts outdoors ahead of the adult couple, his mouth open and his arms raised in panic. He runs up the street, seemingly assailed by diagonal lines (away from which he turns his head, and toward whose apparent source he points). Finally, back in an interior space, the woman points to a bell inscribed with the Ave Maria: she reaches out to the still apprehensive-looking child as the man speaks to him.

Together these images tell a story of communication within a nurturing family. As the boy enters the basilica, he turns his head toward the adults who accompany him, including a woman whose hands rest protectively on his shoulders; his hand gestures are perhaps his "sign" that he wishes to pray at the royal tomb. At the far right, the boy communicates more directly with the adult couple who accompany him. The timing of this scene relative to the prayer is not altogether clear. Given the adults' prayerful gestures and the evident interest of the onlookers, this scene is probably meant to depict the boy's first speech after the miracle; but it is not impossible that this scene could take place before the prayer, showing the boy expressing his desire to pray—in which case it would constitute a very early attempt to represent signed communication. Either way, this scene makes a spectacle of intimate but witnessed conversation. In the lower register, the boy breaks away from his parents and runs alone but is ultimately brought back into the family fold as both parents speak to him, his father with a verbal explanation and his mother with gesture. The boy's separation from his family is brief, and their reunion is achieved through teaching. Reinstated into normate "teleologies of living,"[84] Loÿs has become the able-bodied Child to whom parents can pass knowledge or other legacies.[85]

Given the author's stated goal of "eliminating the superfluous," it is worth noting all that has been eliminated from the visual story. Gone is any hint of the youth's experiences prior to his arrival in Saint-Denis: his abandonment, the childhood tests of his impairment, the state of ignorance in which he arrived at the shrine. Gone, too, are the slow processes of language-learning and socialization. Instead, the key elements of this story are the youth of the *miraculé*, the instantaneity of the miracle (as proven by the reaction to the bells), and the rapid reintegration into the social unit. Indeed, the process of reintegration is a primary compositional focus. Each of the two registers shows the boy three times: first in the company of his parents (with his face turned toward them), then alone, then communicating with his parents. This symmetrical structure dramatizes the miracle as a solitary experience punctuating a transition between two distinctive kinds of social belonging (first as a disabled person, then as an able-bodied person). A further mirroring effect, between the Loÿs images (fig. 5.2) and the facing page (fig. 5.1), indicates another way in which the multisensory phenomenon of miracle unfolds over time: both pages place the visible miracle up top and its audible aftermath—testimony, bells, teaching—below. A miracle is a seen phenomenon, but its proof after the fact is *heard*.

The visual story is reinforced in the text, the first half of which is suspended in rectangular frames that divide the space of the lower visual register; the latter half of the text is on the verso, amid a depiction of a different miracle. Given the text's brevity, I will reproduce it in full:

Autre miracle. Ung enfant de Bourgongne qui estoit sourt et muet dès la nativité fut apporté le jour de la sepulture dudit glorieux saint Loys audit lieu de saint Denis, lequel par aucuns signes externes demonstroit qu'il desiroit et queroit a avoyr l'aide du glorieus saint Loys. Pour laquelle cause en la presence et voyant grant multitude de peuple illecq assistens on le porta pres du tombeau avecques autres plusieurs malades. Et apres ung peu d'entervalles de temps il fut tout net [84v] guery, et lui qui iamais en la vie n'avoit veu[86] ne aussi n'avoit eu la langue desliee parla bon francoys. Et quant il ouyt sonner les cloches il s'en espoenta merveilleusement et s'en fouy hors du moustier et ne le povoyt-on retenir n'arrester n'appaiser iusques a ce que par bonnes introductions et raisons on lui eut donné congnoyssance des cloches et de la tonnerre.

Plusieurs autres grans miracles ont esté faiz par les merites dudit glorieux saint Loys qui cy apres seront demonstrez et par lettre et par ystoyre.

Other miracle. A child from Burgundy who was deaf and mute from birth was brought on the day of the glorious Saint Louis's burial to the aforementioned site of Saint Denis; by means of some external signs he demonstrated that he desired and sought the aid of the glorious Saint Louis. For which reason, in the presence and the sight of a great multitude of people who were there, he was brought close to the tomb along with several other sick people. And after a brief interval of time he was completely [fol. 84v] cured, and he who had never in his life seen nor had ever had his tongue unbound spoke good French. And when he heard the bells ring he was marvelously frightened by it and he fled outside the church, and he could not be held, stopped, or calmed until, with good explanations and reasoning, he had been given acquaintance with bells and thunder.

Many other great miracles were performed through the merits of the said glorious Saint Louis, which will be demonstrated hereafter in letters and in images.

The words support the interpretation of the images, and vice versa, but neither tells the full story on its own. The narrative introduces the *miraculé* simply as "ung enfant," a term imprecise enough that it can apply equally well to a youth in his twenties or to a child of the age depicted in this illustration. The text clearly presents its protagonist as a part of a social network but never provides any details about the nature of those social bonds. We read that the youth "fut apporté" (was brought) to Saint-Denis (but by whom?), that he expressed his desire for help with "signes externes" (external signs; but made to whom?), then "on le porta pres du tombeau" (he was brought close to the tomb; by whom?). The text is clear about the *miraculé*'s affirmative desire to visit the shrine, but is silent on the nature of his social ties; it is only the images, introducing adult male and female companions, that imply a nuclear family.

The second half of the text likewise supports the images' focus on social integration. The bell episode, for instance, is framed as occurring within a social network—and a pedagogically oriented one at that. For while the identities of the boy's teachers are not revealed, we are told that he could not be held, stopped, or calmed (which implies that *someone* tried to do so) until he had been taught what bells and thunder were (which implies he had at least one teacher). This is a far cry from the solitary fear Saint-Pathus describes, which leads Loÿs to flee Saint-Denis, whereupon "il entra en un champ et dormi ilecques" (he entered a field and slept there; p. 53) on his way back to the only home he has ever known. Though the *enfant* of the *Livre des faiz* speaks "bon francoys" without being taught language, he does need to be taught other things in order to make his way in the world.

The unique formatting of the *miracle par ystoyre* causes a peculiar asynchronization of text and image, as the visual text appears only on the recto, while the verbal text continues onto the verso. The two tellings of the story occupy parallel narrative time frames. At the page break, the verbal narrative is suspended at the moment of the miracle: "tout net // guery" (completely cured). Thus, both image and words are divided into "before" and "after," but by different mechanisms: the image is bisected by the text; the text is bisected by the page break. These are, from a visual standpoint, two very different forms of separation, as the full image-story is communicated on a single surface, while only half of the verbal story can be seen at any given time: disability and wholeness are visually continuous but linguistically disjoined. It is of particular import, then, that the distinctive features of this story, as developed in the abbreviated version, occur *after* the healing: the immediate ability to speak proper French, the extreme reaction to the sound of the bells. These are precisely the elements that, in the *Livre des faiz*, are dislocated from their corresponding images.

The asynchrony of word and image is heightened on the verso, where the latter half of Loÿs's story is suspended above the illustration of a different miracle—a miracle whose corresponding verbal narrative begins only on the following page (fig. 5.3). Rather than bisecting the image, these text boxes appear near the top of the page, immediately below a decorative clock. Though the resonance is surely

FIGURE 5.3 Conclusion of the narrative of the deaf and mute boy (ca. 1480–88). From *Livre des faiz monseigneur saint Loys* (BnF MS fr. 2829, fol. 84v). Photograph: Bibliothèque nationale de France.

coincidental, the placement of the text beneath the image of a clock calls to mind the peculiar temporal dislocations of crip time. As Ellen Samuels has pointed out, "*Crip time is time travel,*" inasmuch as "disability and illness have the power to extract us from linear, progressive time with its normative life stages and cast us into a wormhole of backward and forward acceleration, jerky stops and starts, tedious intervals and abrupt endings."[87] Which is precisely what happens when Loÿs, a young adult at the time of his miracle, is depicted as a child. The character's life cycle is disrupted and entire phases of the historical Loÿs's lived childhood bypassed, erased. History has been rewritten and refigured precisely so that the *miraculé*'s bodily condition and cultural naïveté will cohere better with normative expectations about the human life cycle. In this way, as Kafer puts it, "crip time bends the clock to meet disabled bodies and minds."[88] And so, while the decision to represent Loÿs as a child within a family unit is an apparent gesture to chrononormativity—that is, the culturally enforced model of time "necessary for genealogies of descent and for the mundane workings of domestic life"[89]—it also, less obviously, bends time to meet Loÿs's nonnormate experience. The chrononormative or "chronobionormative" process "simultaneously regulates the narrative expectations for the [. . .] body but also erodes these attempts at regulation" when a nonnormate body such as Loÿs's provides the impetus for narration.[90]

When the *miracle par ystoyre* "bends the clock" to give Loÿs an alternate childhood, it also eliminates the other children who, in Saint-Pathus's telling, were instrumental in Loÿs's socialization as disabled: the older boy who first led him to Orgelet, the children who cruelly tested his muteness with hot coals, and the neighbors, probably including people of all ages, who taught the youth to speak. It is apparent that the decision to represent Loÿs as a child reflects not a valorization of childhood, but a valorization of childhood as a tool with which to normalize (and, inadvertently, to "crip") an atypical life course. This representational shortcut is possible precisely because of the child's universal alterity, his humanity, which is marginal yet (in most cases) embedded within a family structure.

The *miracle par hystoyre* is a format that, like Loÿs, speaks few words and depends instead on visual cues. The essence of the story, as conveyed in the visually immersive narration, is this: a vulnerable person, with community support and in the presence of community witnesses, is cured of a serious infirmity. His new bodily state disrupts his experience of the world, until his family imparts the everyday practical knowledge of the world that will allow him to reenter the social fold. The reaction to ordinary yet unfamiliar stimuli both confirms the prior disability and signals the assimilability of the *miraculé* (and therefore the saint's ability to heal not just individuals but communities). Reading the story in this way, the representational logic of this *miracle par ystoyre* becomes apparent. There is no visual shorthand for a deaf and mute person,[91] but there is a readily available and visually distinctive human type that is vulnerable, is both separate from and integrated into the social order, speaks imperfectly, and is assimilable through instruction: the child. Representing Loÿs as a child eases the path toward using the same figure to represent the "before" and the "after": while the deaf and mute *adult* is at once invisible and incurable, the deaf and mute *child* exemplifies the key characteristics of the essential miracle subject. In keeping with Jacques Rancière's observation that to displace an event chronologically "is to transform it into its own metaphor,"[92] the chronological displacement of Loÿs from young adulthood to childhood metaphorizes him, allowing him to stand in for the mechanics of miracles themselves—but writing the adult Loÿs's own voice, his testimony, out of the story entirely.

Every child is a miracle in the making—not because of any cliché relating to "the miracle of life," but because theirs is a visible alterity ripe for transformation. Developing children incarnate the passage of time. When formerly mute child *miraculés* hint at how language works, they are also exposing the mechanisms of time, and of miracle itself. Any cure or "restoration" brings with it a temporal dislocation, as the *miraculé* moves into the future with a body that has been returned to a prior state—of "wholeness," but sometimes, of a not-yet-socialized second infancy. The *Livre des faiz*, in particular, helps us see that healing miracles counterintuitively crip human developmental time, turning back the biological clock to realign it with the divinely ameliorated body. Moreover, the episode of the bells shows that language is a way of existing in time and that muteness is construed as an existence out of time. Muteness and miracle can both scramble the ages of man, and when this cultural construct comes undone, it takes more than a miracle to put it together again.

Medieval cultural scripts likening disabled adults to children abound, from the proverbial affinity between *folz* and *enfants* to the legal disenfranchisement of people with speech impairments,[93] such as the Norman youth Henri, whose speech and property were restored by Thomas Becket. The disabled adult's uncanny occupation of two phases of life can be hard to think about until the disabled adult is turned into a child, as literally (and figurally) occurs in the *Livre des faiz*. The infantilization of adults with disabilities is a social problem that persists today. The medieval form of infantilization I have highlighted in this chapter, however, has enabled a sustained reflection on the relations between disability and the special form of humanity that children inhabit. Mute children like Guillot and Loÿs are sometimes abused as if they were "bestes mues," then trained to parrot language, yet they are sufficiently human to communicate important insights: not just about human life, but about the ineffable world of miracle, and the inadequacy of normative representational and narrative conventions to capture its untimely truths. Indeed, if infants' proximity to animal existence makes them an especially valuable test case with which to assess the capacity of language to signify experience, as I argued in chapter 2, then mute children's marginalization likewise affords a privileged position from which to meditate on the community's role in socializing children *into* as well as *out of* disability: a developmental paradox that highlights the irreconcilability of biographical time and the temporality of miracle.

KNOWING INFANCY

This book has been an exercise in seeking knowledge from the unknowable. Modern readers cannot attain medieval infants' speech (and neither could medieval readers and writers, for that matter); what we *can* more readily begin to appreciate is the intellectual work that infants' universal alterity could do in medieval literature. The truth to be found in literary infant voices—like the truth found in other seemingly impossible narratives, such as accounts of language-deprivation experiments, as Karl Steel points out—is in their revelation of "the conceptual problems that led to their writing in the first place."[1] What we find, when we attend to imagined infant voices with this in mind, is that infants' physical vulnerability is an epistemic advantage; the conceptual problems their voices address are those best answered by people denuded of the strengths, the experiences, and the pretensions of adulthood.

As I stated in the introduction to this book, discourses about children and child-rearing reveal what a society finds most troubling. The substance of imagined infant speech suggests that for the medieval writers I have considered, such topics include female autonomy, injustice, and disability. Infants can speak to such a wide range of unsettling matters thanks to the radical relationality of their existence. Infants' relations with their mothers often proceed through a wearing away of maternal autonomy, with the infant co-opting her voice or the woman descending to a childlike state. Infants exist largely outside of the legal and social systems that construct class and other forms of privilege and are moved to speak when the ideal human equality their birth represents bumps up against a reality that denies justice to the "little guy." Infants are marginalized social actors owing to physical incapacities that they are expected to outgrow as they become full participants in adult social life; but this normate *infirmitas* underscores that able-bodiedness cannot be more than a temporary and imaginary state.

Any one of these embryonic conclusions could have been developed into a study of its own. I have chosen, however, to subsume these to what I see as the most fundamental questions that infant voices provoke — questions that are not sociocultural, but epistemic. Do we truly know what we think we know? What if learning has denatured us to the point of a paradoxical loss of knowledge? How can we reattain varieties of wisdom that humankind has forgotten? If infant vocalizations provide a means with which to explore these unsettling ideas, it is because of the infant's lack of acculturation, which allows him to bypass experiential knowledge and tap directly into a more universal store of wisdom. In other words, the infant's lack of prior knowledge is itself a form of epistemic privilege. This privilege can be conceived as deriving from the infant's universal alterity, which manifests in his greater proximity, relative to other humans, to a number of boundary conditions that test the limits of human experience:

The infant remains closest to the oblivion of bare life, of life as it is experienced prior to the advent of remembered and rememberable thought, because of the continuity of his existence with fetal development. The fetus, as imagined by medieval writers, is the only form of human that can know what it is merely to exist, merely to *be,* unburdened by reason. Fetal existence inaugurates what will become humans' pathways to knowing: sensory perception, affective responses, and rational thought. But theirs is a life without age and a life largely forgotten after birth, suggesting that forgetting is integral to the creation of new knowledge. Our earliest experiences are irretrievable, unknown even to ourselves, and are thus a space of unbounded imaginative possibility.

The infant remains close to the threshold of life and death, already poised to slip away even as she comes into existence. This makes the infant a powerful *memento mori,* because she is such a paradoxical one: the child who exhorts us to remember our future demise is a being who herself has no lived experience to remember, and no future to anticipate. But speaking infants also show that one can be "born" many times, emerging into the nursery, then into language, and finally into a broader social world. Each of these new beginnings grants us access to different forms of knowledge and different means of expression, all with an untimely power to reach across the full breadth of the human life span.

The infant remains closest to his origin *within another person*, and by extension, to the relationality of personhood—an interdependency that early education will rely upon but later acculturation will obscure. The infant literally and figuratively feeds from his mother or his wet nurse, either of whom can nurture him naturally. Together, the infant, the mother, and the nurse expose the inadequacy of a binary "nature and nurture" to capture the multidirectional flow of linguistic influences in a nursery space. The language shared by infants and their caregivers also tests our understanding of what it is to belong, and what it is to be an outsider. Often it is the mother, the "outside" within whom the infant has developed, who ends up as the "outsider"; indeed, given the priority infant voices enjoy in medieval fictions, wherein they frequently can contaminate or supersede their mother's verbal expression, it is perhaps more appropriate to speak of a child-mother dyad rather than a mother-child dyad. Infant voices remain potent within an epistemic system that discounts women's ways of knowing. At the same time, however, mute and orphaned children expose how contingent the dyadic experience is and exemplify a much more precarious kind of infancy. When no mother is present to domesticate baby babble and socialize a child into language—when a baby prematurely loses or is unable to hear and respond to his *doulce nourriture*—the normally temporary alterity of infancy threatens to become a permanent state.

The infant remains closest to an imaginary line between ability and disability. Because this stage of life is defined by a lack—an inability that becomes a disability if it persists beyond the typical end of the stage—infancy in particular points to the contingency and sometime negotiability of life stages and developmental markers. A neonate born with teeth is nonetheless an infant, as is a five-year-old endowed with precocious verbal skills; an adolescent or adult who is unable to speak, while no longer considered a child, does not accede to the full legal rights of adulthood either. Infants who speak and older people who are unable to speak both highlight the disjuncture between age and ability and also hint at the ways the norms of both age and ability can be wielded to marginalize those whose development diverges from cultural scripts. A careful attention to discourses around infant muteness demonstrates that even when they are developing normally, young children are the ultimate "disabled" subjects: socially limited, utterly disenfranchised regardless of social status, physically weak, unable to advocate for themselves.

The infant remains closest to an ideal of purity unsullied by worldly experience. Innocent infants ostensibly can neither speak (*in-fans*) nor do harm (*in-nocens*)—but small children *can* perpetrate epistemic injustice, and even when fictions grant them the power to speak out about injustice, they lack the power to rectify the greater systemic inequities that have given rise to it. Infant innocence unyokes truth claims from experience, suggesting that evidence-based ways of knowing can be inferior to the simpler "home truths" that children reveal when they observe the world without interpreting it, or when they voice their unmitigated dependency. Innocence implies ignorance of the adult *social* world, but a clear vision of the core values that adults have often lost sight of.

Above all, **the infant remains closest to the possibility of knowledge unmediated by language.** Theirs is, in some regards, perceived as an animal existence: what separates humans from beasts is not our intelligence or reason, but our pretension to superiority—a superiority that the infant, unique among humans, cannot claim. The possibility of assigning profound signification to infant vocalizations shows that language is a signal of humanity, but not necessarily of reason—a distinction that belies cultural commonplaces about reason demarcating humans from beasts. Moreover, if baby babbling is an experimental process, it is one that helps us see how to know beyond the illusions of experience. The idea that infant cries tap into a shared store of knowledge to express a general human state means that even before we are socialized, humans already belong to an affective and intellectual community, demonstrating that the collective and the intersubjective, not the individual, form the basis of self-knowledge.

This series of proximities allows us to conclude that for the medieval writers who find them "good to think with," infants may not enjoy the full personhood and agency of adults, but they are more overtly and honestly human. While infancy as a life stage is temporary, the disability and dependency that define infant experience are not. Rather, the disability that the infant embodies is a permanent part of the human condition, one that socialization and acculturation will mask in the course of time. Thus children, especially helpless infants—weaker even than other newborn animals—offer the truest representation and expression of what it means to be human. Infancy lasts only a few years, but as imagined by medieval writers, the alterity that the infant voice expresses is perpetual: it remains within all of us, though it may eventually be obscured by the veneer of adult civilization. The infant gives voice to the stranger within, crying out not the *sum quod eris* of the dead (I am what you will be), but a *sum quod eras* (I am what you were) meant to remind us of our fundamental bodily and moral truths, our natural state. Infants' imagined words are stories through which we remind ourselves *about ourselves*.

And so, instead of debating whether medieval children were perceived as "little adults," it is more productive—and more faithful to the core ideas that medieval imaginings of the infant voice reveal—to reposition children as full and even central players in human experience: central not in terms of their everyday activities, that is, but in their status as sources of knowledge and as crucial instruments for adult reflections. Doing so allows us to see that when infants speak in medieval literature, they redefine the adult in their own terms, as a denatured child. Some denaturing is desirable—we call it "education" and "good manners"—but acculturation also gives rise to delusions of superiority, and thus a fundamental misunderstanding of what it is to be human. Only language can bring us back: literary language, that is, which can reconfigure human biological development and lived time, through the paradox of infant speech.

ACKNOWLEDGMENTS

This book has benefited enormously from the collegial warmth and intellectual generosity of a remarkable cohort of medievalists. Special thanks must go to Helen Solterer, Charlie Samuelson, Jessica Rosenfeld, Deborah McGrady, and Peggy McCracken: your consistent support and unfailingly high standards have spurred me to do my best work, as have rigorous readings from the anonymous evaluators of this manuscript. I am grateful, too, for insights gleaned from conversations with some very smart people, including Wolfram Aichinger, Wendy Love Anderson, Marilynn Desmond, Jane Gilbert, Miranda Griffin, Noah Guynn, Alani Hicks-Bartlett, Katherine Kong, David Lawton, Lise Leet, Jeanette Patterson, Michael Sherberg, Akiko Tsuchiya, and Anna Zayaruznaya. You've pointed me in all sorts of helpful directions, though we may not have known it at the time. Sincere thanks go to Micol Bez, whose inclusion of me in her law and literature seminar at the 2023 American Comparative Literature Association annual conference helped me wrap my mind around the silence of Merlin's mother. I must also express my enormous appreciation for the indefatigable Kevin Brady and the other powerhouses at the Washington University Libraries who kept the books coming (and, in my case, coming and coming and coming) even in the early and uncertain days of the COVID-19 pandemic.

The completion of this book would not have been possible without the generous support of the dean of Arts and Sciences and the Department of Romance Languages and Literatures at Washington University in St. Louis. Chapters 2 and 3 were drafted during a spring 2019 faculty fellowship at Washington University's Center for the Humanities and benefited enormously from the insights of the workshop's participants: Jean Allman, Daniel Bornstein, Ignacio Infante, Ling Kang, Rose Miyatsu, Ashley Pribyl, Luis Salas, Alex Stefaniak, and Rebecca Wanzo. Other material from this project has been presented at numerous venues, including invited lectures at Duke University (2019), the University of Virginia (2021), and Brown University (2021); a keynote address to the interdisciplinary virtual conference of the Centre of Medieval Studies of the Universities of York and Leeds (2021); and conferences including the Vienna edition of A Meeting of Medievalists (2018), the Silver Colloquium at Washington University in St. Louis (2020), the 2023 meeting of the American Comparative Literature Association, and the 2019, 2020, 2022, and 2023 annual meetings of the Modern Language Association. I am grateful to all those in attendance at these presentations for their questions and their interest in this long-gestating project.

My deepest gratitude goes to Michael, Pachook, and Budabec. My game is nothing, but you are everything.

Earlier versions of parts of chapter 1 were previously published in "Fetal Personhood and Voice in Medieval French Literature," *PMLA* 136, no. 5 (October 2021): 696–710, published by Cambridge University Press on behalf of the Modern Language Association of America, © 2021 by Julie Singer, reprinted with permission. Earlier versions of parts of chapter 3 were previously published in "Christine de Pizan's *doulce nourriture*," *Medium Aevum* 89, no. 1 (2020): 93–114, reprinted with permission from the Society for the Study of Medieval Languages and Literature.

NOTES

INTRODUCTION

1. Sermon by Jean l'Agneau quoted in Nicole Bériou, *L'avènement des maîtres de la Parole: La prédication à Paris au XIIIᵉ siècle* (Paris: Institut d'Études Augustiniennes, 1998), vol. 1, p. 336 n. 162. This and subsequent English translations are my own unless otherwise noted.

2. Philippe Ariès, *L'enfant et la vie familiale sous l'Ancien Régime* (Paris: Plon, 1960). Published in English as *Centuries of Childhood: A Social History of Family Life*, trans. Robert Baldick (New York: Knopf, 1962).

3. On the figure of the *jongleur*, see esp. Edmond Faral, *Les jongleurs en France au Moyen Âge*, 2nd ed. (Paris: Champion, 1964); John W. Baldwin, "The Image of the Jongleur in Northern France around 1200," *Speculum* 72 (1997): pp. 635–63; Christopher Page, *The Owl and the Nightingale: Musical Life and Ideas in France, 1100–1300* (Berkeley and Los Angeles: University of California Press, 1990); and Martine Clouzot, "Un intermédiaire culturel au XIIIᵉ siècle: Le jongleur," *Bulletin du centre d'études médiévales d'Auxerre*, hors-série 2 (2008), accessed 22 April 2024, http://journals.openedition.org/cem/4312.

4. Carla Casagrande and Silvana Vecchio, "Clercs et jongleurs dans la société médiévale (XIIᵉ et XIIIᵉ siècles)," *Annales: Économies, sociétés, civilisations* 34 (1979): pp. 913–28.

5. Philippe Ménard, *Le rire et le sourire dans le roman courtois en France au Moyen Âge (1150–1250)* (Geneva: Droz, 1969), p. 149.

6. Bk. 11, chap. 2 of Isidore of Seville, *Etymologiarum Sive Originum*, ed. W. M. Lindsay (Oxford and New York: Oxford University Press, 1911), vol. 2, p. 22.

7. Isidore of Seville, *The Etymologies of Isidore of Seville*, trans. Stephen A. Barney, W. J. Lewis, J. A. Beach, and Oliver Berghof with Muriel Hall (Cambridge: Cambridge University Press, 2006), p. 241.

8. Jean Maillart, *Le roman du comte d'Anjou*, ed. Mario Roques (Paris: Champion, 1931), pp. 124–25, ll. 4079–85.

9. Philippe de Navarre, *Les quatre âges de l'homme*, ed. Marcel de Fréville, SATF (Paris: Firmin Didot, 1888; rpt., New York: Johnson, 1968), pp. 4–5, para. 6.

10. On the simultaneous meaningfulness and irrationality of play, see the opening pages of Johan Huizinga, *Homo ludens: A Study of the Play-Element in Culture* (Boston: Beacon, 1950).

11. Huizinga, *Homo ludens*, p. 4.

12. In this regard I have remained mindful of William F. MacLehose's well-founded criticism of studies that "collapse time, space, texts, and contexts in order to create a homogeneous medieval idea of childhood"; MacLehose, *"A Tender Age": Cultural Anxieties over the Child in the Twelfth and Thirteenth Centuries* (New York: Columbia University Press, 2008), p. 53.

13. Nor was "epistemology" present as a distinct branch of philosophical inquiry in the Middle Ages: Robert Pasnau, *After Certainty: A History of Our Epistemic Ideals and Illusions* (Oxford and New York: Oxford University Press, 2017).

14. As emphatically argued in James A. Schultz, *The Knowledge of Childhood in the German Middle Ages, 1100–1350* (Philadelphia: University of Pennsylvania Press, 1995), p. 40.

15. Didier Lett, *L'enfant des miracles: Enfance et société au Moyen Âge (XIIᵉ–XIIIᵉ siècle)* (Paris: Aubier, 1997), p. 18.

16. Danièle Alexandre-Bidon and Monique Closson, *L'enfant à l'ombre des cathédrales* (Lyon: Presses Universitaires de Lyon, 1985), p. 231.

17. Christiane Klapisch-Zuber, "Introduction: Attitudes devant l'enfant," *Annales de démographie historique 1973: Enfant et Sociétés* (1973): pp. 63–67, at p. 64; Didier Lett, "L'enfance: Aetas infirma, aetas infima," *Médiévales* 15 (1988): pp. 85–95, at p. 85. Similar ideas underlie Ottavia Niccoli, ed., *Infanzie: Funzioni di un gruppo liminale dal mondo classico all'età moderna* (Florence: Ponte alle Grazie, 1993).

18. While I note James A. Schultz's contention that "learned schemes for the ages of man [...] can offer little help in understanding the [vernacular] knowledge of childhood," I disagree: the vernacular French writers with whom I engage often allude quite specifically to these models of the human life course; Schultz, *Knowledge*, p. 39.

19. Elizabeth Sears, *The Ages of Man: Medieval Interpretations of the Life Cycle* (Princeton, NJ: Princeton University Press, 1986), p. 125. See also J. A. Burrow, *The Ages of Man: A Study in Medieval Writing and Thought* (Oxford: Clarendon Press, 1986); Deborah Youngs, *The Life Cycle in Western Europe, c. 1300–c. 1500* (Manchester: Manchester University Press, 2006). On the general exclusion of women from "ages of man" schemas, see Cordelia Beattie, "The Life Cycle: The Ages of Medieval Women," in *A Cultural History of Women in the Middle Ages*, ed. Kim Phillips (London: Bloomsbury, 2013), pp. 15–37.

20. "Infantia dicitur etas, in qua non loquitur puer: infans enim quasi non fans. Hec etas se extendit, usque dum loqui possit"; Thomas of Cantimpré, *Liber de natura rerum. 1. Text*, ed. H. Boese (Berlin: de Gruyter, 1973), p. 80. Sears briefly discusses this passage in *Ages of Man: Medieval Interpretations* (p. 125).

21. Shulamith Shahar, *Childhood in the Middle Ages* (New York: Routledge, 1990), p. 23.

22. Luke Demaitre, "The Idea of Childhood and Child Care in Medical Writings of the Middle Ages," *Journal of Psychohistory* 4 (1977): pp. 461–90, at p. 466.

23. Lett, *L'enfant*, p. 29. Klaus Arnold likewise underscores medical texts'

tendency to distinguish "die Zeit der eigentlichen *infantia*, der Sprachlosigkeit," lasting until weaning, from the rest of early childhood to age seven. Arnold, "Kindheit im europaïschen Mittelalter," in *Zur Sozialgeschichte der Kindheit*, ed. Jochen Martin and August Nitschke (Freiburg: Karl Alber, 1986), pp. 443–67, at p. 447.

24. Alain Chartier, *Le livre de l'Espérance*, ed. François Rouy (Paris: Champion, 1989), Prose IX, p. 71, ll. 151–52.

25. Ivan Pauli studies the vocabulary of childhood across a broad range of Romance dialects (though mostly citing attestations from more modern periods) in *"Enfant," "garçon," "fille" dans les langues romanes* (Lund: Lindstedts, 1919). On this vocabulary in medieval Occitan, see Linda Paterson, "L'enfant dans la littérature occitane avant 1230," *Cahiers de civilisation médiévale* 32, no. 127 (1989): pp. 233–45.

26. For analysis of Corbechon's metadiscourse on translation, see Bernard Ribémont, "Jean Corbechon, un traducteur encyclopédiste au XIVe siècle," *Cahiers de recherches médiévales et humanistes* 6 (1999): pp. 75–97.

27. BnF MS fr. 1968, fol. 141.

28. Like many Latinate neologisms, *puericie* initially appears in translations executed for Charles V in the late fourteenth century but largely disappears thereafter: *Dictionnaire du Moyen Français* [hereafter *DMF*], s.v. "puericie," accessed 22 April 2024, http://www.atilf.fr/dmf/definition/puericie. One of the translations making the most extensive use of this neologism is Jean Daudin's *De la erudition ou enseignement des enfans nobles*, a vernacular rendering of an educational treatise by Vincent of Beauvais.

29. Phyllis Gaffney, "The Ages of Man in Old French Verse Epic and Romance," *Modern Language Review* 85 (1990): pp. 570–82, at p. 572.

30. In his gloss incorporated into his translation of aphorism III.26 of the *Amphorismes Ypocras* (1362–65), Martin de Saint-Gille defines "l'aage d'enfance" as that which extends "depuis que les dens sont plantees jusques a l'aage de puberté — c'est de XII ou XIII ans"; *Les Amphorismes Ypocras de Martin de Saint-Gille*, ed. Germaine Lafeuille (Cambridge, MA: Harvard University Press, 1954), p. 115.

31. Youngs, *Life Cycle in Western Europe*, p. 40.

32. Alexandre-Bidon and Closson, *L'enfant*, p. 7; Barbara Hanawalt, *Growing Up in Medieval London: The Experience of Childhood in History* (Oxford and New York: Oxford University Press, 1993) and *The Ties that Bound: Peasant Families in Medieval England* (Oxford and New York: Oxford University Press, 1986); Annie Saunier, "L'enfant victime: Une représentation de l'enfance au travers de quelques sources religieuses, judiciaires et hospitalières," *Medium Aevum Quotidianum* 52 (2005): pp. 6–19; Lett, *L'enfant*, pp. 93–98.

33. Shahar, *Childhood*, p. 97.

34. For an especially cogent response to Ariès and a review of the critiques of his argument, especially with reference to the Middle Ages, see Schultz, *Knowledge*, pp. 2–9. One of the most detailed critiques of Ariès remains Adrian Wilson, "The Infancy of the History of Childhood: An Appraisal of Philippe Ariès," *History*

and Theory 19, no. 2 (1980): pp. 132–53. For a more recent medievalist reaction, see Barbara Hanawalt, "Medievalists and the Study of Childhood," *Speculum* 77, no. 2 (2002): pp. 440–60. Danièle Alexandre-Bidon surveys work on medieval childhood published in reaction to Ariès in the 1980s in "Grandeur et renaissance du sentiment de l'enfance au Moyen Âge," *Histoire de l'éducation* 50 (1991): pp. 39–63. See also Pierre Riché and Danièle Alexandre-Bidon, "L'enfant au Moyen Âge: État de la question," in *La petite enfance dans l'Europe médiévale et moderne*, ed. Robert Fossier (Toulouse: Presses Universitaires du Mirail, 1997), pp. 7–29.

35. *The History of Childhood*, ed. Lloyd DeMause (New York: Psychohistory Press, 1974).

36. Shahar, *Childhood*; Danièle Alexandre-Bidon and Didier Lett, *Les enfants au Moyen Âge: V^e–XVe siècles* (Paris: Hachette, 1998). On Germany: Schultz, *Knowledge*. On England: Nicholas Orme, *Medieval Children* (New Haven, CT: Yale University Press, 2001).

37. Doris Desclais Berkvam, *Enfance et maternité dans la littérature française des XIIe et XIIIe siècles* (Paris: Champion, 1981); Jens N. Faaborg, *Les enfants dans la littérature française du Moyen Âge* (Copenhagen: Museum Tusculanum Press, 1997); Pierre Riché, *Être enfant au Moyen Âge: Anthologie de textes consacrés à la vie de l'enfant du Ve au XVe siècle* (Paris: Fabert, 2010).

38. Alexandre-Bidon and Closson, *L'enfant*; Pierre Riché and Danièle Alexandre-Bidon, *L'enfance au Moyen Âge* (Paris: Bibliothèque Nationale, 1994).

39. Lett, *L'enfant*; MacLehose, "A Tender Age."

40. Ariès, *L'enfant et la vie familiale*, p. iii; translation from Ariès, *Centuries*, p. 10.

41. In this view I build on the approach of James A. Schultz, who defends literary texts as "essential, perhaps even privileged sources of information" (*Knowledge*, p. 14). However, my interest is less in showing how literary representations build and reflect *cultural* knowledge, as Schultz does, than in exploring literary uses of imagined child voices as a tool for what a modern reader might think of, for lack of a better term, as "existential" inquiries.

42. On the history of the phrase "good to think with" and its uses in humanities scholarship, see Marjorie Garber, *Loaded Words* (New York: Fordham University Press, 2012), pp. 94–103.

43. Giorgio Agamben, *Infancy and History: The Destruction of Experience*, trans. Liz Heron (London: Verso, 1993).

44. Jacques Rancière remarks that "the historian must begin by returning to the source, by once again becoming a child to understand the state of *in-fancy*, in the sense of not speaking, inscribed in the texture of things"; Rancière, *The Names of Poetry: On the Poetics of Knowledge*, trans. Hassan Melehy (Minneapolis: University of Minnesota Press, 1994), p. 60.

45. Adriana Cavarero, *For More than One Voice: Toward a Philosophy of Vocal Expression*, trans. Paul A. Kottman (Stanford, CA: Stanford University Press, 2005).

46. Susan Fraiman, *Extreme Domesticity: A View from the Margins* (New York: Columbia University Press, 2017).

1. Claude Thomasset, "Quelques principes de l'embryologie médiévale (de Salerne à la fin du XIIIᵉ siècle)," in *L'enfant au Moyen Âge: Littérature et civilisation* (Aix-en-Provence: Presses Universitaires de Provence, 1980).

2. Barbara Johnson, *A World of Difference* (Baltimore, MD: Johns Hopkins University Press, 1987), p. 192.

3. On the iconography of the soul depicted as a baby, see Jacques Le Goff and Jérôme Baschet, "Anima," in *Enciclopedia dell'arte medievale*, vol. 1 (Rome: Istituto della enciclopedia italiana, 1991), pp. 798–815, esp. pp. 812–13. Baschet also discusses the "somatomorphic" figuration of the soul at great length, along with other conventions for the representation of the soul, in *Corps et âmes: Une histoire de la personne au Moyen Âge* (Paris: Flammarion, 2016), pp. 123–72. Some late medieval images depicting ensoulment have even been interpreted as representing the soul as an embryo. See Marie-France Morel, "Embryons glorieux: Iconographie des conceptions et des grossesses sacrées dans l'art occidental (XIVᵉ–XVIᵉ siècles)," in *L'embryon humain à travers l'histoire: Images, savoirs et rites; Actes du colloque international de Fribourg, 27–29 octobre 2004*, ed. Véronique Dasen (Gollion: Infolio, 2007), pp. 107–26. See also Jérôme Baschet, "La parenté partagée: Engendrement charnel et infusion de l'âme (à propos d'une miniature de la fin du XVᵉ siècle)," in *Anima e corpo nella cultura medievale: Atti del V convegno di studi della Società Italiana per lo Studio del Pensiero Medievale (Venezia, 25–28 settembre 1995)*, ed. Carla Casagrande and Silvana Vecchio (Florence: SISMEL/Galluzzo, 2017), pp. 123–37.

4. Baschet, *Corps et âmes*; Baschet, "La parenté partagée," p. 125.

5. Joseph W. Koterski, "Boethius and the Theological Origins of the Concept of Person," *American Catholic Philosophical Quarterly* 78, no. 2 (2004): pp. 203–24, at p. 210.

6. Anne Lefebvre-Teillard, "*Infans conceptus*: Existence physique et existence juridique," *Revue historique du droit français et étranger* 72, no. 4 (1994): pp. 499–525.

7. Jean-Paul Galibert, "Le jeu des temps embryonnaires," in *L'embryon humain à travers l'histoire: Images, savoirs et rites; Actes du colloque international de Fribourg, 27–29 octobre 2004*, ed. Véronique Dasen (Gollion: Infolio, 2007), pp. 257–65, at p. 257.

8. Mladen Dolar, *A Voice and Nothing More* (Cambridge, MA: MIT Press, 2006), p. 66.

9. Brian Kane, *Sound Unseen: Acousmatic Sound in Theory and Practice* (Oxford and New York: Oxford University Press, 2014), p. 6.

10. Kane sees such "reversals of inner and outer" as a hallmark of the "underdetermination" of acousmatic sounds. Kane, *Sound Unseen*, p. 159.

11. Walter J. Ong, S.J., *The Presence of the Word: Some Prolegomena for Cultural and Religious History* (New Haven, CT: Yale University Press, 1967), p. 118. Judith A. Peraino also plays with the image of the sonogram as a tool for thinking about medieval literature in "Sonograms of Desire, Medieval and Modern," *Paragraph* 41, no. 1 (2018): pp. 26–41.

12. Steven Connor, *Dumbstruck: A Cultural History of Ventriloquism* (Oxford and New York: Oxford University Press, 2000), p. 12.

13. Michel Serres, *The Parasite*, trans. Lawrence R. Schehr (Baltimore, MD: Johns Hopkins University Press, 1982).

14. Kane, *Sound Unseen*, p. 149; emphasis in original.

15. The word *né* is omitted from fr. 16993, as well as from a number of other manuscripts, including fr. 217, fr. 22531, and Amiens Bibliothèque municipale 399.

16. It serves as the base manuscript for the edition in progress. See Bartholomaeus Anglicus, *De proprietatibus rerum*, ed. Baudouin Van den Abeele, vol. 1 (Turnhout: Brepols, 2007), p. 14.

17. Isidore, *Etymologiarum*, bk. 11, chap. 2, sent. 2; *Etymologies*, p. 241.

18. A recent study of the illustrated manuscripts of Corbechon's translation is Baudouin Van den Abeele, "Illustrer le *Livre des propriétés des choses* de Jean Corbechon: Quelques accents particuliers," in *Encyclopédie médiévale et langues européennes: Réception et diffusion du De proprietatibus rerum de Barthélemy l'Anglais dans les langues vernaculaires*, ed. Joëlle Ducos (Paris: Champion, 2014), pp. 125–64.

19. Sears, *Ages of Man: Medieval Interpretations*, pp. 129–30.

20. Jean Froissart, *Le joli buisson de jonece*, ed. Anthime Fourrier (Geneva: Droz, 1975), p. 102.

21. The translation is from Jean Froissart, *An Anthology of Narrative and Lyric Poetry*, ed. and trans. Kristen M. Figg and R. Barton Palmer (New York: Routledge, 2001), p. 329. I have corrected Palmer's translation of ".IIII." as "three."

22. This view of the fetus as an individual entity, already distinct from its mother at the moment of conception, is consistent with the dominant theological viewpoint (as expressed by Aquinas). See Fabrizio Amerini, *Aquinas on the Beginning and End of Human Life*, trans. Mark Henninger (Cambridge, MA: Harvard University Press, 2013), p. 107.

23. On the vocabulary of *nourechon* in relation to children's language acquisition, see chap. 3.

24. Gunna Sigurs, "La langue médicale française: Nouvelles datations," *Le français moderne* 33 (1965): pp. 199–208, at p. 207.

25. "Et est cause de nourissement et es embrions et es bestes imparfectes"; Nicole Oresme, *Le livre de éthiques d'Aristote*, ed. Albert Douglas Menut (New York: G. E. Stechert, 1940), p. 142. Menut lists it among the words coined by Oresme in the *Éthiques* (p. 80).

26. *Histoire de la première destruction de Troie*, ed. Paul Roth (Tübingen: Francke, 2000), p. 67.

27. Ana Isabel Martín Ferreira, "Del embrión al niño," in *Medicina y filología*:

Estudios de léxico médico latino en la Edad Media, ed. Ana Isabel Martín Ferreira (Porto: Fédération Internationale des Instituts d'Études Médiévales, 2010), pp. 119–64; Lefebvre-Teillard, "*Infans conceptus,*" p. 504 n. 18.

28. Maaike van der Lugt, "Nature as Norm in Medieval Medical Discussions of Maternal Breastfeeding and Wet-Nursing," *Journal of Medieval and Early Modern Studies* 49, no. 3 (2019): pp. 563–88, at p. 566.

29. Youngs remarks that "the French used *enfant* for boys under twelve and girls under seven," though it is not clear what text(s) she uses as a source for this claim. Youngs, *Life Cycle in Western Europe,* p. 39.

30. For further information on medieval embryological understandings of formation and its relationship to ensoulment, I refer the reader to M. Anthony Hewson, *Giles of Rome and the Medieval Theory of Conception* (London: Athlone, 1975); Romana Martorelli Vico, "Anima e corpo nell'embriologia medievale," in *Anima e corpo nella cultura medievale: Atti del V Convegno di Studi della Società Italiana per lo Studio del Pensiero Medievale,* ed. Carla Casagrande and Silvana Vecchio (Florence: SISMEL/Edizioni del Galluzzo, 1999), pp. 95–106; Romana Martorelli Vico, *Medicina e filosofia: Per una storia dell'embriologia medievale nel XIII e XIV secolo* (Milan: Guerini, 2002), which is mostly about Italian medical texts; Luc Brisson, Marie-Hélène Congourdeau, and Jean-Luc Solère, eds., *L'embryon, formation et animation: Antiquité grecque et latine tradition hébraïque, chrétienne et islamique* (Paris: Vrin, 2008).

31. As Evrart de Conty writes, "Et ce dient les sages philosophes que les enfans masles en moins de temps sont formez et parfaiz ou ventre de leur mere que les filles ne sont"; de Conty, *L'harmonie des sphères: Encyclopédie d'astronomie et de musique extraite du commentaire sur "Les Echecs amoureux" (XVᵉ s.) attribué à Evrart de Conty,* ed. Reginald Hyatte and Maryse Ponchard-Hyatte (New York: Peter Lang, 1985), p. 81.

32. Evrart de Conty points out, however, that women who report that they are able to feel fetal movement at forty days' gestation must be mistaken: "Et pour ce se aucunes femmes dient qu'elles sentent souvent et ont senty leurs enfans remouvoir a .xl. jours, nous pouons dire, supposé qu'il soit vray, ce qui n'est pas bien raisonnable a croire, que il ne advient pas souvent ou que par aventure elles sont deceues"; de Conty, *L'harmonie des sphères,* p. 82.

33. The pseudo-Albertus likewise assigns the beginning of "vie" to ensoulment ("A xl jours il est fourmé et parfait et a l jours Dieu luy donne vie combien que aucuns y en a qui ont vie a xxx jours)"; *Women's Secrets: A Translation of Pseudo-Albertus Magnus' "De Secretis Mulierum" with Commentaries,* trans. Helen Rodnite Lemay (Albany: SUNY Press, 1992), p. 15.

34. I borrow this vocabulary of potential and actual humanity from G. R. Dunstan, "Introduction: Text and Context," in *The Human Embryo: Aristotle and the Arabic and European Traditions,* ed. G. R. Dunstan (Exeter: Exeter University Press, 1990), pp. 1–9, at p. 6.

35. Martín Ferreira, "Del embrión al niño," p. 159.

36. Hewson, *Giles*, 98, 100, 102. See also Pamela M. Huby, "Soul, Life, Sense, Intellect: Some Thirteenth-Century Problems," in *The Human Embryo: Aristotle and the Arabic and European Traditions*, ed. G. R. Dunstan (Exeter: Exeter University Press, 1990), pp. 113–22, at p. 120.

37. Andreea Boboc, "Theorizing Legal Personhood in Late Medieval England," in *Theorizing Legal Personhood in Late Medieval England*, ed. Andreea Boboc (Leiden: Brill, 2015), pp. 1–28, at p. 3.

38. Lefebvre-Teillard, "*Infans conceptus*," esp. p. 505 n. 24.

39. Romana Martorelli Vico, "Il *De formatione corporis humani in utero* di Egidio Romano: Indagine intorno alla metodologia scientifica," *Medioevo* 14 (1988): pp. 291–313. Later she argues that these three discourses represent three successive phases of embryological thought in *Medicina e filosofia*, pp. 34–35. Martorelli Vico's arguments are consistent with the observations of Luke Demaitre and Anthony A. Travill, who write that for Albertus Magnus, "embryology lies at the interface of biology and philosophy"; Demaitre and Travill, "Human Embryology and Development in the Works of Albertus Magnus," in *Albertus Magnus and the Sciences*, ed. James A. Weishepl (Toronto: Pontifical Institute of Medieval Studies, 1980), pp. 405–40, at p. 440.

40. Robert Pasnau, "Souls and the Beginning of Life (A Reply to Haldane and Lee)," *Philosophy* 78 (2003): pp. 521–31, at p. 524.

41. In 2003 this was the subject of an intense debate between John Haldane and Patrick Lee on one side and Robert Pasnau on the other: Haldane and Lee, "Aquinas on Human Ensoulment, Abortion and the Value of Life," *Philosophy* 78 (2003): pp. 255–78; Pasnau, "Souls and the Beginning of Life"; Haldane and Lee, "Rational Souls and the Beginning of Life (A Reply to Robert Pasnau)," *Philosophy* 78 (2003): pp. 532–40. See also Joseph F. Donceel, "Immediate Animation and Delayed Hominization," *Theological Studies* 31 (1970): pp. 76–105.

42. Irven Resnick ingeniously shows how "quodlibetal disputations treating the administration of baptism for conjoined twins became a vehicle for a discussion of the relative priority of the heart or the brain in human physiology, as well as a vehicle for a discussion of the nature of the soul"; Resnick, "Conjoined Twins, Medieval Biology, and Evolving Reflection on Individual Identity," *Viator* 44, no. 2 (2013): pp. 343–68, at p. 360.

43. Giles of Rome, *Aegidii Romani opera omnia*, vol. II.13, *De formatione humani corporis in utero*, ed. Romana Martorelli Vico (Florence: Galluzzo, 2008), p. 183.

44. Avicenna, *Opera philosophica* (1508; rpt., Édition de la bibliothèque S.J., 1961), fol. 44rb.

45. It is sometimes suggested that humans retain a somatic (rather than intellective) memory of fetal experience. Citing Isidore of Seville, Bartholomaeus Anglicus writes that people are apt to cry when kneeling because that position recalls the misery they felt, in the dark womb, with their knees drawn up to their eyes. In Corbechon's translation: "car nature si l'aramentoit en quel estat il estoit ou ventre

de sa mere" (for nature thus reminded him [lit., brought back to his mind] in what state he was in his mother's womb; BnF fr. 16993, fol. 67rb).

46. Tatjana Buklijas and Nick Hopwood, "Acquiring a Soul," *Making Visible Embryos*, University of Cambridge, 2008–10, accessed 22 April 2024, www.sites .hps.cam.ac.uk/visibleembryos/s1_3.html.

47. Cavarero, *For More*, p. 169.

48. Later, Leonardo da Vinci will famously write that "when women say that the foetus is heard to weep sometimes within the uterus, this is rather the sound of some flatus"; Joseph Needham, *A History of Embryology* (New York: Abelard-Schuman, 1959), p. 97. Hewson adds that Dino del Garbo, too, rejects the notion of a fetus laughing at forty days (*Giles*, p. 228).

49. *El "De Secretis mulierum" atribuido a Alberto Magno: Estudio, edición crítica y traducción*, ed. and trans. José Pablo Barragán Nieto (Porto: Fédération Internationale des Instituts d'Études Médiévales, 2012), p. 288.

50. *Women's Secrets*, p. 86. This specific mention of the vocal capacities of the developing fetus is omitted from all of the manuscripts of the French translation (*Secrés des femmes*) that I have been able to consult thus far. This is one of many elements that are inconsistent across the many versions of this text, whose transmission is marked by a great deal of variance. See Lynn Thorndike, "Further Consideration of the *Experimenta, Speculum Astronomiae*, and *De Secretis Mulierum* Ascribed to Albertus Magnus," *Speculum* 30 (1955): pp. 413–43; Monica Green, "'Traittié tout de mençonges': The *Secrés des dames*,'Trotula,' and Attitudes toward Women's Medicine in Fourteenth and Early Fifteenth-Century France," in *Christine de Pizan and the Categories of Difference*, ed. Marilynn Desmond (Minneapolis: University of Minnesota Press, 1998), pp. 146–78; Monica Green, "From 'Diseases of Women' to 'Secrets of Women': The Transformation of Gynecological Literature in the Later Middle Ages," *Journal of Medieval and Early Modern Studies* 30 (2000): pp. 5–39.

51. *The Trotula: An English Translation of the Medieval Compendium of Women's Medicine*, ed. and trans. Monica H. Green (Philadelphia: University of Pennsylvania Press 2001), p. 82.

52. Emmanuel Le Roy Ladurie, *Montaillou, village occitan de 1294 à 1324*, ed. revue et corrigée (Paris: Gallimard, 1975), p. 233.

53. *Placides et Timéo ou Li secrés as philosophes*, ed. Claude Thomasset (Geneva: Droz, 1980), p. 119, para. 263.

54. See the brief discussion of this passage in Sylvie Laurent, *Naître au Moyen Âge* (Paris: Léopard d'Or, 1989), p. 92.

55. For a fascinating overview of medieval bell-founding techniques and how they impacted the sounds of the bells produced, see Elisabetta Neri, "Les cloches: Construction, sens, perception d'un son; Quelques réflexions à partir des témoignages archéologiques des 'fours à cloches,'" in *Les cinq sens au Moyen Âge*, ed. Éric Palazzo (Paris: Cerf, 2016), pp. 369–406.

56. J. Allan Mitchell, *Becoming Human: The Matter of the Medieval Child* (Minneapolis: University of Minnesota Press, 2014), p. xiii.

57. Agamben, *Infancy*, p. 5.

58. "Dante is not translating; he is 'vulgarizing,' by which I mean he is rendering the concepts and language of natural science useful here, now, and for us—or at least for his contemporary readers"; Alison Cornish, "Vulgarizing Science: Vernacular Translation of Natural Philosophy," in *Dante for the New Millennium*, ed. Teodolinda Barolini and H. Wayne Storey (New York: Fordham University Press, 2003), pp. 169–82, at p. 171. Other studies of the use of scientific language in this canto include Simon Gilson, "Medieval Science in Dante's *Commedia*: Past Approaches and Future Directions," *Reading Medieval Studies* 27 (2001): pp. 39–77; Manuele Gragnolati, "From Plurality to (Near) Unicity of Forms: Embryology in *Purgatorio* 35," in *Dante for the New Millennium*, pp. 192–210; Jennifer Fraser, "Dante/Fante: Embryology in Purgatory and Paradise," in *Dante and the Unorthodox*, ed. James L. Miller (Waterloo, Ont.: Wilfrid Laurier University Press, 2005), pp. 290–309.

59. For more on this analogy, see Rachel Jacoff, "'Our Bodies, Our Selves': The Body in the *Commedia*," in *Sparks and Seeds: Medieval Literature and Its Afterlife; Essays in Honor of John Freccero*, ed. Dana E. Stewart and Alison Cornish (Turnhout: Brepols, 2000), pp. 119–37, at p. 130.

60. Text and translation are cited from Dante Alighieri, *Dante Alighieri's Divine Comedy*, vol. 3, *Purgatory*, trans. Mark Musa (Bloomington: Indiana University Press, 2000), pp. 246–47.

61. Bruno Nardi writes that "*fante*, participio del verbo *fari*, significa appunto *parlante*"; Nardi, "Il canto XXV del *Purgatorio*," in *Letture dantesche*, ed. Giovanni Getto (Florence: Sansoni, 1964), pp. 1175–91, at p. 1186.

62. "Conceptual antinomy": Vittorio Russo, *Esperienze e/di letture dantesche* (Naples: Liguori, 1971), p. 155. In a brilliant article, Zygmunt G. Barański provides detailed and overwhelming evidence for canto 25 of the *Purgatorio* as a response to Guido Cavalcanti's "Donna me prega" and argues that "both texts fundamentally focus on what it means to be human"; Barański, "'Per similitudine di abito scientifico': Dante, Cavalcanti and the Sources of Medieval 'Philosophical' Poetry," in *Science and Literature in Italian Culture from Dante to Calvino: A Festschrift for Pat Boyde*, ed. Pierpaolo Antonello and Simon A. Gilson (Oxford: European Humanities Research Centre, 2004), pp. 14–52, at p. 31.

63. In this chapter a messenger from Cyprus complains of "ceste generacion genevoise, de tous ses voisins appellee perverse, laquelle selonc le livre de Dant deveroit estre du monde destruicte et entierement dispersé" (this Genoese race, which, according to Dante's book, should be extinguished from the world and entirely dispersed). Philippe de Mézières, *Songe du vieil pèlerin*, ed. Joël Blanchard (Geneva: Droz, 2015), p. 304.

64. On Christine's response to Dante, see Kevin Brownlee, "Literary Genealogy and the Problem of the Father: Christine de Pizan and Dante," *Journal of Medieval*

and Renaissance Studies 23 (1993): pp. 365–87. The earliest extant French transla-tion of *Purgatorio* of which I am aware dates from the second half of the sixteenth century.

65. Nardi, "Il canto XXV," p. 1186.

66. Ong, *Presence*, p. 117.

67. "Interior 'real' body": Dolar, *A Voice*, p. 71. "The most interior": Ong, *Pres-ence*, p. 163.

68. Connor, *Dumbstruck*, p. 6.

69. "One central, replicated feature of acousmatic listening appears to be that underdetermination of the sonic source encourages imaginative supplementation"; Kane, *Sound Unseen*, p. 9.

70. Elina Gertsman, *Worlds Within: Opening the Medieval Shrine Madonna* (University Park: Penn State University Press, 2015).

71. The most thorough discussion of this episode is Gianmario Raimondi, "*Lec-tio Boethiana*: L'*example* di Nerone e Seneca nel *Roman de la Rose*," *Romania* 120 (2002): pp. 63–98, at pp. 71–77.

72. Jonathan Morton, "Introduction: Textual Experiments, Thinking with Fic-tion," in *Medieval Thought Experiments: Poetry, Hypothesis, and Experience in the European Middle Ages*, ed. Philip Knox, Jonathan Morton, and Daniel Reeve (Turn-hout: Brepols, 2018), pp. 1–20, at p. 5.

73. Mitchell, *Becoming*, p. xiii.

74. Ong, *Presence*, p. 164.

75. de Conty, *L'harmonie des sphères*, p. 81.

76. Several examples are cited in Marie-Christine Pouchelle, *The Body and Sur-gery in the Middle Ages*, trans. Rosemary Morris (New Brunswick, NJ: Rutgers Uni-versity Press, 1990), p. 135.

77. Gervais Du Bus and Chaillou de Pesstain, *Le roman de Fauvel*, ed. Armand Strubel (Paris: Poche, 2012), p. 490, vv. 3830–36.

78. Serres, *Parasite*, p. 195.

79. Michael Camille, "Hybridity, Monstrosity, and Bestiality in the *Roman de Fauvel*," in *Fauvel Studies: Allegory, Chronicle, Music, and Image in Paris, Biblio-thèque Nationale de France, MS français 146*, ed. Margaret Bent and Andrew Wathey (Oxford: Clarendon Press, 1998), pp. 161–74, at pp. 162, 166. On the "iconographie du monstrueux," see also Jean-Claude Mühlethaler, *Fauvel au pouvoir: Lire la satire médiévale* (Paris: Champion, 1994), pp. 119–42.

80. Nigel F. Palmer deftly explicates this passage's discourses on macrocosm and microcosm, ages, and complexions in "Cosmic Quaternities in the *Roman de Fauvel*," in *Fauvel Studies: Allegory, Chronicle, Music, and Image in Paris, Bibliothèque Natio-nale de France, MS français 146*, ed. Margaret Bent and Andrew Wathey (Oxford: Clarendon Press, 1998), pp. 395–419.

81. In this regard the depiction of the uterine space could be added to Mar-gherita Lecco's list of *bestournements* in the *Fauvel*, among which she includes the

subcategory of movements from inside to outside (da *dentro* a *fuori*); Lecco, *Ricerche sul "Roman de Fauvel"* (Alessandria: Edizioni dell'Orso, 1993), p. 22. Mühlethaler's observation of the distance maintained between Fauvel and Fortune, both in the text and in the fr. 146 miniatures, complements this reading; *Fauvel au pouvoir*, pp. 47–51.

82. I cite both text and translation from Heldris de Cornualle, *Silence*, ed. and trans. Sarah Roche-Mahdi (East Lansing, MI: Colleagues Press, 1992).

83. This is a rubric from Pierre Bersuire's translation of Livy's *Decades*, *Des excellens fais des Rommains*, BnF MS fr. 31, fol. 24. Within the chapter thus rubricated, Bersuire renders Livy's wonders of the year 214 BC, when "uns enfes parla ou ventre sa mere et cria yo triumphe" (a child spoke in its mother's womb and cried out, "Hail, triumph"; BnF MS fr. 31, fol. 56rb). Cf. Livy, *History of Rome*, vol. 6, *Books 23–25*, trans. Frank Gardner Moore, Loeb Classical Library 355 (Cambridge, MA: Harvard University Press, 1940), pp. 208–9.

84. Maaike van der Lugt, *Le ver, le démon et la vierge: Les théories médiévales de la génération extraordinaire* (Paris: Les Belles Lettres, 2004), pp. 379–470.

85. Maaike van der Lugt has extensively studied the "debate over the embryological interpretation of the miraculous conception of Christ," which grew to prominence, she shows, from the late 1230s through the early fourteenth century; *Le ver*, p. 379. See also Joseph Ziegler, "The Sciences of the Body around 1300 as a Locus of Theological and Spiritual Thought," in *The Medieval Paradigm: Religious Thought and Philosophy*, ed. Giulio d'Onofrio (Turnhout: Brepols, 2012), vol. 2, pp. 577–92.

86. Jacqueline Tasioulas, "'Heaven and Earth in Little Space': The Foetal Existence of Christ in Medieval Literature and Thought," *Medium Aevum* 76 (2007): pp. 24–48.

87. Charles Taylor, "The Person," in *The Category of the Person: Anthropology, Philosophy, History*, ed. Michael Carrithers, Steven Collins, and Steven Lukes (Cambridge: Cambridge University Press, 1985), pp. 257–81, at p. 273.

88. *Bible historiale*, BnF MS fr. 20090, fol. 462va.

89. This cannot be dismissed as an error or a peculiarity of the cited manuscript; others display the same pattern, including the earlier fourteenth-century BnF MS fr. 157, which reads "li fans de ton ventre" (fol. 180rb).

90. This discussion appears in *Multi in nativitate ejus gaudebunt*, a sermon for the nativity of St. John the Baptist, probably dated 24 June 1403. Jean Gerson, *Oeuvres complètes*, vol. 7.2, ed. Palémon Glorieux (Paris: Desclée, 1968), pp. 717–20, at p. 718, no. 360.

91. Jaroslav Polc, "La festa della Visitazione e il giubileo del 1390," *Rivista di storia della chiesa in Italia* 29 (1975): pp. 149–72, at p. 153.

92. Anne Marie Velu, *La Visitation dans l'art: Orient et Occident V^e–XVIe siècle* (Paris: Cerf, 2012).

93. Velu, *La Visitation*, p. 119.

94. The term is borrowed from Maureen Boulton, who examines all three of the texts I discuss here, though to rather different ends, in *Sacred Fictions of Medieval France: Narrative Theology in the Lives of Christ and the Virgin, 1150–1500* (Woodbridge: D. S. Brewer, 2015).

95. "Le romanz de saint Fanuel," ed. Camille Chabaneau, *Revue des langues romanes* 28 (1885): pp. 118–23, 157–258, and 32 (1888): pp. 360–409.

96. Daniele Ruini, "*Le Romanz de Saint Fanuel*: Note su fonti, struttura e tradizione manoscritta," *Cultura neolatina* 74 (2014): pp. 95–143.

97. Dolar, *A Voice*, p. 15.

98. Boulton, *Sacred Fictions*, p. 48. Cf. Chabaneau's edition, p. 190, vv. 1333–44.

99. The text thus addresses a contemporary theological question as outlined by Maaike van der Lugt: "Aux yeux des théologiens médiévaux, la scène de la visitation pose plutôt la question de savoir si l'âme de l'enfant à naître peut déjà exercer ses sens" (In the eyes of medieval theologians, the Visitation scene poses, rather, the question of whether the soul of the unborn child can already use its senses). Maaike van der Lugt, "L'animation de l'embryon humain et le statut de l'enfant à naître dans la pensée médiévale," in *L'embryon, formation et animation: Antiquité grecque et latine tradition hébraïque, chrétienne et islamique*. ed. Luc Brisson, Marie-Hélène Congourdeau, and Jean-Luc Solère (Paris: Vrin, 2008), at p. 263 n. 15.

100. Iacopo da Varazze, *Legenda aurea*, ed. Giovanni Paolo Maggioni, second edition (Florence: SISMEL/Galluzzo, 1998), p. 542.

101. Jacques de Voragine, *La légende dorée: Édition critique, dans la révision de 1476 par Jean Batallier, d'après la traduction de Jean de Vignay (1333–1348) de la "Legenda aurea" (c. 1261–1266)*, ed. Brenda Dunn-Lardeau (Paris: Champion, 1997), p. 547.

102. On the history of the text and its fortunes in the late medieval French-speaking sphere see Pierre Courroux, *L'écriture de l'histoire dans les chroniques françaises (XIIᵉ–XVᵉ siècle)* (Paris: Garnier, 2016), pp. 292–99.

103. Courroux, *L'écriture*, p. 323 n. 1.

104. Boulton, *Sacred Fictions*, pp. 206–17.

105. This episode is cited without further analysis in O. Colson, "L'enfant qui parle avant d'être né IX," in *Mélusine* V (1890–91), col. 36.

106. Jean d'Outremeuse, *Ly mireur des histors*, ed. Adolphe Borgnet, vol. 1 (Brussels: Hayez, 1864), pp. 340–41.

107. Borgnet's base text for his edition is the so-called Stavelot Manuscript, Brussels KBR 10455. He corrects with his ms B, the so-called Berlaymont Manuscript, KBR 19303, which is the manuscript cited above. However, Stanislas Bormans, who completed the edition and wrote the intro, remarks that "Le texte du manuscrit de Berlaymont n'a pas la valeur de celui de Jean de Stavelot. Il fourmille de fautes, souvent grossières, qui dénotent une main inhabile" ("Introduction," vol. 7, p. CXCVI). In this case, the Stavelot Manuscript (correctly, biblically speaking) has Mary singing the Magnificat; it is, however, difficult to reconcile Mary's singing

with the assertion (present in both manuscripts) that John was actually the one reciting—which is perhaps why Borgnet chose the lesson from Berlaymont.

108. On the importance of dialogue to the advancement of the narrative, see Maureen Boulton, "Digulleville's *Pèlerinage de Jésus Christ*: A Poem of Courtly Devotion," in *The Vernacular Spirit: Essays on Medieval Religious Literature*, ed. Renate Blumenfeld-Kosinski, Duncan Robertson, and Nancy Bradley Warren (New York: Palgrave, 2002), pp. 125–144, at p. 128; Pamela Sheingorn, "Performing the Illustrated Manuscript: Great Reckonings in Little Books," in *Visualizing Medieval Performance: Perspectives, Histories, Contexts*, ed. Elina Gertsman (Aldershot: Ashgate, 2008), pp. 57–82, at p. 61.

109. Stürzinger reproduces rubrics from *Le romant des trois pelerinages* (Paris: Barthole [Rembolt] & Jehan Petit, c. 1517).

110. Guillaume de Deguileville, *Le pèlerinage de Jesus Christ*, ed. J. J. Stürzinger (London: Nichols for the Roxburghe Club, 1897), p. 44, ll. 1282–86.

111. The first *la* is an adverb marking a place (equivalent to the modern French *là*), the second is the definite article, the third is a direct-object pronoun, and the last is again an adverb.

112. Mary Hayes, *Divine Ventriloquism in Medieval English Literature: Power, Anxiety, Subversion* (New York: Palgrave Macmillan, 2011), p. 90.

113. Ong, *Presence*, p. 324. Hence the iconographic tradition wherein "at the Annunciation a minuscule Christ had entered the Virgin's body through her ear" (Tasioulas, "Heaven and Earth," p. 26).

114. Connor, *Dumbstruck*, p. 15.

115. Sheingorn, "Performing," pp. 75–76.

116. Sheingorn, "Performing"; Robert L. A. Clark and Pamela Sheingorn, "Performative Reading: Experiencing through the Poet's Body in Guillaume de Digulleville's *Pèlerinage de Jhesucrist*," in *Cultural Performances in Medieval France: Essays in Honor of Nancy Freeman Regalado*, ed. Eglal Doss-Quinby, Roberta L. Krueger, and E. Jane Burns (Woodbridge: D. S. Brewer, 2007), pp. 135–51; Agnès Le Bouteiller, "Le procès de paradis du *Pèlerinage de Jésus-Christ*: Un débat allégorique, juridique et théologique porté au seuil de la dramatisation," in *Guillaume de Digulleville: Les "Pèlerinages" allégoriques*, ed. Frédéric Duval and Fabienne Pomel (Rennes: Presses Universitaires de Rennes, 2008), pp. 131–58.

117. Kane, *Sound Unseen*, p. 138.

118. For a detailed study of incubus lore and its "perverted analogy" to the conception of Christ, see van der Lugt, *Le ver*, pp. 195–208. On the medical *incubus* (which combines elements of what would today be called night terrors, sleep apnea, and SIDS), as opposed to the demonological one, see Maaike van der Lugt, "The *Incubus* in Scholastic Debate: Medicine, Theology, and Popular Belief," in *Religion and Medicine in the Middle Ages*, ed. Peter Biller and Joseph Ziegler (York: York Medieval Press, 2001), pp. 175–200.

119. Alban Georges, *Tristan de Nanteuil. Écriture et imaginaire épiques au XIVᵉ siècle* (Paris: Champion, 2006), p. 630.

120. According to legend, Charlemagne committed incest with his sister, and Roland was the product of this union; the emperor refused to confess his sin for fear of naming it aloud, but Saint Giles was finally able to absolve him after an angel delivered a scroll detailing Charlemagne's actions. The fullest account of this legend is in Rita Lejeune, "Le péché de Charlemagne et la *Chanson de Roland*," in *Studia Philologica: Homenaje ofrecido a Dámaso Alonso* (Madrid: Gredos, 1961), vol. 2, pp. 339–71. See also Charles Vulliez, "Orléans, saint Gilles et la légende du pardon de Charlemagne: Présentation d'un dossier," in *Haut Moyen Âge: Culture, éducation et société; Études offertes à Pierre Riché*, ed. M. Sot (La Garenne-Colombes: Éditions européennes Érasme, 1990), pp. 575–89; Hans Erich Keller, "Le péché de Charlemagne," in *L'imaginaire courtois et son double: Actes du VIᵉ Congrès Triennal de la Société Internationale de Littérature Courtois* (Salerno: Pubblicazioni dell'Università degli Studi di Salerno, 1992), pp. 39–54; Elizabeth Archibald, *Incest and the Medieval Imagination* (Oxford: Clarendon Press, 2001), pp. 201–2. While Keller concludes that the legend was not especially widespread, Lejeune's, Vulliez's, and Archibald's accounts suggest otherwise.

121. Most of the recent scholarship on *Tristan de Nanteuil* has focused on trans studies, gender studies, and interspecies relationships. See, for example, Francesca Canadé Sautman, "What Can They Possibly Do Together? Queer Epic Performances in *Tristan de Nanteuil*," in *Same Sex Love and Desire among Women in the Middle Ages*, ed. Francesca Canadé Sautman and Pamela Sheingorn (New York: Palgrave, 2001), pp. 199–232; Alban Georges, "Entre le héros et le saint: L'androgyne; Androgynie et médiation dans *Tristan de Nanteuil*," in *Entre l'ange et la bête: L'homme et ses limites au Moyen Âge*, ed. Marie-Étiennette Bély, Jean-René Valette, and Jean-Claude Vallecalle (Lyon: Presses universitaires de Lyon, 2003), pp. 151–65; Kimberlee Campbell, "Acting like a Man: Performing Gender in *Tristan de Nanteuil*," in *Cultural Performances in Medieval France: Essays in Honor of Nancy Freeman Regalado*, ed. Eglal Doss-Quinby, Roberta L. Krueger, and E. Jane Burns (Woodbridge: D. S. Brewer, 2007), pp. 79–89; Peggy McCracken, "The Wild Man and His Kin in *Tristan de Nanteuil*," in *L'humain et l'animal dans la France médiévale (XIIᵉ– XVᵉ s.)*, ed. Irène Fabry-Tehranchi and Anna Russakoff (Amsterdam: Rodopi, 2014), pp. 21–42; Blake Gutt, "Transgender Genealogy in *Tristan de Nanteuil*," *Exemplaria* 30 (2018): pp. 129–46.

122. On the "sins of the tongue," see Edwin D. Craun, "Introduction," pp. ix–xviii, in *The Hands of the Tongue: Essays on Deviant Speech*, ed. Edwin D. Craun (Kalamazoo, MI: Medieval Institute Publications, 2007); Carla Casagrande and Silvana Vecchio, *Les péchés de la langue: Discipline et éthique de la parole dans la culture médiévale*, trans. Philippe Baillet (Paris: Cerf, 1991), especially the discussion of "crimes against truth," p. 187ff.

123. For further development of medieval "age expectations" regarding the first age of man, see Youngs, *Life Cycle in Western Europe*, p. 21.

124. Following accepted practice, laisse and line number will be given as a roman numeral, followed by a period and an arabic numeral.

125. Connor, *Dumbstruck*, p. 24.

126. Dolar, *A Voice*, p. 62.

127. Nico H. van den Boogaard has identified traces of the text's division into fifteen oral performance sessions; van den Boogaard, "Le caractère oral de la chanson de geste tardive," *Rapports/Het franse Boek* 48 (1978): pp. 61–74.

128. Serres, *Parasite*, p. 185.

129. See Keith V. Sinclair, *Tristan de Nanteuil: Thematic Infrastructure and Literary Creation* (Tübingen: Niemeyer, 1983), esp. p. 121. More generally, Alexander Haggerty Krappe characterizes *Tristan de Nanteuil* as a "composite" work woven together from disparate textual and folkloric sources in "Tristan de Nanteuil," *Romania* 61 (1935): pp. 55–71.

130. Frederic C. Tubach, *Index exemplorum: A Handbook of Medieval Religious Tales* (Helsinki: Suomalainen Tiedeakatemia, 1969). See especially nos. 408 (p. 37), 648 (p. 54), and 1460 (p. 117). C. Grant Loomis remarks that this motif appears frequently in saints' lives, but he cites no specific examples: Loomis, *White Magic: An Introduction to the Folklore of Christian Legend* (Cambridge, MA: Medieval Academy of America, 1948), p. 24.

131. Sinclair remarks, "In the matter of sources the author is only specific when narrating sections of the life of his own hermit character, Gilles," and he points out that the two saints' lives cited comprise the source for nearly an eighth of the chanson's total bulk. *Tristan de Nanteuil: Thematic Infrastructure*, p. 133.

132. Alban Georges has noted the connection, without exploring it in depth: Georges, *Tristan de Nanteuil*, p. 633. The *Merlin* episode is discussed at length below in chap. 4.

133. Robert de Boron, *Merlin: Roman du XIIIe siècle*, ed. Alexandre Micha (Geneva: Droz, 1979), pp. 68–69. On the divine origins of Merlin's prophetic speech and the contrast with the perverse and seductive speech of his diabolical father, see Christine Ferlampin-Acher, "La parole dans le Merlin de Robert de Boron," in *Merlin, Roman du XIIIe siècle*, ed. Danielle Quéruel and Christine Ferlampin-Acher (Paris: Ellipses, 2000), pp. 89–104.

134. Robert de Boron, *Merlin*, p. 57. Earlier the eighteen-month-old Merlin had promised his mother that "vos ne morroiz por pechié qui de moi vos soit avenuz" (You will not die for the sin that happened to you through me; p. 53).

135. Connor, *Dumbstruck*, p. 25.

136. Serres, *Parasite*, p. 79.

137. The diabolically engendered fetus is not born, but it does exit its mother's body. In this regard it offers an interesting parallel to the legend of the Antichrist's delivery by Caesarean section, studied by Renate Blumenfeld-Kosinski in *Not of Woman Born: Representations of Caesarean Birth in Medieval and Renaissance Culture* (Ithaca, NY: Cornell University Press, 1990). As the mother of two imps delivered by Caesarean, I can attest to the verisimilitude of this legend.

138. Mitchell, *Becoming*, p. 14.

139. Ong, *Presence*, pp. 41–42.

140. Angela Leighton, *Hearing Things: The Work of Sound in Literature* (Cambridge, MA: Belknap Press of Harvard University Press, 2018), p. 5.

141. Tasioulas, "Heaven and Earth," p. 35.

142. Connor, *Dumbstruck*, p. 36.

CHAPTER TWO

1. Rachel May Golden and Katherine Kong, "Introduction," in *Gender and Voice in Medieval French Literature and Song* (Gainesville: University Press of Florida, 2021), pp. 1–28, at p. 2.

2. Jeffrey Jerome Cohen, "Kyte oute yugilment: An Introduction to Medieval Noise," *Exemplaria* 16, no. 2 (2004): pp. 267–76, at p. 269.

3. Dolar, *A Voice*, p. 26.

4. My thinking about representations of infant cries as "thought experiments" is informed by Dolar as well as by Giorgio Agamben, who reflects on infancy as "an *experimentum linguae* [...] in which the limits of language are to be found not outside language, in the direction of its referent, but in an experience of language as such, in its pure self-reference"; Agamben, *Infancy*, 5. See also the thoughtful framing in Morton, "Introduction."

5. For the Latin grammarian Priscian, who remained authoritative throughout the Middle Ages, "Far from being sound alien to language, voice-noise as a subset of vocal utterance inhabits grammar, as dissonance within"; Valerie J. Allen, "Broken Air," *Exemplaria* 16, no. 2 (2004): pp. 305–22, at p. 306. An overview of Priscian's *Institutiones* and their influence in the Middle Ages is provided in Rita Copeland and Ineke Sluiter, eds., *Medieval Grammar and Rhetoric: Language Arts and Literary Theory, AD 300–1475* (Oxford and New York: Oxford University Press, 2009).

6. See, for example, Albert the Great, *Questions Concerning Aristotle's On Animals*, trans. Irven M. Resnick and Kenneth F. Kitchell, Jr. (Washington, DC: Catholic University Press, 2008), bk. 4, pp. 160–62, question 8: "Whether every voice is significative."

7. Voice is also robustly theorized in medieval theology, physiology, and music theory. For a far more thorough survey of medieval theories of voice I refer the reader to David Lawton, *Voice in Later Medieval English Literature: Public Interiorities* (Oxford and New York: Oxford University Press, 2017), esp. pp. 12–41. See also Jean-Marie Fritz, *Paysages sonores du Moyen Âge: Le versant épistémologique* (Paris: Champion, 2000), pp. 190–204.

8. Isidore, *Etymologies*, p. 39. "Litterae autem sunt indices rerum, signa verborum, quibus tanta vis est, ut nobis dicta absentium sine voce loquantur. Verba enim per oculos non per aures introducunt"; *Etymologiarum*, bk. 1, chap. 3, sent. 1.

9. The fullest study of the interjection in medieval theories of language is Irène Rosier, *La parole comme acte: Sur la grammaire et la sémantique au XIIIᵉ siècle* (Paris: Vrin, 1994), pp. 57–122.

10. Isidore, *Etymologies*, p. 96.

11. Bartholomaeus Anglicus, *De rerum Proprietatibus* (Frankfurt 1601; facs., Frankfurt: Minerva, 1964), p. 1253.

12. On tree structures, see Franco Moretti, *Graphs, Maps, Trees: Abstract Models for Literary History* (London: Verso, 2005). As in Moretti's discussion, medieval natural philosophers display evident "pleasure in the pattern." For overviews of these divisions, especially from a musical perspective, see Elizabeth Eva Leach, *Sung Birds: Music, Nature, and Poetry in the Later Middle Ages* (Ithaca, NY: Cornell University Press, 2007), pp. 24–40; Emma Dillon, *The Sense of Sound: Musical Meaning in France, 1260–1330* (Oxford and New York: Oxford University Press, 2012), pp. 36–43.

13. Irven M. Resnick and Kenneth F. Kitchell, Jr., "Albert the Great on the 'Language' of Animals," *American Catholic Philosophical Journal* 70 (1996): pp. 41–61, at p. 42. My summary of Albert's schema owes a heavy debt to their article.

14. Albertus Magnus, *De animalibus libri XXVI*, ed. Hermann Stadler, Beiträge zur Geschichte der Philosophie des Mittelalters 15 (Münster: Aschendorff, 1916), p. 397, ll. 92–93.

15. Albertus, *De animalibus*, p. 398, ll. 3–5.

16. Dolar, *A Voice*, p. 15.

17. For further comment on medieval iterations of this idea, notably as expressed by Abelard, see Umberto Eco, Roberto Lambertini, Costantino Marmo, and Andrea Tabarroni, "On Animal Language in the Medieval Classification of Signs," in *On the Medieval Theory of Signs*, ed. Umberto Eco and Costantino Marmo (Amsterdam: Benjamins, 1989), pp. 3–41, at p. 15.

18. Eco, Lambertini, Marmo, and Tabarroni, "On Animal Language."

19. Julie Orlemanski, "Margery's 'Noyse' and Distributed Expressivity," in *Voice and Voicelessness in Medieval Europe*, ed. Irit Ruth Kleiman (New York: Palgrave Macmillan, 2015), pp. 123–38, at p. 125.

20. See Rosier, *La parole*, especially chaps. 2 and 3; Fritz, *Paysages*, pp. 190–91.

21. Priscian, *Grammaire: Livres XIV, XV, XVI—Les invariables*, ed. and trans. Marc Baratin, Frédérique Biville, Guillaume Bonnet, Bernard Colombat, Cécile Conduché, Alessandro Garcea, Louis Holtz, Séverine Issaeva, Madeleine Keller, and Diane Marchand (Paris: Vrin, 2013), pp. 214–16.

22. Peter Helie differentiates between "interiectiones significativas ad placitum" and those "quae sunt soni litterati, et imitatorias" in his commentary on Priscian: see Jan Pinborg, "Interjektionen und Naturlaute: Petrus Heliae und ein Problem der antiken und mittelalterlichen Sprachphilosophie," *Classica et Mediaevalia* 22 (1961): pp. 117–38, at p. 122. Bacon distinguishes between involuntary and conventional expressions of pain (the "groan" and the "ouch") in *De signis* I.9: discussed in Eco, Lambertini, Marmo, and Tabarroni, "On Animal Language," p. 14.

23. As Rosier notes, the interjection plays a major role in the speculative grammarians' definitions of "modes"; Rosier, *La parole*, p. 82.

24. Isidore, *Etymologiarum*, bk. 1, chap. 14; *Etymologies*, pp. 46–47.

25. Cavarero expands on the infant voice as an invocation entrusting itself to the voice that responds in *For More*, p. 169. On the ethics of the maternal response to that call, see Adriana Cavarero, *Inclinations: A Critique of Rectitude*, trans. Amanda Minervini and Adam Sitze (Stanford, CA: Stanford University Press, 2016), esp. pp. 56–58.

26. Isidore, *Etymologarium*, bk. 1, chap. 4, sent. 3; *Etymologies*, p. 40.

27. Isidore, *Etymologarium*, bk. 1, chap. 4, sent. 16; *Etymologies*, p. 41; emphasis added.

28. Cited in Anna Zayaruznaya, "'Sanz note' & 'sanz mesure': Toward a Premodern Aesthetics of the Dirge," in *Voice and Voicelessness in Medieval Europe*, ed. Irit Ruth Kleiman (New York: Palgrave Macmillan, 2015), pp. 155–75; Lambertini, Marmo, and Tabarroni, "On Animal Language," p. 165.

29. Cavarero, *For More*, p. 132.

30. Albert the Great, *Questions*, p. 161.

31. Henry Suso, *Heinrich Seuses Horologium Sapientiae* (Freiburg: Universitätsverlag Freiburg Schweiz, 1977), I.16, pp. 512–13.

32. Henry Suso, *Wisdom's Watch upon the Hours*, trans. Edmund Colledge (Washington, DC: Catholic University Press, 1994), p. 224.

33. About fifty manuscripts of the full French translation survive, along with many more that reproduce some of the *Horologium*'s content in *Tresor* or digest form. *Dictionnaire des lettres françaises: Le Moyen Âge* (hereafter *DLFMA*), s.v. "Henri Suso," p. 676.

34. *Dragmaticon* VI.10, para. 3; cited and discussed in Fritz, *Paysages sonores*, p. 278.

35. *Women's Secrets*, p. 107.

36. BnF MS fr. 16993, fol. 75vb.

37. Robert Jacob, *Les époux, le seigneur et la cité: Coutume et pratiques matrimoniales des bourgeois et paysans de France du Nord au Moyen Âge* (Brussels: Facultés universitaires Saint-Louis, 1990), p. 361. His discussion of this matter responds to Heinrich Brunner, "Die Geburt eines lebenden Kindes und das eheliche Vermögensrecht," *Zeitschrift der Savigny Stiftung für Rechtsgeschichte—Germanistische Abteilung* 16 (1895): pp. 65–108.

38. E.-M. Meijers and J.-J. Salverda de Grave, *Des lois et coutumes de Saint-Amand* (Haarlem: Tjeenk Willink & Zoon, 1934), p. 65.

39. Philippe de Beaumanoir, *Coutumes de Beauvaisis*, ed. Amédée Salmon, 2 vols. (Paris: Picard, 1899–1900), vol. 1, p. 306, no. 618.

40. *The Coutumes de Beauvaisis of Philippe de Beaumanoir*, trans. F. R. P. Akehurst (Philadelphia: University of Pennsylvania Press, 1992), p. 221, no. 618.

41. The Perugian jurist Baldus de Ubaldis makes a similar move, as Lefebvre-Teillard discusses in "*Infans conceptus*," p. 511.

42. Elsewhere, when discussing the means by which young people can prove

they have reached the age of majority, Beaumanoir writes that testimony can be offered by "les nourices" (wet nurses) and "les mesnies qui estoient entour la mere ou tans qu'il fu nes" (people of his mother's household when he was born), among others. No. 556, pp. 266–67 in Salmon, p. 195 in Akehurst. As for witnesses to establish a live birth, Beaumanoir specifies only that they must be truthful.

43. This is another major meaning of *vox* in medieval grammar: a quotable piece of text. Lawton, *Voice*, p. 3 and passim.

44. *Le Roman de Thèbes*, ed. Guy Raynaud de Lage (Paris: Champion, 1966), p. 4, vv. 107–14. Ménard cites similar scenes in the *chansons de geste La Bataille Loquifer, Jourdain de Blayes*, and *Daurel et Beton: Le rire et le sourire*, p. 33. The same plot device is used, with a slightly older child (in this case the titular character, at age five or six), in *L'histoire de Guillaume le Maréchal*, ll. 525–60. *History of William Marshal*, ed. A. J. Holden, trans. S. Gregory (London: Anglo-Norman Text Society, 2002).

45. On the infant's age in this story, as visible in the romance's frequent repetitions that the countess has not yet completed her lying-in, see Peggy McCracken, *The Curse of Eve, the Wound of the Hero: Blood, Gender, and Medieval Literature* (Philadelphia: University of Pennsylvania Press, 2003), pp. 64–76.

46. Christine de Pizan, *Le livre du corps de policie*, ed. Robert H. Lucas (Geneva: Droz, 1967), p. 5. This line is also quoted by Jesus in Matthew 21:16. Lett points out that hagiographers, in recounting miraculous healings of children, often quote this verse; *L'enfant*, p. 80.

47. English Bible citations are from the American Douay-Rheims translation.

48. *Le Roman de Cassidorus*, ed. Joseph Palermo, vol. 2 (Paris: Picard for the SATF, 1964), p. 485.

49. *Patrologia Latina*, p. 198, col. 1071B; emphasis added.

50. Lotario dei Segni, *De miseria condicionis humane*, ed. and trans. Robert E. Lewis (Athens: University of Georgia Press, 1978). For an overview of this text's thematics and a contextualization of it within Innocent's other writings, see Robert Bultot, "Mépris du monde, misère et dignité de l'homme, dans la pensée d'Innocent III," *Cahiers de civilisation médiévale* 4 (1961): pp. 441–56.

51. Christine Martineau-Génieys, *Le thème de la mort dans la poésie française de 1450 à 1550* (Paris: Champion, 1978), pp. 112, 126. Jean Delumeau contests Martineau-Génieys's argument that the text grew in popularity after the Black Death, pointing out that a substantial proportion of surviving manuscripts date from the thirteenth century. Delumeau, *Sin and Fear: The Emergence of a Western Guilt Culture, 13th–18th Centuries*, trans. Eric Nicholson (New York: Saint Martin's Press, 1990), p. 45.

52. For R. Howard Bloch, this is "deadly serious wordplay" that betokens broad patterns of misogynistic thinking. Bloch, *Medieval Misogyny and the Invention of Western Romantic Love* (Chicago: University of Chicago Press, 1991), p. 25.

53. Note the etymology of *eiulatu*, from the interjection *ei*, an exclamation of pain and sorrow. *Lateinisches Etymologisches Wörterbuch (LEW)*, s.v. "ei."

54. On the significance of the name Eva in early linguistic discussions, see

Umberto Eco, *The Search for the Perfect Language*, trans. James Fentress (Oxford: Blackwell, 1995), p. 8. The meaning of the name Eva was not arcane knowledge in the Middle Ages: it is cited, for instance, by the so-called *mesnagier de Paris* in his late fourteenth-century manual for his young wife. This bourgeois lay writer states that "apres ce qu'ilz orent pechié elle ot nom Eva, qui vault autant que *vita*: car toutes les creatures humaines qui puis ont eu vie et avront sont venues d'elle" (after they had sinned she had the name Eva, which means life: for all human creatures who have lived since then or who will ever live came from her). *Le mesnagier de Paris*, ed. Georgina E. Brereton and Janet M. Ferrier (Paris: Poche Lettres Gothiques, 1994), p. 156.

55. Fritz draws a number of similar conclusions from Comestor's description of the name Eva (*Paysages*, p. 279). However, these come through much more clearly in Lotario's modified account, as the latter provides causal rationales for resemblances that Comestor attributes at least partly to happenstance.

56. Lawton, *Voice*, p. 5.

57. Even this brief look at the manuscript variants reveals a striking visual similarity between the words *nez* (born) and *vois* (voice) as written in late medieval French hands: beyond the strong cultural association between birth and voice that I am laying out in this chapter, the two words also look enough alike that they are easily mistaken for each other.

58. See Mary Sirridge, "The Wailing of Orphans, the Cooing of Doves, and the Groans of the Sick: The Influence of Augustine's Theory of Language on Some Theories of the Interjection," in *Vestigia, Imagines, Verba: Semiotics and Logic in Medieval Theological Texts (XIIth–XIVth Century)*, ed. Costantino Marmo (Turnhout: Brepols, 1997), pp. 99–116.

59. The *Besant de Dieu* survives in a unique manuscript (BnF fr. 19525), and the leaf containing the adaptation of *De miseria* chap. 6 (fol. 105v) is damaged; while the A/E discussion was probably not raised in that part of the text, I cannot entirely rule it out. Guillaume Le Clerc, *Le besant de Dieu*, ed. Pierre Ruelle (Brussels: Éditions de l'Université de Bruxelles, 1973).

60. The verb *se guarmenter* refers often, but not exclusively, to verbal laments. In Middle French it is often paired with the verb *pleurer*, *complaindre*, or *se plaindre*: DMF, s.v. "guermenter," accessed 22 April 2024, http://www.atilf.fr/dmf/definition/guermenter. The word is also used, in *Les Livres du roy Modus et de la royne Ratio*, to refer to the call a stag makes to a doe: *Dictionnaire étymologique de l'ancien français*, s.v. "garmenter."

61. While an inscription in the manuscript (in a different hand from the rest) states that it was presented to Charles V, the date makes that dedication impossible: see Patricia Michon, "Une édition manuscrite d'Eustache Deschamps: Le *Double lay de fragilité humaine*," in *L'écrivain éditeur*, vol. 1, *Du Moyen Âge à la fin du XVIIIe siècle*, ed. F. Bessire, special issue, *Travaux de littérature* 14 (2001): pp. 27–42.

62. Daniel Poirion, in his classic study of late medieval courtly poetry, calls the *Double lay* "un ensemble d'interprétations poétiques, de méditations lyriques"

(a set of poetic interpretations, lyric meditations): Daniel Poirion, *Le poète et le prince: L'évolution du lyrisme courtois de Guillaume de Machaut à Charles d'Orléans* (Paris: Presses Universitaires de France, 1965), p. 404. Martineau-Génieys calls it "une interprétation, dans le sens où l'on parle de l'interprétation de l'oeuvre d'un musicien par un autre artiste" (an interpretation, in the sense in which one speaks of the interpretation of one musician's work by another performer): Martineau-Génieys, *Le thème de la mort*, p. 128. And G. Matteo Roccati calls it not a translation but "une réélaboration assez poussée" (a fairly extensive reworking) in "La culture latine d'Eustache Deschamps," *Le Moyen Age* 111, no. 2 (2005): pp. 259–74.

63. BnF MS fr. 20029 gives the Latin text—but only of the passages Deschamps chose to adapt—alongside the French text. Differences in size and lettering suggest a reading of the Latin as a gloss of the French. See Geneviève Hasenohr, "Discours vernaculaire et autorités latines," in *Mise en page et mise en texte du livre manuscrit*, ed. Henri-Jean Martin and Jean Vezin (Paris: Éditions du cercle de la Librairie-Promodis, 1990), pp. 288–315; Laura Kendrick, "The Monument and the Margin," *South Atlantic Quarterly* 91, no. 4 (1992): pp. 835–64. The manuscript of Deschamps's complete works, made by Raoul Tainguy after the poet's death, does not replicate this easily legible two-column layout, instead alternating French and Latin in a less systematic manner. This problem is discussed in paragraph 24 of Clotilde Dauphant, "L'organisation du manuscrit des Œuvres complètes d'Eustache Deschamps par Raoul Tainguy," *Babel* 16 (2007), accessed 18 December 2018, http://journals.openedition.org/babel/702; DOI: 10.4000/babel.702.

64. Deschamps, *Oeuvres complètes*, vol. 2, p. 259, vv. 189–90, 193–94.

65. There is but one recent study of this author: Sylvie Lefèvre, "Guillaume Alecis: Une oeuvre entre manuscrits et imprimés," in *Au prisme du manuscrit: Regards sur la littérature française du Moyen Âge (1300–1500)*, ed. Sandra Hindman and Elliot Adam (Turnhout: Brepols, 2019), pp. 270–87.

66. In Middle French texts, the word *aspiration* is used mainly in rhetorical manuals. A prime example is Jacques Legrand's *Archiloge Sophie*, in which *aspirations* are cited as evidence of the primitive imperfection of the Hebrew language: "Par quoy il appert que hebrieu fut le premier langage: lequel quant a aucuns cas est moult imparfait, car il a pluseurs lectres sans necessité et use moult de aspiracions . . ."; Legrand, *Archiloge Sophie, Livre de bonnes moeurs*, ed. Evencio Beltran (Geneva: Slatkine, 1986), p. 59, ll. 11–14.

67. Hewson, *Giles*, p. 52.

68. *La phisionomie de maistre Michel Lescot, compilee par luy, & depuis traduicte de latin en vulgaire francoys par maistre Nicole Volkyr de Serouille, secretaire du duc de Lorraine* (Paris: Vincent Sertenas, 1540), fol. 28r–28v.

69. As Émile Benveniste noted, "From the sign to the sentence there is no transition, neither by syntagmation nor by any other means. A gap separates them." Cited in Giorgio Agamben, *The Signature of All Things: On Method*, trans. Luca D'Isanto and Kevin Attell (New York: Zone Books, 2009), p. 61.

70. Agamben characterizes the statement (as elaborated by Foucault in *Archaeology of Knowledge*) thus: "Neither semiotic nor semantic, not yet discourse and no longer mere sign, statements, like signatures, do not institute semiotic relations or create new meanings; instead, they mark and 'characterize' signs at the level of their existence, thus actualizing and displaying their efficacy"; Agamben, *Signature*, p. 64.

71. "Larger than a sound (so more than a phoneme or even most single words other than the imperatives of verbs), *vox* is the smallest free-standing unit of discourse, a phrase or clause, a snatch of conversation or text;" Lawton, *Voice*, pp. 26–27.

72. This analogy is especially clear in a *Meditatio de humana conditione*, probably by Hugh of St. Victor, that Lotario used as a source for *De miseria*: at birth "I was thrown out into the exile of this world, wailing and crying"; quoted in Delumeau, *Sin and Fear*, p. 44.

73. *Placides et Timéo*, incidentally, posits an etymological relationship to the *babil* of infants. Fritz, *Paysages*, p. 283.

74. On the philosophical history of Adam as never-infant, see Cavarero, *Inclinations*, p. 17.

75. *Women's Secrets*, p. 107. In commenting upon this passage Mitchell—not accounting for the larger *A/E* tradition—dismisses the infant cry as non-speech: "The cry is a noise that is hard to manage in any case, denoting the agony and humiliation of a babbling, bare life: a not-yet-rational or redeemed humanity"; Mitchell, *Becoming*, p. 32.

76. As Alexandre-Bidon and Closson note, in medieval France cultural gender distinctions also commence immediately after birth. Alexandre-Bidon and Closson, *L'enfant*, p. 65.

77. Peggy McCracken, *In the Skin of a Beast: Sovereignty and Animality in Medieval France* (Chicago: University of Chicago Press, 2017), p. 1.

78. Ballade MCVI, *Oeuvres complètes*, vol. 6, pp. 11–13.

79. On Philippe de Novare's literary culture, see Elisabeth Schulze-Busacker, "Philippe de Novare, les *Quatre âges de l'homme*," *Romania* 127 (2009): pp. 104–46. Because he appears to have been largely self-taught and to have undertaken his readings while living in the Holy Land, Schulze-Busacker argues that the study of Philippe's citations offers precious insight into what books were circulating among French-speakers in thirteenth-century *Outremer*.

80. *Les quatre âges*, pp. 2–3, para. 3. Similar sentiments are expressed in the thirteenth-century prose *Riote du monde*, but without the underlying affection, as the version of the text in BnF MS fr. 1553 reads, "Si n'amai onques petit anfant ne moien ne grant: li petis est anieus a norir, et si ne lait la gent dormir par nuit" (And I have never loved little children nor mid-sized ones nor big ones: the little one is a pain to raise, and it doesn't let people sleep at night . . .). "La riote du monde," ed. J. Ulrich, *Zeitschrift für romanische Philologie* 8 (1884): pp. 275–89, at p. 282. Similar

complaints about the noise of infant cries are to be found in works as diverse as Abelard's letters, Rutebeuf's poetry, and the antifeminist *Quinze joies de mariage.*

81. *Les quatre âges*, pp. 4–5, para. 6.

82. *Les quatre âges*, p. 5, para. 6.

83. Karl Steel, *How Not to Make a Human* (Minneapolis: University of Minnesota Press, 2019), p. 10.

84. *Oeuvres complètes*, vol. 2, p. 258, vv. 179–88.

85. This move is typical of French adaptations. See also Besançon MS 434.

86. "There is melancholy here in both the image and the French verse that is totally lacking in the Latin original"; Michael Camille, *Master of Death: The Lifeless Art of Pierre Remiet, Illuminator* (New Haven, CT: Yale University Press, 1996), p. 89.

87. Most French versions of Lotario's text do remain largely faithful to his language, aside from BnF fr. 461, which reduces the description of children with deformities to a single sentence ("Aucuns en naissent si deffourme et si tres lait que ilz n'apperent mie comme homme mais contre nature de fourme d'omme" [Some are born so deformed and so very ugly that they don't appear at all like humans but against the nature of the human form], fol 97r). At the other end of the spectrum, Guillaume Alexis (characteristically) offers an expansive rendering of this passage, devoting no fewer than sixteen lines to the subject.

88. "Nam illa ut statim orta sunt gradiantur; nos autem non solum erecti pedibus non incedimus, verum eciam curvati manibus non reptamus" ("for they walk as soon as they are born; but we do not only not walk upright on our feet, we do not even crawl bent over on our hands"), pp. 102–3. Locomotion and a deliberate ambiguity between human and nonhuman animals also lie at the core of the Sphinx's riddle, solved by Oedipus: "D'une beste ai oÿ parler: / quant primes doit par terre aler / a quatre piez vet . . ." (I have heard tell of a beast that, when it first has to move about on the ground, goes on four legs . . .). *Roman de Thèbes*, p. 11, vv. 317–19.

89. In this way, healthy newborns are the "humans whose bodies diverge from the stereotypical 'human' bodies of the tradition by not allowing them to gaze at the heavens or walk upright without assistance," whom Karl Steel seeks as "marginal cases" that would test medieval ides about the association of human reason with upright posture. Karl Steel, *How to Make a Human* (Columbus: Ohio State University Press, 2011), pp. 47–48.

90. Likewise the question of nudity—present in Deschamps and especially in the anonymous French prose translation—magnifies this sense of social alienation: "Et moins encore assez avons nous que bestes mues en plusieurs choses, quar si tost comme elles sont nees elles vont toutes droites **et si sont vestues**, et nous sommes **touz nuz** et ne nous poons soustenir ne de piez ne de mains"; Besançon MS 434, fol. 379rb.

91. On this manuscript and its illustrations, see, notably, Michon, "Une édition manuscrite"; Camille, *Master of Death*; *Paris 1400: Les arts sous Charles VI* (Paris: Réunion des musées nationaux, 2004), pp. 53–55.

92. Camille, *Master of Death*, p. 88.

93. Corbechon, BnF MS fr. 16993, fol. 77va. Also: "Quant l'enfant ist hors, le nombril est rompu ou couppé pres de la marris et ist avec l'enfant et le lient les ventrieres a la longueur de .iiii. dois et de ceste lieure se fait la ronde boce qui est au dehors du nombril"; fol. 66ra–b.

94. BnF MS fr. 16993, fol. 66rb.

95. Bartholomaeus devotes a substantial portion of his chapter on navels to the difference between human and avian navels. The prominent place of the umbilical cord in this image may also offer a faint allusion to female sexuality (which is the source of all human suffering, for if not for women's lustful nature, children would not be conceived in the first place). Corbechon, following Bartholomaeus, writes that a woman's genitals are concealed beneath her navel (BnF MS fr. 16993, fol. 66rb).

96. I follow Michael Camille (*Master of Death*, p. 88) in identifying this animal as an ass. However, it should be noted that according to medieval lore, jennies rarely birth twins: "Il est pou souvent trové que l'anesse ait porté .ii. faons a une foiz"; Corbechon, BnF MS fr. 16993, fol. 293ra.

97. Corbechon explains this in his chapter on asses; additionally, he writes that fumigation with smoke from either burning dung or burning hooves could help accelerate childbirth (BnF MS fr. 16993, fols. 292va–293va). On the ass as an emblem of parental self-sacrifice, see Nicole Bozon, *Les contes moralisés*, ed. Lucy Toulmin Smith and Paul Meyer (Paris: Firmin Didot for the SATF, 1889), pp. 155–56. Christopher Lucken traces the symbolism of the donkey in biblical texts and in medieval encyclopedias and bestiaries, especially as an emblem of humility, in "L'âne ou le corps silencieux d'une parole en souffrance," *Micrologus* 8 (2000): pp. 511–35. Additionally, Alexandre-Bidon and Closson note that the composition of jenny's milk is more similar to human milk than is that of other barnyard animals: *L'enfant*, p. 135.

98. Fritz, *Paysages*, pp. 196, 340.

99. *Oeuvres complètes*, vol. 9, p. 9, ll. 171–72.

100. Camille, *Master of Death*, p. 65.

101. Corbechon, BnF MS fr. 16993, fol. 77ra. Here he translates Bartholomaeus's "Mater, secundum Isido. Sicitur eo, quod foetui nutriendo mammam porrigat," p. 241. However, this does not make sense, nor is it at all what Isidore says; Isidore derives *mater* from *materia*. Isidore, *Etymologarium*, bk. 9, chap. 5, sent. 4; *Etymologies*, p. 206.

102. Cavarero, *Inclinations*, p. 56; emphasis in original.

103. Cavarero, *Inclinations*, p. 56.

104. P. 79, vv. 252–54, 261–63.

105. The phrase "un autre petit feon" indicates a nonbinary and nonanthropocentric view of human/animal comparisons, creating an obvious point of contact with critical animal studies approaches—especially given Susan Crane's suggestion that practitioners of medieval animal studies must abandon human/animal binaries

in favor of "a multiplicity of intersecting and competing distinctions that better re-flect medieval ways of thinking"; Crane, *Animal Encounters: Contacts and Concepts in Medieval Britain* (Philadelphia: University of Pennsylvania Press, 2013), p. 8. Also see Joyce E. Salisbury's foundational study *The Beast Within: Animals in the Middle Ages* (New York: Routledge, 1994), esp. chap. 5, "Humans as Animals." While I will not further pursue the potential of animal studies to enrich this study of newborn humanity, I wish to signal this as a potentially fruitful avenue for future inquiry.

106. "Digression de la foiblesce, fragilité et grans passibilité de humaine créa-ture"; Olivier de la Haye, *Poème sur la grande peste de 1348*, ed. Georges Guigue (Lyon: Henri Georg, 1888), p. 63. The poem draws on the 1349 French prose trans-lation of the Paris medical faculty's 1348 consultation on the Black Death, though the source does not include this "digression"; it does state that children are among those most prone to be infected with the plague, and it is just after that section that Olivier inserts it. See Rudolf Sies, *Das "Pariser Pestgutachten" von 1348 in alt-französischer Fassung*, Würzburger medizinhistorische Forschungen 7 (Hannover: Horst Wellm, 1977), p. 34.

107. Dolar, *A Voice*, p. 60; emphasis in original.

108. The debate is helpfully summarized in *Trésor de la langue française* (here-after *TLF*), s.v. "macabre."

109. "Item, l'an 1424, fut faite la Danse Macabre aux Innocents, et fut com-mencée environ le mois d'août et achevée au Carême ensuivant"; *Journal d'un bourgeois de Paris*, ed. Colette Beaune (Paris: Poche Lettres Gothiques, 1990), p. 220.

110. My account of the *danse macabre* tradition is necessarily incomplete. The reader will find full bibliographies in several outstanding recent scholarly works: Elina Gertsman, *The Dance of Death in the Middle Ages: Image, Text, Performance* (Turnhout: Brepols, 2010); Sophie Oosterwijk, "Dance, Dialogue, and Duality: Fatal Encounters in the Medieval *Danse Macabre*," in *Mixed Metaphors: The Danse Macabre in Medieval and Early Modern Europe*, ed. Sophie Oosterwijk and Stefanie Knöll (Newcastle upon Tyne: Cambridge Scholars, 2011), pp. 9–42; Ashby Kinch, *Imago Mortis: Mediating Images of Death in Late Medieval Culture* (Leiden: Brill, 2013); Seeta Chaganti, *Strange Footing: Poetic Form and Dance in the Late Middle Ages* (Chicago: University of Chicago Press, 2018).

111. Megan Leigh Cook and Elizaveta Strakhov, *John Lydgate's Dance of Death and Related Works* (Kalamazoo, MI: Medieval Institute, 2019).

112. A 1449 performance in Bruges is mentioned in Pasquale Morabito's intro-duction to Jean Miélot, *Mors de la pomme* (Messina: Peloritana, 1967), p. 115. The *danse macabre* furnished the subject for one of many snow or ice sculptures erected in Arras during the bitterly cold winter of 1434–35: "Item, devant les Loé Dieu estoit la dansse machabre où estoient en figure de nege l'Empereur, le Roy, le Mort et Manouvrier" (*Item*, in front of the *Loé Dieu* [a convent] was the *danse machabre* in which there were snow figures of the Emperor, the King, the Cadaver, and the

Laborer). Robert Muchembled, *Culture populaire et culture des élites dans la France moderne (XVᵉ–XVIIIᵉ siècles)* (Paris: Flammarion, 1978), p. 162.

113. There is a recent, accessible edition of Marchant's first edition, with an English translation: *The Danse Macabre Printed by Guyot Marchant, 1485*, trans. David A. Fein (Tempe, AZ: ACMRS, 2013).

114. Jane H. M. Taylor, "Danse Macabré and Bande Dessinée: A Question of Reading," *Forum for Modern Language Studies* 25, no. 4 (1989): pp. 356–69, at p. 357.

115. See above, n. 111. Also by Chaganti: "*Danse macabre* and the Virtual Churchyard," *Postmedieval* 3, no. 1 (2012): pp. 7–26. A few other scholars, notably Taylor and Eustace and King, have thought about the text in conjunction with dance practice. Jane H. M. Taylor, "Que signifiait *danse* au quinzième siècle? Danser la Danse macabré," *Fifteenth Century Studies* 18 (1991): pp. 259–77. Frances Eustace with Pamela M. King, "Dances of the Living and the Dead: A Study of *Danse Macabre* Imagery within the Context of Late-Medieval Dance Culture," in Oosterwijk and Knöll, *Mixed Metaphors*, pp. 43–71.

116. Cited from Marchant, as shown in Fein, *The Danse Macabre*, p. 48. Fein errs in transcribing the first word of the last line as "Ainsi" (p. 49).

117. Sophie Oosterwijk, "'Muoz ich tanzen und kan nit gun?' Death and the Infant in the Medieval *danse macabre*," *Word & Image* 22, no. 2 (2006): pp. 146–64, at p. 152.

118. Gertsman, *Dance*, p. 92; Oosterwijk, "Muoz," p. 152.

119. Like the other characters being pulled away by the dead, the infant peppers his speech with a great many negations: four over the eight lines of his stanza. In the case of the baby who dies as soon as he was born, his existence can be affirmed only by its opposite. I am reminded of Roman Jakobson's famous reading of Poe's "The Raven," in which he observes that "semantically, the author prepares us for the unlimited negation *nevermore* by repeating the restrictive negation *merely this and nothing more*"; Jakobson, "Language in Operation," in *Language in Literature*, ed. Krystyna Pomorska and Stephen Rudy (Cambridge, MA: Harvard University Press, 1987), pp. 50–61, at p. 59. In this case the restrictive negation "Ie ne fais quentree et yssue" points toward both the more absolute "Rien nay meffait" and the ultimate negations that are divine judgment and Death: "Lordonnance dieu ne se mue."

120. Chaganti, *Strange*, p. 22.

121. Cavarero, *For More*, p. 169.

122. Dolar, *A Voice*, p. 147.

123. Jane H. M. Taylor, "Poésie et prédication: La fonction du discours proverbial dans la *Danse macabre*," *Medioevo romanzo* 14, no. 2 (1989): pp. 215–26.

124. *For More*, p. 138.

125. See David A. Fein, "Text and Image Mirror Play in Guyot Marchant's 1485 *Danse macabre*," *Neophilologus* 98, no. 2 (2014): pp. 225–39.

126. "The beholder, in other words, is offered the opportunity to identify with

each figure whose status most closely resembles his own, and this identification is furthered by the conversational way Death addresses them"; Gertsman, *Danse*, p. 92.

127. The phrase *sum quod eris* is associated especially with the legend of the three living and the three dead—a scene that was sculpted on the portal of the Cemetery of the Innocents. See Ashby Kinch, "The *Danse Macabre* and the Medieval Community of Death," *Mediaevalia* 23, no. 1 (2002): pp. 159–202.

128. The *Danse macabre* infant taps into a long tradition—from Solomon and Job through *De miseria*—holding that we begin preparing for death while still in utero, and that people are better off bypassing earthly life, instead going straight from the womb to the tomb. These ideas are expressed notably in Denys the Carthusian's *De iudicio mortis*, which is quoted on fol. 25v. of the *Danse macabre des femmes*: "Ex utero natis pedetentim calle sub ipso / Subdola mors comes est nos laqueare studens" (From the mother's womb on, stealthy death is a constant companion seeking to ensnare us, on our very path); text and translation from *The Danse Macabre of Women*, ed. and trans. Susan Stukey (Kent, OH: Kent State University Press, 1994), p. 54.

129. In this I differ from Maja Dujakovic, who interprets the infant as being positioned "at the very bottom of the social ladder"; Dujakovic, "The Dance of Death, the Dance of Life: Cemetery of the Innocents and the Danse Macabre," in *Out of the Stream: Studies in Medieval and Renaissance Mural Painting*, ed. Luis Urbano Afonso and Vitor Serrão (Newcastle upon Tyne: Cambridge Scholars, 2007), pp. 206–32, at p. 213.

130. The paradox of the preambulatory dance is perhaps also the reason for an important distinction, observed by Eustace and King, between the infant and all of the other *danse* figures: Death grasps him with a different handhold: "It is only the infant whom he actually holds firmly by the hand; the other illustrations show a range of familiarity, firmness or coercion"; Eustace and Kind, "Dances," p. 60. Eustace and King also note the unusual, flowing drapery of Death in the infant image; again, this appears designed to introduce movement to the scene showing the only character who could not possibly dance.

131. Gertsman, *Dance*, p. 123.

132. Chaganti, *Strange*, p. 106. Her discussion of "verticality" alludes mostly to the Guild Chapel in Stratford-upon-Avon.

133. Medieval viewers were accustomed to the vertical reading required by the typological iconography of the Old and New Testaments. Literary *memento mori* discourses such as Villon's stanzas of the *Testament* devoted to the Cemetery of the Innocents also encourage the "reading" of living humans under the Innocents' arcades in conjunction with the skeletal remains above.

134. It was believed that bodies decomposed at an accelerated rate in the consecrated ground of the Innocents. Eventually, when the Cemetery of the Innocents was destroyed, the bones were transferred to the city's system of underground tunnels and mine shafts, parts of which are now a tourist trap known as the Catacombs of Paris.

135. On the vogue for representations of the massacre of the Innocents see Alexandre-Bidon and Closson, *L'enfant*, p. 227.

136. Anna Benvenuti Papi, "Il culto degli Innocenti nell'immaginario medievale," in *Infanzie: Funzioni di un gruppo liminale dal mondo classico all'Età moderna*, ed. Ottavia Niccoli (Florence: Ponte alle Grazie, 1993), pp. 113–43, at p. 119.

137. Dolar, *A Voice*, p. 71.

138. "Essentially, when the Dance of Death entered the format of book illustration, it transformed the uninterrupted, continuous representation of a perpetual allegory, meant to be taken in all at once, into a temporal story, with a beginning and end"; Gertsman, *Dance*, p. 165. I think she overstates this—the frescoes and their text also had an implied beginning and end—but it is still a point well taken.

139. Lawrence L. Besserman, *The Legend of Job in the Middle Ages* (Cambridge, MA: Harvard University Press, 1979), p. 57.

140. Dillon, *Sense of Sound*, p. 216.

141. Besserman, *Legend*, pp. 58–59.

142. On the interpretation of phylacteries as "speech balloons," see Danièle Alexandre-Bidon, "Écrire le son au Moyen Âge," *Ethnologie française* n.s. 20, no. 3 (1990): pp. 319–28, at pp. 320–21.

143. Besserman details changes in the prevailing ways of reading Job over course of Middle Ages: *Legend*, p. 79. See the fourteenth-century *Hystore Job* for a clear vernacular example of how "Naked came I out of my mother's womb, and naked shall I return thither" (Job 1:21) becomes the pretext for an extended rumination on equality before death: Joseph Gildea, ed., *L'Hystore Job: An Old French Verse Adaptation of Compendium in Job by Peter of Blois*, 2 vols. (Liège: Vaillant-Carmanne, 1974), vol. 1, p. 135.

144. The iconography of the Office of the Dead undergoes a major shift in early fifteenth century and remains more fluid than the generally rigid iconographic programs illustrating other sections of the Book of Hours; Millard Meiss, "La mort et l'Office des Morts à l'époque du Maître de Boucicaut et des Limbourgs," *Revue de l'art* 1–2 (1968): pp. 17–25. On the "accidents," see Mary Beth Winn, "Gathering the Borders in Hardouyn's Hours: From the 'Accidents de l'homme' to the 'Dis des Estas,'" *Papers of the Bibliographical Society of America* 103, no. 2 (2009): pp. 141–97.

145. Sophie Oosterwijk, "'I Cam but Now, and Now I Go My Wai': The Presentation of the Infant in the Medieval *Danse Macabre*," in *Essays on Medieval Childhood: Responses to Recent Debates*, ed. Joel T. Rosenthal (Donington: Shaun Tyas, 2007), pp. 124–50, at p. 135. The image is available online at http://ica.themorgan.org/manuscript/page/298/76807, accessed 22 April 2024.

146. A famous example is the marginal "alphabet game" found in the Hours made for Marguerite d'Orléans in the 1420s or 1430s (BnF MS Lat. 1156B, fol. 135r). Another particularly fine example is a Book of Hours printed by Guillaume Godard around 1514 (PML 18561), which contains both a marginal Dance of Death and an "a.b.c. pour les petiz enfans," discussed in Roger S. Wieck, *Painted Prayers: The Book of Hours in Medieval and Renaissance Art* (New York: Braziller, 1997), p. 13

and fig. 4. For extended discussion of ABC primers, including alphabets in Books of Hours, see the essays collected in Michael Clanchy, *Looking Back from the Invention of Printing: Mothers and the Teaching of Reading in the Middle Ages* (Turnhout: Brepols, 2018).

147. See Danièle Alexandre-Bidon, "La lettre volée: Apprendre à lire à l'enfant au Moyen Âge," *Annales: Histoire, Sciences Sociales* 44, no. 4 (1989): pp. 953–92, esp. pp. 971, 980, 988.

148. Karl Steel describes a twelfth-century manuscript depicting a bear saying "A" in imitation of his human master who says "ABC"; Steel, *How to*, p. 52. Marie de France's fable 81 features a priest trying to teach the alphabet to a wolf, but the pupil expresses his animal hunger by supposing that the alphabet spells *aignel* (lamb). For Crane, this fable "heightens its species incongruities by evoking them in the context of an exclusively human accomplishment, the acquisition of letters"; *Animal Encounters*, p. 47.

149. Pierre Champion, "Pièces joyeuses du XVe siècle," *Revue de philologie française* 21 (1907): pp. 161–96, at pp. 191–92.

150. Recent scholars of medieval literary representations of the dead, notably Jane Gilbert, *Living Death in Medieval French and English Literature* (Cambridge: Cambridge University Press, 2011), and Helen Swift, *Representing the Dead: Epitaph-Fictions in Late Medieval France* (Woodbridge: Boydell & Brewer, 2016), have offered compelling evidence that medieval death is not entirely a postlinguistic state.

151. "The non-structured voice miraculously starts to represent the structure as such, the signifier in general. For the signifier in general, as such, is possible only as a non-signifier"; Dolar, *A Voice*, p. 29.

152. José Esteban Muñoz, *Disidentifications: Queers of Color and the Performance of Politics* (Minneapolis: University of Minnesota Press, 1999), p. 12.

CHAPTER THREE

1. Elinor Ochs and Bambi B. Schieffelin, "The Theory of Language Socialization," in *The Handbook of Language Socialization*, ed. Alessandro Duranti, Elinor Ochs, and Bambi B. Schieffelin (Malden, MA: Wiley-Blackwell, 2012), pp. 1–21, at p. 7.

2. Hélène Cixous, *La jeune née* (1975), quoted in Toril Moi, *Sexual/Textual Politics: Feminist Literary Theory* (London: Methuen, 1985), p. 114.

3. Hélène Cixous, "The Laugh of the Medusa," in *New French Feminisms*, ed. Elaine Marks and Isabelle de Courtivron (New York: Schocken, 1981), pp. 245–64, at p. 251.

4. Hélène Cixous, *"Coming to Writing" and Other Essays*, trans. Deborah Jenson (Cambridge, MA: Harvard University Press, 1991), p. 21.

5. Cixous, "Coming," p. 22.

6. The mother tongue is even referred to as "la langue nutritive" (nourishing language) in a fifteenth-century poem by the Savoyard Jacques de Bugnin, cited in

Jacqueline Cerquiglini-Toulet, *The Color of Melancholy*, trans, Lydia G. Cochrane (Baltimore, MD: Johns Hopkins University Press, 1997), p. 11.

7. Contemporary discussions of "motherese" in the fields of linguistics and evolutionary psychology still center on questions of pitch and tone. See, in particular, Anne Fernald, "Human Maternal Vocalizations to Infants as Biologically Relevant Signals: An Evolutionary Perspective," in *The Adapted Mind: Evolutionary Psychology and the Generation of Culture*, ed. John Tooby, Leda Cosmides, and Jerome H. Barkow (Oxford and New York: Oxford University Press, 1992), pp. 391–428; Laurel J. Trainor, Caren M. Austin, and Renée N. Desjardins, "Is Infant-Directed Speech Prosody a Result of the Vocal Expression of Emotion?" *Psychological Science* 11, no. 3 (2000): pp. 188–95; Rosemarie Sokol Chang and Nicholas S. Thompson, "The Attention-Getting Capacity of Whines and Child-Directed Speech," *Evolutionary Psychology* 8, no. 2 (2010): pp. 260–74. Pitch is an important element of the "BT register" that Charles A. Ferguson defines in "Baby Talk as a Simplified Register," in *Talking to Children: Language Input and Acquisition*, ed. Catherine E. Snow and Charles A. Ferguson (Cambridge: Cambridge University Press, 1977), pp. 209–35. On BT as a high-pitched register, see also Olga Solomon, "Rethinking Baby Talk," in *The Handbook of Language Socialization*, ed. Alessandro Duranti, Elinor Ochs, and Bambi B. Schieffelin (Malden, MA: Wiley-Blackwell, 2012), pp. 121–49.

8. *Trotula*, p. 54.

9. "And this language I know, I don't need to enter it, it surges from me, it flows, it is the milk of love, the honey of my unconscious. The language that women speak when no one is there to correct them"; Cixous, *"Coming,"* p. 21.

10. For a general introduction to this text, see Margaret Wade Labarge, "The Regime du Corps of Aldebrandino of Siena: A Thirteenth Century Regimen for Women," in *A Medieval Miscellany* (Ottawa: Carleton University Press, 1997), pp. 273–80. On the manuscript tradition, see the series of articles by Françoise Fery-Hue: "Le Régime du corps d'Aldebrandin de Sienne: Tradition manuscrite et diffusion," in *Santé, médecine et assistance au Moyen Âge*, vol. 1 (Paris: Comité des travaux historiques et scientifiques, 1987), pp. 113–34; "Le régime du corps d'Aldebrandin de Sienne: Complément à la tradition manuscrite," *Romania* 117 (1999): pp. 51–77; "Le régime du corps d'Aldebrandin de Sienne: Complément à la tradition manuscrite (suite)," *Scriptorium* 58, no. 1 (2004): pp. 99–108.

11. Aldobrandino of Siena, *Le régime du corps*, ed. Roger Pépin (Paris: Champion, 1911).

12. Michele Bellotti discusses Aldobrandino's debts to and modifications of Rhazes's text in "Un traité de diététique écrit dans la langue des nourrices: Sur l'insertion du langage des enfants dans le *Régime du corps* d'Aldebrandin de Sienne," in *Sciences et langues au Moyen Âge*, ed. Joëlle Ducos (Heidelberg: Universitätsverlag, 2012), pp. 137–56, at p. 140.

13. Roman Jakobson observed that "since the time of Buffon the principle of least effort has often been invoked: those sounds which are the easiest to articulate

are acquired first. But there is one fact crucial to the linguistic development of the child which clearly contradicts this hypothesis. During the babbling period the child easily produces the widest variety of sounds [. . .] almost all of which he eliminates [. . .] upon assigning to his sound productions their first semantic values." Obviously the principle goes back much further than Buffon, but otherwise Jakobson's point stands. Roman Jakobson, "The Sound Laws of Child Language and Their Place in General Phonology," *Studies on Child Language and Aphasia* (The Hague: Mouton, 1971), pp. 7–20, at p. 8.

14. Bellotti, "Un traité." He notes that other branches of the French text give three examples—*mama*, *papa*, and a third term such as *babou*, *babeu*, or *baba* (p. 150)—as do Latin and Tuscan translations.

15. The medieval Tuscan translation gives *pappa* and the Latin gives *papa*: Bellotti, "Un traité," pp. 149–50.

16. On such repetitions as a cross-linguistic characteristic of baby talk, see Charles A. Ferguson, "Baby Talk in Six Languages," *American Anthropologist* 66, no. 6, part 2 (1964): pp. 103–14.

17. Dolar, *A Voice*, p. 186.

18. Jean Petit, *Le livre du champ d'or et autres poèmes inédits*, ed. P. Le Verdier (Rouen: Cagniard, 1895), pp. 124–25, vv. 2673–85.

19. Oresme, *Éthiques*, p. 483.

20. As Yasmina Foehr-Janssens points out, "Il faut avoir enfanté pour être une nourrice: [. . .] il y a toujours un enfant mort, sacrifié ou du moins tenu à l'écart, dans les coulisses d'un allaitement mercenaire" (One has to have given birth in order to be a wet nurse; [. . .] there is always a child who is dead, sacrificed, or at least shunted aside, in the wings of any breastfeeding for hire); Foehr-Janssens, "Fées, nourrices et superstitions: les soins aux nourrissons au prisme de la fiction médiévale," *Annales de Bretagne et des Pays de l'Ouest* 124, no. 3 (2017): pp. 109–33, at p. 130. While there is no physiological reason a woman could not nurse both her own child and someone else's, this does not appear to have been the medieval norm. Women were often available as wet nurses because their own infant had died, especially given the insistence that best wet nurse was one who had given birth to a son a few months earlier. See Christiane Klapisch-Zuber, *Women, Family, and Ritual in Renaissance Italy*, trans. Lydia Cochrane (Chicago: University of Chicago Press, 1985), pp. 132–64.

21. Did the apostles become *gentle* or did they become *children?* See the discussions in *The Letters to the Thessalonians*, ed. and trans. Abraham J. Malherbe, Anchor Bible, vol. 32B (New York: Doubleday, 2000), pp. 144–45; Trevor J. Burke, *Family Matters: A Socio-Historical Study of Kinship Metaphors in 1 Thessalonians* (London: T&T Clark, 2003), pp. 151–57; Reidar Aasgaard, "Paul as a Child: Children and Childhood in the Letters of the Apostle," *Journal of Biblical Literature* 126, no. 1 (2007): pp. 129–59, at p. 147.

22. Beverly Roberts Gaventa has characterized it as an "inverted metaphor"

because it implicates not just a "mixture" but a role reversal; Gaventa, "Apostles as Babes and Nurses in 1 Thessalonians 2:7," in *Faith and History: Essays in Honor of Paul W. Meyer*, ed. John T. Carroll, Charles H. Cosgrove, and E. Elizabeth Johnson (Atlanta, GA: Scholars Press, 1990), pp. 193–207.

23. Gaventa cites numerous examples, mostly drawn from sermons, in "Our Mother St Paul: Toward the Recovery of a Neglected Theme," in *A Feminist Companion to Paul*, ed. Amy-Jill Levine with Marianne Blickenstaff (Cleveland, OH: Pilgrim Press, 2004), pp. 85–97. The image also appears in popular devotional texts such as the German Dominican Henry Suso's *Horologium sapientiae* (c. 1339), which was translated into eight medieval languages and survives in hundreds of manuscripts.

24. Louis Mourin has argued that this undated sermon must date from early in Gerson's career, the late 1380s or early 1390s. *Six sermons français inédits de Jean Gerson*, ed. Louis Mourin (Paris: Vrin, 1946), pp. 437–39.

25. Stuttering is often described in the Middle Ages as a characteristic of small children's speech. For example, Jean-Marie Fritz cites Firmin Le Ver's 1440 Latin-French dictionary, which defines *balbutio* as "besguier, baubeter, si come parlers de petits enfans qui ne scevent parler" (to stutter, to stammer, like the speech of little children who do not know how to talk); Fritz, *Paysages*, p. 278 n. 2. See also Roman Jakobson, "Why 'Mama' and 'Papa'?," *Studies on Child Language and Aphasia* (The Hague: Mouton, 1971), p. 21–29, at p. 25.

26. Dolar, *A Voice*, p. 27. Likewise, Cavarero has focused on babbling-to-infant as act of pure relation: *For More*, p. 170.

27. Cavarero, *For More*, p. 171.

28. "Baby Talk is part of situated cultural activities where caregivers' actions are guided by their ontological understandings of self and others" and is therefore an act of both "self- and other- fashioning"; Solomon, "Rethinking," p. 122. It has also been noted that "in mother-child interactions, it is not only the child who is being socialized—the child, through its actions and verbalizations, is also actively (if not necessarily consciously) socializing the mother as a mother"; Don Kulick and Bambi B. Schieffelin, "Language Socialization," in *A Companion to Linguistic Anthropology*, ed. Alessandro Duranti (Oxford: Blackwell, 2004), pp. 349–68, at p. 350.

29. Cavarero has argued in *Inclinations* for the inclined posture as a sign of a female relational ethic of care. This resonates with Christine de Pizan's statement in *Trois Vertus* I.XV that as compared to fathers, "Nature de mere est communement plus *encline* au regart de ses enfans." Cited in Marie-Thérèse Lorcin, "Mère nature et le devoir social: La mère et l'enfant dans l'oeuvre de Christine de Pizan," *Revue historique* 282.1, no. 571 (1989): pp. 29–44, at p. 41.

30. On medieval and early modern debates about whether nurses ought to pre-chew children's food—a practice that Avicenna allows but that later writers such as Vallambert condemn—see Marie-Madeleine Fontaine, "L'alimentation du jeune enfant au XVIᵉ siècle," in *Pratiques et discours alimentaires à la Renaissance*, ed.

Jean-Claude Margolin and Robert Sauzet (Paris: Maisonneuve & Larose, 1982), pp. 57–68, at p. 62.

31. On the cultural valences of digestion, see Marie-Christine Pouchelle, "Une parole médicale prise dans l'imaginaire: Alimentation et digestion chez un maître-chirurgien du XIVe siècle," in *Pratiques et discours alimentaires à la Renaissance: Actes du colloque de Tours de mars 1979*, ed. Jean-Claude Margolin and Robert Sauzet (Paris: Maisonneuve & Larose for the Centre d'Études supérieures de la Renaissance, 1982), pp. 179–92.

32. Christine de Pizan, *La città delle dame*, ed. Earl Jeffrey Richards, trans. Patrizia Caraffi (Milan: Luni, 1998), p. 84.

33. Cixous, "Laugh," p. 246.

34. BnF MS fr. 12575, fol. 89v. Compare Roach's edition, which gives the less logical reading "Coyement et mot se sonnoit"; Coudrette, *Le Roman de Mélusine ou Histoire de Lusignan*, ed. Eleanor Roach (Paris: Klincksieck, 1982), p. 253, l. 4377.

35. Dillon, *Sense of Sound*, p. 4.

36. Susan Boynton, "Women's Performance of the Lyric before 1500," in *Medieval Woman's Song: Cross-Cultural Approaches*, ed. Anne L. Klinck and Ann Marie Rasmussen (Philadelphia: University of Pennsylvania Press, 2002), pp. 47–65, at p. 60.

37. Jacqueline Sachs, "The Adaptive Significance of Linguistic Input to Prelinguistic Infants," in *Talking to Children: Language Input and Acquisition*, ed. Catherine E. Snow and Charles A. Ferguson (Cambridge: Cambridge University Press, 1977), pp. 51–61, at p. 58.

38. Ulrike Wiethaus, "The Death Song of Marie d'Oignies: Mystical Sound and Hagiographical Politics in Medieval Lorraine," in *The Texture of Society: Medieval Women in the Southern Low Countries*, ed. Ellen E. Kittell and Mary A. Suydam (New York: Palgrave Macmillan, 2004), pp. 153–79, at p. 154.

39. John Haines, *Medieval Song in Romance Languages* (Cambridge: Cambridge University Press, 2010), p. 156.

40. Leach, *Sung Birds*, chap. 5.

41. MS fr. 16993 omits the word "dormir"; a different hand has written "joye" in the margin following the word "faire" (fol. 77v).

42. *Brun de la Montagne*, ed. Paul Meyer (Paris: Firmin Didot for the SATF, 1875).

43. The same physiological process, in which smoke rises to the brain and causes a sleepy feeling, occurs in drunken adults. See Julie Singer, "Lyrical Humor(s) in the 'Fumeur' Songs," in *The Oxford Handbook of Music and Disability Studies*, ed. Blake Howe, Stephanie Jensen-Moulton, Neil Lerner, and Joseph Straus (Oxford and New York: Oxford University Press, 2015), pp. 497–516.

44. "The voice is sound, not speech. But speech constitutes its essential destination"; Cavarero, *For More*, p. 12.

45. Cohen, "Kyte oute yugilment," p. 270.

46. Bruce Holsinger, *Music, Body, and Desire in Medieval Culture* (Stanford, CA: Stanford University Press, 2001), p. 17.

47. Cavarero, *For More*, p. 6.

48. Christine de Pizan, *Oeuvres poétiques*, ed. Maurice Roy, vol. 3 (Paris: Firmin Didot for the SATF, 1896), p. 168.

49. "*Sefer Hasidim* mentions the possible dangers of having a Jewish child hear a Christian lullaby sung by his or her wet nurse. R. Judah the Pious does not recommend, however, firing the wet nurse, but rather that the wet nurse not sing"; Elisheva Baumgarten, *Mothers and Children: Jewish Family Life in Medieval Europe* (Princeton, NJ: Princeton University Press, 2004), pp. 136–37. See also Miri Rubin, *Gentile Tales: The Narrative Assault on Late Medieval Jews* (New Haven, CT: Yale University Press, 1999), p. 33; Simha Goldin, "Jewish Society under Pressure: The Concept of Childhood," in *Youth in the Middle Ages*, ed. P. J. P. Goldberg and Felicity Riddy (York: York Medieval Press, 2004), pp. 25–43.

50. Valerie Fildes, *Wet Nursing: A History from Antiquity to the Present* (Oxford: Blackwell, 1988), p. 41.

51. Elisheva Baumgarten, "Jewish Conceptions of Motherhood in Medieval Christian Europe: Dialogue and Difference," *Micrologus* 17 (2009): pp. 149–65, at p. 155.

52. The French text is rather unclear on this point, and other versions of the story, notably the Spanish *Flores y Blancaflor* and Lope García de Salazar's account in *Las bienandanzas e fortunas*, specify that the Christian slave breastfeeds both children. See Patricia E. Grieve, *Floire and Blancheflor and the European Romance* (Cambridge: Cambridge University Press, 1997), esp. pp. 43–46, 96–98.

53. *La bataille loquifer*, ed. Monica Barnett (Oxford: Blackwell, 1975), p. 140 laisse LXXXIX.

54. Berkvam, *Enfance*, p. 51.

55. Baumgarten, *Mothers and Children*, p. 138.

56. Fildes, *Wet Nursing*, pp. 42–43. The infant in question is often identified as Godefroy de Bouillon, as in Jean Petit's *Livre du champ d'or*, but the same story is also told about the title character in the fifteenth-century prose romance *Ysaÿe le Triste*.

57. "In women's speech, as in their writing, that element which never stops resonating, which, once we've been permeated by it, profoundly and imperceptibly touched by it, retains the power of moving us—that element is the song: first music from the first voice of love which is alive in every woman"; Cixous, "Laugh," p. 251.

58. Haines, *Medieval Song*, p. 158.

59. *Le mistere de Saint Quentin*, ed. Henri Chatelain (Saint-Quentin: Imprimerie Générale, 1907), pp. 10–11, ll. 609–40. The verse form stands out from the surrounding rhymed couplets.

60. Petit de Julleville describes them as such in *Histoire du théâtre en France: Les mystères* (Paris: Hachette, 1880), vol. 2, p. 651. One other theatrical text that has

been cited as a possible lullaby is the episode of the *Mistere du Viel Testament* in which the Egyptian wet nurses refuse to kill their newborn Hebrew charges (Exodus 1). Pierre Riché identifies these lines as a lullaby in his *Être enfant*, p. 76 — but Riché has altered the versification to make these lines appear more songlike. Compare to *Mistere du Viel Testament*, ed. James de Rothschild, vol. 3 (Paris: Firmin Didot for the SATF, 1881), pp. 230–31.

61. Other medieval Romance languages, and English, tend to use words derived from the roots *lall-* or *nann-*. See Aline Smeesters, "Les berceuses latines de G. G. Pontano (1429–1503)," *Revue belge de philologie et d'histoire* 83, no. 1 (2005): pp. 149–66, at p. 153.

62. BnF MS fr. 12323, fol. 98v. Similarly, the late twelfth- or early thirteenth-century Occitan *chanson de geste Daurel et Beton* describes a nurse signing ".i. bel so" (a pretty song); Paterson, "L'enfant," p. 235.

63. *On the Properties of Things: John Trevisa's translation of Bartholomaeus Anglicus De proprietatibus rerum; A critical text*, ed. M. C. Seymour and G. M. Liegey, vol. 1 (Oxford: Clarendon Press, 1975), p. 299.

64. *DMF*, s.v. "niner," accessed 22 April 2024, http://www.atilf.fr/dmf/definition/niner.

65. Haines, *Medieval Song*, p. 161.

66. Kathleen Palti, "Singing Women: Lullabies and Carols in Medieval England," *Journal of English and Germanic Philology* 110, no. 2 (2011): pp. 359–82. Orme notes that *lulla* (the song) and *lell* (the verb) are attested in English by the fourteenth century; *Medieval Children*, p. 132.

67. Guido Mazzoni, "Sull'antica cantilena 'Ninna nanna li miei begli fanti,'" *Studi medievali* 2 (1929): pp. 409–16.

68. Gabriela Nogueira, "L'origine de la berceuse: Quelques regards," in *La berceuse*, ed. Marina Altmann de Litvan (Toulouse: Érès 2008), pp. 85–93, at p. 86. Haines notes that in the early thirteenth century, Bishop Sicard of Cremona likened *Gloria in excelsis Deo* to the songs (*cantilenis*) that nurses sing for infants: Haines, *Medieval Song*, p. 159.

69. Rancière, *Names*, p. 58.

70. Renate Haas, "*Femina*: Female Roots of 'Foreign' Language Teaching and the Rise of Mother-Tongue Ideologies," *Exemplaria* 19, no. 1 (2007): pp. 139–62, at p. 142. On maternal pedagogical modes as nonintellectual, see also Bernard Ribémont, "Christine de Pizan et la figure de la mère," in *Christine de Pizan 2000: Studies of Christine de Pizan in Honour of Angus J. Kennedy*, ed. John Campbell and Nadia Margolis (Amsterdam: Rodopi, 2000), pp. 149–61.

71. Henri de Gauchy, *Li livres du gouvernement des rois*, ed. Samuel Paul Molenaer (New York: Macmillan, 1899), p. 197.

72. This idea continues into the Renaissance: Giulio Lepschy cites Benedetto Varchi's definition of "lingue natie" (native languages) as "quelle, in somma le quali si suol dire che si succiano col latte e s'apprendono nella culla" (those, in short, of

which it is typically said that they are sucked in with milk and learned in the cradle); Lepschy, *Mother Tongues and Other Reflections on the Italian Language* (Toronto: University of Toronto Press, 2002), p. 7.

73. Robert Hollander, "Babytalk in Dante's *Commedia*," in *Studies in Dante* (Ravenna: Longo, 1980), pp. 115–29, at p. 116. Gary P. Cestaro goes even further, reading *De vulgari eloquentia* as a dialectical text constructed around "that primal border which separates infancy from speech, the maternal breast from the moment of weaning"; Cestaro, ". . . quanquam Sarnum biberimus ante dentes: The Primal Scene of Suckling in Dante's *De vulgari eloquentia*," *Dante Studies* 109 (1991): pp. 119–47, at p. 122.

74. Oresme, *Éthiques*, p. 101. For Jean Batany, "Il est significatif que cette expression, employée dans ce texte pour la première fois, semble-t-il, en langue française, n'y concerne le français que par le ricochet d'une comparaison structurale et anoblissante" (It is significant that this expression, used for the first time in French, so it seems, in this text, concerns French only indirectly, via a structural and ennobling comparison); Batany, "L'amère maternité du français médiéval," *Langue française* 54 (1982): pp. 29–39, at p. 37. On the implications of Oresme's "feminizing" neologism, see also Thelma Fenster, "'Perdre son latin': Christine de Pizan and Vernacular Humanism," in *Christine de Pizan and the Categories of Difference*, ed. Marilynn Desmond (Minneapolis: University of Minnesota Press, 1998), pp. 91–107, at p. 101.

75. Pierre Col, *Le débat sur le Roman de la Rose*, trans. Virginie Greene (Paris: Champion, 2006), p. 211.

76. *Le mirouer et exemple moralle des enfans ingratz pour lesq[ue]lz les pères et mères se destruisent pour les augme[n]ter, qui en la fin les descongnoissent* (Aix: Pontier, 1836). This is a facsimile of the 1530 print edition; though the text does not survive in any earlier version, it draws heavily on medieval source material. See Alan Hindley, "La prédication dans un fauteuil? Sermon et moralité: le cas des *Enfants ingrats*," in *Prédication et performance du XIIᵉ au XVIᵉ siècle*, ed. Marie Bouhaïk-Girones and Marie Anne Polo de Beaulieu (Garnier 2013), pp. 189–214.

77. Women could, however, acquire Latinity through miracle: see Christine F. Cooper-Rompato, *The Gift of Tongues: Women's Xenoglossia in the Later Middle Ages* (University Park: Pennsylvania State University Press, 2010). This phenomenon is part of a broader trend of "mystical acoustic experiences" as discussed in Wiethaus, "Death Song."

78. However, it appears that in Jewish communities motherese was less uniformly perceived to be an exclusively feminine register. Rabbi Isaac b. Yedayah, active in Provence in the mid-thirteenth century, writes in his commentary on *Ethics of the Fathers* that fathers love their small children (not yet weaned) more than they love the older ones, because "the child teaches or causes the father to speak of idle matters, perhaps to talk baby talk, and whatever the child says is pleasing to the father"; Ephraim Kanarfogel, "Attitudes toward Childhood and Children in Medieval Jewish Society," in *Approaches to Judaism in Medieval Times*, vol. 2, ed. David R.

Blumenthal (Chico, CA: Scholars Press, 1985), pp. 1–34, at p. 4. Note, too, that this type of talk is attributed to both mothers and fathers in *Paradiso* XV.

79. Cestaro, ". . . quanquam Sarnum biberimus ante dentes," p. 126.

80. On Cixous's critique of the nature/culture binary, see Moi, *Sexual/Textual*, p. 104.

81. The at times paradoxically gendered hierarchies of Latin versus vernacular, and of formal schooling versus home training, are implicit in the common personification of the liberal art Grammar as a wet nurse, which illustrates the importance of breastfeeding as a figure not just for nurture, but specifically for language teaching—even in the context of an all-male school. The trope of Grammar as wet nurse reappears in two of the most influential high medieval literary treatments of the liberal arts: John of Salisbury's *Metalogicon* (1159) and Alain of Lille's *Anticlaudianus* (c. 1182). Gary P. Cestaro highlights a long history of discussions of nurses in Latin pedagogical discourses: Cestaro, *Dante and the Grammar of the Nursing Body* (South Bend, IN: University of Notre Dame Press, 2003). This imagery has a long afterlife in vernacular literature as well, including in the *Mutacion de Fortune*, wherein Christine de Pizan highlights the unnaturalness of the three-breasted Grammar's nurture. Even if the lactating mother figure remains a culturally preferred figure for the transmission of linguistic knowledge, this metaphor is explicitly acknowledged to be an artifice that exceeds nature.

82. The earlier *Femina* is more commonly called the *Tretiz* in recent scholarship. An overview of both texts and their titles is provided in Haas, "*Femina.*" For the latest resources see the website of the *Learning French in Medieval England* project, led by Thomas Hinton, which aims to produce an electronic edition of all seventeen witnesses: *Learning French in Medieval England*, accessed 22 April 2024, http://tretiz.exeter.ac.uk/.

83. William Rothwell, "Anglo-French and Middle English Vocabulary in 'Femina nova,'" *Medium Aevum* 69, no. 1 (2000): pp. 34–58. Thomas Hinton provides a needed update to Rothwell's interpretation of the *Tretiz* readers' linguistic competencies in "Anglo-French in the Thirteenth Century: A Reappraisal of Walter de Bibbesworth's *Tretiz*," *Modern Language Review* 112, no. 4 (2017): pp. 855–81.

84. As Maria Colombo Timelli and Giovanni Iamartino note, *Femme* is the first word of the *Tretiz*, which is titled *Ffemme* in one manuscript explicit: "*Liber iste vocatur femina* . . . : Le français et les dames dans l'Angleterre du XVᵉ siècle," *Documents pour l'histoire du français langue étrangère ou seconde* 47–48 (2012), para. 7, https://doi.org/10.4000/dhfles.3136.

85. *Femina*, ed. William Aldis Wright (Cambridge: Cambridge University Press, for the Roxburghe Club, 1909).

86. Doris Desclais Berkvam, "Nature and Norreture: A Notion of Medieval Childhood and Education," *Mediaevalia* 9 (1983): pp. 165–80.

87. Thomas Wright, ed., *A Volume of Vocabularies* (privately printed, 1857), pp. 142–74, at p. 142.

88. Walter de Bibbesworth, *Le tretiz*, ed. William Rothwell (London: Anglo-Norman Text Society, 1990), p. 3.

89. Or, as Karen K. Jambeck puts it, "Language acquisition is an innate, biologically-triggered behavior with a relatively predictable timetable"; Jambeck, "The *Tretiz* of Walter of Bibbesworth: Cultivating the Vernacular," in *Childhood in the Middle Ages and the Renaissance*, ed. Albrecht Classen (Berlin: de Gruyter, 2005), pp. 159–84.

90. For further discussion of Walter's conception of "naturele noise," see William Sayers, "Animal Vocalization and Human Polyglossia in Walter of Bibbesworth's Thirteenth-Century Domestic Treatise in Anglo-Norman French and Middle English," *Sign Systems Studies* 37 (2009): pp. 525–41.

91. *Le tretiz*, p. 3, vv. 27–28.

92. This observation holds despite Thomas Hinton's astute assertion that the *Tretiz's* domestic frame may merely be a rhetorical device; Hinton, "Anglo-French," p. 858.

93. *Femina*, p. 1.

94. *Femina*, p. 83.

95. *Femina*, p. 1, vv. 6, 8. Haas notes the "peculiar ambiguity" of this *naturalment*—does it refer to a natural order, or to a fluent quality of speech? Haas, "*Femina*," p. 152.

96. The situation of the medieval mother or nurse is not without parallels to the modern "gender paradox," defined by William Labov, whereby women conform more to prescribed or "prestige" linguistic forms than men do, but they also show more linguistic innovation when linguistic forms are not overtly prescribed. The result is that, as Labov writes, several decades of linguistic studies have shown that "women are the principal innovators in the process of change"; Labov, *Principles of Linguistic Change*, vol. 2, *Social Factors* (Malden, MA: Blackwell, 2001). The findings of these modern studies are seemingly confirmed in studies of early modern English by Terttu Nevalainen and Helena Raumolin-Brunberg, especially as they describe in *Historical Sociolinguistics: Language Change in Tudor and Stuart England* (New York: Longman, 2003).

97. Batany, "L'amère maternité," p. 33.

98. Cixous, *Coming*, pp. 36, 21.

99. This section includes material developed more fully in Julie Singer, "Christine de Pizan's 'doulce nourriture,'" *Medium Aevum* 89, no. 1 (2020): pp. 93–114.

100. See Anne Grondeux's fascinating study of the emergence of the phrase *lingua materna* in Northern France in the twelfth century; Grondeux, "La notion de langue maternelle et son apparition au Moyen Âge," in *Zwischen Babel und Pfingsten/Entre Babel et Pentecôte*, ed. Peter Von Moos (Zurich: Lit Verlag, 2008), pp. 339–56.

101. Oresme coined the phrase during the period that Nadia Margolis has called the "golden age of neologism"; Margolis, "Les terminaisons dangereuses: Lyrisme,

féminisme et humanisme néologiques chez Christine de Pizan," *Moyen Français* 39–40–41 (1996–97): pp. 381–404, at p. 381. The expressions *langage maternel* and *langue materne* also appear in the works of Philippe de Mézières and of Jean Molinet, among others—belying Thomas Paul Bonfiglio's claim, in *Mother Tongues and Nations: The Invention of the Native Speaker* (New York: De Gruyter Mouton, 2010), p. 82, that the first recorded usage of the phrase *langue maternelle* dates from the sixteenth century.

102. The essential study of Christine's deliberate "foreignness" remains Jacqueline Cerquiglini-Toulet, "L'étrangère," *Revue des langues romanes* 92 (1988): pp. 239–51.

103. For an overview of the ways in which these discourses of nurture articulate with the broader thematics of lineage and heritage in Christine's works, see the essays collected in Dominique Demartini and Claire Le Ninan, eds., *Genèses et filiations dans l'oeuvre de Christine de Pizan* (Paris: Garnier, 2021).

104. Christine de Pizan, *Oeuvres poétiques*, ed. Maurice Roy, vol. 1 (Paris: Firmin Didot for the SATF, 1886), p. 16. Not only does the subject matter (weaning) mark the voice as that of an infant; so too do the repeated interjection and the verb pair "crier et braire," both of which are typical in medieval representations of infant cries. Given the utter clarity of these cues, it is puzzling that as insightful a critic as James C. Laidlaw should repeatedly refer to this persona as a "young man." See Laidlaw, "L'unité des *Cent balades*," in *The City of Scholars: New Approaches to Christine de Pizan*, ed. Margarete Zimmermann and Dina De Rentiis (Berlin: de Gruyter, 1994), pp. 97–106, at p. 101; Laidlaw, "The *Cent balades*: The Marriage of Content and Form," in *Christine de Pizan and Medieval French Lyric*, ed. Earl Jeffrey Richards (Gainesville: University Press of Florida, 1998), pp. 53–82, at p. 69.

105. One may note that though the ballade features rhymes in *-ure*, the word *nature* never appears; while such negative evidence is not in itself meaningful, it is consistent with my reading of the poem. Christine does elsewhere rhyme *nature* and *norriture*, most notably in stanza XXIV of the *Ditié de Jeanne d'Arc*.

106. Peter V. Davies remarks that this rejet receives "particular emphasis" in a manner consistent with the tendency of Christine's ballades to "acquire impact from a sparing (and therefore more emphatic) use" of enjambement. Davies, "'Si bas suis qu'a peine / Releveray': Christine de Pizan's Use of Enjambement," in *Christine de Pizan 2000*, ed. John Campbell and Nadia Margolis (Amsterdam: Rodopi, 2000), pp. 77–90, at p. 89 and p. 314 n. 56. Fenster also discusses Christine's use of enjambements for "experimenting with rupture" in "'Perdre son latin,'" p. 104.

107. This squares with Jonathan Culler's theorizing of the refrain as an element that "disrupts narrative and brings it back to a present of discourse"; Culler, *Theory of the Lyric* (Cambridge, MA: Harvard University Press, 2015), p. 24.

108. "Prendre la cure de" means to care for or to take care of someone, and that is clearly the sense in which it is used here. However, the Middle French "prendre en cure" can also be used to refer to medical interventions, and the medical connotation

ought not to be discounted as a possible subtext here. *DMF*, s.v. "cure," accessed 22 April 2024, http://www.atilf.fr/dmf/definition/cure.

109. *Malons* are ulcers, buboes, or diseases that manifest as such: Godefroy, *Dictionnaire de l'ancienne langue française*, s.v. "malan." Julia Simms Holderness explains that "although 'enfonture' normally describes an illness caused by overeating, we may understand 'pouvre enfonture' as one caused by undereating"; Holderness, "Fiction and Truth in Ballad 15 of the *Cent balades*," in *Contexts and Continuities*, ed. Angus J. Kennedy, Rosalind Brown-Grant, James C. Laidlaw, and Catherine M. Müller (Glasgow: University of Glasgow Press, 2002), vol. 2, pp. 421–29, at p. 426. *Enfonture* also provides an aural echo of *enfant* that reinforces the alterity of this poem's first-person lyric voice.

110. This is consistent with Connor's assertion that "the voice is the auditory apparition of the breast, the sound that swells to fill the void opened by the breast's absence"; Connor, *Dumbstruck*, p. 31.

111. "A child comes into language through the mother's address. It is her job to transform a little animal into a little human being. The fact that she does this by teaching the child to speak indicates that, however dependent on her the child may be in fact, her most important lesson will be to turn 'into signifying form' everything that unites them. Might poetry be an attempt not to address the mother but to *hear her voice*? Is poetry perhaps a way of *being addressed*?" Barbara Johnson, *Mother Tongues: Sexuality, Trials, Motherhood, Translation* (Cambridge, MA: Harvard University Press, 2003), p. 66.

112. On "good translation" as "domestication" see Lawrence Venuti, *The Scandals of Translation: Towards an Ethics of Difference* (New York: Routledge, 1998), especially chap. 1, "Heterogeneity."

113. Venuti, *Scandals*, p. 11.

114. On the usefulness of the widow identity for a literary beginner, see Barbara Altmann, "L'art de l'autoportrait littéraire dans les *Cent ballades* de Christine de Pizan," in *Une femme de lettres au Moyen Âge: Études autour de Christine de Pizan*, ed. Liliane Dulac and Bernard Ribémont (Orléans: Paradigme, 1995), pp. 327–36, at p. 332. On the sexlessness of the widow and of the child, respectively, see Kevin Brownlee, "Widowhood, Sexuality and Gender in Christine de Pizan," *Romanic Review* 86, no. 2 (1995): pp. 339–53; Cerquiglini-Toulet, "Le goût de l'étude: Saveur et savoir chez Christine de Pizan," in *Au champ des escriptures*, ed. Eric Hicks, Diego Gonzalez, and Philippe Simon (Paris: Champion, 2000), pp. 597–608, at p. 602.

115. Christine de Pizan, *Le livre de l'advision Christine*, ed. Christine Reno and Liliane Dulac (Paris: Champion, 2001).

116. Grondeux, "La notion de langue maternelle," esp. p. 350.

117. Brownlee, "Widowhood," pp. 351–52.

118. "Femme ytalienne": Christine de Pizan, *The Book of Deeds of Arms and of Chivalry*, ed. Charity Cannon Willard, trans. Sumner Willard (University Park: Penn State University Press, 1999), p. 13. "Estrangement instituee": Christine de

Pizan, *Le livre de la mutacion de Fortune*, ed. Suzanne Solente, 2 vols. (Paris: Picard for the SATF, 1959–66).

119. Lori Walters, "*Translatio studii*: Christine de Pizan's Self-Portrayal in Two Lyric Poems and in the *Livre de la mutacion de Fortune*," in *Christine de Pizan and Medieval French Lyric*, ed. Earl Jeffrey Richards (Gainesville: University Press of Florida, 1998), pp. 155–67, at p. 162.

120. Fraiman, *Extreme Domesticity*, p. 123.

121. Cerquiglini-Toulet describes Christine as "l'écrivain de la distance [...] distance à sa langue maternelle"; Cerquiglini-Toulet, "L'étrangère," p. 239.

122. Ochs and Schieffelin, "Theory," p. 16.

123. Margolis, "Les terminaisons dangereuses," p. 383.

124. Fraiman, *Extreme Domesticity*, p. 5.

125. The authorship of Charles's English lyrics has been a topic of great debate. Advocates of an attribution to Charles include John Fox, "Charles d'Orléans, poète anglais?" *Romania* 86 (1965): pp. 433–62; Mary-Jo Arn, *Fortunes Stabilnes: Charles of Orleans's English Book of Love; A critical edition* (Binghamton, NY: Medieval and Renaissance Texts and Studies, 1994), pp. 29–37; and the essays in R. D. Perry and Mary-Jo Arn, *Charles d'Orléans's English Aesthetic: The Form, Poetics, and Style of "Fortunes Stabilnes,"* Medieval and Renaissance Texts & Studies 138 (Cambridge: Boydell & Brewer, 2020). Arguments against Charles's authorship are summed up in William Calin, "Will the Real Charles of Orleans Please Stand! Or Who Wrote the English Poems in Harley 682?," in *Conjunctures: Medieval Studies in Honor of Douglas Kelly*, ed. Keith Busby and Norris J. Lacy (Amsterdam: Rodopi, 1994), pp. 69–86.

126. This late compilation is studied brilliantly by Anne E. B. Coldiron in *Canon, Period, and the Poetry of Charles of Orleans: Found in Translation* (Ann Arbor: University of Michigan Press, 2000).

127. Fraiman, *Extreme Domesticity*, p. 121.

128. This poem offers the first known written attestation of the French forms *dodo, bobo, jojo* [joujou], and *à gogo*, and the only attestation of *gnogno*. Claudio Galderisi, *Le lexique de Charles d'Orléans dans les "rondeaux"* (Geneva: Droz, 1993), pp. 159, 180, 200, 207.

129. The rondeau is often cited as an example of Charles's lexical expansion; it is called "famous" but is little discussed. Pierre Champion interpreted it as a coded satire on Italian manners. Alice Planche suggests it may have only a literal meaning: *Charles d'Orléans ou la recherche d'un langage* (Paris: Champion, 1975), pp. 133–34. John Fox briefly reads it as a macaronic poem in "Glanures," in *Charles d'Orléans in England, 1415–1440*, ed. Mary-Jo Arn (Cambridge: D. S. Brewer, 2000), pp. 89–108. I am aware of no other scholarly engagements with this poem.

130. *Poetry of Charles d'Orléans and His Circle*, ed. John Fox and Mary-Jo Arn, trans. R. Barton Palmer (Tempe, AZ: ACMRS, 2010), pp. 526–27. I provide my own translation, as Palmer's does not capture the tone of the "baby talk" or the

texture of its contrast with more adult forms. I have sacrificed a small measure of exactitude (for example, in translating the refrain as "when they haven't gone beddy-bye" instead of a more literal "when they haven't slept enough") in favor of what I believe to be a greater fidelity to the rondeau's overall tone.

131. See Paul Zumthor, "Charles d'Orléans et le langage de l'allégorie," in *Mélanges offerts à Rita Lejeune* (Gembloux: J. Duculot, 1969), vol. 2, pp. 1481–1502; Claudio Galderisi, "Personnifications, réifications et métaphores créatives dans le système rhétorique de Charles d'Orléans," *Romania* 114 (1996): pp. 385–412.

132. "Et ces nouvelles acquisitions, parfois même des néologismes comme 'fons,' 'descriée,' 'dodo,' et quelques autres, appartiennent toutes, ou presque, aux champs sémantiques de l'activité quotidienne, du monde concret, de l'appréciation de la réalité"; Galderisi, *Lexique*, p. 12. On the landscape, see Jacqueline Cerquiglini-Toulet, "Espèces d'espaces: Espace physique et espace mental dans la poésie de Charles d'Orléans," *Moyen Français* 70 (2012): pp. 7–20.

133. Unless it is meant to evoke the mother's or caregiver's scolding, which John Fox's proposed derivation from *gnongnon* would admit as a possibility—in which case this poem, like Gerson's sermon, executes a remarkable "condescension" and flattening of baby's and female caregiver's speech.

134. Fox, "Glanures," p. 90.

135. For a list of autograph poems, see Mary-Jo Arn, *The Poet's Notebook: The Personal Manuscript of Charles d'Orléans (Paris, BnF MS fr. 25458)* (Turnhout: Brepols, 2008), pp. 121–23.

136. Arn, *Poet's Notebook*, p. 168.

137. Planche, *Charles d'Orléans*, p. 105.

138. Enid McLeod, *Charles d'Orléans, Prince and Poet* (New York: Viking, 1969), pp. 4–5.

139. On Valentina's library, see Thierry Crepin-Leblond, "Le mécénat et les collections de Valentine Visconti: une autre approche des rapports franco-italiens," in *La création artistique en France autour de 1400*, ed. Élisabeth Taburet-Delahaye (Paris: École du Louvre, 2006), pp. 95–101; Tracy Adams, "Valentina Visconti, Charles VI, and the Politics of Witchcraft," *Parergon* 30 (2013): pp. 11–32.

140. Virelai DLXIV; *Oeuvres complètes*, vol. 4, pp. 21–22, vv. 18–21.

141. Pierre Champion, *Vie de Charles d'Orléans* (Paris: Champion, 1911), p. 4. Elizabeth Gonzalez notes that the governesses and other female members of Valentina's household were often the spouses of members of duke Louis of Orléans's household and were therefore mostly French; Gonzalez, *Un prince en son hôtel: Les serviteurs des ducs d'Orléans au XVe siècle* (Paris: Publications de la Sorbonne, 2004), pp. 82–83.

142. This is the term Ardis Butterfield uses to characterize Anglo-French literary relations in the same period; Butterfield, *The Familiar Enemy: Chaucer, Language, and Nation in the Hundred Years War* (Oxford and New York: Oxford University Press, 2008).

143. Alain Marchandisse, "Milan, les Visconti, l'union de Valentine et de Louis d'Orléans, vus par Froissart et par les auteurs contemporains," in *Autour du XVᵉ siècle: Journées d'étude en l'honneur d'Alberto Vàrvaro*, ed. Paola Moreno and Giovanni Palumbo (Liège: Bibliothèque de la Faculté de Philosophie et Lettres de l'Université de Liège, 2008), pp. 93–116; Adams, "Valentina Visconti."

144. Juan F. García Bascuñana, "Traduction et plurilinguisme au XVᵉ siècle: À propos de Charles d'Orléans," in *Actes du XXVᵉ Congrès international de linguistique et de philologie romanes, Innsbruck 2007*, ed. Maria Iliescu, Heidi Siller-Runggaldier, and Paul Danler (Berlin: de Gruyter, 2010), vol. 1, pp. 565–73.

145. Arn, *Poet's Notebook*, pp. 77–84. Arn rejects idea that space was left for music, pointing out that both the ruling and the *mise en page* preclude this. It is possible that these pages were meant to be illustrated.

146. Cixous, *Coming*, p. 21.

147. Arn describes this "very interesting part of the manuscript in which the poet seems to cluster a number of kinds of experimental lyrics on the upper portions of successive leaves"; *Poet's Notebook*, pp. 139–40.

148. Galderisi, *Lexique*, p. 120. Fox highlights the unusual character of the *-o* rhyme and uses it to account for the posited transformation of *gnangnan* to *gnogno*; "Glanures," p. 90.

149. *Avoglé et assourdy* is the last of several rondeaux mislabeled as chansons in the manuscript's original genre labels. Arn, *Poet's Notebook*, p. 91.

150. Arn, *Poet's Notebook*, p. 115.

151. Galderisi, *Lexique*, p. 13. This corresponds to what Anne L. Klinck calls his "denial of the existence of a stable self" in "Making a Difference: Bilingualism and Re-creation in Charles d'Orléans," *Neophilologus* 99 (2015): pp. 685–96.

152. Poirion, "La cour des princes comme milieu poétique," in *Le poète et le prince*, pp. 177–90. Jane H. M. Taylor, *The Making of Poetry: Late-Medieval French Poetic Anthologies* (Turnhout: Brepols, 2007), chap. 2.

153. Taylor, *The Making of Poetry*, p. 114; emphasis in original.

154. Cavarero, *For More*, pp. 170, 179.

155. Ferguson, "Baby Talk as a Simplified Register," p. 232.

156. Elinor Ochs and Bambi Schieffelin, "Language Acquisition and Socialization: Three Developmental Stories and Their Implications," in *Culture Theory: Essays on Mind, Self, and Emotion*, ed. Richard A. Shweder and Robert A. LeVine (Cambridge and New York: Cambridge University Press, 1984), pp. 276–320, at p. 309.

157. "La petite enfance n'a pas, comme la jeunesse, un traditionnel droit de cité dans la poésie médiévale"; Planche, *Charles d'Orléans*, p. 133.

158. Taylor writes that the manuscript's interlocutors become a community "who thereby acquire a group identity in which certain poetic idioms come to act as signs of cultural sophistication and rhetorical mastery" (*The Making of Poetry*, p. 112) — but unlike macaronic French-Latin, baby talk does not come to take on that sort of sociolinguistic currency.

159. Cavarero, *For More*, p. 132.

160. According to Venuti, translation "domesticates foreign texts, inscribing them with linguistic and cultural values that are intelligible to specific domestic constituencies"; *Scandals*, p. 67.

161. Serres, *Parasite*, p. 89.

162. André Tissier, *Recueil de farces* (Geneva: Droz, 1988), vol 3, p. 158, vv. 262–69.

163. For Édouard Fournier, the words are devoid of meaning ("dépourvus de sens"). Fournier, *Le théâtre français avant la Renaissance, 1450–1550: Mystères, moralités et farces* (Paris: Laplace, Sanchez, 1872), p. 281. L.-Émile Chevaldin proposed, rather fancifully, that this was supposed to "donner à sa prière la force d'une conjuration diabolique" (lend his prayer the force of an incantation to the devil); Chevaldin, *Les jargons de la Farce de Pathelin* (Paris: Fontemoing, 1903), p. 58. The English clown Johan Bouset utters a nearly identical string of pseudo-Latin (*Teram nos mineterus, alabastra, pillatores*) in the late sixteenth-century German play *Hibaldeha*, but I haven't yet found any earlier potential source for this specific language. Luis Salas has suggested that the form *pillatores* might offer an echo of *pilatrix* (female thief) but has confirmed that this string of pseudo-Latin is largely meaningless. I thank him for his assistance with this intriguing problem.

164. Cavarero, *For More*, p. 182.

165. Dolar, *A Voice*, p. 26.

166. On babbling as a call for attention, see Andreea Marculescu, "The Voice of the Possessed in Late Medieval French Theater," in *Voice and Voicelessness in Medieval Europe*, ed. Irit Ruth Kleiman (New York: Palgrave Macmillan, 2015), pp. 139–52, at p. 148.

167. Similarly, the *Sottie des menus propos* (Rouen, February 1461) includes one of the fools declaring, "Se tu as papa ou memmen, / Il puisse mescheoir a l'enfant" (If you have *papa* or *mama*, it might bring misfortune to the child). *Recueil général des sotties*, ed. Émile Picard, vol. 1 (Paris: Firmin Didot for the SATF, 1902), p. 96. The convergence of the language of the fool and the language of the small child is not unlike the effect achieved in *Calbain*. For a discussion of the *Menus propos* and its *propos sans suite*, see Heather Arden, *Fools' Plays: A Study of Satire in the Sottie* (Cambridge: Cambridge University Press, 1980), esp. pp. 22–23, 58–60.

168. Cavarero, *For More*, p. 134.

169. Dean Falk, *Finding Our Tongues: Mothers, Infants and the Origins of Language* (New York: Basic Books, 2009), p. 134.

170. Thanks to Deborah McGrady for her helpful reframing of my reading of Charles d'Orléans in these terms. Personal communication, 20 February 2019.

171. On the fundamentality of the distinction of voicing and voice, and the role of the former in lyric's status as an event rather than a representation of an event, see Culler, *Theory*, p. 35.

172. Leighton, *Hearing Things*, p. 6.

CHAPTER FOUR

1. Jean-François Lyotard, *Le différend* (Paris: Minuit, 1983), p. 24. The English translation is from Jean-François Lyotard, *The Differend: Phrases in Dispute*, trans. Georges Van Den Abbeele (Minneapolis: University of Minnesota Press, 1988), p. 9.

2. Éric Berthon, "À l'origine de la spiritualité médiévale de l'enfance: Les saints innocents," in *La petite enfance dans l'Europe médiévale et moderne*, ed. Robert Fossier (Toulouse: Presses Universitaires du Mirail, 1997), pp. 31–38.

3. Isidore, *Etymologarium*, bk. 11, chap. 2, sent. 10; *Etymologies*, p. 241.

4. *DMF*, s.v. "Innocence," accessed 22 April 2024, http://www.atilf.fr/dmf /definition/innocence.

5. Lee Edelman, *No Future: Queer Theory and the Death Drive* (Durham, NC: Duke University Press, 2004), p. 21.

6. Michael D. Burroughs, "Navigating the Penumbra: Children and Moral Responsibility," *Southern Journal of Philosophy* 58 (2020): pp. 77–101, at p. 93; emphasis in original.

7. Edelman, *No Future*, p. 13.

8. As Roy J. Pearcy points out, John of Salisbury's *Metalogicon* cites the idea that the fact of a woman giving birth proves she has engaged in sex as a previously accepted axiom that must be logically rejected due to the counterevidence of the Virgin. Roy J. Pearcy establishes a fascinating connection between this proposition and adulterous fabliau wives in the form of an allusion to the fabliau *L'enfant qui fu remis au soleil* in one of the Coventry Plays; Pearcy, *Logic and Humour in the Fabliaux: An Essay in Applied Narratology* (Cambridge: D. S. Brewer, 2007), pp. 7–8.

9. Jamie K. Taylor, *Fictions of Evidence: Witnessing, Literature, and Community in the Late Middle Ages* (Columbus: Ohio State University Press, 2013), p. 8. On the use of the word *testimony* to refer to "any kind of telling in and through which the expression and transmission of knowledge becomes possible," see José Medina, *The Epistemology of Resistance: Gender and Racial Oppression, Epistemic Injustice, and Resistant Imaginations* (Oxford and New York: Oxford University Press, 2013), p. 28.

10. Miranda Fricker, *Epistemic Injustice: Power and the Ethics of Knowing* (Oxford and New York: Oxford University Press, 2007), p. 1.

11. Kristie Dotson, "Conceptualizing Epistemic Oppression," *Social Epistemology* 28, no. 2 (2014): pp. 115–38, at p. 115.

12. Ishani Maitra, "The Nature of Epistemic Injustice," *Philosophical Books* 51, no. 4 (2010): pp. 195–211, at p. 208.

13. On the silencing that results from epistemic injustice, see especially Kristie Dotson, "Tracking Epistemic Violence, Tracking Practices of Silencing," *Hypatia* 26., no. 2 (2011): pp. 236–57, in which Dotson adapts the term "epistemic violence" from Gayatri Spivak's essay "Can the Subaltern Speak?"; see also José Medina, "Hermeneutical Injustice and Polyphonic Contextualism: Social Silences and Shared Hermeneutical Responsibilities," *Social Epistemology* 26 (2012): pp. 201–20. On

silencing as both a symptom and a cause of epistemic harm, see Wesley Buckwalter, "Epistemic Injustice in Social Cognition," *Australasian Journal of Philosophy* 97 (2019): pp. 294–308.

14. Fricker, *Epistemic Injustice*, pp. 2–3.

15. Daniel Lord Smail, *The Consumption of Justice: Emotions, Publicity, and Legal Culture in Marseille, 1264–1423* (Ithaca, NY: Cornell University Press, 2003), p. 208.

16. On silence as an appeal for interpretation, see the insightful remarks in Jelica Sumic-Riha, "Testimony and the Real: Testimony between the Impossibility and Obligation," *Parallax* 10, no. 1 (2004): pp. 17–29, at pp. 20–21.

17. As the philosopher Elizabeth Fricker points out, most children's acquisition of both language and knowledge of the world depends on "simple trust in [their] teachers"; children therefore serve as a reminder that "each of us is causally reliant on others' testimony in the historical process by which she acquires her system of concepts and beliefs" because language, and the basic knowledge of the world acquired with it, is learned through a testimonial process. Fricker, "Testimony and Epistemic Autonomy," in *The Epistemology of Testimony*, ed. Jennifer Lackey and Ernest Sosa (Oxford: Clarendon Press, 2006), pp. 225–50, at pp. 225–26.

18. Gaile Polhaus, Jr., "Relational Knowing and Epistemic Injustice: Toward a Theory of 'Willful Hermeneutical Ignorance,'" *Hypatia* 27, no. 4 (2012): pp. 715–35, at p. 720.

19. Medina, *Epistemology*, p. 46.

20. Marie-Louise Fabre, *Suzanne ou les avatars d'un motif biblique* (Paris: L'Harmattan, 2000); Valerie Flint, "Susanna and the Lothar Crystal: A Liturgical Perspective," *Early Medieval Europe* 4 (1995): pp. 61–86.

21. The most complete overview of literary treatments of the legend, albeit one focused primarily on English materials, is Lynn Staley, "Susanna's Voice," in *Sacred and Profane in Chaucer and Late Medieval Literature*, ed. Robert Epstein and William Robins (Toronto: University of Toronto Press, 2010), pp. 46–67.

22. Alan E. Knight, "The Stage as Context: Two Late Medieval French Susanna Plays," in *The Stage as Mirror: Civic Theatre in Late Medieval Europe*, ed. Alan E. Knight (Cambridge: D. S. Brewer, 1997), pp. 201–16.

23. Monica H. Green, "Masses in Remembrance of 'Seynt Susanne': A Fifteenth-Century Spiritual Regimen," *Notes and Queries* (December 2003): pp. 380–84; Sara Ritchey, "Prayer as Obstetric Practice at Thirteenth-Century La Cambre," in *Pregnancy and Childbirth in the Premodern World: European and Middle Eastern Cultures, from Late Antiquity to the Renaissance*, ed. Costanza Gislon Dopfel, Alessandra Foscati, and Charles Burnett (Turnhout: Brepols, 2019), pp. 171–94.

24. Catherine Brown Tkacz, "Susanna as a Type of Christ," *Studies in Iconography* 20 (1999): pp. 101–53.

25. According to Christian Gnilka, the church fathers generally agree that Daniel is twelve years old; Christian Gnilka, *Aetas Spiritalis* (Bonn: Peter Hanstein, 1972), p. 238. Patristic writings tend to focus on Daniel's age as a sign of his virginity;

Régis Courtray, "La 'chaste Suzanne' chez les Pères latins," *Latomus* 68, no. 2 (2009): pp. 442–57, at p. 448. Earlier medieval visual representations of the tale, as well as typological pairings of the boy Daniel and the twelve-year-old Jesus in the Temple, suggest that Daniel continued to be portrayed well into the Middle Ages as a child on the cusp of adolescence. Catherine Brown Tkacz, "*Susanna Victrix, Christus Victor*: Lenten Sermons, Typology, and the Lectionary," in *Speculum sermonis: Interdisciplinary Reflections on the Medieval Sermon*, ed. Georgiana Donavin, Cary J. Nederman, and Richard Utz (Turnhout: Brepols, 2004), pp. 55–79; Tkacz, "Susanna as a Type of Christ," p. 128; Fabre, *Suzanne*, p. 92 n. 34.

26. Jonathan Stavsky, "'Gode in all thynge': *The Erle of Tolous*, Susanna and the Elders, and Other Narratives of Righteous Women on Trial," *Anglia* 131, no. 4 (2013): pp. 538–61, at p. 538.

27. A recent reading of both is Glenn D. Burger, *Conduct Becoming: Good Wives and Husbands in the Later Middle Ages* (Philadelphia: University of Pennsylvania Press, 2018).

28. Diane Bornstein memorably describes the chevalier as a misogynist seeking to form wives "who would cause men the least possible trouble and expense," whereas she finds the Mesnagier "much more 'chivalric' toward women than [the] knight"; Bornstein, *The Lady in the Tower: Medieval Courtesy Literature for Women* (Hamden, CT: Archon, 1983), pp. 49, 59.

29. *Le livre du chevalier de la Tour Landry pour l'enseignement de ses filles*, ed. Anatole de Montaiglon (Paris: Jannet, 1854), pp. 191–92; *Le mesnagier*, pp. 132–41.

30. Danielle Regnier-Bohler, "L'honneur des femmes et le regard public: L'accusé et son juge; Une étude de cas; le *Livre du Chevalier de La Tour Landry* (1371)," in *Das Öffentliche und Private in der Vormoderne*, ed. Gert Melville and Peter Von Moos (Cologne: Böhlau, 1998), pp. 411–33, at p. 420.

31. Anne Marie De Gendt, "'Mors et vita in manu linguae': Paroles dévastatrices et lénifiantes dans le *Livre du Chevalier de La Tour Landry*," *Mediaeval Studies* 58 (1996): pp. 351–63. See also Anne Marie de Gendt, *L'art d'éduquer les nobles damoiselles: Le Livre du Chevalier da la Tour Landry* (Paris: Champion, 2003).

32. Staley, "Susanna's Voice." Work on the medieval English Susanna focuses mainly on Lollard texts. In addition to Staley, see Jonathan Stavsky, "As the Lily among Thorns: Daniel 13 in the Writings of John Wyclif and his Followers," *Viator* 46, no. 1 (2015): pp. 249–76.

33. "Ideologies of injustice [. . .] promote distorted conceptions of virtue that commend attacks on or oppression of the victims of injustice"; Elizabeth Anderson, "The Epistemology of Justice," *Southern Journal of Philosophy* 58 (2020): pp. 6–29, at p. 9.

34. Martha Wallen, "Biblical and Mythological Typology in Machaut's *Confort d'ami*," *Res publica litterarum* 3 (1980): pp. 191–206, at p. 193.

35. Guillaume de Machaut, *Le Confort d'ami (Comfort for a Friend)*, ed. and trans. R. Barton Palmer (New York: Garland, 1992). The translation is modified:

I changed *enfançon* from "boy" to "little child" to preserve the apparently redundant doubling of this meaning that Machaut creates with the expression *juene enfançon*.

36. Alasdair MacIntyre, *Dependent Rational Animals: Why Human Beings Need the Virtues* (London: Bloomsbury, 2009).

37. In raising the hue and cry, Susanna is actively building her own defense. As F. R. P. Akehurst notes with reference to the late thirteenth-century *Coutumes de Beauvaisis*, in order to argue that a rape has occurred, "The woman must demonstrate that she did not agree to the act, by showing that she cried out, and that her cry was heard (thus making the incident *notoire*), unless she was in fear of her life"; Akehurst, "Good Name, Reputation, and Notoriety in French Customary Law," in *Fama: The Politics of Talk and Reputation in Medieval Europe*, ed. Thelma Fenster and Daniel Lord Smail (Ithaca, NY: Cornell University Press, 2003), pp. 75–94, at p. 89.

38. Fabre, *Suzanne*, p. 92.

39. Medina underlines the etymology of *resist* "from the Latin *resistere*, to take a stand"; Medina, *Epistemology*, p. 48.

40. Moreover, "Daniel's first words in the story of Susanna are virtually the same as those of Pilate when he washes his hands"; Tkacz, "Susanna as a Type of Christ," p. 108.

41. R. Barton Palmer, "Guillaume de Machaut and the Classical Tradition: Individual Talent and (Un)Communal Tradition," in *A Companion to Guillaume de Machaut*, ed. Deborah McGrady and Jennifer Bain (Leiden: Brill, 2012), pp. 241–60, at p. 249.

42. William Calin, *A Poet at the Fountain: Essays on the Narrative Verse of Guillaume de Machaut* (Lexington: University Press of Kentucky, 1974), p. 133.

43. Giorgio Agamben, *Remnants of Auschwitz: The Witness and the Archive*, trans. Daniel Heller-Roazen (New York: Zone, 2002), p. 18.

44. Oresme, *Éthiques*, p. 319.

45. For an overview of the epistemic problems framing such situations, see Sanford C. Goldberg, "Testimonially Based Knowledge from False Testimony," *Philosophical Quarterly* 51 (2001): pp. 512–26.

46. On the former, see Catherine E. Léglu and Stephen J. Milner, "Introduction: Encountering Consolation," in *The Erotics of Consolation: Desire and Distance in the Late Middle Ages*, ed. Catherine E. Léglu and Stephen J. Milner (New York: Palgrave Macmillan, 2008), pp. 1–18. On the latter, see Deborah McGrady, *The Writer's Gift or the Patron's Pleasure? The Literary Economy in Late Medieval France* (Toronto: University of Toronto Press, 2019).

47. Sarah Kay, "Touching Singularity: Consolation, Philosophy, and Poetry in the French *Dit*," in *The Erotics of Consolation: Desire and Distance in the Late Middle Ages*, ed. Catherine E. Léglu and Stephen J. Milner (New York: Palgrave Macmillan, 2008), pp. 21–38, at p. 36.

48. Alexandre Leupin, "The Powerlessness of Writing: Guillaume de Machaut,

the Gorgon, and Ordenance," trans. Peggy McCracken, *Yale French Studies* 70 (1986): pp. 127–49, at p. 137.

49. "Un tort serait ceci: un dommage accompagné de la perte des moyens de faire la preuve du dommage. C'est le cas si la victime est privée de la vie, ou de toutes les libertés, ou de la liberté de rendre publiques ses idées ou ses opinions, ou simplement du droit de témoigner de ce dommage, ou encore plus simplement si la phrase du témoignage est elle-même privée d'autorité." Para. 7; pp. 18–19 (original), p. 5 (translation).

50. For Lyotard, "le 'délit parfait' ne consisterait pas à tuer la victime ou les témoins [. . .] mais à obtenir le silence des témoins, la surdité des juges et l'inconsistance (l'insanité) du témoignage." Para. 9; p. 23 (original), p. 8 (translation).

51. Agamben, *Remnants*, p. 145. The compounding factors of Daniel's age and Susanna's gender shed new light on Agamben's theorization of testimony, from which gender is notably absent.

52. Andrea Frisch, *The Invention of the Eyewitness: Witnessing and Testimony in Early Modern France* (Chapel Hill: University of North Carolina Press, 2004), pp. 40, 13. Daniel, as a baby in his mother's arms, is a particularly "intersubjective" figure.

53. *Oeuvres complètes*, vol. 9. The main Susanna narrative is told on pp. 145–50, ll. 4400–4544; it is alluded to again on pp. 173–74, ll. 5295–5312.

54. Exodus 23:7.

55. Deschamps also addresses this topic in lyric poems including Ballade CCXL (vol. 2, pp. 171–72), in which he criticizes "les drois civilz" for their pursuit of the poor, and Ballade MCCI (vol. 6, pp. 186–87), which laments that "le povre est en tous lieux despité / Et reprouchés de droit en tesmoinage / Injuste en soy" (ll. 5–7).

56. "*Epistemic power* refers to relations of privilege and underprivileged afforded via different social positions, relevant resources and/or epistemological systems with respect to knowledge production. It is often bound up with social, political, and economic power"; Dotson, "Conceptualizing," 125. Medina defines *epistemic vice* as "a set of corrupted attitudes and dispositions that get in the way of knowledge"; Medina, *Epistemology*, p. 30.

57. Sylvia Huot has argued that Deschamps may have been inspired to use Susanna's judges as an exemplum of injustice and corruption because of a similar discussion in Gui de Mori's interpolation to the *Roman de la Rose*. Huot, "The *Miroir de mariage*: Deschamps Responds to the *Roman de la Rose*," in *Eustache Deschamps, French Courtier-Poet: His Work and His World*, ed. Deborah M. Sinnreich-Levi (New York: AMS Press, 1998), pp. 131–44.

58. Such processes "can result in new possibilities for knowing, providing new tools for organizing and making sense of experience"; Polhaus, "Relational Knowing," p. 719.

59. Earl Jeffrey Richards has argued that Christine's use of *droiture* reveals a substantial engagement with legal commentaries, and with Italian sources in particular; Richards, "Christine de Pizan and Medieval Jurisprudence," in *Contexts and*

Continuities: Proceedings of the IVth International Colloquium on Christine de Pizan, ed. Angus J. Kennedy, Rosalind Brown-Grant, James C. Laidlaw, and Catherine M. Müller (Glasgow: University of Glasgow Press, 2002), vol. 3, pp. 747–66. Bernard Ribémont disputes Richards's interpretation of *droiture* in "Christine de Pizan, la justice et le droit," *Le Moyen Âge* 118, no. 1 (2012): pp. 129–68, esp. pp. 154–57.

60. Christine de Pizan, *La città delle dame*, p. 58.

61. Here I differ from Thelma Fenster's view that "the word heroine does not seem to apply to Christine's view of her female protagonists"; Fenster, "Who's a Heroine? The Example of Christine de Pizan," in *Christine de Pizan: A Casebook*, ed. Barbara K. Altmann and Deborah L. McGrady (New York: Routledge, 2003), pp. 115–28, at p. 123.

62. "À travers les exemples de femmes vertueuses qui peuplent la cité, Christine s'assimile à un juge"; Delphine Reix, "Christine de Pizan et la justice," in *Christine de Pizan et son époque: Actes du Colloque international des 9, 10 et 11 décembre 2011 à Amiens*, ed. Danielle Buschinger, Liliane Dulac, Claire Le Ninan, and Christine Reno (Amiens: Presses du Centre d'études médiévales, Université de Picardie–Jules Verne, 2012), pp. 125–36, at p. 134.

63. See Maureen Curnow, "*La Pioche d'Inquisicion*: Legal-Judicial Content and Style in Christine de Pizan's *Livre de la cité des dames*," in *Reinterpreting Christine de Pizan*, ed. Earl Jeffrey Richards and Joan Williamson (Athens: University of Georgia Press, 1992), pp. 157–72.

64. Text and translation from Christine de Pizan, *The Book of Peace*, ed. and trans. Karen Green, Constant J. Mews, Janice Pinder, and Tania Van Hemelryck, with Alan Crosier (University Park: Penn State University Press, 2008).

65. She cites the psalm in the section on the early education of princes, *Cy dit comment on doit nourir a leur commencement les enfans des princes*: "dit le psalmiste que en la bouche des enfans et des alaittans Dieux a parfaite sa loenge, c'est a dire qu'il l'a agreable"; Christine de Pizan, *Le livre du corps de policie*, ed. Angus J. Kennedy (Paris: Champion, 1998), p. 3, ll. 19–20.

66. Tracy Adams, *Christine de Pizan and the Fight for France* (University Park: Penn State University Press, 2014), p. 164.

67. Mews, in Christine de Pizan, *The Book of Peace*, p. 34.

68. "Although epistemic resources are resources of the mind, they are resources of the embodied mind that coordinate one's attention with other knowers in lived situations." Polhaus, "Relational Knowing," p. 721, identifies relational epistemic practices as a means for empowerment of marginalized knowers in particular.

69. Christine de Pizan, *Le Livre des trois vertus*, ed. Charity Cannon Willard (Paris: Champion, 1989), pp. 33–36. Tania Van Hemelryck discusses the trope of woman as mediatrix in "Christine de Pizan et la paix: La rhétorique et les mots pour le dire," in *Au champ des escriptures: IIIe Colloque international sur Christine de Pizan*, ed. Eric Kicks with Diego Gonzalez and Philippe Simon (Paris: Champion, 2000), pp. 663–89.

70. The text is edited in Angus J. Kennedy, "Christine de Pizan's *Epistre à la reine* (1405)," *Revue des langues romanes* 92 (1988): pp. 253–64. See also the discussion in Angus J. Kennedy, "Christine de Pizan's *Epistre a la reine*: A Woman's Perspective on War and Peace?," in *War and Peace: Critical Issues in European Societies and Literature 800–1800*, ed. Albrecht Classen and Nadia Margolis (Berlin: De Gruyter, 2011), pp. 395–423.

71. Tracy Adams, "*Moyennerresse de traictié de paix*: Christine de Pizan's Mediators," in *Healing the Body Politic: The Political Thought of Christine de Pizan* (Turnhout: Brepols, 2005), pp. 177–200; Nathalie Nabert, "La mère dans la littérature politique à la fin du Moyen Âge," *Bien dire et bien aprandre* 16 (1998): pp. 191–202. On Christine's use of maternity as a rhetorical strategy in her communications to Queen Isabeau in particular, see Lori J. Walters, "Birth Imagery in Manuscripts Produced by Christine de Pizan for the Queen of France," in *Genèses et filiations dans l'oeuvre de Christine de Pizan*, ed. Dominique Demartini and Claire Le Ninan (Paris: Garnier, 2021), pp. 225–44.

72. Karen Green, "Isabeau de Bavière and the Political Philosophy of Christine de Pizan," *Historical Reflections/Réflexions historiques* 32, no. 2 (2006): pp. 247–72, at p. 265. See also Katherine Kong, *Lettering the Self in Medieval and Early Modern France* (Cambridge: D. S. Brewer, 2010), pp. 140–41.

73. Edited in Angus J. Kennedy, "La lamentacion sur les maux de la France de Christine de Pisan," in *Mélanges de langue et littérature françaises du Moyen Âge et de la Renaissance offerts à Monsieur Charles Foulon*, vol. 1 (Rennes: Institut de français, Université de Haute-Bretagne, 1980), pp. 177–85.

74. Berenice A. Carroll, "On the Causes of War and the Quest for Peace: Christine de Pizan and Early Peace Theory," in *Au champ des escriptures: IIIe Colloque International sur Christine de Pizan*, ed. Eric Hicks, with Diego Gonzalez and Philippe Simon (Paris: Champion, 2000), pp. 337–58, at p. 356.

75. Susan Sered and Samuel Cooper, "Sexuality and Social Control: Anthropological Reflections on the Book of Susanna," in *The Judgment of Susanna: Authority and Witness*, ed. Ellen Spolsky (Atlanta, GA: Scholars Press, 1996), pp. 43–55, at p. 46. The ungendering or even feminization of Daniel is visible in some late medieval French works, notably Jean Gerson's *De quadam puella* (1429), written in defense of Joan of Arc: here Gerson groups Daniel with Deborah, Esther, and Judith as unlikely (because physically weak) liberators of the faithful; H. G. Francq, "Jean Gerson's Theological Treatise and Other Memoirs in Defence of Joan of Arc," *Revue de l'Université d'Ottawa* 41 (1971): pp. 58–80. Benjamin Cornford observes that their physical weakness is what unites this group; Cornford, "Christine de Pizan's *Ditie de Jehanne d'Arc*: Poetry and Propaganda at the Court of Charles VII," *Parergon* 17, no. 2 (2000): pp. 75–106, at p. 81. It is worth pointing out, however, that Christine cites Deborah, Esther, and Judith in her *Ditié de Jehanne d'Arc*, but not Daniel.

76. On liminality as a desirable quality in a mediator or peacemaker see Adams, "*Moyennerresse*," esp. p. 180.

77. "To say that a given epistemological system is highly resilient is to say that it can absorb extraordinarily large disturbances without redefining its structure"; Dotson, "Conceptualizing," p. 121. If divine intervention isn't a large disturbance, what is?

78. Paul Ricoeur, *The Just*, trans. David Pellauer (Chicago: University of Chicago Press, 2000), p. 127.

79. This is a key distinction but one that is often overlooked in the *Merlin* scholarship: witness Christine Acher's statements that the author "insiste sur l'innocence de sa mère" and that "Merlin est sauvé par une mère innocente"; Acher, "Le *Merlin* de Robert de Boron, roman des origines et origines du roman," in *Fils sans père: Études sur le Merlin de Robert de Boron*, ed. Denis Hüe (Orléans: Paradigme, 2000), pp. 5–10, at pp. 8, 9.

80. Anne Berthelot, "Merlin *puer senex* par excellence," in *Old Age in the Middle Ages and the Renaissance: Interdisciplinary Approaches to a Neglected Topic*, ed. Albrecht Classen (Berlin: de Gruyter, 2007), pp. 251–61. Philippe Walter, "Merlin, l'enfant-vieillard," in *L'imaginaire des âges de la vie*, ed. Danièle Chauvin (Grenoble: ELLUG, 1996), pp. 117–33. James A. Schultz points out that "such a topos [the *puer senex*] is only meaningful in cultural contexts where children are ordinarily expected to be foolish, for it is only where children are thought to be *tump* [foolish] by nature that a child can give evidence of her special nature by being *wis* [wise]"; Schultz, *Knowledge*, p. 64.

81. Stephen Knight argues that Merlin's salvation at his mother's initiative is an early example of the "role of women's agency" that becomes increasingly vital "in the developing French version of the Arthur story"; Knight, *Merlin: Knowledge and Power through the Ages* (Ithaca, NY: Cornell University Press, 2009), p. 50.

82. Robert Baudry has argued that this notion of diabolical paternity in Robert de Boron's romance stems from a misreading (perhaps deliberate) of Geoffrey of Monmouth, in "Merlin, fils du diable? Une légende tenace née d'un contre-sens latin!," *Bien dire et bien aprandre* 24 (2007): pp. 99–108. Mónica Nasif discusses Robert de Boron's *Merlin* in light of contemporaneous demonology in "La historia del mago Merlín desde la perspectiva demonológica de la baja edad media," *Letras* 48–49 (2004): pp. 117–24.

83. Medina, *Epistemology*, p. 47.

84. On the "realism" of the trial, see Alexandre Micha, *Étude sur le "Merlin" de Robert de Boron* (Geneva: Droz, 1980), pp. 114–18. Along similar lines, Stephen Knight remarks that the trial scene, far from evoking a mythical past, is "located in the here and now"; Knight, *Merlin*, p. 50.

85. Jean-René Valette, "Merveilleux et production du sens: Le cas du *Merlin* de Robert de Boron," *Littératures* 43 (2000): pp. 35–45, at p. 38.

86. Agamben, *Remnants*, p. 12.

87. This is consistent with real-world practices by which "older women and widows, in particular, acted as the enforcers of proper behavior, based on standards that reflected gendered notions of good and bad deportment"; Susan Alice McDonough,

Witnesses, Neighbors, and Community in Late Medieval Marseille (New York: Palgrave Macmillan, 2013), p. 34.

88. This translation is my own; other English translations (those with page numbers) are taken from the partial translation "*The Prose Merlin* and *The Suite du Merlin* (Episodes)," trans. Samuel N. Rosenberg, in *The Romance of Arthur*, new expanded ed., ed. James J. Wilhelm (New York: Garland, 1994), pp. 305–63.

89. Fricker, *Epistemic Injustice*, p. 149.

90. Not only is Merlin's mother never named in the text, but Micha, in his *Étude*, does not include her in his list of the romance's characters. Jean-Marie Fritz notes that only a few texts in the Arthurian corpus give the character a name: "Excessivement rares sont les textes à nommer la mère de l'enchanteur; elle s'appelle *Optima* dans *Le roman des fils du roi Constant* de Bauduin Butor, alors qu'un *Brut* en prose de la fin du XIIIᵉ siècle la nomme curieusement *Adhan*: Merlin serait le fils d'Adam, mais d'un Adam au féminin, autre forme de subversion"; Fritz, "Les détenteurs du savoir généalogique dans le roman arthurien: Merlin, les mères et les ermites," in *L'imaginaire de la parenté dans les romans arthuriens (XIIᵉ–XIVᵉ siècles)*, ed. Martin Aurell and Catalina Gîrbea (Turnhout: Brepols, 2010), pp. 131–140, at p. 136.

91. "Le nom de Merlin, dans une interprétation immédiate du signifiant selon la tradition des 'étymologies populaires' si vivace au Moyen Âge, conduit à *Mer-lin*, au lignage de la mère. Robert de Boron précise bien d'ailleurs que ce nom de Merlin est un matronyme, et qu'il fut porté par l'ancêtre maternel"; Francis Dubost, *Aspects fantastiques de la littérature narrative médiévale (XIIᵉᵐᵉ–XIIIᵉᵐᵉ siècles)* (Geneva: Slatkine, 1991), p. 738.

92. Fricker, "Testimony and Epistemic Autonomy," p. 230.

93. Ricoeur, *The Just*, p. 6.

94. Jennifer E. Looper, "L'*Estoire de Merlin* and the Mirage of the Patrilineage," *Arthuriana* 12, no. 3 (2002): pp. 63–85.

95. E. Jane Burns, *Arthurian Fictions: Rereading the Vulgate Cycle* (Columbus: Ohio State University Press, 1985), p. 166.

96. R. Howard Bloch, "Merlin and the Modes of Medieval Legal Meaning," in *Archéologie du signe*, ed. Lucie Brind'Amour and Eugene Vance (Toronto: PIMS, 1983), pp. 127–44, at p. 130.

97. In this respect the narrative is "realistic," conforming to Didier Lett's observation that the time of pregnancy is a time during which human justice cannot be applied; Lett, *L'enfant*, p. 253.

98. The definition of a juridical interval (the suspension of a sentence) in terms of maternal embodiment dovetails with Kaitlin Sager's arguments about "lacteal time" in medieval French narrative. Sager, "Embodied Temporalities: Reproduction, Illness, and Chronobiopolitics in Medieval France" (Ph.D. diss., Tulane University, 2023).

99. Moreover, as Richard Trachsler observes, the trial ultimately turns into a test of Merlin's prophetic abilities, with the priest's suicide constituting the decisive

proof. Trachsler, *Merlin l'enchanteur: Étude sur le Merlin de Robert de Boron* (Paris: SEDES, 2000), p. 95.

100. R. Howard Bloch, *Etymologies and Genealogies* (Chicago: University of Chicago Press, 1983), p. 213.

101. Bloch, "Merlin," pp. 134, 139. Kate Cooper, "Merlin Romancier: Paternity, Prophecy and Poetics in the Huth *Merlin*," *Romanic Review* 77, no. 1 (1986): pp. 1–24, at p. 10.

102. Oresme, *Éthiques*, p. 301.

103. Polhaus, "Relational Knowing," p. 731.

104. Bruno Roy, ed., "Devinettes françaises du Moyen Âge," special issue, *Cahier d'études médiévales* 3 (1977): p. 79, riddle 130.

105. James Woodrow Hassell, Jr., *Middle French Proverbs, Sentences and Proverbial Phrases* (Toronto: Pontifical Institute of Medieval Studies, 1982), pp. 122–23.

106. Marie-Thérèse Lorcin, *Façons de sentir et de penser: Les fabliaux français* (Paris: Champion, 1979), p. 27.

107. For one take on these knowledge differentials with respect to bodily impairments, see M. Andia Augustin, "The Disabled Body in the Fabliaux," *Postmedieval* 3, no. 2 (2012): pp. 158–67.

108. Brent A. Pitts, "Truth-Seeking Discourse in the Old French Fabliaux," *Medievalia et Humanistica* n.s. 15 (1987): pp. 95–117, at p. 96.

109. Mary Jane Schenck, "Orality, Literacy, and the Law: Judicial Scenes in the Fabliau," *Reinardus* 8 (1995): pp. 63–75. See also Per Nykrog, *Les fabliaux* (Copenhagen: Munksgaard, 1957), p. 57.

110. On medieval mistrust of children due to their unpredictability, see Jean Batany, "Regards sur l'enfance dans la littérature moralisante," in "Enfant et sociétés," special issue, *Annales de démographie historique* (1973): pp. 123–27, at p. 125. In his reading of these fabliaux Didier Lett opines that fabliau authors often include children aged between three and seven years because this is such a disordered age, an age of speech less fettered by reason; Lett, *L'enfant*, pp. 104–5.

111. *No Future*, p. 13.

112. "Celui qui bota la pierre," in *Nouvau recueil complet des fabliaux*, vol. 6, ed. Willem Noomen (Assen: Van Gorcum, 1991), pp. 125–44.

113. The description of the boy as "medisans" makes it difficult to accept Jean Subrenat's characterization of this as a sympathetic portrait of a child. Subrenat, "La place de quelques petits enfants dans la littérature médiévale," in *Mélanges de littérature du Moyen Âge au XXᵉ siècle offerts à Mademoiselle Jeanne Lods par ses collègues, ses élèves, et ses amis* (Paris: École Normale Supérieure de Jeunes Filles, 1978), pp. 547–57, at p. 556.

114. Dotson presents the hypothetical case of a three-year-old, concluding that "whether our three-year-old is acting in epistemically violent ways depends upon whether the [child's] reliable ignorance is, in fact, harmful in the specific linguistic exchange"; Dotson, "Tracking," p. 240.

115. The word *plait* doesn't always have a juridical connotation, but it often does. See *DMF*, s.v. "plaid," accessed 22 April 2024, http://www.atilf.fr/dmf/definition /plaid.

116. Roy J. Pearcy's structural analysis of this fabliau presumes the child's revelation of the infidelity to be strictly unintentional: "the sexual negotiation provokes a *foolish act* by an infant whose naivety leads him to suppose that punishment and voluntary acquiescence are discrete phenomena"; Pearcy, *Logic and Humour*, p. 159.

117. Alain Corbellari, *Des fabliaux et des hommes* (Geneva: Droz, 2015), pp. 121–35.

118. Nykrog noted that *Celui qui bota la pierre* is unusual in that it (along with *Braies au prestre*) recounts the revelation of the affair but not the aftermath of that revelation. Nykrog, *Les fabliaux*, p. 110.

119. Ricoeur, *The Just*, p. 131.

120. Jürgen Beyer, "The Morality of the Amoral," in *The Humor of the Fabliaux*, ed. Thomas D. Cooke and Benjamin L. Honeycutt (Columbia: University of Missouri Press, 1974), pp. 15–42, at pp. 39, 40.

121. Schenck, "Orality."

122. This fabliau, with its stanzas of four pentasyllables and four decasyllables, is described by Jean Dufournet as a "unique specimen"; *Fabliaux du Moyen Âge*, ed. and trans. Jean Dufournet (Paris: Flammarion, 1998), p. 357. *Baillet* is edited on pp. 90–99 of that volume, with notes (including a misidentification of the manuscript) on pp. 357–58. On the *Rosarius*—a curious combination of Marial poetry, moralized natural philosophy, and secular tales that was made c. 1330 and appears later to have belonged to Charles V—see Arthur Langfors, "Notice du manuscrit français 12483 de la Bibliothèque nationale," *Notices et extraits des manuscrits de la Bibliothèque nationale et autres bibliothèques* 39, no. 2 (1916): pp. 503–665. Further remarks on the fabliau's manuscript context are to be found in Pearcy, *Logic and Humour*, pp. 164–65. Oddly, Pearcy analyzes the structure of this fabliau at some length without ever mentioning the child character.

123. Nykrog, *Les fabliaux*, p. 58.

124. Lett, *L'enfant*, pp. 98–100, reads *Baillet le savetier* in parallel with *Celui qui bota la pierre*, focusing mainly on the children's ages as indicative of differential responsibility for their words.

125. The child, so key to the plot of *Baillet le savetier*, is absent from the other medieval French version of the same story (that of Étienne de Bourbon, who situates it in the diocese of Grenoble). See A. Lecoy de La Marche, ed., *Anecdotes historiques, légendes et apologues tirés du recueil inédit d'Étienne de Bourbon, dominicain du XIIIe siècle* (Paris: Renouard for the SHF, 1877), p. 405. The relationship between this exemplum and *Baillet* is briefly discussed in Jacques Berlioz, "Résumé et amplification: Une fausse question? Le premier témoignage du fabliau *Du Prestre qui fu mis au lardier* chez Étienne de Bourbon († v. 1261)," *PRIS-MA* 13, no. 2 (1997): pp. 137–45.

126. Judith Butler thus describes the "bodily acts" of gender performativity in *Undoing Gender* (New York: Routledge, 2004), p. 199.

127. An interpretative injustice is a wrongful act whereby a hearer attributes a message to a speaker other than the message that the speaker meant to communicate. Andrew Peet, "Epistemic Injustice in Utterance Interpretation," *Synthese* 194 (2017): pp. 3421–43.

128. Medina, *Epistemology*, p. 27.

CHAPTER FIVE

1. On the origins of "normalcy" with the emergence of modern statistical methods, see Lennard Davis, *Enforcing Normalcy: Disability, Deafness, and the Body* (New York: Verso, 1995). Karma Lochrie makes a similar point about the non-existence of "norms" with particular reference to medieval sexuality in *Heterosyncrasies: Female Sexuality when Normal Wasn't* (Minneapolis: University of Minnesota Press, 2005), esp. pp. x–xxiv and 1–25.

2. Marcus Tullius Cicero, *De senectute; De amicitia; De divinatione*, trans. William Armistead Falconer, Loeb Classical Library 154 (Cambridge, MA: Harvard University Press, 2014), pp. 42–43.

3. Anna Benvenuti Papi and Elena Giannarelli, "Santi bambini, santi da bambini," in *Bambini santi: Rappresentazioni dell'infanzia e modelli agiografici*, ed. Anna Benvenuti Papi and Elena Giannarelli (Turin: Rosenberg & Sellier, 1991), pp. 7–24, at p. 12. Irina Metzler likewise remarks that "childhood itself can be seen as a disability, in the context of the Ages of Man theme"; Metzler, "Disabled Children: Birth Defects, Causality, and Guilt," in *Medicine, Religion and Gender in Medieval Culture*, ed. Naoë Kukita Yoshikawa (Cambridge: D. S. Brewer, 2015), pp. 161–80, at p. 164 n. 13.

4. See Silvia Nagel and Silvana Vecchio, "Il bambino, la parola, il silenzio nella cultura medievale," *Quaderni storici* n.s. 19, no. 57 (1984): pp. 719–63, at p. 722. Wendy J. Turner discusses the analogies established in medieval English law books between children and adults deemed mentally incompetent in *Care and Custody of the Mentally Ill, Incompetent, and Disabled in Medieval England* (Turnhout: Brepols, 2013), esp. pp. 131–33.

5. The term *normate* was coined and explicated by Rosemarie Garland-Thomson in *Extraordinary Bodies* (New York: Columbia University Press, 1997): "As I examine the disabled figure, I will also trouble the mutually constituting figure this study coins: the normate. This neologism names the veiled subject position of cultural self, the figure outlined by the array of deviant others whose marked bodies shore up the normate boundaries. The term normate usefully designates the social figure through which people can represent themselves as definitive human beings" (p. 8).

6. This is a question briefly touched on by Didier Lett, who notes that twelfth- and thirteenth-century miracle narratives rarely identify muteness as a problem in

children below the age of six or seven years, and by Jenni Kuuliala, who cites the example of one three-year-old whose parents identify his lack of speech as a cause for concern. Lett, *L'enfant*, p. 107; Kuuliala, *Childhood Disability and Social Integration in the Middle Ages: Constructions of Impairments in Thirteenth- and Fourteenth-Century Canonization Processes* (Turnhout: Brepols, 2016), p. 109.

7. Alison Kafer, *Feminist, Queer, Crip* (Bloomington: Indiana University Press, 2013).

8. Karin Ljuslinder, Katie Ellis, and Lotta Vikström, "Cripping Time—Understanding the Life Course through the Lens of Ableism," *Scandinavian Journal of Disability Research* 22, no. 1 (2020): pp. 35–38, at p. 35.

9. Adam W. Davidson, "Stasis-Maintenance-(Un)productive-Presence: Parenting a Disabled Child as Crip Time," *Disability Studies Quarterly* 40, no. 3 (2020), https://doi.org/10.18061/dsq.v40i3.6693.

10. Elena Giannarelli, "Infanzia e santità: Un problema della biografia cristiana antica," in *Bambini santi: Rappresentazioni dell'infanzia e modelli agiografici*, ed. Anna Benvenuti Papi and Elena Giannarelli (Turin: Rosenberg & Sellier, 1991), pp. 25–58, at p. 45.

11. Benedicta Ward, *Miracles and the Medieval Mind. Theory, Record, and Event, 1000–1215* (Philadelphia: University of Pennsylvania Press, 1982), p. 2.

12. Anne E. Bailey, writing of English miracle narratives from the long twelfth century, claims that "hagiographers were little interested in children's perspectives"; Bailey, "Miracle Children: Medieval Hagiography and Childhood Imperfection," *Journal of Interdisciplinary History* 47, no. 3 (2017): pp. 267–85, at p. 281.

13. The standard work of reference on the evolution of the canonization process is André Vauchez, *La sainteté en Occident aux derniers siècles du Moyen Âge* (Rome: École française de Rome, 1988); see also the essays in Gábor Klaniczay, ed., *Procès de canonisation au Moyen Âge: Aspects juridiques et religieux/Medieval Canonization Processes: Legal and Religious Aspects* (Rome: École française de Rome, 2004). See also Michael Goodich, *Miracles and Wonders: The Development of the Concept of Miracle, 1150–1350* (Aldershot: Ashgate, 2007); M. Cecilia Gaposchkin, *The Making of Saint Louis: Kingship, Sanctity, and Crusade in the Later Middle Ages* (Ithaca, NY: Cornell University Press, 2008), pp. 22–23.

14. This question is inspired by Geoffrey Baker's inverse question, posed of nineteenth-century forensic fiction: "In an age of evidence, what is it to believe?" Geoffrey Baker, "'Who Is to Believe Me?' The Epistemology of Wrongful Accusation and Character Testimony in Elizabeth Gaskell's *Mary Barton*," paper presented to the American Comparative Literature Association, 19 March 2023.

15. Kisha G. Tracy, "Speech: Medieval Representations of Speech Impairments," in *A Cultural History of Disability in the Middle Ages*, ed. Jonathan Hsy, Tory V. Pearman, and Joshua R. Eyler (London: Bloomsbury, 2020), pp. 99–113, at p. 101. The tenth-century Persian physician Rhazes (Al-Razi), one of the most important medical authorities for late medieval Europe, is a major source for this point of view; see

Denyse Rockey and Penelope Johnstone, "Medieval Arabic Views on Speech Disorders," *Journal of Communications Disorders* 12 (1979): pp. 229–43.

16. Pierre-André Sigal, *L'homme et le miracle dans la France médiévale (XIe–XIIe siècle)* (Paris: Cerf, 1985), p. 234.

17. On the adaptation as a means of asserting the primacy of Chartres as a pilgrimage site, see Marie-Thérèse Lorcin, "Les miracles de Notre-Dame de Chartres: Du latin au français," in *Mélanges de langue et de littérature médiévales offerts à Alice Planche*, ed. Maurice Accarie and Ambroise Queffélec (Nice: Les Belles Lettres 1984), vol. 2, pp. 319–26.

18. Jean le Marchant, *Miracles de Notre-Dame de Chartres*, ed. Pierre Kunstmann (Chartres: Société Archéologique d'Eure-et-Loir, 1973).

19. Ll. 25, 31, and 37.

20. On the capacity to narrate as a social capacity learned from caregivers and indicative of full moral status, see Elizabeth Purcell, "Disability, Narrative, and Moral Status," *Disability Studies Quarterly* 36, no. 1 (2016), https://doi.org/10.18061 /dsq.v36i1.4375.

21. Agata Sobczyk also points out that the opening scene grabs attention by creating expectations of a different textual genre, then defying those expectations, though she places the knight and the girl in the realm of romance rather than fabliau. Sobczyk, "Langue, texte, image: L'enfant muet dans les recueils et le vitrail des *Miracles de Notre-Dame de Chartres*," *Cahiers de civilisation médiévale* 58 (2015): pp. 113–21, at p. 116.

22. Marie-Thérèse Lorcin argues that this collection was written to move its readers rather than to provide documentation, and that to this end it plays up the affective power of the mother-child pair. Lorcin, "Le couple privilégié mère-enfant dans les *Miracles de Notre-Dame de Chartres*," *Médiévales* 19 (1990): pp. 71–75, at p. 73.

23. On Gautier de Coinci's child characters, see Daniel E. O'Sullivan, "Reading Children in Gautier de Coinci's *Miracles de Nostre Dame*," *Neophilologus* 89 (2005): pp. 201–19. Children are also discussed in Brigitte Cazelles, *La faiblesse chez Gautier de Coinci* (Saratoga, CA: Anma Libri, 1978), pp. 82–90.

24. Lett, *L'enfant*, p. 79.

25. Sobczyk, "Langue," p. 115.

26. Lett, "Aetas infirma," p. 94.

27. Lett, *L'enfant*, p. 77.

28. Lett, *L'enfant*, p. 79; Sobczyk, "Langue," p. 117.

29. Kafer, *Feminist, Queer, Crip*, p. 43.

30. Julie Singer, "Deafness: Reading Invisible Signs," in *A Cultural History of Disability in the Middle Ages*, ed. Jonathan Hsy, Tory Pearman, and Joshua Eyler (London and New York: Bloomsbury, 2020), pp. 83–98, at p. 88.

31. Jenni Kuuliala, "Unlikely Heroes: A Study on Three Miracle Narratives of Disabled Beggar Children in Late Thirteenth-Century Hagiographic Sources,"

in *Agents and Objects: Children in Pre-Modern Europe*, ed. Katariina Mustakallio and Jussi Hanska (Rome: Institutum Romanum Finlandiae, 2015), pp. 147–67, at p. 158 n. 64.

32. Suger, *Oeuvres*, vol. 1, ed. and trans. Françoise Gasparri (Paris: Les Belles Lettres, 1996), p. 98.

33. This miracle is not included in Pierre de Beauvais's early thirteenth-century life of Saint Josse.

34. Claude Thiry discusses the relationship between the verse and prose sections in "Vie et miracles de st Josse," *Le Moyen Français* 67 (2010): pp. 101–10.

35. Jean Miélot, *Vie et miracles de saint Josse*, ed. Nils-Olof Jönsson (Turnhout: Brepols, 2004), p. 7, ll. 11–14.

36. Thiry notes picardisms in the quatrains: "Vie," p. 103.

37. *Materials for the History of Thomas Becket, Archbishop of Canterbury*, ed. James Craigie Robertson, vol. 1 (London: Longman, 1875).

38. Michael Staunton, *Thomas Becket and His Biographers* (Woodbridge: Boydell Press, 2006), p. 51.

39. Becket is an international saint, as discussed in Staunton, *Thomas Becket*, pp. 9, 49. His miracles increasingly occur away from Canterbury: see Didier Lett, "Deux hagiographes, un saint et un roi: Conformisme et créativité dans les deux recueils de *miracula* de Thomas Becket," in *Auctor et auctoritas: Invention et conformisme dans l'écriture médiévale*, ed. Michel Zimmermann (Paris: École des Chartes, 2001), pp. 201–16, at p. 204 n. 17. On the diffusion of his cult in France in particular, see Raymonde Foreville, "La diffusion du culte de Thomas Becket dans la France de l'Ouest avant la fin du XIIe siècle," *Cahiers de civilisation médiévale* 19 (1976): pp. 347–69, reprinted in *Thomas Becket dans la tradition historique et hagiographique* (London: Variorum, 1981).

40. The narrative does, however, include the commonplace that the saint was moved to act when the youth "in auribus ejus querimoniam lacrymabilem deposuisti" (placed the complaint of [his] tears in the saint's ears; p. 507).

41. The use of the term *lingua materna* to describe an idiom not learned in a social context highlights an alienation from the female teaching subject analogous to the book as woman in the *Femina* and *Femina nova*; see chap. 3 for discussion.

42. This story is mentioned in Lett, *L'enfant*, p. 104.

43. I borrow these terms from Sara Wasson, who explores the tensions between these temporalities in contemporary transplant memoirs. Wasson, "Waiting, Strange: Transplant Recipient Experience, Medical Time and Queer/Crip Temporalities," *Medical Humanities* 47, no. 4 (2021): pp. 447–55.

44. Kafer, *Feminist, Queer, Crip*, pp. 27–28; see also the helpful reframing of this concept in the introduction to Eunjung Kim, *Curative Violence: Rehabilitating Disability, Gender, and Sexuality in Modern Korea* (Durham, NC: Duke University Press, 2017).

45. Kim, *Curative Violence*, p. 9.

46. Guillaume de Saint-Pathus, *Miracles de saint Louis*, ed. Percival B. Fay (Paris: Champion, 1931), pp. 50–55. A partial English translation and brief commentary are to be found in Sharon Farmer, "A Deaf-Mute's Story," in *Medieval Christianity in Practice*, ed. Miri Rubin (Princeton, NJ: Princeton University Press, 2009), pp. 203–8.

47. The tests are harsh but not atypical, either of the miracle genre or of Saint-Pathus's renditions of the miracles of Saint Louis in particular. See Julie Singer, "Able-Bodied Fragility," *Digital Philology* 9, no. 1 (2020): pp. 47–68.

48. Louis Carolus-Barré, "Guillaume de Saint-Pathus, confesseur de la reine Marguerite et biographe de saint Louis," *Archivum Franciscanum historicum* 79 (1986): pp. 142–52; Gaposchkin, *Making*, pp. 38–40.

49. A study of the illustrations (examining mainly the "life" images) is Jane Geein Chung-Apley, "The Illustrated 'Vie et Miracles de Saint Louis' of Guillaume de Saint-Pathus (Paris, B.N., ms. Fr. 5716)" (Ph.D. diss., University of Michigan, 1998).

50. Farmer, "A Deaf-Mute's Story," p. 207.

51. Irina Metzler, *A Social History of Disability in the Middle Ages* (New York: Routledge, 2015), p. 3; see also the more extended discussion of Loÿs on pp. 199–202.

52. Kuuliala, *Childhood*, pp. 190, 257.

53. M. Cecilia Gaposchkin, "Place, Status, and Experience in the Miracles of Saint Louis," *Cahiers de recherches médiévales et humanistes* 19 (2010): pp. 249–66, at pp. 252–53.

54. He calls it "a hermeneutic process which is facilitated by the lack of an established written text"; Thomas J. Heffernan, *Sacred Biography: Saints and Their Biographers in the Middle Ages* (Oxford and New York: Oxford University Press, 1988), p. 34.

55. Farmer thinks the youth's deafness cannot have been congenital, or else he would not have been able to learn to speak ("A Deaf-Mute's Story," p. 207 n. 2). The question is also taken up by Metzler and by Kuuliala, and in Maria Wittmer-Butsch and Constanze Rendtel, *Miracula: Wunderheilungen im Mittelalter* (Cologne: Böhlau, 2003).

56. Jacques Le Goff, "Saint Louis et la prière," in *Horizons marins, itinéraires spirituels (Ve–XVIIIe siècles)*, vol. 1, *Mentalités et sociétés*, ed. Henri Dubois, Jean-Claude Hocquet, and André Vauchez (Paris: Publications de la Sorbonne, 1987), pp. 85–94, at p. 91.

57. *The Teachings of Saint Louis*, ed. David O'Connell (Chapel Hill: University of North Carolina Press, 1972), p. 56, para. 8. The passage is commented on in Le Goff, "Saint Louis et la prière," p. 86.

58. "The gestures of prayer and prostration were so clearly prescribed that a young man, both deaf and mute, was able to effect Louis' intercession through their imitation without understanding the faith that they signified"; Gaposchkin, "Place," p. 258.

59. Sharah Chennai and Odile Redon, "Les miracles de Saint Louis," in *Les miracles miroirs des corps*, ed. Jacques Gelis and Odile Redon (Paris: Presses Universitaires de Vincennes, 1983), pp. 55–85, at p. 76.

60. Wittmer-Butsch and Rendtel, *Miracula*, p. 274.

61. Such falls into disability are theorized in the critical-autobiographical essay by Eliza Chandler, "Sidewalk Stories: The Troubling Task of Identification," *Disability Studies Quarterly* 30, nos. 3–4 (2010), https://doi.org/10.18061/dsq.v30i3/4.1293.

62. Lorcin, "Le couple privilégié," p. 72.

63. Save, perhaps, the slightly older boy who first led him to Orgelet; this child's identity is never established.

64. This process is related to the one described by Hannah Skoda: "The onset and experience of impairment [...] are not presented as purely medical phenomena, but as shaped by the reactions of families, friends and neighbors"; Skoda, "Representations of Disability in the Thirteenth-Century *Miracles de Saint Louis*," in *Disability in the Middle Ages: Reconsiderations and Reverberations*, ed. Joshua R. Eyler (Aldershot: Ashgate, 2010), pp. 53–66, at p. 54. The torturous tests inflicted upon Loÿs are similar to the tests to which mute children are subjected in earlier miracle narratives; see Bailey, "Miracle Children," p. 283.

65. As Jenni Kuuliala puts it, "He remained disabled and his socialization incomplete until he was taught, in his twenties, the things that children usually learn at a very early age"; Kuuliala, *Childhood*, p. 257.

66. The pun isn't explicitly made in the text, but it presents itself in the rich aural echoes of the opening rubric: "Ce quinzieme miracle est d'un vallet de huit anz qui n'avoit onques **oÿ** ne parlé, qui recovra s'**oïe** au tombel saint **Loÿs**" (p. 50, ll. 1–3; emphasis added).

67. Ato Quayson, *Aesthetic Nervousness: Disability and the Crisis of Representation* (New York: Columbia University Press, 2007).

68. For the date: Carolus-Barré, *Procès*, p. 129. See also Gaposchkin, *Making*, p. 35 n. 83.

69. Guillaume de Chartres, *De vita et miraculis sancti Ludovici*, in *Recueil des historiens des Gaules et de la France*, vol. 20, ed. Pierre-Claude-François Dannou and Joseph Nandet (Paris: Imprimerie Royale, 1840), p. 38.

70. The earliest version of which I'm aware that does *not* include the deaf and mute youth is the 1514 play by Pierre Gringore.

71. *Recueil des historiens des Gaules et de la France*, vol. 23, ed. Natalis de Wailly, Léopold Delisle, and Charles Jourdain (Paris: Imprimerie Royale, 1840), p. 69.

72. *Recueil des historiens*, vol. 23, p. 165.

73. A digitized example is *La vie des saints en francoys*, printed by Antoine Vérard (1493), fol. 293r, accessed 22 April 2024, https://gallica.bnf.fr/ark:/12148/bpt6k9909876.

74. *Le mystère de saint Louis roi de France*, ed. Francisque Michel (Westminster: Nichols for the Roxburghe Club, 1871).

75. Reinhard Strohm, *Music in Late Medieval Bruges* (Oxford: Clarendon Press, 1985).

76. Alain Corbin, *Village Bells: Sound and Meaning in the 19th-Century French Countryside*, trans. Martin Thom (New York: Columbia University Press, 1998), p. 97.

77. The one volume devoted to the *Livre des faiz* is Marie-Thérèse Gousset, François Avril, and Jean Richard, *Saint Louis, roi de France: Livre des faits de Monseigneur saint Louis* (Paris: Chêne, 1990); it contains three essays and reproduces all the images from the life section, as well as a few from the miracles. The book is also alluded to in Colette Beaune, *Le miroir du pouvoir* (Paris: Hervas, 1990), p. 178; Olivier Mattéoni, *Un prince face à Louis XI: Jean II de Bourbon, une politique en procès* (Paris: Presses Universitaires de France, 2012), pp. 209–10; Nicole Fleurier, *Paris: Enluminures* (Paris: Bibliothèque nationale de France, 2009), p. 65.

78. This constitutes, according to François Avril, "le plus important corpus d'images destiné à commémorer les actions et les bienfaits *post mortem* du grand saint capétien"; Gousset, Avril, and Richard, *Saint Louis*, p. 86. In the same volume Marie-Thérèse Gousset claims, surprisingly, that "le cycle des miracles [. . .] n'ajoute, en dehors de son côté anecdotique, rien de nouveau à l'iconographie du culte du saint capétien" (p. 93).

79. For Jean Richard, the anonymous writer is "plus 'historiographe' qu'hagiographe" (Gousset, Avril, and Richard, *Saint Louis*, p. 12), which may be true of the life section, though the miracle section defies any attempt to distinguish the one from the other.

80. "According to theories of narrative time current in the fifteenth century, the natural order of narration could be disrupted by miraculous events"; Matthew Champion, *The Fullness of Time: Temporalities of the Fifteenth-Century Low Countries* (Chicago: University of Chicago Press, 2015), p. 113.

81. This depiction of family unit counters James A. Schultz's conclusions about the unimportance in Middle High German literature of "a category that would designate the coresidential unit of parents and children that we consider so important to psychic health and social stability"; Schulz, *Knowledge*, p. 115.

82. Alexandre Baril offers a helpful history of concepts of "crip time" in "'Doctor, Am I an Anglophone Trapped in a Francophone Body?' An Intersectional Analysis of 'Trans-crip-t Time' in Ableist, Cisnormative, Anglonormative Societies," *Journal of Literary & Cultural Disability Studies* 10, no. 2 (2016): pp. 155–72, at pp. 157–60.

83. On the particular temporalities of speech impairment in relation to "clock time," see Joshua St. Pierre, "Distending Straight-Masculine Time: A Phenomenology of the Disabled Speaking Body," *Hypatia* 30, no. 1 (2015): pp. 49–65.

84. The term is borrowed from Elizabeth Freeman, *Time Binds: Queer Temporalities, Queer Histories* (Durham, NC: Duke University Press, 2010), p. 5.

85. This observation is inspired by Kafer's reflections on the differential futurity of the disabled child and the idealized nondisabled Child; Kafer, *Feminist, Queer, Crip*, p. 29.

86. The boy's ertswhile impairment is misidentified. This is likely just a scribal error, but one reinforcing that the particulars of the boy's prior physical impairment are not important to this rendition of the story, either in the text or in the images.

87. Ellen Samuels, "Six Ways of Looking at Crip Time," *Disability Studies Quarterly* 37, no. 3 (2017), https://doi.org/10.18061/dsq.v37i3.5824; emphasis in original.

88. Kafer, *Feminist, Queer, Crip*, p. 27.

89. Freeman, *Time Binds*, p. xxii.

90. Sager, "Embodied Temporalities," p. 72. Sager adopts the term "chrono-bionormative" from Dana Luciano's work on nineteenth-century America, extending it to a compelling discussion of reproductive temporalities in medieval French literature.

91. Singer, "Deafness," pp. 90–93.

92. Rancière, *Names*, p. 11.

93. On the latter, see Turner, *Care and Custody*. The legal implications of muteness are also discussed in less detail in Cory Rushton, "Philomela Accuses," *Disability and Medieval Law*, ed. Cory Rushton (Cambridge: Cambridge Scholars, 2013), pp. 157–73.

CONCLUSION

1. Steel, *How Not*, p. 49.

INDEX

Page numbers in italics refer to figures.

nurture (*continued*)
105; and relationality, 128. *See also*
nature
Nykrog, Per, 184

Oedipus, 72, 102
Office of the Dead, 99–102, 271n144
Old French, 23, 133. *See also* French
language; Middle French
Olivier de la Haye, 90
Ong, Walter, 34, 47
Oosterwijk, Sophie, 94
Oresme, Nicole, 23, 110, 122–23, 159,
178
Orléans. *See* Charles d'Orléans
Orlemanski, Julie, 67
Outremeuse, Jean d', 41, 44
Ovid, 123

Palmer, R. Barton, 158
pantomime, 70
parasitic relationships, 17, 35, 145
Pasnau, Robert, 27
*Passe temps de tout homme et de toute
femme* (Alexis), 79
paternity anxieties, 58
Pauli, Ivan, 245n25
Pearcy, Roy J., 288n8, 298n116
Pèlerinage de Jhesucrist (Deguileville),
41, 45–46, 48–50, 58–59
personhood: beginning of, 12; of children, 195; definitions of, 16–19, 55,
57, 59; discourses of, 17; loss of, 55–
56; and relationality, 10–11, 238; and
voice acquisition, 26–27. *See also*
ensoulment; humanity; subjectivity
Petit, Jean, 110
Philippe III, 206
Philippe de Mézières, 32
Philippe de Novare, 4, 83, 265n79
Physionomia (Scot), 80
Pizan. *See* Christine de Pizan

Placides et Timéo, 30–32, 37, 59
play, 4, 143–44, 243n10
"Poème sur la grande peste de 1348"
(Olivier de la Haye), 90
poetic language, 132–33, 135, 141–42,
144
Poet's Notebook, The (Arn), 141
Pontano, Giovanni Gioviano, 121
postmodernism, 151
prayer: effectiveness of, 199–200; imitation of, 206–9, 303n58; as spoken
activity, 197–98; and understanding, 211–13, 216–18, 220–21; in
visual narrative, 226–28
prestre qui fut mis au lardier, Le. *See
Baillet le savetier*
Primat de Saint Denis, 219
Priscian, 67, 259n5
pronunciation, 109
Purgatorio (Dante), 31–32, 252n62

Quant n'ont assez fait dodo, 142–43
Quayson, Ato, 216
queer theory, 103
Quentin, Saint, 120

Rancière, Jacques, 10, 121, 234, 246n44
rationality, 3, 17, 24–28, 57, 66, 70, 76,
104, 237
régime du corps, Le, 109
relationality, 16, 110–11, 120–21, 128,
195–96, 238
Remiet, Pierre, 86–88
Rendtel, Constanze, 209
Resnick, Irven, 250n42
Rhazes, 109
rhyme, 79–80, 92, 94, 129, 282n105
Richard, Jean, 305n79
Ricoeur, Paul, 170, 175–76
Riote du monde, 265n80
Robert de Boron, 14, 51, 56, 150,
170–78

Printed in Dunstable, United Kingdom